W9-CHD-509

lonely planet

Edinburgh

Neil Wilson
Tom Smallman

LONELY PLANET PUBLICATIONS
Melbourne • Oakland • London • Paris

Edinburgh
2nd edition – January 2002
First published – March 1999

Published by
Lonely Planet Publications Pty Ltd ABN 36 005 607 983
90 Maribyrnong St, Footscray, Victoria 3011, Australia

Lonely Planet Offices
Australia Locked Bag 1, Footscray, Victoria 3011
USA 150 Linden St, Oakland, CA 94607
UK 10a Spring Place, London NW5 3BH
France 1 rue du Dahomey, 75011 Paris

Photographs
Many of the images in this guide are available for licensing from
Lonely Planet Images.
email: lpi@lonelyplanet.com.au
Web site: www.lonelyplanetimages.com

Front cover photograph
Fringe Festival Office (Pat Yale/Gareth McCormack)

ISBN 1 86450 378 5

Printed by Craft Print International Ltd, Singapore

Contents – Text

2 Contents – Text

Contents – Maps

The Authors

Neil Wilson

After working as a geologist in Australia and the North Sea and doing geological research at Oxford University, Neil gave up the rock business for the more precarious life of a freelance writer and photographer. Since 1988 he has travelled in five continents and written around 30 travel and walking guidebooks for various publishers. He has worked on Lonely Planet's *Georgia, Armenia & Azerbaijan*, *Malta*, *Czech & Slovak Republics*, *Prague*, *Slovenia* and *Scotland* guides. Although he was born in Glasgow, in the west of Scotland, Neil defected to the east at the age of 18 and has lived in Edinburgh ever since.

Tom Smallman

Tom lives in Melbourne, Australia, and had a number of jobs before joining Lonely Planet as an editor. He now works full-time as an author and has worked on Lonely Planet guides to *Australia*, *Britain*, *Canada*, *Dublin*, *Edinburgh*, *Ireland*, *New South Wales*, *Pennsylvania*, *Scotland* and *Sydney*.

FROM THE AUTHOR

Many thanks to the various people who supplied assistance and advice (both wanted and unwanted), but especially to Carol for help with restaurants and shopping, and to Michael and Charlie for the nitty gritty on the gay scene.

This Book

This is the 2nd edition of LP's *Edinburgh* city guide and was written and updated by Neil Wilson. It also incorporates material written by Tom Smallman for the 1st edition.

From the Publisher

This edition of *Edinburgh* was produced in Lonely Planet's London office. Heather Dickson was the coordinating editor and Jolyon Philcox handled the mapping, design and layout. Arabella Shepherd, Emma Sangster and Amanda Canning helped with editing and proofing. Jimi Ellis drew the climate chart, Annika Roojun designed the cover and Lachlan Ross drew the back-cover map. Lonely Planet Images provided the photographs and illustrations were drawn by Asa Andersson and Jane Smith.

Many thanks to Emma Koch for the 'Scottish Gaelic' boxed text and Tom Hall for getting there and away information. Thanks also to Amanda Canning and Tim Fitzgerald for all their help and to Neil Wilson for his contagious Scottish humour.

Thanks

Many thanks to the travellers who used the last edition and contacted us with helpful hints, advice and interesting anecdotes:

Bob Bolia, Rebecca Brown, Kate Cogill, Erik Einbeck, Rachelle Garland, Justin Green, Wolfgang Guenther, Sandra Hampel, Ingrid Johansson, Arthur Knight, Yvonne Lake, Keith Murray, Elizabeth Neazor, Louise Ngaei, Edward Nicol, Eugene Sheyn, Derek Stewart, Claire Swain and Jennifer Young.

Foreword

ABOUT LONELY PLANET GUIDEBOOKS

The story begins with a classic travel adventure: Tony and Maureen Wheeler's 1972 journey across Europe and Asia to Australia. Useful information about the overland trail did not exist at that time, so Tony and Maureen published the first Lonely Planet guidebook to meet a growing need.

From a kitchen table, then from a tiny office in Melbourne (Australia), Lonely Planet has become the largest independent travel publisher in the world, an international company with offices in Melbourne, Oakland (USA), London (UK) and Paris (France).

Today Lonely Planet guidebooks cover the globe. There is an ever-growing list of books and there's information in a variety of forms and media. Some things haven't changed. The main aim is still to help make it possible for adventurous travellers to get out there – to explore and better understand the world.

At Lonely Planet we believe travellers can make a positive contribution to the countries they visit – if they respect their host communities and spend their money wisely. Since 1986 a percentage of the income from each book has been donated to aid projects and human rights campaigns.

Updates Lonely Planet thoroughly updates each guidebook as often as possible. This usually means there are around two years between editions, although for more unusual or more stable destinations the gap can be longer. Check the imprint page (following the colour map at the beginning of the book) for publication dates.

Between editions up-to-date information is available in two free newsletters – the paper *Planet Talk* and email *Comet* (to subscribe, contact any Lonely Planet office) – and on our Web site at www.lonelyplanet.com. The *Upgrades* section of the Web site covers a number of important and volatile destinations and is regularly updated by Lonely Planet authors. *Scoop* covers news and current affairs relevant to travellers. And, lastly, the *Thorn Tree* bulletin board and *Postcards* section of the site carry unverified, but fascinating, reports from travellers.

Correspondence The process of creating new editions begins with the letters, postcards and emails received from travellers. This correspondence often includes suggestions, criticisms and comments about the current editions. Interesting excerpts are immediately passed on via newsletters and the Web site, and everything goes to our authors to be verified when they're researching on the road. We're keen to get more feedback from organisations or individuals who represent communities visited by travellers.

Lonely Planet gathers information for everyone who's curious about the planet – and especially for those who explore it first-hand. Through guidebooks, phrasebooks, activity guides, maps, literature, newsletters, image library, TV series and Web site we act as an information exchange for a worldwide community of travellers.

Research Authors aim to gather sufficient practical information to enable travellers to make informed choices and to make the mechanics of a journey run smoothly. They also research historical and cultural background to help enrich the travel experience and allow travellers to understand and respond appropriately to cultural and environmental issues.

Authors don't stay in every hotel because that would mean spending a couple of months in each medium-sized city and, no, they don't eat at every restaurant because that would mean stretching belts beyond capacity. They do visit hotels and restaurants to check standards and prices, but feedback based on readers' direct experiences can be very helpful.

Many of our authors work undercover, others aren't so secretive. None of them accept freebies in exchange for positive write-ups. And none of our guidebooks contain any advertising.

Production Authors submit their raw manuscripts and maps to offices in Australia, USA, UK or France. Editors and cartographers – all experienced travellers themselves – then begin the process of assembling the pieces. When the book finally hits the shops, some things are already out of date, we start getting feedback from readers and the process begins again…

WARNING & REQUEST

Things change – prices go up, schedules change, good places go bad and bad places go bankrupt – nothing stays the same. So, if you find things better or worse, recently opened or long since closed, please tell us and help make the next edition even more accurate and useful. We genuinely value all the feedback we receive. A well-travelled team reads and acknowledges every letter, postcard and email and ensures that every morsel of information finds its way to the appropriate authors, editors and cartographers for verification.

Everyone who writes to us will find their name in the next edition of the appropriate guidebook. They will also receive the latest issue of *Planet Talk*, our quarterly printed newsletter, or *Comet*, our monthly email newsletter. Subscriptions to both newsletters are free. The very best contributions will be rewarded with a free guidebook.

Excerpts from your correspondence may appear in new editions of Lonely Planet guidebooks, the Lonely Planet Web site, *Planet Talk* or *Comet*, so please let us know if you *don't* want your letter published or your name acknowledged.

Send all correspondence to the Lonely Planet office closest to you:

Australia: Locked Bag 1, Footscray, Victoria 3011
USA: 150 Linden St, Oakland, CA 94607
UK: 10a Spring Place, London NW5 3BH
France: 1 rue du Dahomey, 75011 Paris

Or email us at: talk2us@lonelyplanet.com.au

For news, views and updates see our Web site: www.lonelyplanet.com

HOW TO USE A LONELY PLANET GUIDEBOOK

The best way to use a Lonely Planet guidebook is any way you choose. At Lonely Planet we believe the most memorable travel experiences are often those that are unexpected, and the finest discoveries are those you make yourself. Guidebooks are not intended to be used as if they provide a detailed set of infallible instructions!

Contents All Lonely Planet guidebooks follow roughly the same format. The Facts about the Destination chapters or sections give background information ranging from history to weather. Facts for the Visitor gives practical information on issues like visas and health. Getting There & Away gives a brief starting point for re-searching travel to and from the destination. Getting Around gives an overview of the transport options when you arrive.

The peculiar demands of each destination determine how sub-sequent chapters are broken up, but some things remain constant. We always start with background, then proceed to sights, places to stay, places to eat, entertainment, getting there and away, and getting around information – in that order.

Heading Hierarchy Lonely Planet headings are used in a strict hierarchical structure that can be visualised as a set of Russian dolls. Each heading (and its following text) is encompassed by any preceding heading that is higher on the hierarchical ladder.

Entry Points We do not assume guidebooks will be read from beginning to end, but that people will dip into them. The tradi-tional entry points are the list of contents and the index. In addition, however, some books have a complete list of maps and an index map illustrating map coverage.

There may also be a colour map that shows highlights. These highlights are dealt with in greater detail in the Facts for the Visitor chapter, along with planning questions and suggested itin-eraries. Each chapter covering a geographical region usually begins with a locator map and another list of highlights. Once you find something of interest in a list of highlights, turn to the index.

Maps Maps play a crucial role in Lonely Planet guidebooks and include a huge amount of information. A legend is printed on the back page. We seek to have complete consistency between maps and text, and to have every important place in the text captured on a map. Map key numbers usually start in the top left corner.

Although inclusion in a guidebook usually implies a recommen-dation we cannot list every good place. Exclusion does not necessarily imply criticism. In fact there are a number of reasons why we might exclude a place – sometimes it is simply inappropriate to encourage an influx of travellers.

Introduction

You can always tell something about the character of a city by the nicknames it has picked up. Appropriately for the city that inspired *The Strange Tale of Dr Jekyll and Mr Hyde*, Edinburgh has two contradictory – but complementary – ones.

The Athens of the North, a name inspired by the great thinkers of the Scottish Enlightenment, invokes images of high culture and high ideals, of art and literature, and of scientific achievement. It is here that each summer the world's biggest arts festival rises, phoenix-like, from the ashes of last year's rave reviews and broken box-office records to produce yet another string of superlatives. And it was here, in 2000, beneath the Greek temples of Calton Hill – Edinburgh's acropolis – that the Scottish parliament convened for the first time in almost 300 years.

But Edinburgh is also Auld Reekie, an altogether earthier place that thumbs its nose at the pretensions of the literati. Auld Reekie is a city of bars and clubs, of all-night parties and overindulgence, of loud singing in pubs and impromptu music sessions, of wandering home through cobbled streets at dawn. It is the city that inspired Robert Louis Stevenson, that tempted him from his law lectures at the university to explore the drinking dens and lurid street life of 19th-century Old Town. And it is the city of Beltane, the resurrected pagan May Day festival where half-naked revellers dance in the flickering firelight of bonfires beneath the stony indifference of Calton Hill's pillared monuments.

Despite – or more probably because of – this split personality, Edinburgh consistently comes out top in travellers' polls and in surveys measuring the quality of life in UK cities. It was voted second only to London in *Condé Nast Traveller* magazine's Best UK City 2000 poll, and readers of the *Guardian* newspaper voted it their favourite city for three years running (1999–2001).

Quite apart from its lively cultural and social life, one of its many attractions is the way the city is intertwined with the surrounding countryside – Edinburgh is a town entangled in its landscape. The rocky peak of Arthur's Seat overlooks the Old Town and the battlements of Salisbury Crags, a natural counterpart to the castle walls, while the leafy corridor of the Water of Leith snakes along only yards from the elegant Georgian terraces of New Town. It's possible to walk or cycle from the city centre to the Pentland Hills almost without touching a Tarmac road.

Above all, Edinburgh is a city that begs to be explored. From the warren of the wynds that riddle the Old Town to the urban villages of Stockbridge, Duddingston and Cramond, it beckons you to walk just a little farther, to take a look around the next bend. Every corner turned reveals sudden views and unexpected vistas – green sunlit hills, a glimpse of rust-red crags, a blue flash of distant sea.

Whether you tastes tend towards Athens or Auld Reekie, Edinburgh is there to be experienced and takes visitors far beyond the Fringe (and the Festival).

9

Facts about Edinburgh

HISTORY
First Immigrants

Scotland's earliest inhabitants were hunter-gatherers, who began pushing northwards from England, Ireland and northern Europe as the glaciers retreated in the wake of the last Ice Age around 10,000 BC. Over the next few thousand years these colonisers came in waves to different parts of the country. There are indications of Baltic cultures in eastern Scotland and Irish cultures on the western islands. Mesolithic flints from northern France have been found at many sites.

Recent archaeological investigations at Cramond, on the north-western edge of Edinburgh, have uncovered evidence of habitation there dating to 8500 BC – the earliest known traces of human activity in Scotland.

The Neolithic era, beginning in the 4th millennium BC, brought a new way of life, with agriculture, stock breeding and trading. These changes caused an increase in population and more complex patterns of social organisation evolved to control them. With organised groups of workers, more ambitious construction projects became possible.

Edinburgh's Castle Rock, a volcanic crag with three vertical sides, dominates the city centre. This natural defensive position attracted the first settlers; the earliest signs of habitation on the rock date back to around 900 BC. There is also evidence of ancient habitation on Arthur's Seat, Blackford Hill and Craiglockhart Hill. The Iron Age reached Scotland around 500 BC with the arrival of Celtic settlers from Europe.

Roman Attempts at Colonisation

The Roman invasion of Britain began in 55 BC, when Julius Caesar's legions first crossed the English Channel. However, the Roman onslaught ground to a halt in the north. Between AD 78 and 84, the Roman governor Agricola (whose son-in-law, Tacitus, named the northern part of Scotland Caledonia after the Caledones – the first tribe he came across) marched northwards and spent several years trying to subdue the wild tribes the Romans called the Picts (from the Latin *pictus*, meaning painted).

By the 2nd century, Emperor Hadrian had decided that this inhospitable land of mist, bogs, midges and warring tribes had little to offer the Roman Empire and built the wall (AD 122–28) that took his name (close to the modern border between Scotland and England). Two decades later Hadrian's successor, Antoninus Pius, invaded Scotland again and built a turf rampart, the Antonine Wall, between the Firth of Forth and the River Clyde. An important Roman fort and supply station was built at Cramond, with other garrisons at Inveresk and Dalkeith, but they were only manned for about 40 years before the Romans again withdrew.

Celts & Northumbrians

When the Romans first arrived in the Lothian region, the chief tribe they encountered was the Votadini, who had settlements on Castle Rock, Arthur's Seat and Blackford Hill. Little is known about them but it seems likely that these ancient Britons were the ancestors of the Gododdin, who are mentioned by the Welsh bard Aneirin in a 7th-century manuscript. Aneirin relates how Mynyddog Mwynfawr, king of the Gododdin, feasted with his warriors in the 'halls of Eidyn' before going into battle with the Angles (the tribe who gave their name to Angle-land, or England) at Catraeth.

The 'capital' of the Gododdin was called Dun Eiden, which means 'Fort on the Hill Slope', and almost certainly referred to Castle Rock. The Angles, from the kingdom of Northumbria in north-eastern England, defeated the Gododdin and captured Dun Eiden in 638. It is thought that the Angles took the existing Celtic name 'Eiden' and tacked it onto their own Old English word for fort, 'burh', to create the forerunner of the name Edinburgh.

The historian Bede attributes Christianity's arrival in Scotland to St Ninian who established a centre in Whithorn, in the south-west, in 397. St Columba set up his mission on the island of Iona in the 6th century, and spread the Gospel in the west and north. By the late 8th century, most Scottish tribes had converted to Christianity.

The MacAlpin Kings

The name Scotland is thought to be derived from the Scotti, or Scots, a Gaelic-speaking Irish tribe who colonised the west of Scotland (Dalriada) in the 6th century. The Scots and Picts were drawn together by the threat of invasion by the Norsemen (Vikings) and by their common Christianity.

In 843 Kenneth MacAlpin, the king of Dalriada (modern-day Kintyre and Argyll) and son of a Pictish princess, took advantage of the Picts' custom of matrilineal succession to take over the Pictish throne, thus uniting Scotland north of the Firth of Forth into a single kingdom. He made Scone (near Perth) his capital and brought to it the sacred Stone of Destiny used in the coronation of Scottish kings. Thereafter the Scots gained cultural and political ascendancy.

Nearly 200 years later, Kenneth Mac-Alpin's great-great-great-grandson, Malcolm II (reigned 1005–18), defeated the Northumbrian Angles led by King Canute at the Battle of Carham (1018) near Roxburgh on the River Tweed. This victory brought Edinburgh and Lothian under Scottish control and extended Scottish territory as far south as the Tweed.

The Canmore Dynasty

Malcolm II's grandson was Malcolm III Canmore (reigned 1057–93). Malcolm III's father Duncan was murdered by Macbeth (as described in Shakespeare's eponymous play), and Macbeth himself was killed by Malcolm at Lumphanan in 1057. With his Saxon queen, Margaret, Malcolm Canmore founded a solid dynasty of able Scottish rulers. They introduced new Anglo-Norman systems of government and religious foundations. Malcolm and Margaret had their main home in Dunfermline but regularly visited the fort at Edinburgh.

Until this period there was no record of a town at Edinburgh – just the fort – but from the 11th century a settlement grew along the ridge to the east of Castle Rock. It was made into a royal burgh (a self-governing town with commercial privileges) no later than 1124, when Malcolm's son, David I (reigned 1124–53), held court at the castle and founded the abbey at Holyrood.

David's mother Margaret had been a deeply religious woman and either he or his brother, Alexander I (reigned 1107–24), built a church in her honour on Castle Rock. It survives today as St Margaret's Chapel, the city's oldest building. David I increased his power by adopting the Norman feudal system, granting land to noble Norman families in return for their acting as what amounted to a royal police force.

The royal burghs – which included Edinburgh and Canongate – were permitted to conduct foreign trade, for which purpose Edinburgh created a port at nearby Leith. Edinburgh at the beginning of the 12th century was still something of a backwater, playing second fiddle to the wealthy burghs of Stirling, Perth and Berwick. That altered when David I's successor Malcolm IV (reigned 1153–65) made the castle in Edinburgh his chief residence and royal treasury.

During this period, the Highland clans remained an inaccessible law unto themselves in their glens. A cultural and linguistic divide grew up between the Gaelic-speaking Highlanders and the Scots-speaking Lowlanders, and still persists to the present day.

Wars of Independence

Two centuries of the Canmore dynasty came to an end in 1286 when Alexander III fell to his death over a sea-cliff at Kinghorn in Fife. He was succeeded by his four-year-old granddaughter, Margaret (the Maid of Norway), who was engaged to the son of King Edward I of England.

Sadly, Margaret died in 1290 during the sea voyage to Scotland from her home in Norway, and there followed a dispute over the succession to the throne. There were no less than 13 'tanists' or claimants, but in the end it came down to two: Robert de Brus, lord of Annandale, and John Balliol, lord of

Galloway. As the greatest feudal lord in Britain, Edward I of England was asked to arbitrate – he chose Balliol, whom he thought he could manipulate more easily. Instead of withdrawing, as the Scots nobles expected, Edward tightened his feudal grip on Scotland, treating the Scots king as his vassal rather than his equal. The humiliated Balliol finally turned against Edward and allied Scotland with France in 1295, thus beginning the enduring 'Auld Alliance'.

The English king responded with a bloody attack. In 1296 he marched on Scotland with an army of 30,000 men, razed the ports of Berwick and Dunbar and butchered the citizens, and captured the castles of Berwick, Edinburgh, Roxburgh and Stirling. Balliol was incarcerated in the Tower of London, oaths of allegiance were demanded from Scottish nobles and, in a final blow to Scottish pride, Edward I removed the Stone of Destiny, the coronation stone of the kings of Scotland, from Scone and took it back to London (see the boxed text 'The Stone of Destiny' in the Things to See & Do chapter).

Bands of rebels led by local warlords attacked and harried the English occupiers. One such band, led by William Wallace, defeated the English army at the Battle of Stirling Bridge in 1297, but Wallace was captured and executed in London in 1305. The Scots nobles, inspired by Wallace's example, looked around for a new leader and turned to Robert the Bruce, grandson of the lord of Annandale who had been rejected by Edward in 1292. Bruce murdered his rival, John Comyn, in February 1306 and had himself crowned king of Scotland at Scone the following month.

Bruce mounted a campaign to drive the English out of Scotland but suffered repeated defeats. According to legend, while Bruce was on the run he was inspired by a spider's persistence in spinning its web to renew his own efforts. He went on to win a famous victory over the English, led by Edward II, at the Battle of Bannockburn in 1314. Continued raids on the north of England forced Edward II to sue for peace and, in 1328, the Treaty of Northampton (also known as the Treaty of Edinburgh) gave

The Declaration of Arbroath

During the Wars of Independence, a group of Scottish nobles sent a letter to Pope John XXII requesting support for the cause of Scottish independence. Bearing the seals of eight earls and 31 barons, and written in Latin by the abbot of Arbroath in 1320, it is the earliest document that seeks to place limits on the power of a king.

Having railed against the tyranny of Edward I of England and having sung the praises of Robert the Bruce, the Declaration of Arbroath famously concludes:

> Yet even the same Robert, should he turn aside from the task and yield Scotland or us to the English king or people, him we should cast out as the enemy of us all, and choose another king to defend our freedom; for so long as a hundred of us remain alive, we will yield in no least way to English dominion. For we fight, not for glory nor for riches nor for honour, but only and alone for freedom, which no good man surrenders but with his life.

Scotland its independence, with Robert I, the Bruce, as its king.

One of Robert's last acts before his death in 1329 was to grant Edinburgh a charter giving it control over the port of Leith, the mills on the Water of Leith and much of the surrounding countryside, effectively making it Scotland's most important burgh.

The Stewart Dynasty

Bannockburn and the Treaty of Northampton had no lasting effect. After the death of Robert I, the country was ravaged by civil disputes and continuing wars with England. Edinburgh was occupied several times by English armies, and in 1385 the Kirk of St Giles was burnt to the ground. Robert was succeeded by his five-year old son, David II (reigned 1329–71), who returned from exile in France in 1341 and made Edinburgh his main residence, building a tower house on the site of what is now the Half Moon Battery in Edinburgh Castle. When David II died without a son, the crown passed to his nephew, Robert II (1371–90), the child of his sister Marjory and her husband Walter, the third high steward of Scotland. Thus was born the Stewart dynasty, which would rule Scotland and Britain for the next 300 years.

By the mid-15th century, Edinburgh was the de facto royal capital and political centre of Scotland. The coronation of James II (reigned 1437–60) was held in the abbey at Holyrood and the Scottish parliament met in the Tolbooth on High St or in the castle. The city's first effective town wall was constructed at about this time and enclosed Old Town as far east as Netherbow and the area around Grassmarket. This overcrowded area – now the most populous town in Scotland – became a medieval Manhattan, forcing its densely packed inhabitants to build upwards instead of outwards, and creating tenements soaring up to 12-storeys high.

James IV & the Renaissance

James IV (reigned 1488–1513) married the daughter of Henry VII of England, the first of the Tudor monarchs, thereby linking the two royal families through 'the Marriage of the Thistle and the Rose'. This didn't prevent the French from persuading James to go to war against his in-laws, and he was killed at the Battle of Flodden in 1513, along with 10,000 of his subjects. To protect Edinburgh from a feared English invasion its citizens hurriedly built another wall – the Flodden Wall – around the city. The wall, which took over 40 years to build, was over 1¼-miles long, 7.5m high and 1.5m thick.

James IV's death ended a golden era that had seen the foundation of the Royal College of Surgeons, the establishment of a supreme law court and the introduction of printing in Edinburgh. Much graceful Scottish architecture dates from this time, and the Renaissance style can be seen in the alterations and additions made to the royal palaces at Holyrood, Stirling, Linlithgow and Falkland. The building of collegiate churches and universities brought opportunities for education along French lines.

Renaissance ideas flourished throughout James IV's reign. Scottish poetry thrived, created by 'makars' (makers of verses) such

as William Dunbar, the court poet of James IV, and Gavin Douglas. The intellectual climate provided fertile ground for the rise of Protestantism, a reaction against the perceived wealth and corruption of the medieval Roman Catholic Church, which would eventually lead to the Reformation.

Mary Queen of Scots & the Reformation

In 1542, King James V lay on his deathbed in Falkland Palace in Fife – broken-hearted, it is said, after his defeat by the English at Solway Moss. His French wife, Mary of Guise, had borne him two sons but both had died in infancy. On 8 December a messenger brought word that his wife had given birth to a baby girl at the Palace of Linlithgow. Fearing the end of the Stewart dynasty and recalling its origin through Robert the Bruce's daughter, James sighed, 'It cam' wi' a lass, and it will gang wi' a lass.' He died a few days later, leaving his week-old daughter Mary to inherit the throne as queen of Scots.

In 1548 Mary (reigned 1542–67) was sent to France, leaving the country to be ruled by regents who rejected overtures from Henry VIII of England urging them to wed the infant queen to his son. Henry was furious and sent his armies to take vengeance on the Scots. Parts of Edinburgh were razed, Holyrood Abbey was sacked and the Border

Mary Queen of Scots

abbeys of Melrose, Dryburgh and Jedburgh were burnt down. The Rough Wooing, as it was called, failed to persuade the Scots of the error of their ways. In 1558, Mary was married to the French dauphin and became queen of France as well as Scotland.

While Mary was in France, being raised as a Roman Catholic, the Reformation tore through Scotland. The wealthy Catholic Church was riddled with corruption and the preachings of John Knox, a pupil of the Swiss reformer Calvin, found sympathetic ears. In 1560 the Scottish parliament created a Protestant church that was independent of Rome and the monarchy. The Latin Mass was abolished and the pope's authority denied.

Following the death of her sickly husband, the 18-year-old Mary returned to Scotland, arriving at Leith on 19 August 1561. A week later she was formally welcomed to her capital city, dining in Edinburgh Castle before proceeding down the Royal Mile to the Palace of Holyroodhouse, where she held a famous audience with John Knox. The great reformer harangued the young queen and tried her Catholic faith; she later agreed to protect the Protestant Church in Scotland while continuing to hear Mass in private.

She married Henry Stewart, Lord Darnley, in the Chapel Royal at Holyrood and gave birth to a son (later James VI) in Edinburgh Castle in 1565. Any domestic bliss was short-lived and, in a scarcely believable train of events, Darnley was involved in the murder of Mary's Italian secretary Rizzio (rumoured to be her lover). Darnley himself was then murdered at his Edinburgh home, probably by Mary's new lover and second-husband-to-be, the earl of Bothwell.

Mary's enemies – led by her bastard half-brother Lord James Stewart, the earl of Moray – finally confronted her at Carberry Hill, just east of Edinburgh, and Mary was forced to abdicate in 1567. Her son, the infant James VI (reigned 1567–1625), was crowned at Stirling and a series of regents ruled in his place. When Queen Elizabeth I of England died childless in 1603, James VI of Scotland inherited the English throne in the so-called Union of the Crowns, thus becoming James I of Great Britain (usually written as (VI/I). James moved his court to London and, for the most part, the Stewarts ignored Edinburgh from then on. Indeed, when Charles I (reigned 1625–49) succeeded James in 1625, he couldn't be bothered to come north to Edinburgh to be formally crowned as king of Scotland until 1633.

Covenanters & Civil War

The 17th century was a time of civil war in Scotland and England. The arrogant attempts by Charles I to impose episcopacy (the rule of bishops) and an English liturgy on the Scottish Church set off public riots in Edinburgh. The Presbyterian Scottish Church believed in a personal bond with God that had no need of mediation through priests, popes and kings, and on 28 February 1638 hundreds gathered in Greyfriars Kirkyard to sign a National Covenant, affirming their rights and beliefs. Scotland was divided between the Covenanters and those who supported the king.

Edinburgh remained mostly unaffected by the civil wars of the 1640s but was laid low by the plague that raged between 1644 and 1645, when a fifth of the population died. Although the Scots opposed Charles I's religious beliefs and autocratic rule, they were appalled when Oliver Cromwell's parliamentarians executed the king in 1649. They offered his son the Scottish crown as long as he signed the Covenant, which he did. Charles II (reigned 1649–85) was crowned at Scone on 1 January 1651 but was soon forced into exile by Cromwell, who invaded Scotland and captured Edinburgh.

Following Charles II's restoration in 1660, he reneged on the Covenant; episcopacy was reinstated and hard-line Presbyterian ministers were deprived of their churches. Many clergymen rejected the bishops' authority and started holding outdoor services, or conventicles. Charles' brother and successor, James VII/II (1685–89) was a Catholic who made worshipping as a Covenanter a capital offence. It was during this period that Greyfriars Kirkyard was used as a Covenanters prison (see the boxed text 'The MacKenzie Poltergeist' in the Things to See & Do chapter).

With the arrival in England of the Protestant William of Orange in 1688, the Catholic Stuart monarchy was doomed (the spelling 'Stuart' was preferred to 'Stewart' after 1603, in deference to their French allies, whose alphabet has no 'w'). Scottish royalists held on to Edinburgh Castle in the name of King James during the Long Siege of 1689. Their leader, the duke of Gordon, held a famous conference with John Graham of Claverhouse (known as 'Bonnie Dundee') at the western postern of the castle. Dundee then rode off to raise a Jacobite army and began five more months of civil war that ended with his death at the Battle of Killiecrankie.

Union with England
By the end of the 17th century, Edinburgh was indisputably Scotland's most important city. It had been made a cathedral city by Charles I in 1633; the Parliament Hall was built next to St Giles in 1639; and the Bank of Scotland was founded there in 1695. But civil war had left the country and its economy ruined. In the 1690s, famine killed up to a third of the population in some areas. The situation was exacerbated by the failure of an investment venture in Panama (the so-called Darien Scheme, set up by the Bank of England to boost the economy), which resulted in widespread bankruptcy.

The failure of the Darien Scheme made it clear to wealthy Scottish merchants and stockholders that the only way to gain access to the lucrative markets of developing colonies was through union with England. The English parliament favoured union through fear of Jacobite sympathies in Scotland being exploited by their French enemies, and threatened to end the Scots' right to English citizenship and ban the duty-free export of their goods to England. They also offered a financial incentive to those who lost money in the Darien Scheme. Despite opposition, the Act of Union – which brought the two countries under one parliament, one sovereign and one flag, but preserved the independence of the Scottish Church and legal system – took effect on 1 May 1707.

On receiving the Act in Edinburgh, the chancellor of Scotland, Lord Seafield – leader of the parliament that the Act abolished – is said to have murmured, 'Now there's an end to an auld sang.' Robert Burns later castigated the wealthy politicians who engineered the Union in characteristically stronger language: 'We're bought and sold for English gold – such a parcel of rogues in a nation!'

The Jacobites
The Jacobite rebellions of the 18th century sought to displace the Hanoverian monarchy (chosen by the English parliament in 1701 to succeed the house of Orange) and restore a Stuart king to Britain's throne. (The name Jacobite comes from Jacob, the Latin form of James – the Jacobites were originally supporters of the exiled James VII/II.)

James Edward Stuart, known as the Old Pretender, was the son of James VII/II. With French support he arrived in the Firth of Forth with a fleet of ships in 1708, causing panic in Edinburgh, but was seen off by English men-o-war. Another attempt in 1715 fizzled out after the inconclusive Battle of Sheriffmuir but prompted the building of stronger defences at Edinburgh Castle.

In 1745 the Old Pretender's son, Charles Edward Stuart (Bonnie Prince Charlie), landed in Scotland to claim the crown for his father. Supported by an army of Highlanders, he marched southwards and captured Edinburgh (except for the castle) in September 1745, holding court at Holyrood before defeating the Hanoverian forces of Sir John Cope at Prestonpans (near Musselburgh, just east of the capital). He got as far south as Derby in England but success was short-lived; a Hanoverian army led by the duke of Cumberland harried him all the way back to the Highlands, where Jacobite dreams were finally extinguished at Culloden in 1746. Jacobite prisoners were held in Edinburgh Castle, which became an important military garrison.

The Scottish Enlightenment
Increasing stability in the second half of the 18th century allowed Edinburgh to expand.

Desperate to relieve the pressure on over-crowded and insanitary Old Town, the city council proposed to 'boldly enlarge Edinburgh to the utmost'. The council sponsored an architectural competition to design a 'New Town'; the winner was the unknown, 23-year-old James Craig. Over the next 50 years, elegant Georgian terraces spread across the low ridge to the north of the castle. Many of the finest houses were designed by architect Robert Adam, whose neoclassical style – a revival of Greek and Roman forms – swept through Europe in the late 18th and early 19th centuries.

Following the removal of the Scottish parliament in 1707, Edinburgh declined in political importance but its cultural and intellectual life flourished. During the period known as the Scottish Enlightenment (roughly 1740–1830), Edinburgh became known as 'a hotbed of genius'. The philosophers David Hume and Adam Smith and the sociologist Adam Ferguson emerged as influential thinkers, nourished on generations of theological debate. Medic William Cullen produced the first modern pharmacopeia, chemist Joseph Black advanced the science of thermodynamics, and geologist James Hutton challenged long-held beliefs about the age of the Earth.

After centuries of bloodshed and religious fanaticism, people applied themselves with the same energy and piety to the making of money and the enjoyment of leisure. There was a revival of interest in Scottish history and vernacular literature, reflected in Robert Fergusson's satires and Alexander MacDonald's Gaelic poetry. The poetry of Robert Burns, a man of the people, achieved lasting popularity. Sir Walter Scott, the prolific novelist and ardent patriot, unearthed the Scottish crown jewels and had them put on public display in the castle.

The 19th Century

The renaissance of Scottish culture brought about by the Enlightenment awakened interest in Scotland elsewhere. In 1822, King George IV (reigned 1820–30) made the first state visit to Scotland by a reigning monarch since Charles II's coronation visit during December 1650 and January 1651. His procession through Edinburgh, clad in Highland dress, was stage-managed by Sir Walter Scott and marked the beginnings of Edinburgh's tourist industry. The royal association was cemented by Queen Victoria (reigned 1837–1901), who was famously besotted with all things Scottish, and wrote, 'The impression Edinburgh has made on me is very great; it is quite beautiful, totally unlike anything else I have ever seen.'

Religious tensions, never far from the surface, broke out again over who had the right to appoint Church of Scotland ministers. Since 1712, the civil authorities had held that power; the dissenters supported the right of the congregation to appoint their own minister. It all came to a head in Edinburgh in 1843, when 190 clergymen walked out of the General Assembly, then being held in the Church of St Andrew and St George on George St. The Disruption, as it came to be known, marked the founding of the Free Church of Scotland.

Although the Industrial Revolution affected Edinburgh on a much smaller scale than Glasgow, it brought many changes to the capital. Ironworks, potteries, glass factories and light engineering were added to the traditional industries of baking, brewing, distilling and publishing. Edinburgh's population increased rapidly, quadrupling in size to 400,000 – not much less than it is today. The Union Canal was completed in 1822, allowing coal from the Midlothian mines to be transported by barge to the Forth and Clyde canal and on to Glasgow. No sooner had the canal gone into operation than it was rendered largely obsolete by the arrival of the railways. New suburbs of Victorian tenement blocks spread over the country estates south of Old Town as the city grew, swallowing up nearby villages.

The 20th Century

In the 1920s the city's borders expanded again to encompass Leith in the north, Cramond in the west and the Pentland Hills in the south. Following the reorganisation of Scottish local government in 1975, the city expanded westwards to absorb South

Striking Edinburgh Castle sits regally atop the volcanic remains of Castle Rock.

Edinburgh's silhouetted towers from Calton Hill

Nae knickers? A thick tartan kilt for a chilly day

NEIL SETCHFIELD

Designed to set cogs whirring: Our Dynamic Earth takes you from the Big Bang to the 21st century.

MARTIN MOOS

The Royal Museum of Scotland's modern facade

JONATHAN SMITH

Going Greek: the unfinished National Monument

BETHUNE CARMICHAEL

Fancy bridge-spotting? The Forth Rail Bridge's three cantilevers span 1447m and have 8 million rivets

Queensferry, Ratho and Kirkliston. Inner-city slum-dwellers were moved into new housing estates ringing the city; these now foster massive social problems.

Following WWII, the city's cultural life blossomed, initiated by the Edinburgh International Festival and its fellow traveller the Fringe, both held for the first time in 1947 and now recognised as world-class arts festivals. The University of Edinburgh established itself as a teaching and research centre of international importance in areas such as medicine, electronics and artificial intelligence.

Ill-conceived development plans in the 1960s and '70s resulted in the demolition of large parts of Greenside (at the top of Leith Walk, St Leonards, Dalry and Tollcross) and the construction of various concrete monstrosities in and around the city centre, notably the St James Centre at the eastern end of Princes St. Fortunately, not all of the plans were realised, and Edinburgh was spared the horror of a motorway running the length of Princes St Gardens. In reaction, a strong conservation movement emerged to preserve and restore the city's old buildings and to control the impact of any new developments on the city's character. In 1995 both the Old and New Towns were declared UNESCO World Heritage Sites.

Scottish Self-Rule

In 1967 the Scottish National Party (SNP) won a landmark election victory when it took the Hamilton seat away from Labour, and support for independence grew when oil – and the revenues it generated – began to flow from the Scottish sector of the North Sea in the 1970s.

Both Labour and Conservative governments had toyed with the idea of offering Scotland devolution, or a degree of self-government, and in 1979 a referendum was held on whether to set up a directly elected Scottish Assembly. Fifty-two percent of those who voted said 'yes' to devolution but the Labour prime minister, James Callaghan, decided that everyone who didn't vote should be counted as a 'no'. By this devious reasoning, only 33% of the electorate had voted 'yes', so the Scottish Assembly was rejected.

From 1979 to 1997, Scotland was ruled by a Conservative government in London for which the majority of Scots hadn't voted. Separatist feelings, always present, grew stronger. Following the landslide victory of the Labour Party in May 1997, another referendum was held over the creation of a Scottish parliament. This time the result was overwhelmingly and unambiguously in favour.

Elections to the new parliament took place on 6 May 1999 and the Scottish parliament convened for the first time on 12 May in the Assembly Rooms of the Church of Scotland at the top of the Royal Mile. Donald Dewar (1937–2000), formerly the Secretary of State for Scotland, was nominated as first minister (the Scottish parliament's equivalent of prime minister). The parliament was officially opened by Queen Elizabeth II on 1 July 1999. A new parliament building is being constructed at Holyrood (see the boxed text 'The Bottomless Pit?' in the Things to See & Do chapter).

GEOGRAPHY & GEOLOGY

Edinburgh's latitude is 55° 57' north, its longitude 3° 13' west. The city is draped over and around a series of hills – the deeply eroded stumps of ancient volcanoes – between the Pentland Hills in the south and the broad Firth of Forth estuary to the north. During the last Ice Age (around 12,000 years ago) a vast ice sheet flowed from west to east around Castle Rock, creating a 'crag and tail' feature on which the Old Town was built.

Holyrood Park provides a strong touch of countryside in the city centre, with a varied landscape of hills, lochs and moorland. Edinburgh's only river, the Water of Leith, runs from the Pentlands northwards to the Firth of Forth at Leith, along the north-western border of New Town.

CLIMATE

Edinburgh has a cool temperate climate. Given just how far north the city lies (Edinburgh is on the same latitude as Labrador in Canada), you might expect the climate to

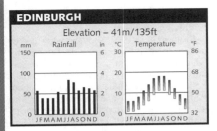

be colder than it is but the winds from the Atlantic are warmed by the Gulf Stream. The eastern coast tends to be warmer and drier than the western. July and August are the warmest months, when temperatures average a high of 18°C, but are also the wettest; winter temperatures rarely drop below 0°C, although winds off the North Sea can rattle your teeth. The average annual rainfall is around 650mm.

The weather changes quickly – a rainy day can often be followed by a sunny one. May and June are generally the best bet for dry, sunny weather but you can expect rain at any time. A distinctive feature of Edinburgh's weather is the 'haar' – a dense, chilly fog that often blows in from the North Sea when the wind is in the east. You can usually escape by heading just a few miles inland.

ECOLOGY & ENVIRONMENT

Edinburgh earned its sobriquet of Auld Reekie (Old Smoky) in the 17th century from the pall of smoke above the city, which was caused by the huge concentration of domestic fires. With the coming of the Industrial Revolution, pollution from factories and steam trains added to the grime. Beginning in the 1950s, a series of smokeless zones were set up that now encompass the whole city. This has encouraged the cleaning of soot-blackened stonework on many of its buildings, restoring them to their original colour. Others have not been cleaned because of the danger of damage to delicate stonework – it may be hard to believe, but the Scott Monument on Princes St was originally pale grey in colour.

With the aim of reducing traffic congestion and vehicle pollution, a system of dedicated bus lanes has been set up and a growing network of cycling routes has been built (see the boxed texts 'Amazing Technicolour Roadways' and 'Cycling Edinburgh' in the Getting Around chapter).

Edinburgh is the first city in the UK to introduce a 'car-free' housing development, 2 miles from the city centre on Gorgie Rd. Space usually allocated to car parking will be given to children's playgrounds, sports facilities and cycle paths. Solar power is used to augment the electricity supply and 'grey water' (waste water from baths and kitchen sinks) is recycled through a reed bed and reused for domestic washing.

The Water of Leith and the River Almond, formerly industrialised and polluted, have been cleaned up in the last two decades; the Almond is now so clean that otters and salmon have been sighted in recent years.

Organisations

A number of organisations concerned with the environment have their headquarters in Edinburgh. These include:

John Muir Trust (JMT; ☎ 554 0114, **W** www .jmt.org) 41 Commercial St, Leith, Edinburgh EH6 6JD. The JMT aims to bring wilderness areas of Scotland (recent acquisitions include Ben Nevis) into stable, long-term conservation ownership.

Royal Society for the Protection of Birds (RSPB; ☎ 311 6500, **W** www.rspb.org.uk) Dunedin House, 25 Ravelston Terrace, Edinburgh EHD4 3TP. The RSPB has nature reserves around Scotland that are open to the public.

Scottish Natural Heritage (SNH; ☎ 447 4784, **W** www.snh.org.uk) 12 Hope Terrace, Edinburgh EH9 2AS. SNH is a government agency responsible for the conservation of Scotland's wildlife, habitats and landscapes; it designates and manages National Nature Reserves (NNRs and Sites of Special Scientific Interest (SSSIs)

Scottish Wildlife Trust (SWT; ☎ 312 7765, **W** www.swt.org.uk) Cramond House, 16 Cramond Glebe Rd, Edinburgh EHD4 6NS. SWT is a voluntary agency that owns and runs over 120 nature reserves in Scotland.

GOVERNMENT & POLITICS

The Scottish parliament is a single-chamber system with 129 members (known as MSPs) elected through proportional representation and led by a first minister, currently Henry McLeish. It sits for four-year terms (the next elections are in 2003) and is responsible for education, health, housing, transport, economic development and other domestic affairs. It also has the power (as yet unused) to increase or decrease the rate of income tax in Scotland by up to 3%. The Scottish Executive – composed of the first minister, Scottish ministers, junior ministers and Scottish law officers – is the Scottish government, which proposes new laws and deals with the areas of responsibility outlined above, while the body of MSPs constitutes the Scottish legislature, which debates, amends and votes on new legislation.

Westminster still controls areas such as defence, foreign affairs and social security. Scotland is represented in Westminster by 72 Scottish members of parliament (MPs) in the House of Commons, out of a total of 659. The Scotland Office, headed by the Secretary of State for Scotland, is the Westminster department charged with ensuring Scotland's interests are represented in the UK government.

In contrast to Westminster, where the main political contest is between the Labour and Conservative parties with the Liberal Democrats coming a poor third, Scotland's has four main parties – the Labour Party, the Scottish National Party, the Scottish Conservative and Unionist Party (also known as the Tory Party or just the Tories) and the Liberal Democrats (Lib Dems) – and the main struggle for power is between Labour and the SNP.

The Conservative Party was predominantly opposed to devolution (the transfer of government powers from Westminster to Scotland), a policy proposed by the Labour Party in the hope of appeasing demands for independence. The long-term goal of Scottish Nationalists is complete independence for Scotland.

In the 1997 general elections, Scotland returned no Conservative MPs at all and in the 2001 UK elections the Tories managed

The Storm Over Section 28

Having convened for the first time in May 1999, the new Scottish parliament lost no time in miring itself in controversy. The subject in contention was the infamous Section 28, introduced by Margaret Thatcher's Conservative government in 1988, and widely perceived as discriminating against homosexuals. It was introduced into UK law as part of the Local Government Act of 1988. It states:

A local authority shall not: a) intentionally promote homosexuality or publish material with the intention of promoting homosexuality; b) promote the teaching in any maintained school of the acceptability of homosexuality as a pretended family relationship.

The effect of the Section was to prevent teachers discussing homosexuality in schools.

In the autumn of 1999, the Labour government announced its intention to repeal Section 28 and stirred up a veritable hornets' nest of homophobia. In Scotland, a coalition of conservatives, religious leaders and tabloid newspapers, led and funded by Brian Souter the millionaire founder of the Stagecoach global transport group, launched a 'Keep the Clause' campaign. They organised a privately run postal referendum on the question. Over 4 million ballot papers were issued but only 1.26 million were returned; of these, however, 86.8% were in favour of retaining Section 28.

Souter's poll had no legal force and in view of the poor response – over 60% of Scots refused to take part – its democratic credentials were dismissed by Labour ministers. Nevertheless, the Labour Party felt compelled to appease the right-wingers by conceding that statutory guidelines to schools would insist on the central role in society of heterosexual marriage and the nuclear family.

In June 2000, the Scottish parliament voted by 99 to 17, with two abstentions, to abolish Section 28. At the time of research, the clause remains in force in the rest of the UK.

to claw back just one seat in Scotland, with a majority of only 48 votes. In the 1999 Scottish parliament elections, Labour won 56 seats, the SNP 35, Conservatives 18, and the Lib Dems 17; the Scottish Socialist Party and the Green Party took one seat each.

Edinburgh's local government is in the hands of the City of Edinburgh Council, based in the City Chambers in the High St. The council is popularly elected and serves four-year terms.

ECONOMY

Edinburgh has one of the richest urban economies in the UK. Of Edinburgh's traditional industries, only brewing continues on a major scale, although closures, takeovers and 'rationalisations' have reduced the size of the workforce. Publishing and printing also continue on a smaller scale. Electronics and engineering are now the main industrial employers.

Edinburgh's economy is largely based on services (accounting for 85% of employment), mainly finance and tourism; in both sectors Edinburgh is second only to London. The Royal Bank of Scotland, the Bank of Scotland (which merged with Halifax plc in 2001) and many other financial bodies have their headquarters in the city. Other important service industries include retail, education, law, local government and medicine. The city's growth areas are in research, information technology, computer software and biotechnology, with many businesses located in new industrial parks in the west of the city.

Edinburgh's economy received a major boost with the creation of the Scottish parliament. New building and redevelopment projects are taking shape all over the city and the unemployment rate (around 2.8%) is well below the UK average. Edinburgh's per capita GDP is 10% higher than the UK average and economic growth of 21% is predicted for the period 1996–2002.

POPULATION & PEOPLE

Edinburgh's population of 453,430 (June 2000) is made up of white-collar and blue-collar workers in roughly equal proportions. In fact, with so many people employed in education, finance, government, law and medicine, it has Scotland's largest middle-class population. Immigration has added to the city's ethnic mix but on a smaller scale than other European capitals. Following the 19th-century famines in Ireland, many Irish settled here, as have a considerable proportion of English. There are also many smaller ethnic communities including Italians, Poles, Indians and Chinese. For much of the year the large student population adds to Edinburgh's cosmopolitanism, and during the Edinburgh Festival the city's population almost doubles with the influx of visitors.

ARTS

Edinburgh (together with Glasgow) dominates the arts in Scotland. It has an energetic cultural scene, partly reflected by its world-class festivals, which showcase an extraordinary range of artists and performers. Historically, however, the arts (except for literature) never seem to have caught the Scottish popular imagination – or at least not in a form recognised by modern culture vultures. It has been suggested that the need for creative expression perhaps took different, less elitist paths – in the *ceilidh* (see Society & Conduct later in the chapter), in folk music, stories, dance and oral poetry.

Literature

Edinburgh has always been at the heart of the Scottish literary scene, from the days of the medieval makars (makers of verses; poets) William Dunbar and Gavin Douglas to the modern 'brat pack' of Iain Banks, Irvine Welsh, Ian Rankin and Christopher Brookmyre.

Gavin Douglas (1476–1522) was the son of the earl of Angus and served as Provost of St Giles between 1502 and 1514. His poetic style ranged from colloquial to courtly and his major works include the *Tretis of the Tua Mariit Wemen and the Wedoe* (Treatise of the Two Married Women and the Widow) and a masterful translation of Virgil's *Aeneid*.

Though born in the Southern Uplands village of Leadhills, the poet Allan Ramsay (1686–1758) spent most of his life in Edinburgh. His best-known work is *The Gentle Shepherd*, a pastoral comedy that was much admired by Robert Burns. The house he built for himself on Castle Hill survives in Ramsay Garden.

Another poet who earned Burns' admiration was Robert Fergusson (1750–74), who was born in Edinburgh and wrote wittily in broad Scots about everyday city life, notably in the poem *Auld Reekie*. Tragically, he suffered a head injury after falling down stairs and died soon afterwards in a mental institution at the age of only 24.

Robert Burns (1759–96) himself spent only a few short spells in the capital between 1786 and 1788 and again in 1791, but was enthusiastically received by Edinburgh society, who hailed him 'the ploughman poet'. His love affair with the Edinburgh lady Mrs Agnes MacLehose inspired one of Burns' finest love poems, *Ae Fond Kiss*.

From the sublime to the ridiculous – if Burns was famous for the excellence of his poetry, William Topaz McGonagall (c.1825–1902) was renowned for the excruciating awfulness of his. Born in Edinburgh, he grew up in Orkney and Dundee, and lived most of his life in the latter. His *Poetic Gems* – including the appalling *Railway Bridge of the Silvery Tay* – are so bad they have become internationally famous.

James Boswell (1740–95), an Edinburgh advocate, is best known for his *Life of Johnson*, a biography of Dr Samuel Johnson, the English lexicographer who compiled the first dictionary of the English language. His *Journal of a Tour to the Hebrides* is a lively and engaging account of his expedition with Johnson to the western isles of Scotland.

Sir Walter Scott (1771–1832) is Scotland's greatest and most prolific novelist. The son of an Edinburgh lawyer, Scott was born in Guthrie St (off Chambers St; the house no longer exists) and lived at various New Town addresses before moving to his country house at Abbotsford (see the Excursions chapter). In 1787, the young Scott met Robert Burns in the house of an Edinburgh University professor. Scott's early works were rhyming ballads, such as *The Lady of the Lake*, and his first historical novels – Scott effectively invented the genre – were published anonymously. He almost single-handedly revived interest in Scottish history and legend in the early 19th century, and was largely responsible for organising King George IV's visit to Scotland in 1822. Plagued by debt in later life, he wrote obsessively – to the detriment of his health – in order to make money, but will always be best remembered for classic tales such as *The Antiquary*, *The Heart of Midlothian*, *Ivanhoe*, *Redgauntlet* and *Castle Dangerous*.

Along with Scott, Robert Louis Stevenson (1850–94) ranks as Scotland's best-known novelist. Born at 8 Howard Place in Inverleith, into a family of famous lighthouse engineers, Stevenson studied law at Edinburgh University but was always intent on pursuing the life of writer. An inveterate traveller, though dogged by ill-health, he settled in Samoa in 1889, where he was revered by the natives as 'Tusitala' – the teller of tales. Stevenson is known and loved around the world for those tales – *Kidnapped*, *Catriona*, *Treasure Island*, *The Master of Ballantrae* and *The Strange Case of Dr Jekyll and Mr Hyde*.

Sir Arthur Conan Doyle (1859–1930), the creator of Sherlock Holmes, was born in Edinburgh and studied medicine at Edinburgh University. He based the character of Holmes on one of his lecturers, the surgeon Dr Joseph Bell, who had employed his forensic skills and powers of deduction on several murder cases in Edinburgh.

Scotland's finest modern poet was Hugh MacDiarmid (1892–1978). Born Christopher Murray Grieve, and originally from the Dumfriesshire town of Langholm, he moved to Edinburgh in 1908 where he trained as a teacher and later a journalist, but spent most of his life in Montrose, Shetland, Glasgow and Biggar. His masterpiece is *A Drunk Man Looks at the Thistle*, a 2685-line Joycean monologue.

Born in Edinburgh and educated at the university, Norman MacCaig (1910–96) is widely regarded as the greatest Scottish poet of his generation. A primary-school teacher for almost 40 years, MacCaig wrote poetry that is witty, adventurous, moving, evocative and filled with sharp observation; poems such as 'November Night, Edinburgh' vividly capture the atmosphere of his home city. MacCaig could often be found enjoying a pint of beer with his contemporaries Robert Garioch (1909–81) and Sydney Goodsir Smith (1915–75) in Milne's Bar on the corner of Rose and Hanover Sts.

Dame Muriel Spark (b.1918) was born in Edinburgh and educated at James Gillespie's High School for Girls, an experience which provided material for perhaps her best-known novel *The Prime of Miss Jean Brodie*, a shrewd portrait of 1930s' Edinburgh. A prolific writer, Dame Muriel's latest novel *Aiding and Abetting*, based on the mysterious disappearance of Lord Lucan in 1974, was published in 2000.

Dorothy Dunnett (b.1923) was born in Fife but went to school in Edinburgh, overlapping with Muriel Spark at Gillespie's. She is best known for her two series of historical novels, *The Lymond Chronicles* and *The House of Niccolo*.

The novels of Irvine Welsh (b.1961), who grew up in Edinburgh's working-class district of Muirhouse, describe a very different world from that inhabited by Miss Jean Brodie – the modern city's underworld of drugs, drink, despair and violence. Famous for his debut novel *Trainspotting*, Welsh's best work is probably *Marabou Stork Nightmares*, in which a soccer hooligan – paralysed and in a coma – reviews his violent and brutal life.

Architecture

Edinburgh and its surroundings have a remarkable heritage of superb architecture from the 12th century to the present day.

Romanesque (12th century)

The Normans were great builders and their Romanesque style – with its characteristic round arches – can be seen in the old western door of Duddingston Parish Church and in St Margaret's Chapel (built by David I or his brother Alexander I around 1130), the oldest surviving building in Edinburgh.

Gothic (12th to 16th century)

As the Gothic style developed in England and Europe, it was brought to Scotland and adapted by the religious orders as they built the great Border abbeys of Melrose, Dryburgh and Jedburgh. The nave of Holyrood Abbey (13th century) is all that remains in Edinburgh from the early-Gothic period, while the interior of St Giles Cathedral is the only survivor from the 14th century. The more flamboyant late-Gothic style of the 15th and early 16th centuries, with its pointed arches, pinnacles and elaborate tracery, can be seen in the Trinity Apse (all that remains of the Trinity College Church), just off the Royal Mile, and in the parish churches of Restalrig and Corstorphine.

Post-Reformation (17th century)

After 1560 most churches were modified to suit the new religion, which frowned on ceremony and ornament. Greyfriars Kirk (built in 1620 and renovated in 1722) was the first new church to be built in Edinburgh after the Reformation. The unusual Canongate Kirk (1691) also dates from this period.

Georgian (18th to early 19th century)

Edinburgh has a rich legacy of Georgian architecture. The greatest exponents of the austere, symmetrical style in Scotland were the Adam family, in particular Robert Adam (1728–92). Among many of the neoclassical buildings he designed are the Old College of the University of Edinburgh, Register House on Princes St, Charlotte Square (possibly the finest examples of Georgian architecture anywhere) and also Hopetoun House near South Queensferry.

Victorian (19th century)

As the Scottish identity was reaffirmed by writers such as Burns and Scott, architects turned to the towers and turrets of the past for inspiration, and produced the so-called Scottish Baronial style. Fanciful buildings such as Fettes College (built between 1864 and 1870) were created and the fashion was also displayed in many of Edinburgh's civic buildings, such as the Royal Infirmary (built between 1872 and 1879) on Lauriston Place.

Victorian architects also looked to Europe for inspiration, but whereas the Georgians looked towards Greece, the Victorians tended to look towards Italy. The Royal Museum in Chambers St (built between 1861 and 1889) has a Venetian Renaissance facade, for example, while the Scottish National Portrait Gallery (built between 1885 and 1890) is modelled on Venice's Doge's Palace.

The 20th Century & Beyond The massive, modernist pile of St Andrews House (built between 1936 and 1939), sitting imperiously on Calton Hill, is one of the most impressive pieces of pre-WWII architecture in Edinburgh. Contemporary architecture has appeared all over Edinburgh in the last decade, as the city's building boom continues. The Edinburgh International Conference Centre on Morrison St, with its huge circular auditorium, is a modern showpiece, but the building everyone is waiting to see is the new Scottish parliament building at Holyrood, designed by the Catalan architect, the late Enric Miralles.

Edinburgh, like other cities in the UK, suffered badly from the onslaught of the motor car, shoddy council housing and bad planning in the late 20th century. Many citizens still haven't forgiven the university for replacing much of George Square with featureless tower blocks. Much of Princes St's northern side has given way to bland shopfronts and the St James Shopping Centre round the corner on Leith St is just plain ugly. A few fine 19th-century buildings have survived on Princes St, notably the glorious Renaissance palace of Jenners (1895), the world's oldest department store.

Painting
Scottish painting only really emerged in the mid-17th century with portraits by George Jameson (c.1589–1644), an Aberdonian who moved to Edinburgh in 1633 to paint decorations for Charles II's visit, and his pupil John Wright (1617–1700).

Scottish portraiture reached its peak during the Scottish Enlightenment in the second half of the 18th century with the Edinburgh-born figures of Allan Ramsay the Younger (1713–84), son of the poet Allan Ramsay, and Sir Henry Raeburn (1756–1823). Alexander Nasmyth (1758–1840), a pupil of Allan Ramsay, set up as a portraitist in 1778 but emerged as an important landscape painter, whose work had a great impact on 19th-century Scottish art.

A Fife lad who learned his craft at the Trustees' Academy in Edinburgh between 1799 and 1805, Sir David Wilkie (1785–1841) spent most of his life in London. One of the top Scottish artists of the 19th century, his paintings depict simple scenes of Scottish rural life.

The Trustees' Academy, particularly under the direction of Robert Scott Lauder (1803–69), was very influential and produced many of the great 19th-century painters, most notably William McTaggart (1835–1910). Exhibitions at the Royal Scottish Academy (RSA) in Edinburgh also helped to promote Scottish painters. David Octavius Hill (1801–70), a portrait painter and secretary of the RSA, was an important early pioneer of portrait photography. He and his partner Robert Adamson (1821–48) produced around 1800 magnificent photographs of Edinburgh people, from Newhaven fishwives to Church of Scotland ministers.

Three out of the four artists known as the Scottish Colourists – Samuel J Peploe (1871–1935), Francis CD Cadell (1883–1937) and John D Fergusson (1874–1961) from Leith – were born in Edinburgh. Their striking paintings drew upon French post-impressionism and Fauvism.

The Edinburgh School of the 1930s was a group of modernist painters who depicted the Scottish landscape. Chief among them were William Gillies (1898–1973), Sir William MacTaggart (1903–81; grandson of his earlier namesake) and Anne Redpath (1895–1965). Following WWII, artists such as Alan Davie and Sir Eduardo Paolozzi gained international reputations in abstract expressionism and pop art. Today, the focus of Scottish painting has swung back to the west, where the 'New Glasgow Boys' are producing work characterised by a concern for social issues.

Music

Sir John Clerk of Penicuik (1676–1755), a leading Scottish patron of the arts, was a notable composer, violinist and harpsichordist, who studied in Europe under the master Arcangelo Corelli. He paved the way for a flowering of Scottish music during the Enlightenment, when Edinburgh composers William McGibbon (c.1690–1756) and James Oswald (1710–69) adapted traditional Scots tunes to the classical Italian style. Thomas Erskine (1732–81), sixth earl of Kelly (known as 'Fiddler Tam'), was one of the most important British composers of the 18th century and a noted Edinburgh *bon viveur*. He was the first Scottish musician to produce a symphony.

Sir Alexander Campbell MacKenzie (1847–1935), the son of a noted Edinburgh violinist, and himself a professional violinist by the age of 11, was one of the finest British musicians and composers of his time; his best works include his *Piano Quartet* and the choral oratorio *Rose of Sharon*.

Scotland did not have a full-time symphony orchestra until the mid-1930s, and

Tartanalia

Bagpipes The bagpipe is one of the oldest musical instruments still in use today. Although no piece of film footage on Scotland is complete without the drone of the pipes, their origin probably lies outside the country.

The Highland bagpipe comprises a leather bag kept inflated by the blowpipe and held under the arm; the piper forces air through the pipes by squeezing the bag. Three of the pipes, appropriately known as the drones, play all the time without being touched by the piper. The fourth pipe, the chanter, is the one on which the melody is played.

Queen Victoria did much to repopularise the bagpipes with her patronage of all things Scottish. When staying at Balmoral she liked to be wakened by a piper playing outside her window.

Ceilidh The Gaelic word *ceilidh* (pronounced 'kaylee') means 'visit' – a ceilidh was originally a social gathering after the day's work was over. A local bard (poet) presided over the telling of folk stories and legends, and there was also music and song. These days, a ceilidh means an evening of entertainment including music, song and dance.

institutions such as the Scottish Opera and Scottish Ballet (based in Glasgow) were not founded until the 1960s.

Scotland has always had a strong folk tradition, which underwent an Edinburgh-based revival in the 1960s and '70s. Robin Hall and Jimmy MacGregor, the Corries and the hugely talented Ewan McColl worked the pubs and clubs in the capital and up and down the country. During this time the Incredible String Band and the Boys of the Lough successfully combined folk and rock and have been followed by Runrig

(who write songs in Gaelic), the Battlefield Band, Alba, Capercaillie and others.

Edinburgh rock musicians who made their names in the 1970s and '80s include Iain Anderson, front man for Jethro Tull, and Mike Scott of the Waterboys. Fish, the lead singer in Marillion, now produces solo albums and runs a successful recording studio in East Lothian. Barbara Dickson and Nazareth hail from Dunfermline, across the Forth.

When it comes to new bands, Edinburgh tends to be eclipsed by the hipper metropolis of Glasgow and the temptations of London.

Tartanalia

Highland Games Highland games are held in Scotland throughout the summer, and not just in the Highlands – the Edinburgh International Highland Games take place in late July and early August. Assorted sporting events with piping and dancing competitions attract locals and tourists alike.

Some events are peculiarly Scottish, particularly those that involve bouts of strength testing. The apparatus used can be pretty primitive – tossing the caber involves heaving a tree trunk into the air. Other popular events are throwing the hammer and putting the stone.

Tartan The oldest surviving piece of tartan – a patterned woollen material now made into everything from kilts to key-fobs – dates back to the Roman period. Today, tartan is popular the world over, and beyond – astronaut Al Bean took his MacBean tartan to the moon and back. Particular *setts* (tartan patterns) didn't come to be associated with particular clans until the 17th century, although today every clan, and indeed every Scottish football team, has one or more distinctive tartans.

The Kilt The original Scottish Highland dress was not the kilt but the *plaid* – a long length of tartan cloth wrapped around the body and over the shoulder. The wearing of Highland dress was banned after the Jacobite rebellions but revived under royal patronage in the following century. George IV and his English courtiers donned kilts for their visit to Scotland in 1822. Sir Walter Scott, novelist, poet and dedicated patriot, did much to rekindle interest in Scottish ways. By then, however, many of the old setts had been forgotten – some tartans are actually Victorian creations. The modern kilt only appeared in the 18th century and was reputedly invented by Thomas Rawlinson, an Englishman!

The Scottish Flag Scottish football and rugby supporters can never seem to make up their minds which flag to wave – the Saltire or the Lion Rampant. The Saltire, or St Andrew's Cross – a diagonal white cross on a blue ground – is one of the oldest national flags in the world, dating from the 12th century. Originally a religious emblem – St Andrew was crucified on a diagonal cross – it became a national emblem in the 14th century. According to legend, white clouds in the form of a saltire appeared in a blue sky during a battle between Scots and Saxons, urging the Scots to victory. It was incorporated in the Union Flag of the United Kingdom following the Act of Union in 1707.

The Lion Rampant – a red lion on a golden-yellow ground – is the Royal Banner of Scotland. It is thought to derive from the arms of King William the Lion (reigned 1165–1214), and strictly speaking should be used only by a Scottish monarch. It is incorporated in the British Royal Standard, quartered with the three lions of England and the harp of Ireland.

The city's contribution to the contemporary music scene includes: the rock band Idlewild; reggae-soul-pop singer Finlay Quaye; Shirley Manson, lead singer of Garbage; and the red-hot jazz saxophonist Tommy Smith.

Cinema

Scotland has never really had its own film industry but in recent years the government-funded agency Scottish Screen (☎ 0141-302 1730) has been created to nurture native talent and promote and develop all aspects of film and TV in Scotland.

Film-maker Bill Douglas (1934–91), the director of an award-winning trilogy of films documenting his childhood and early adult life, was born in the former mining village of Newcraighall, situated just south of Edinburgh.

Screen-writer John Hodge, who wrote the scripts for *Shallow Grave*, *Trainspotting* and *A Life Less Ordinary*, in collaboration with director Danny Boyle and producer Andrew Macdonald, is actually a qualified doctor who studied medicine at Edinburgh University from 1982 to 1987. Michael Caton-Jones, director of *Memphis Belle* and *Rob Roy* (and another graduate of Edinburgh University), was born in West Lothian.

Edinburgh's most famous son – in or out of the cinema – is of course the actor Sir Sean Connery, the original and best James Bond, and star of countless hit movies since. Connery started life as 'Big Tam' Connery, sometime milkman and brickie, born in a tenement in Fountainbridge.

Edinburgh hosts a highly regarded international film festival, based at the Filmhouse in Lothian Rd (see The Festival City special section for details).

Theatre & Music Hall

These days not everyone will have heard of the Scottish music-hall entertainer Sir Harry Lauder (1870–1950), but they almost certainly will have heard one or more of his songs. Born in Portobello, he worked as a flax spinner in Arbroath while still at school, then as a pitboy in a Lanarkshire coal mine in his teens. He won several talent competitions before achieving pro-fessional success in Glasgow. When he moved to London he was an immediate hit and then went on to wow audiences in the USA and around the world.

Two of his most famous songs, *Roamin' in the Gloamin* and *I Love a Lassie*, were written for his wife. Another, *Keep Right on to the End of the Road*, was written after their only son was killed in battle in WWI. Although he continued to perform he never fully recovered from this tragedy. Sometimes derided for his stage persona of a stereotypical bekilted Scot, he was enormously talented and his musical legacy lives on.

Edinburgh's world-famous Traverse Theatre has a well-deserved reputation for producing contemporary drama of the finest quality. It was founded during the 1962 Edinburgh Festival in a former brothel in James Court, off the Royal Mile, and from 1969 to 1992 was based in West Bow in Grassmarket. It is now housed in a purpose-built theatre next to the Usher Hall in Lothian Rd (see Theatre, Musicals and Comedy in the Entertainment chapter).

SCIENCE & PHILOSOPHY

The Scots have made a contribution to modern civilisation that is out of all proportion to the size of their country. Although Scotland accounts for only 10% of the British population, it has produced more than 20% of Britain's leading scientists, philosophers, engineers and inventors. Scots pioneered the modern disciplines of economics, sociology, geology, electromagnetic theory, anaesthesiology and antibiotics, and invented the steam engine, the pneumatic tyre, the telephone and the television.

Founded in 1583, Edinburgh University is one of the world's leading academic institutions. Its alumni include Charles Darwin (1809–82), who formulated the theory of evolution through natural selection, and James Burnett, Lord Monboddo (1714–99), who published a pre-Darwinian treatise, *On the Origin and Progress of Language*, which proposed that humans were descended from orang-utans.

Famous Edinburgh-born scientists include John Napier (1550–1617), the inventor of logarithms; James Hutton (1726–97), the founder of modern geology; James Clerk Maxwell (1831–79), who developed the theory of electromagnetism and is widely recognised as the 'father of electronics'; and the inventor of the telephone, Alexander Graham Bell (1847–1922).

Edinburgh's medical schools have produced the likes of William Hunter (1718–83), the pioneering surgeon and anatomist; Sir James Young Simpson (1811–70), who discovered the anaesthetic properties of chloroform; Joseph Lister (1827–1912), a leader in the field of antisepsis; and Dr Elsie Inglis (1864–1917), a pioneering woman doctor and founder of the Scottish suffragette movement.

The list of famous Scots goes on and on: James Watt (1736–1819), who revolutionised steam power; John McAdam (1756–1836), who developed road-building and surfacing techniques; Sir Alexander Fleming (1881–1955), co-discoverer of penicillin; Thomas Telford (1757–1834), one of the greatest civil engineers of his time; Charles Macintosh (1766–1843), inventor of rainproof material; John Dunlop (1840–1921), who invented the pneumatic tyre; John Logie Baird (1888–1946), pioneer of television; and Sir Robert Watson-Watt (1892–1973), a direct descendant of James Watt, who aided the development of the radar system that helped Britain gain victory in WWII.

Among his many achievements – notably becoming a student at Glasgow University at age 10, and becoming a professor by age 22 – William Thomson (Lord Kelvin; 1824–1907) formulated the second law of thermodynamics and supervised the laying of the first transatlantic telegraph cable.

The city's greatest philosophers and thinkers include David Hume (1711–76), author of *A Treatise on Human Nature*, and Adam Smith (1723–90), who wrote *The Wealth of Nations*.

In 1996, a team of Scottish embryologists working at the Roslin Institute near Edinburgh scored a first when they successfully cloned a sheep, Dolly, from the breast cell of an adult sheep. They added to his success when Dolly mated naturally with a Welsh ram; in April 1998 she gave birth to a healthy lamb, Bonnie.

SOCIETY & CONDUCT

Outside Scotland, Scots are often stereotyped as being a tight-fisted bunch, but nothing could be further from the truth – most are in fact extremely generous. Scots may appear reserved but they are passionate in their beliefs, whether they're about politics, religion or football. They generally treat visitors courteously, and class distinctions that so bedevil England are far less prevalent.

Edinburgh is Scotland's most middle-class city and those with the financial wherewithal enjoy the highest quality of urban life in the UK. The city's social problems have largely been pushed out to the large public housing estates surrounding the city, where unemployment, drug abuse and AIDS are endemic.

Dos & Don'ts

Though using the term 'British' is fine, the Scots understandably don't like being called English. If subjects such as religion or Scottish nationalism come up in a pub conversation, as a visitor it's probably best to practise your listening skills and not interject, at least till you're totally sure of the situation.

RELIGION

It's probably true that religion has played a more influential part in Scotland's history than in other parts of Britain. This remains true today: while barely 2% of people in England and Wales regularly attend church services, the attendance figure for Scotland is 10%.

Two-thirds of Scots belong to the Presbyterian Church (or Kirk) of Scotland, which is also the largest religious denomination in Edinburgh. There are two Presbyterian minorities: the Free Church of Scotland (known as the Wee Frees) and the United Free Presbyterians, found mainly in the Highlands and islands. In Edinburgh, other denominations include Episcopalians, Roman Catholics, Methodists and Baptists. There are also small communities of Jews, Muslims and Hindus.

LANGUAGE

The language of modern Edinburgh is, of course, English. However, from the 8th to the 19th centuries the common language of the city's inhabitants was 'Scots tung'.

Lowland Scots (sometimes called Lallans), like modern English, evolved from Old English and has Dutch, French, Gaelic, German and Scandinavian influences. As distinct from English as Norwegian is from Danish, it was the official language of the state in Scotland until the Act of Union in 1707, and was the language used by Robert Burns in his poetry. English rose to predominance as the language of government and of 'polite society' following the Union.

The spread of education and literacy in the 19th century eventually led to the Scots language being perceived as backward and unsophisticated – school children were often beaten for using Scots instead of English.

The Scots tongue persisted, however, and today it is undergoing a revival – Scots language dictionaries have been published, there are university degree courses in Scots language and literature, and Scots is studied as part of the school curriculum.

English spoken with a broad Scottish accent can be difficult for visitors to understand, and there are numerous Scots and Gaelic words that linger on in everyday English speech. Ye ken?

Scottish Gaelic

Greetings & Civilities

Good morning.
    Madainn Mhath.
    madding va
Good afternoon/Good evening.
    Feasgar math.
    feskurr ma
Good night.
    Oidhche mhath.
    uh eech uh va
How are you?
    Ciamar a tha thu?
    kimmer uh ha oo?
Very well, thank you.
    Glè mhath, tapadh leat.
    gley va tappuh leht
Please.
    Mas e do thoil e.
    mahs eh doh hawl eh
Thank you.
    Tapadh leat.
    tappuh leht

Small Talk

Do you speak Gaelic?
    A bheil Gàidhlig agad?
    uh vil gaa lick ackut?
Yes, a little.
    Tha, beagan.
    ha bake-an

What's your name?
    De an t-ainm a tha ort?
    jae an tannam uh ha orsht?
I'm ...
    Is mise ...
    is meeshuh ...
Good health! (Cheers!)
    Slàinte mhath!
    slahntchuh va!
Goodbye.
    Beannachd leat. (lit: Blessings go with you)
    byan achk leht
Goodbye.
    Mar sin leat. (lit: The same with you)
    mar shin leht

English Borrowings from Gaelic

Bard (poet)
    bard   *baard*
ben (hill)
    beinn   *bayn* or *been*
bog (soft, wet)
    bog   *bohk*
brogue (shoe)
    bròg   *bro-ck*
Sassenach (Englishman)
    Sasannach   *Sasunach*
Sporran (purse)
    sporan   *sporan*
whisky (water of life)
    uisge beatha   *ooshkuk behuh*

Facts for the Visitor

WHEN TO GO

Edinburgh is a year-round destination – no matter what time of year you visit there is always something to do.

In terms of weather the best times to explore Edinburgh are May and June, which are usually the sunniest months, and September, which often sees some 'Indian summer' sunshine. Although July and August are the busiest months in terms of tourist numbers, they are also often the wettest. However, Edinburgh enjoys the benefits of lying in a 'rain shadow' – the prevailing westerly winds dump most of their moisture in the west of Scotland, and the east is noticeably drier and sunnier. The winter months can be dull, grey and wet but during the occasional spell of clear, frosty weather the city sparkles in the sun like a jewel.

Another thing to think about is daylight. In midsummer, daylight hours are long and Edinburgh evenings are seemingly endless – the sun doesn't set till around 10.30pm and in late June/early July there's a glow in the sky all night. The downside of Edinburgh's high latitude is the midwinter blues – in late December/early January the sun doesn't come up until 9.30am and sets again around 3.30pm. People go to work in the dark and come home in the dark. However, that won't stop you enjoying the city's museums, galleries, shops, pubs and restaurants.

The city is overwhelmed with visitors during the main festival period (August to early September) and during the Hogmanay celebrations (around 1 January). If you plan to visit during these times, you should think about booking accommodation as far ahead as possible – a year ahead in the case of the festival.

For more climate details see that section in the Facts about Edinburgh chapter.

ORIENTATION

Central Edinburgh is dominated by Edinburgh Castle, perched atop its black, volcanic crag. Old Town stretches for a mile to the east of the castle, along a gently sloping ridge. The crest of the ridge is followed by the Old Town's main street, known as the Royal Mile, which leads to the Palace of Holyroodhouse. In the valley to the south of the Royal Mile lie Grassmarket, with its pubs and restaurants, and the narrow defile of Cowgate.

New Town lies on the crest of another ridge, only 300m north of Old Town. Princes St, New Town's main street (and the city's main shopping street), runs parallel to the Royal Mile. It helps to remember that the huge, pale grey Balmoral Hotel, with its clock tower, is at the eastern end of Princes St, and the huge, red-sandstone Caledonian Hotel is at the western end. In the valley between Old and New Towns lie the main railway line, Waverley train station and Princes St Gardens. The streets known as The Mound and North Bridge link Old and New Towns.

At the eastern end of Princes St rises Calton Hill, crowned by prominent monuments, and to its south-east lies the higher, rocky summit of Arthur's Seat (251m).

The Tourist Information Centre (TIC) lies between Waverley train station and Princes St, above the Princes Mall shopping centre. The bus station in the New Town is trickier to find; it's off the north-eastern corner of St Andrew Square, north of Princes St.

Bear in mind that long streets are known by different names at different points along their length. For example, following North Bridge southwards from Princes St it becomes South Bridge, Nicolson St, Clerk St, South Clerk St, Newington Rd, Minto St, Mayfield Gardens and Craigmillar Park, all in the space of 2 miles. Leith Walk stretches for over a mile between Edinburgh city centre and Leith, and although it is called Leith Walk for its entire length, different blocks of buildings have different names: for example, at the southern end you will see Union Place and Antigua St on one side; Elm Row and Greenside Place on the other.

MAPS

Lonely Planet's fold-out *Edinburgh City Map* is perfect for sightseeing. It is plastic-coated, virtually indestructible and indicates all the major landmarks, museums and shops. There's also a street index.

The ESIC (see Tourist Offices later) issues a handy, free pocket map of the city centre. For coverage of the whole city, the most detailed maps are Nicolson's *Edinburgh Citymap* (£3.50) and the Ordnance Survey's (OS) *Edinburgh Street Atlas* (£5.99). You can

Exploring Your Scottish Roots

It has often been said that Scotland's biggest export is its people – according to the Museum of Scotland, some 60 million people around the world claim to be of Scottish descent. Genealogy is hugely popular these days and many visitors to Edinburgh take the opportunity to do some detective work on their Scottish ancestry.

The main records used in Scottish genealogical research – the Statutory Registers of births, marriages and deaths (1855 to the present day), the Old Parish Registers (1533–1854) and the 10-yearly census returns from 1841 to 1901 – are held at the General Register Office (GRO) at the eastern end of Princes Street. The registration of births, marriages and deaths became compulsory in Scotland on 1 January 1855 – prior to that date, the ministers of the Church of Scotland kept registers of baptisms and marriages. The oldest surviving parish registers date back to 1553 but these records are far from complete and many births and marriages before 1855 went unrecorded. Next door to the GRO is the National Archives of Scotland (NAS), which holds records of wills, property transactions and many other items of interest to genealogists.

You can consult all these records yourself but make sure to do some research before leaving home – gather as much information as possible from birth, marriage and death certificates and other family papers in your possession, and interview elderly relatives. You will need full names, dates and places of birth, marriage or death in Scotland. One of the best guides is the book *Tracing Your Scottish Ancestry* by Kathleen B Cory, and there are many useful Web sites too – GenUKI (W www.genuki.org.uk) is a good starting point.

At the Scots Origins Web site (W www.origins.net/GRO) you can search the indexes to the Old Parish Registers and the Statutory Registers up to 100 years ago (75 years ago for deaths), and the indexes to the 1881 and 1891 census returns, on a pay-per-view basis. The International Genealogical Index (W www.familysearch.com), compiled by the Mormon Church, includes freely searchable records of Scottish baptisms and marriages from 1553 to 1875.

The **General Register Office for Scotland** (Map 3; ☎ 334 0380, fax 314 4400, W www.gro-scotland.gov.uk), New Register House, 3 West Register St, Edinburgh EH1 3YT, opens 9am to 4.30pm Monday to Friday. A full day's research costs £17; a half-day (from 1pm to 4.30pm) costs £10. If you book and pay for a place two to six weeks in advance (☎ 314 4433 from 2pm to 4pm Monday to Friday) the cost for a day's research is only £13.

The **National Archives of Scotland** (☎ 535 1334, fax 535 1328, W www.nas.gov.uk), 2 Princes St, Edinburgh EH1 3YY, opens 9am to 4.45pm Monday to Friday. On your first visit you must ask for a reader's ticket (free) – you will need some form of ID bearing your name and signature (for example, passport, driving licence, bank card). Use of the Historical Search Room is free and operates on a first-come, first-served basis – you can't reserve a seat here.

Another useful resource is the **Scottish Genealogy Society Library & Family History** (Map 8; ☎/fax 220 3677, W www.scotsgenealogy.com), 15 Victoria Terrace, Edinburgh EH1 2JL, which opens 10.30am to 5.30pm Tuesday and Thursday, 10.30am to 8.30pm Wednesday and 10am to 5pm Saturday. In addition to books and records, it maintains the world's largest collection of Scottish gravestone inscriptions. Admission is free to society members, £5 to nonmembers.

buy these at the ESIC and at many bookshops and newsagents.

The OS' 1:50,000 Landranger map *Edinburgh, Penicuik & North Berwick* (Sheet No 66; £5.25) covers the city and the surrounding region to the south and east at a scale of 2cm to 1km, and is useful for walking in the Pentland Hills and exploring East Lothian. *Edinburgh Seven Hills* (£3.95) by Harvey Maps is a walker's map with useful enlargements of Arthur's Seat and the other hills that lie within the city.

TOURIST OFFICES
Local Tourist Offices
The Edinburgh and Scotland Information Centre (ESIC; Map 3; ☎ 473 3800, fax 473 3881, e esic@eltb.org), above Princes Mall at 3 Princes St, opens 9am to 8pm Monday to Saturday, 10am to 8pm Sunday in July and August; 9am to 7pm Monday to Saturday, 10am to 7pm Sunday in May, June and September; and 9am to 5pm Monday to Wednesday, 9am to 6pm Thursday to Saturday and 10am to 5pm Sunday the rest of the year. The telephone line is often busy. The centre has an accommodation booking service, a currency exchange, a gift and book shop, and counters selling tickets for Edinburgh city tours and Scottish Citylink bus services (see the Getting There & Away chapter). There are also tourist information desks at Edinburgh airport and at the Old Craighall Junction service area on the main A1 road, about 5 miles east of the city centre.

There are electronic information terminals at various points around the city centre, notably outside the ESIC, at Mound Place (beside the Royal Scottish Academy on Princes St) and in front of the Caledonian Hotel at the eastern end of Princes St.

The Scottish Tourist Board/visitscotland headquarters (STB; ☎ 332 2433, fax 315 4545, e info@stb.gov.uk, w www.visit scotland.com), 23 Ravelston Terrace, Edinburgh EH4 3TP, deals with postal and telephone enquiries only. In London, the STB has a branch at 19 Cockspur St, London SW1 5BL, but for telephone enquiries call the Edinburgh office.

Tourist Offices Abroad
Overseas, the British Tourist Authority (BTA; w www.bta.org.uk) represents the STB and stocks masses of information, much of it free. For information in foreign languages, check out the Web site w www.visitbritain.com.

Contact the BTA before leaving home as some discounts are available only to people who have booked before arriving in Britain. Travellers with special needs (disability, diet and so on) should also contact the nearest BTA office. Addresses are listed on its Web site. Some overseas offices include:

Australia (☎ 02-9377 4400, fax 9377 4499, e visitbritainaus@bta.org.uk) Level 16, The Gateway, 1 Macquarie Place, Circular Quay, Sydney, NSW 2000
Canada (☎ 888 VISIT UK, fax 905-405 1835, e travelinfo@bta.org.uk) 5915 Airport Rd, Suite 120, Mississauga, Ontario L4V 1T1
France (☎ 01 44 51 56 20, fax 01 44 51 56 21) Maison de la Grande Bretagne, 19 Rue des Mathurins, F-75009 Paris (entrance in Rues Tronchet and Auber)
Germany (☎ 01801-468642, fax 069-97 112444, e gbinfo@bta.org.uk) Westendstrasse 16–22, D-60325 Frankfurt
Ireland (☎ 01-670 8000, fax 670 8244) 18–19 College Green, Dublin 2
Netherlands (☎ 020-689 0002, fax 689 0003, e britinfo.nl@bta.org.uk) Aurora Gebouw (5e), Stadhouderskade 2, NL-1054 ES Amsterdam
New Zealand (☎ 09-303 1446, fax 377 6965, e bta.nz@bta.org.uk) 17th Floor, NZI House, 151 Queen St, Auckland 1
USA (☎ 1 800 GO 2 BRITAIN, e travelinfo@ bta.org.uk) 625 N Michigan Ave, Suite 1001, Chicago IL 60611 (personal callers only) 551 Fifth Ave, Suite 701, New York, NY 10176-0799

TRAVEL AGENCIES
There are dozens of travel agencies all over Edinburgh – check the *Yellow Pages* to find the nearest. Two agencies that specialise in budget and student travel are usit Campus (Map 8; ☎ 668 3303), 53 Forrest Rd; and STA Travel (Map 8; ☎ 226 7747), 27 Forrest Rd; both issue ISIC cards.

American Express and Thomas Cook have offices in the city centre (see Money later in the chapter).

VISAS & DOCUMENTS
Passport

Your most important travel document is a passport, which should remain valid until well after your trip. If it's about to expire, renew it before you go. This may not be easy to do abroad and some countries insist your passport remains valid for up to six months after your arrival.

Applying for or renewing a passport can be an involved process, taking from a few days to several months, so don't leave it till the last minute. Bureaucracy usually grinds faster if you do everything in person rather than relying on the postal system or agents. You'll need to supply some or all of the following: passport photos, birth certificate, population register extract, signed statements and payment.

Australian citizens can apply at post offices or the passport office in their state capital; Canadians can apply at regional passport offices; New Zealanders can apply at any district office of the Department of Internal Affairs; and US citizens must apply in person (but may usually renew by mail) at a US Passport Agency office or some courthouses and post offices.

Citizens of EU countries need a national identity card (which usually involves less paperwork and processing time) for travel to Britain but taking a passport is advisable.

Visas

A visa is a stamp in your passport permitting you to enter a country for a specified period of time. Depending on your nationality, the procedure ranges from a mere formality to an endurance test. Sometimes you can get visas at borders or airports but it's better to have paperwork done before arrival.

There are various types of visa for Britain, including tourist, transit, business and work visas. Transit visas are usually cheaper than tourist or business visas but they only allow a very short stay and can be difficult to extend.

Currently, if you're a citizen of Australia, Canada, New Zealand, South Africa or the USA, you're given 'leave to enter' Britain at your place of arrival. Tourists from these countries are permitted to stay for up to six months without a visa but are prohibited from working. The Working Holidaymaker scheme, for Commonwealth citizens aged 17 to 27 inclusive, allows visits of up to two years but arrangements must be made in advance through a British embassy.

EU citizens can live and work in Britain free of immigration control and don't need a visa to enter the country.

The British immigration authorities have always been tough and are getting even tougher; dress neatly and carry proof that you have sufficient funds with which to support yourself. A credit card and/or an onward ticket will help. People have been refused entry because they happened to be carrying papers (such as references) that suggested they intended to work.

There are no immigration controls on entering Scotland from England or Northern Ireland. If you arrive from the Republic of Ireland or any other country, normal British customs and immigration regulations apply.

Visa requirements can change and you should always check with embassies or a reputable travel agent before travelling. For more information on British visa requirements, access the Foreign Office Web site at W visa.fco.gov.uk or the Lonely Planet Web site at W www.lonelyplanet.com.

Visa Extensions To extend your stay in the UK contact the Home Office, Immigration and Nationality Directorate (☎ 0870 606 7766), Block C, Whitgift Centre, Croydon, London CR9 1AT, *before* your existing permit expires. You'll need to send your passport with your application.

Onward Tickets

Although you don't need an onward ticket to be granted 'leave to enter' on arrival (see Visas earlier), it could help if there's any doubt over whether you have sufficient funds to support yourself and purchase an onward ticket in Britain.

Travel Insurance

A travel insurance policy to cover theft, loss and medical problems is a good idea but

ake me to the river, dip me in the Water of Leith.

Victorian palm house at the Royal Botanic Garden

ake a stroll through leafy West Princes St Gardens to St Cuthbert's Parish Church, built in the 1890s.

BETHUNE CARMICHAEL

Watering holes abound...whatever your tipple!

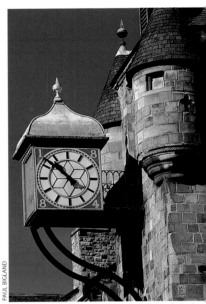

PAUL BIGLAND

Canongate Tolbooth's quaint turrets and clock

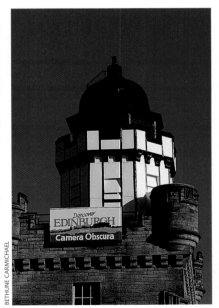

BETHUNE CARMICHAEL

It's all done with mirrors at the Camera Obscura.

JONATHAN SMITH

An old stalwart: John Knox's House (1490)

there is a wide variety available, so check the small print.

Some policies specifically exclude 'dangerous activities', which can include scuba diving, motorcycling and rock climbing. A locally acquired motorcycle licence is not valid under some policies.

You may prefer a policy that pays doctors or hospitals directly rather than you having to pay on the spot and claim later. If you have to claim later, make sure you keep all documentation. Some policies ask you to call back (reverse charges) to a centre in your home country where an immediate assessment of your problem is made.

Check that the policy covers ambulances or an emergency flight home.

For information on medical treatment and the E111 form see Other Documents later in this section.

Driving Licence

Citizens of the EU, Iceland, Norway and Liechtenstein can use their home driving licence until its expiry date. For non-EU citizens, home driving licences are legal for 12 months from the last date of entry to Britain; you can then apply for a British licence at post offices.

Ask your home automobile association for a Letter of Introduction. This entitles you to services offered by British sister organisations (touring maps and information, help with breakdowns, technical and legal advice and so on), usually free of charge.

Camping Card International

Your home automobile association also issues a Camping Card International, which is basically a camp site ID. It's also issued by local camping federations and sometimes at camp sites. It incorporates third-party insurance for damage you may cause and many camp sites offer small discounts if you have one.

Hostel Card

If you're travelling on a budget, membership of the Scottish Youth Hostel Association/Hostelling International (SYHA/HI) is a must. Prices are as follows: £6 for over-

18s; £2.50 for under-18s; and £60 for life membership. There are four SYHA hostels in Edinburgh (see the Places to Stay chapter) and over 70 SYHA hostels around Scotland. Members are eligible for a wide range of discounts.

Student & Youth Cards

The most useful card is the plastic ID-style International Student Identity Card (ISIC), which displays your photograph. This can perform wonders, including producing discounts on many forms of transport. Even if you have your own transport, the card soon pays for itself through reduced or free admission to attractions and cheap meals in some student restaurants.

There's a worldwide industry in fake student cards and many places now stipulate a maximum age for student discounts or, more simply, substitute a 'youth discount' for a 'student discount'. If you're aged under 26 but not a student, you can apply for the Euro<26 card, which goes by various names in different countries, or a GO25 card issued by the Federation of International Youth Travel Organisations (FIYTO). These cards are available through student unions, hostelling organisations or youth-oriented travel agencies. They don't automatically entitle you to discounts but you won't find out until you flash the card.

Seniors Cards

Some discounts are available to travellers aged 60 and over. The Rail Europe Senior Card (RES) entitles you to around a 30% discount on international journeys and domestic journeys connecting with an international service. To be eligible for this card, you must have a local senior citizens' railcard, the availability of which depends on the country you're in. In Britain, railcards (£16) and RES Cards (£5) are sold at mainline train stations. For details contact Rail Europe (☎ 08705 848848), French Rail House, 10 Leake Street, London SE1 7NN.

Other Documents

Nationals of EU countries should carry Form E111, which allows free emergency medical treatment in Scotland. Ask your national health service or travel agent well in advance of your trip. Australian Medicare does not cover any medical treatment in Scotland.

If you're visiting Britain on the Working Holidaymaker scheme bring any course certificates or letters of reference that might help you find a job.

Copies

All important documents (passport data page and visa page, credit cards, travel insurance policy, air/bus/train tickets, driving licence and so on) should be photocopied before you leave home. Leave one copy with someone at home and keep another with you, separate from the originals; stash some cash alongside, just in case.

It's also a good idea to store details of your vital travel documents in Lonely Planet's free online Travel Vault in case you lose the photocopies or can't be bothered with them. Your password-protected Travel Vault is accessible online anywhere in the world – create it at [W] www.ekno.lonely planet.com.

EMBASSIES & CONSULATES
UK Embassies & Consulates Abroad

Following are some of the countries where the UK has diplomatic representation:

Australia
High Commission: (☎ 02-6270 6666) Commonwealth Ave, Yarralumla, Canberra, ACT 2600

Canada
High Commission (☎ 613-237 1530) 80 Elgin St, Ottawa, Ontario K1P 5K7

France
Embassy: (☎ 01 44 51 31 00) 35 rue du Faubourg St Honoré, 75383 Paris

Germany
Embassy: (☎ 030-204570) Wilhelmstrasse 70, 10117 Berlin

Japan
Embassy: (☎ 03-5211 1100) 1 Ichiban-cho, Chiyoda-ku, Tokyo 102-8381

New Zealand
High Commission: (☎ 04-472 6049) 44 Hill St, Wellington 1

South Africa
High Commission: (☎ 21-461 7220) 91 Parliament St, Cape Town 8001

USA
Embassy: (☎ 202-588 6500) 3100 Massachusetts Ave NW, Washington DC 20008

Consulates in Edinburgh

It's important to realise what your own consulate – the consulate of the country of which you are a citizen – can and can't do to help you if you get into trouble in Scotland. Generally speaking, it won't be much help in emergencies if the trouble you're in is remotely your own fault. Remember that you are bound by the laws of the country you are in. Your consulate will not be sympathetic if you end up in jail after committing a crime locally, even if such actions are legal in your own country.

In genuine emergencies you might get some assistance but only if other channels have been exhausted. For example, if you need to get home urgently, a free ticket home is exceedingly unlikely – the consulate would expect you to have insurance to cover this type of emergency. If you have all your money and documents stolen, it might assist with getting a new passport but a loan for onward travel is certainly out of the question.

Edinburgh's consulates include:

Australia
Honorary Consulate: (Map 3; ☎ 624 3333) 69 George St, EH2 2JG (NB For passport applications and document witnessing only for emergencies contact the Australian High Commission in London on ☎ 020-7887 5335)

Belgium
Consulate: (☎ 01968-679970) 2 West S Penicuik, Midlothian, EH26 9DL

Canada
Consulate: (Map 3; ☎ 220 4333) Standard Life House, 30 Lothian Rd, EH1 2DH

Denmark
Consulate: (Map 1; ☎ 337 6352) 215 Balgree Rd, EH11 2RZ

France
Consulate: (Map 2; ☎ 225 7954) 11 Randolph Crescent, EH3 7TT

Germany
Consulate: (Map 2; ☎ 337 2323) 16 Eglinto Crescent, EH12 5DG

Ireland
Consulate: (Map 2; ☎ 226 7711) 16 Randolph Crescent, EH3 7TT
Italy
Consulate: (Map 2; ☎ 226 3631) 32 Melville St, EH3 7HA
Japan
Consulate: (Map 2; ☎ 225 4777) 2 Melville Crescent, EH3 7HW
Netherlands
Consulate: (Map 3; ☎ 220 3226) Thistle Court, 1–2 Thistle St, EH2 2HT
Spain
Consulate: (Map 3; ☎ 220 1843) 63 North Castle St, EH2 3LJ
Sweden
Consulate: (☎ 220 6050) 22 Hanover St, EH2 2EP
Switzerland
Consulate: (Map 3; ☎ 226 5660) 66 Hanover St, EH2 1HH
USA
Consulate: (Map 3; ☎ 556 8315) 3 Regent Terrace, EH7 5BW

CUSTOMS

Travellers arriving in the UK from other EU countries do not have to pay tax or duty on goods bought for personal use. The maximum amounts of tobacco and alcohol that each person can bring into the country, duty free, are 800 cigarettes, 400 cigarillos, 200 cigars, 1kg of smoking tobacco, 10L of spirits, 20L of fortified wine (eg sherry), 90L of wine and 110L of beer. Those aged under 17 are not allowed to import alcohol or tobacco.

Travellers from outside the EU can bring in, duty free, a maximum of 200 cigarettes or 100 cigarillos or 50 cigars or 250g of tobacco; 2L of still table wine; 1L of spirits or 2L of fortified wine, sparkling wine or liqueurs; 60ml of perfume; 250ml of toilet water; and £145-worth of all other goods, including gifts and souvenirs. Any items over this limit must be declared to customs officers on arrival.

Restricted goods, which you cannot bring into the UK without a special licence, include: firearms; CB radios; animals and birds (including pets); certain plants; most meats and meat products; dairy products (eggs, milk, cream and so on). For more details of restrictions, see the HM Customs and Excise Web site at [W] www.hmce.gov.uk.

MONEY
Currency

The unit of currency in the UK is the pound sterling (£), with 100 pence (p) to a pound. One and 2p coins are copper; 5p, 10p, 20p and 50p coins are silver; the £1 coin is gold-coloured; and the £2 coin is gold- and silver-coloured. Like its written counterpart, the word pence is usually abbreviated and is pronounced 'pee'.

Notes (bills) come in £5, £10, £20, £50 and £100 denominations and vary in colour and size. Notes issued by several Scottish banks (the Clydesdale Bank, Royal Bank of Scotland and Bank of Scotland), including a £1 note, are sometimes not accepted in other parts of the UK, although they are exactly equivalent to Bank of England notes. You shouldn't have trouble using them in shops and so on immediately south of the Scotland-England border but elsewhere, including London, it may be difficult. Although all UK banks will accept them, foreign banks will not.

Exchange Rates

The following currencies convert at these approximate rates:

country	unit		sterling
Australia	A$1	=	£0.36
Canada	C$1	=	£0.46
euro zone	€1	=	£0.61
Japan	¥100	=	£0.57
New Zealand	NZ$1	=	£0.29
USA	US$1	=	£0.70

For up-to-date exchange rates, check the Internet at [W] www.oanda.com.

Exchanging Money

You can exchange foreign cash and travellers cheques at banks, travel agencies, some post offices and at private currency exchange counters (usually known in the UK by the French term 'bureaux de change').

The bureau de change in the ESIC (see Tourist Offices earlier in the chapter) opens the same hours as the ESIC. It charges no commission for changing foreign cash or travellers cheques into sterling but you'll get a better rate at a bank or American Express (Amex). There's also a bureau de change in Waverley train station (beside Platform 1/19) but it charges high commission rates – 2% with a £3.50 minimum on travellers cheques, and a whopping £3.50 on cash amounts from £13 to £50, and 9% on cash amounts from £51 to £500.

Amex (Map 3; ☎ 718 2501), 139 Princes St, opens 9am to 5.30pm Monday to Friday and to 4pm Saturday. It charges no commission on cash and Amex travellers cheques, and generally offers a good rate of exchange (slightly better on cash than on cheques).

Thomas Cook (Map 3; ☎ 226 5500), 52 Hanover St, opens 9am to 5.30pm Monday to Saturday and charges 2% commission, with a minimum charge of £3, on both cash and travellers cheques. Rates of exchange are the same for both cash and cheques.

Most banks also exchange money. The Royal Bank of Scotland (Map 3; ☎ 556 8555) and the Bank of Scotland (Map 3; ☎ 442 7777) have branches on St Andrew Square. Banks generally charge 2% commission on foreign cash (minimum charge £2) and foreign-currency travellers cheques (minimum charge £3). Sterling travellers cheques can be cashed free of charge.

Cash Nothing can beat cash for convenience... or risk. It's still a good idea, though, to travel with some local currency in cash, if only to tide you over until you get to an exchange facility. Edinburgh, Glasgow, Glasgow Prestwick and Aberdeen airports all have good-value exchange counters open for incoming flights.

If you're travelling in several countries, some extra cash is a good idea; it can be easier to change a small amount of cash (just before leaving a country, for example) than a travellers cheque.

Banks rarely accept foreign coins, although some airport foreign exchanges will. Before you leave one country for the next, try to use up your change.

Travellers Cheques In Scotland, travellers cheques are usually only accepted by banks, bureaux de change and travel agencies – unlike the USA, you can't use them in shops and restaurants.

Take most cheques in large denominations, say £100; commissions are usually charged per cheque. It's only towards the end of a stay that you may want to change a small cheque to make sure you don't get left with too much local currency.

Credit Cards, Debit Cards & ATMs Visa, MasterCard, Amex and Diners Club cards are widely recognised and accepted throughout Scotland, although some place (usually smaller shops) make a charge fo accepting them (generally for small trans actions). B&Bs usually require cash.

You can use Visa, MasterCard, Amex Cirrus, Plus and Maestro in ATMs belong ing to the Royal Bank of Scotland, Clydes dale Bank, Bank of Scotland and TSB These banks also accept cards from Englis banks, including HSBC, Lloyds and Bar clays. There are ATMs on almost ever street corner in central Edinburgh.

Combine plastic and travellers cheque so you have something to fall back on i local banks don't accept your card or a ATM swallows it.

Here are some numbers for cancellin your cards should you lose them:

Amex	☎ 01273-689955
Diners Club	☎ 01252-516261
MasterCard	☎ 01702-362988
Visa	☎ 0800 895082

International Transfers You can instruc your home bank to send you a draft. Spec ify the city, the bank and the branch t which you want your money directed o ask your home bank to tell you wher there's a suitable one. The whole procedur will be easier if you've authorised someon back home to access your account.

Money sent by telegraphic transfer (usu ally at a cost of £7) should reach you withi a week; by mail, allow at least two week When it arrives, it will most likely be cor verted into local currency – you can take as it is or buy travellers cheques.

You can also transfer money by eithe Moneygram or Thomas Cook. America travellers can also use Western Union (☎ 0800 833833 in the UK).

Security

Keep your money in a money-belt or something similar, out of easy reach of snatch thieves. You might want to stitch an inside pocket into your skirt or trousers to keep emergency cash. Take care in crowded places and never leave wallets sticking out of trouser pockets or bags.

Costs

There's no denying that Edinburgh is an expensive city – second only to London in the UK cost-of-living league.

In Edinburgh you'll need to budget at least £20 to £25 per day for bare survival. Hostel accommodation costs from £10 to £16 per night, a one-day bus travel card costs £2.20, and food and drink will cost at least £6, with any sightseeing or nightlife costs (around £10 to £15) extra. That most basic of human needs, a pint of beer, costs £2.10 and upwards.

Costs obviously rise if you stay in a central B&B or hotel and eat restaurant meals. B&B rates range from £20 to £25 per person and a bar or restaurant meal will be at least £10 per head. Add a couple of pints of beer and admission fees to a tourist attraction or nightclub and you could easily spend £50 per day – without being extravagant.

Some typical high-season (July and August) costs are listed below:

Hostel bed	£14 per person
B&B	£20 per person
Mid-range hotel	£45 per person
Top-end hotel	£90 per person
Budget burger meal	£3
Nice restaurant	£15 per head
Gourmet restaurant	£25 per head
Loaf of bread	80p
Pint of beer	£2.20
Bottle of wine	£4 (in supermarket)
Bottle of quality wine	£15 (in restaurant)
1L petrol	78p
Bus journey within city	80p
Ticket to Fringe event	£4–10
Admission to Edinburgh Castle	£7.50
Car hire	from £20 per day
Local phone call	20p
Newspaper	30p

Tipping & Bargaining

In general, if you eat in an Edinburgh restaurant you should leave a tip of at least 10% unless the service was unsatisfactory. Waiting staff are often paid derisory wages on the assumption that the money will be supplemented by tips. If the bill already includes a service charge (usually 10%), you needn't add a further tip.

Taxis in Edinburgh are expensive, and drivers rarely expect a tip unless they have gone out of their way to help you.

Bargaining is virtually unheard of, although it's fine to ask if there are discounts for students, young people, or youth-hostel members.

Taxes & Refunds

Value-added tax (VAT) is a 17.5% sales tax that is levied on all goods and services except fresh food, children's clothes, books and newspapers. Prices displayed in restaurants must, by law, include VAT.

Non-EU citizens can sometimes claim a VAT refund paid on goods bought within the EU, which makes for a considerable saving. EU residents may also be eligible but must have been in Britain *less* than 365 days out of the two years prior to making the purchase and must leave the EU for at least one year within three months of making the purchase. Non-EU nationals are only required to leave the EU within three months of making the purchase.

The VAT refund scheme is voluntary and not all shops participate. Different shops will have different minimum-purchase conditions (normally around £40).

On request, participating shops give you a special form/invoice (called VAT407); they'll need to see your passport. This form must be presented with the goods and receipts to customs when you depart (VAT-free goods can't be posted or shipped home). After customs has certified the form, it should be returned to the shop for a refund, less an administration fee.

FACTS FOR THE VISITOR

Several companies offer a centralised refunding service to shops. Participating shops carry a sign in their window. You can avoid bank charges for cashing a sterling cheque by using a credit card for purchases and asking to have your VAT refund credited to your card account. Cash refunds are sometimes available at major airports.

For further details, see the HM Customs & Excise Web site at **w** www.hmce.gov.uk/public/travel or pick up the leaflet *Notice 704/2 – Travellers Guide to the Retail Export Scheme*, available from all customs arrival points in the UK.

POST & COMMUNICATIONS
Post

Edinburgh's main post office (☎ 0345 223344) is inconveniently hidden away inside the sprawling St James Centre (Map 3), off Leith St at the eastern end of Princes St. It opens 9am to 5.30pm Monday, 8.30am to 5.30pm Tuesday to Friday and 8.30am to 6pm on Saturday.

There are more convenient city-centre post offices at 40 Frederick St and 7 Hope St in the New Town, and in St Mary's St off the Royal Mile in the Old Town. These and other branches open 9am to 5.30pm weekdays, and 9am to 12.30pm on Saturday.

Mail sent within the UK can go either first or second class. First-class mail is faster (normally next-day delivery) and more expensive (27/41p up to 60/100g) than 2nd-class mail (19/33p). Air-mail postcards/letters (40g to 60g) to European countries cost 36/65p, to South Africa, the USA and Canada 40p/1.35 and to Australia and New Zealand 40p/£1.49. An air-mail letter takes about five days to get to the USA or Canada and a week to Australia or New Zealand.

Poste Restante Mail should be addressed to Poste Restante, Your Name, c/o Post Office, 8–10 St James Centre, Edinburgh EH1 3SR. It will be sent to the main post office in the St James Centre and held for 14 days. Items can be picked up from any counter – take your passport for ID – and the service is free for up to three months. Amex offices also hold card-holders' mail for free.

Parcels Packages and parcels weighing up to 2kg can be sent via airmail using the Small Packet service (anything sent outside of the EU must carry a customs declaration – the post office will give you a sticker to fill in). The rate for a 1kg packet to Europe/America/Australia is £2.67/4.55/4.95.

Larger parcels can be sent using the Parcelforce courier service – a 10kg package to the USA or Canada would cost from £44.95, with delivery expected in three days.

Telephone

There are plenty of public telephones around Edinburgh, all of which have STD or international access. Although British Telecom (BT) is the largest of the telephone operators, operating the majority of public phone booths, there are also several competing companies.

There's a mixture of coin phones and card phones, which take pre-paid phone cards. You can buy phone cards in post offices, newsagents and general stores, in values ranging from £2 to £20. Public phones have clear instructions in several languages.

Local & National Calls The area code for Edinburgh is 0131 but it's only used for calling from outside Edinburgh. To call a number within the city, just dial the seven-digit number.

Calls to phone numbers beginning with ☎ 0800 are free to the caller, while numbers beginning ☎ 0845 are charged at the local call rate no matter where you are phoning from. Numbers beginning with ☎ 0900 or 0901 are for premium rate and multimedia services, which cost up to 60p per minute.

Local calls are charged by time; national calls are charged by time and distance. Daytime rates are from 8am to 6pm, Monday to Friday; the cheap rate is from 6pm to 8am Monday to Friday, and the cheap weekend rate is from midnight Friday to midnight Sunday. The latter two rates offer substantial savings.

For directory enquiries call ☎ 192. These calls are free from public telephones but are charged at 25p from a private phone. To get the operator call ☎ 100.

International Calls Dial ☎ 155 for the international operator. To get an international line (for international direct dialling) dial 00, then the country code, area code (drop the first zero if there is one) and number. Direct dialling is cheaper but some budget travellers prefer the operator-connected reverse-charges (collect) calls.

You can also use the Home Country Direct service to make a reverse-charge or credit-card call via an operator in your home country.

For most countries (including Europe, USA and Canada) it's cheaper to phone overseas between 8pm and 8am Monday to Friday and at weekends; for Australia and New Zealand, however, it's cheapest from 2.30pm to 7.30pm and from midnight to 7am daily. The savings are considerable.

There's a wide range of local and international phonecards.

eKno Communication Service Lonely Planet's eKno Communication Card is aimed specifically at independent travellers and provides budget international calls, a range of messaging services, free email and travel information. For local calls, you're usually better off with a local card. You can join online at 🔲 www.ekno.lonelyplanet.com or by phone from the UK by dialling ☎ 0800 169 8646. Once you have joined, to use eKno from the UK, dial ☎ 0800 376 2366 or ☎ 0800 169 8646.

Check the eKno Web site for joining and access numbers from other countries and updates on super-budget local access numbers and new features.

Mobile Phones The UK uses the GSM 900 network, which covers the rest of Europe, Australia and New Zealand, but is not compatible with the North American GSM 1900 or the totally different system in Japan (though some North Americans have GSM 1900/900 phones that do work here). If you have a GSM phone, check with your service provider about using it in the UK, and beware of calls being routed internationally (very expensive for a local call). It is also possible to rent a phone from various com-

Country-Direct Numbers

Many countries have arrangements for direct-dial connections from the UK to a domestic operator for reverse-charge (collect), account and credit-card calls.

Dial ☎ 080089 then:

Australia/Optus:	☎ 0061
Australia/Telstra:	☎ 0611
Canada:	☎ 0016
France:	☎ 0033
Germany:	☎ 0049
Ireland:	☎ 0353
Japan/Dial Japan:	☎ 0443
Japan/Japan Direct:	☎ 0081
Japan/Japan Straight:	☎ 0080
Japan/Auto Home Dial:	☎ 0860
Netherlands:	☎ 0031
New Zealand/NZ Direct:	☎ 0064
New Zealand/Call NZ:	☎ 0640
South Africa:	☎ 0027
USA/AT&T:	☎ 0011
USA/Hawaii Direct:	☎ 0808
USA/MCI:	☎ 0222
USA/Sprint:	☎ 0877
USA/Worldcom:	☎ 0456

panies, including Mobell (☎ 0800 243524, 🔲 www.mobell.com) and Cellhire (☎ 08705 610610, 🔲 www.cellhire.com) from around £20 per week, depending on the hire period. In this case, however, you can't use your existing number.

Telegrams
The UK no longer has a domestic telegram service but you can still send telegrams to overseas destinations. Dial ☎ 0800 190190 and dictate your message.

Fax, Email & Internet Access
You can send faxes from dozens of copy offices all over town; International Telecom Centre (Map 8) on High St charges £1.50 plus cost of call.

Most hotels have fax machines that their guests can use, and the larger ones have fully fledged business centres with fax, printing, email and Internet access. Most backpacker hostels offer Internet access to their customers and there's Internet access in the ESIC (see Tourist Offices earlier in the chapter).

Alternatively, go to one of the Internet cafes that are scattered all over the city.

easyEverything (Map 3; ☎ 220 3580 , W www .easyeverything.com, 58 Rose St) Open 24 hours. This is a huge place with 450 PCs and a dynamic pricing system – the quieter the place is, the cheaper it gets. Average cost is around £1 for 35 minutes, the minimum charge is £2.

e-corner (Map 3; ☎ 558 7858, W www.e-corner .com, Platform 1, Waverley train station) Open 7.30am to 9pm Monday to Friday, 8am to 9pm Saturday and Sunday. Access costs £1 for 20 minutes and £2 for an hour.

Frugal Cafe (Map 5; ☎ 228 7567, W www.frugal cafe.com, 1a Brougham Place) Open 8.30am to 10pm daily. Best value Internet cafe in town – access costs 1p per minute at all times.

International Telecom Centre (Map 8; ☎ 558 7114, W www.btinternet.com/~itc1, 52 High St) Open 9am to 11pm daily. Access costs 1p per minute before 7pm and £1 for 30 minutes after 7pm. It also offers a fax service and cheap international phone calls.

Web 13 (Map 3; ☎ 229 8883, W www.web13 .co.uk, 13 Bread St) Open 9am to 10pm daily. Access costs £1 per 20 minutes.

DIGITAL RESOURCES
Web Sites

The World Wide Web is a rich resource for travellers. You can research your trip, hunt down bargain air fares, book hotels, check on weather conditions or chat with locals and other travellers about the best places to visit (or avoid!).

There's no better place to start your Web explorations than the Lonely Planet Web site (W www.lonelyplanet.com). Here you'll find succinct summaries on travelling to most places on earth, postcards from other travellers and the Thorn Tree bulletin board, where you can ask questions before you go or dispense advice when you get back. You can also find travel news and updates to many of our most popular guidebooks, and the subWWWay section offers links to the most useful travel resources elsewhere on the Web.

City of Edinburgh Council
W www.edinburgh.gov.uk
This site has more practical information aimed mainly at residents plus lots of useful and interesting stuff for the visitor, including a handy 'what's on in the next seven days' function.

City of Edinburgh Council – Museums and Galleries
W www.cac.org.uk
For details of the city's programme of exhibitions check the 'What's On' sections of this site.

Cruelty-Free Guide to Edinburgh
W www.mulvenna.demon.co.uk/cfg
Formerly available in print, this guide now exists only in its online form. It provides information on vegetarian and vegan cafes, restaurants, shops and accommodation, and other businesses that provide goods and services without involving cruelty to animals.

Edinburgh Architecture
W www.edinburgharchitecture.co.uk
This is an informative site dedicated to the city's contemporary architecture. It includes guided tours and interviews as well as information on current and planned building projects, including the city's most talked about project – the new parliament buildings.

Edinburgh Arts & Entertainment
W www.eae.co.uk
A good listings site for art, music, theatre and other entertainment events in the city.

Edinburgh Evening News
W www.edinburghnews.com
This newspaper-related site covers local news and sport and has articles on the arts, entertainment, things to do and places to go.

Edinburgh Guide
W www.edinburghguide.com
This Yahoo-style directory provides links to Edinburgh-related Web sites.

Edinburgh & Lothians Tourist Board
W www.edinburgh.org
A useful site for rooting out information on accommodation, attractions and events in and around Edinburgh.

National Galleries of Scotland
W www.natgalscot.ac.uk
Check out the 'What's On' section of this site for all the latest exhibitions.

National Museums of Scotland
W www.nms.ac.uk
An easy-to-use site for gathering information on the city's museums.

Scottish Parliament
W www.scottish.parliament.uk
This site covers the workings of the Scottish parliament (including live Webcasts).

The Oracle

[W] www.theoracle.co.uk
This is the most comprehensive and up-to-date listings Web site for Edinburgh, covering live music, theatre, comedy, exhibitions and so on.

CitySync

CitySync Edinburgh is Lonely Planet's digital city guide for Palm OS handheld devices. With CitySync you can quickly search, sort and bookmark hundreds of Edinburgh's restaurants, hotels, attractions, clubs and more – all pinpointed on scrollable street maps. Sections on activities, transport and local events means you get the big picture plus all the little details. Purchase or demo CitySync Edinburgh online at [W] www.citysync.com.

BOOKS
Lonely Planet

If you plan to explore farther afield, consider taking Lonely Planet's *Scotland* or *Scotland's Highlands & Islands* guides. LP's *Walking in Britain* and *Cycling Britain* guides have chapters on Scottish routes. For travel elsewhere in Britain, Lonely Planet publishes *Britain* and *London* guides as well as a *British Phrasebook*. The UK is also covered in the LP guides to *Western Europe* and *Europe on a Shoestring*.

Guidebooks

For walkers there are a few useful books: *Edinburgh & Lothian – 25 Walks* by Roger Smith and *One Hundred Hill Walks Around Edinburgh* by J Chalmers & D Storey.

Andrew Lownie's *The Literary Companion to Edinburgh* is a guide to the corners of Edinburgh associated with famous writers, from Daniel Defoe, Scott and Stevenson, through the WWI poets Wilfred Owen and Siegfried Sassoon to Irvine Welsh of *Trainspotting* fame.

History

Strangely for a capital city, there were no general histories of Edinburgh in print at the time of research. *Edinburgh: Portrait of a City* by Charles McKean is a succinct review of the city's past. *The Edinburgh Encyclopedia,* edited by Sandy Mullay, contains lots of historical detail but in alphabetical, rather than chronological, order.

Traditions of Edinburgh by Robert Chambers was originally published in 1824 but is now widely available as a facsimile edition. It includes many fascinating tales and legends relating to Old Town. *Edinburgh Castle* by Iain MacIvor is a detailed history of the city's best-known landmark.

For more general background, *Scotland: A Concise History* by Fitzroy MacLean provides an interesting and readable introduction to Scotland's past. Michael Lynch's large tome, *Scotland – A New History*, provides a good historical background up to the early 1990s. For detailed popular history you can't beat Professor TC Smout's excellent *A History of the Scottish People 1560–1830* and *A Century of the Scottish People 1830–1950*. Andrew Marr's *The Battle for Scotland* is an interesting political history of Scotland from the 19th century to 1992.

Architecture

A useful companion to Charles McKean's history of the city is his *Edinburgh – an Illustrated Architectural Guide,* with information on many of the city's most notable buildings. A more scholarly guide to the city's architecture is *The Buildings of Scotland: Edinburgh* by John Gifford et al.

Food & Drink

Scottish Cookery by Catherine Brown is an excellent guide, including fascinating historical background as well as dozens of tried-and-tested recipes. *Brander's Original Guide to Scotch Whisky* by Michael Brander, first published in 1975 and completely revised in 2000, is an excellent introduction to Scotland's national drink.

Fiction

Many novelists, from Sir Walter Scott to Irvine Welsh, have used Edinburgh as a setting for their fiction. Scott's *Heart of Midlothian* is a moving tale of personal courage that begins with the Porteous riot of 1736, centred on the infamous Tolbooth Prison that once stood beside St Giles Cathedral.

The city's dual nature – outward respectability concealing a heart of darkness, epitomised by the notorious Deacon Brodie – is said to have inspired Robert Louis Stevenson's classic tale of *Dr Jekyll and Mr Hyde*. The constraints of middle-class conformity in 1930s Edinburgh are explored in *The Prime of Miss Jean Brodie* by Muriel Spark, which tells the story of a romantic, self-obsessed teacher at an Edinburgh girls school and the effect she has on the lives of the 'little gerls' in her care.

Ian Rankin – described by US novelist James Ellroy as the 'King of Tartan Noir' – takes pleasure in revealing the seamier side of the Scottish capital in his novels featuring his alter ego Detective Inspector John Rebus. Rebus made his first appearance in *Knots and Crosses* in 1987, and has aged along with his creator over the space of a dozen novels. The latest Rebus story, *The Falls*, was published in 2001.

Trainspotting by Irvine Welsh was published in 1993 and became a hit movie in 1996. It's a grim but blackly humorous trawl through the depths of Edinburgh's underworld, as hero Renton tries to clean himself up and escape the horrors of heroin addiction.

Paul Johnston's futuristic thrillers *Body Politic* and *Water of Death* are set in a chillingly imagined Edinburgh in the year 2025.

FILMS

Classic films set in Edinburgh include *Tunes of Glory* (1960) starring Alec Guinness and John Mills. Guinness plays troubled soldier Major Jock Sinclair, whose regiment is billeted in Edinburgh Castle. Maggie Smith won an Oscar for Best Actress in *The Prime of Miss Jean Brodie* (1969), in which Edinburgh plays a prominent supporting role along with Gordon Jackson and Pamela Franklin.

The 1990s saw a spate of films shot in Edinburgh, including *Shallow Grave* (1994; with Kerry Fox, Christopher Eccleston and Ewan McGregor), *Mary Reilly* (1996; with Julia Roberts and John Malkovich), *The Debt Collector* (1999; with Billy Connolly and Ken Stott) and, most notably, *Trainspotting*

(1996), which propelled Ewan McGregor to international stardom.

As well as starring as itself, Edinburgh has doubled for Dickensian London in several TV historical dramas, and also as 19th-century Oxford in *Jude,* the 1996 adaptation of Thomas Hardy's *Jude the Obscure,* with Kate Winslet and Christopher Eccleston.

NEWSPAPERS & MAGAZINES

The Scots have been publishing newspapers since the mid-17th century. Edinburgh's home-grown dailies include *The Scotsman* (W www.thescotsman.co.uk), a broadsheet covering Scottish, UK and international news and current affairs, and *The Edinburgh Evening News* (W www.edinburghnews.com), containing news on the city and its environs. *Scotland on Sunday* is the weekend offering from the same stable.

Tabloids the *Daily Record* and the *Sunday Mail* and broadsheets *The Herald* – the longest-running daily newspaper in the English-speaking world (founded in 1783) – and the *Sunday Herald* are published in Glasgow. Competition between *The Herald* and *The Scotsman* for the title of Scotland's 'national daily newspaper' reflects the age-old rivalry between the two cities.

All UK national newspapers are available in Edinburgh, some of them in special editions aimed specifically at the Scottish market (eg, the *Scottish Daily Mail*, the *Scottish Express, The Sunday Times Scotland*).

The List is a useful fortnightly listings magazine that covers music, films, theatre, art, comedy, clubs, shopping and food in both Edinburgh and Glasgow.

Edinburgh pretty much invented the literary magazine in the late 18th century, and the *Edinburgh Review* – founded in 1802 – is still published twice a year. Current Edinburgh-based literary magazines also include the thrice-yearly *Cencrastus* and the quarterly *Chapman*.

The monthly *Scots Magazine,* which includes articles on all aspects of Scottish life from history to hill-walking, has been in circulation since the 18th century. *Scottish Memories* is another monthly mag that highlights people and stories from Scottish history.

Many European, North American and international papers and magazines can be found in newsagents in central Edinburgh, including the *International Herald Tribune*, *Time* and *Newsweek*. You'll find the biggest and best selection at the International Newsagents (Map 8; ☎ 225 4827) at 351 High St on the Royal Mile.

RADIO & TV
Radio and TV stations are linked to the UK-wide networks.

Radio
The BBC (w www.bbc.co.uk) caters for most tastes though much of the material comes from England. Its main music station, Radio 1 (FM 97.6–99.8MHz) aims at a teenage and 20-something audience; Radio 2 (FM 88–90.2MHz) provides music aimed at older listeners; Radio 3 (FM 90.2–92MHz) is for classical music and opera; Radio 4 (FM 92.4–94.6MHz) offers a mix of news, current affairs, drama and comedy; Radio Five Live (AM 693 and 909kHz) intersperses sport with current affairs.

Try BBC Radio Scotland (MW 810kHz, FM 92.4–94.7MHz) for a mix of music, drama, news and sport from a Scottish point of view. It also oversees regional stations in Aberdeen, the Highlands, the Orkneys and the Shetlands, and a Gaelic language channel, Radio nan Gaidheal. Radio Forth (AM 1548kHz, FM 97.3MHz) is a local news, music and talk station covering the region around the Firth of Forth.

UK-wide commercial stations can be picked up in Edinburgh. These include Classic FM (classical music), Virgin Radio (pop) and Talk Radio ('shock jock' chat and phone-ins).

Radio frequencies and programmes are published in the daily press.

TV
Britain still turns out some of the best quality TV programmes in the world. BBC 1 and BBC 2 are publicly funded by an annual TV licence and don't carry advertising. ITV and Channels 4 and 5 are commercial stations and do.

There are two Scottish-based commercial TV broadcasters. Scottish Television (STV) covers southern Scotland and some of the western Highlands. Grampian TV transmits to the Highlands, from Perth to the Western Isles, and to Shetland. Both include Gaelic-language programmes. Border TV covers Dumfries & Galloway and the Borders, as well as north-western England.

These channels are up against stiff competition from Rupert Murdoch's satellite TV company, BSkyB, and assorted cable channels. Cable churns out mostly missable rubbish but BSkyB is monopolising sports coverage with pay-per-view screenings of the most popular events.

VIDEO SYSTEMS
With many tourist attractions selling videos as souvenirs it's worth bearing in mind that Britain, like much of Europe, uses the Phase Alternative Line (PAL) system that isn't compatible with NTSC or SECAM unless converted.

PHOTOGRAPHY & VIDEO
Film & Equipment
Both print and slide film are widely available; if there's no specialist photographic shop around, Boots is the likeliest stockist. Thirty-six exposure print and slide films cost from £4.49, excluding processing. A three-pack of 90-minute Digital 8/Hi8 video cassettes costs around £15; a 30-minute Mini DV cassette costs about £13.

Good photography and video shops in the city include: Jessops Photo & Video Centre (Map 3; ☎ 229 9854) at 27 Shandwick Place, near the western end of Princes St; GD Young (Map 2; ☎ 229 6601) at 250 Morrison St in Haymarket; and Edinburgh Cameras (Map 4; ☎ 447 9977) at 219 Bruntsfield Place in Morningside. All provide processing services as well as film and equipment sales. For repairs to cameras and camcorders, go to Capital Camera Repairs (Map 5; ☎ 228 6812) at 38 Marchmont Rd.

Many shops all over the city can process print films in one hour.

Technical Tips

With dull, overcast conditions common, high-speed film (ISO 200 or ISO 400) is useful. In summer, the best times of day for photography are usually early in the morning and late in the afternoon when the glare of the sun has passed.

Restrictions

Many tourist attractions either charge for taking photos or prohibit photography altogether. Use of flash is frequently forbidden to protect pictures and fabrics. Video cameras are often disallowed because of the inconvenience they can cause to other visitors.

TIME

Edinburgh, along with the rest of Britain and Ireland, follows Greenwich Mean Time (GMT) in the winter and British Summer Time (BST) in the summer. BST is GMT plus one hour – the clocks go forward one hour at 2am on the last Sunday in March, and back again at 2am on the last Sunday in October.

When it's noon in Edinburgh in summer, it's 4am in Los Angeles, 7am in New York, 1pm in Paris (and the rest of Europe), 1pm in Johannesburg, 8pm in Tokyo, 9pm in Sydney and 11pm in Auckland.

Most public transport timetables use the 24-hour clock.

ELECTRICITY

The standard voltage in Scotland, as in the rest of Britain, is 240V, 50Hz AC. Plugs have three square pins and adapters are necessary for non-British appliances; these are widely available in electrical stores in Edinburgh. North American appliances, which run on 110V, will also need a transformer if they don't have one built in.

WEIGHTS & MEASURES

Despite dogged resistance from a minority of the population, Britain has officially moved to the metric system of weights and measures. However, road distances are still quoted in miles, not kilometres, and in pubs draught beer is still sold by the pint (568ml), although spirits are sold in measures of 25ml or 35ml. Petrol (gasoline) is sold by the litre. This book uses miles to indicate distance and the heights of mountains are given in metres.

For conversion tables, see the inside back cover.

LAUNDRY

Most of Edinburgh's backpacker hostels will wash and dry a load of laundry for you for around £3; some have self-service coin-operated washing machines, where you can do the laundry yourself.

There are self-service, coin-operated laundries all over the city – expect to pay around £3 for a wash and dry. Check the *Yellow Pages* under Launderettes to find the nearest. The best of the bunch is the Sundial Launderette (Map 3; ☎ 556 2743) at 7–9 East London St, in New Town. It's bright, clean and has an excellent cafe next door called The Lost Sock Diner. It opens 8am to 7pm Monday to Friday, 8am to 4pm Saturday and 10am to 2pm Sunday.

North-east of the city centre, the Bendix Launderette & Dry Cleaners (Map 6; ☎ 554 2180) is at 342 Leith Walk. Canonmills Dry Cleaners & Launderette (Map 3; ☎ 556 3199), 7 Huntly St, is convenient for those staying in Eyre Place. South of the centre in Marchmont is another Sundial Launderette (Map 5; ☎ 229 2137) at 17 Rosneath St.

TOILETS

There are well-maintained public toilets conveniently spaced around the city centre and most have facilities for the disabled. On Princes St there are toilets (open 10am to 10pm daily) beside St Cuthbert's Church at the western end; on either side of the Royal Scottish Academy (gents to the west, ladies to the east) in the middle; and in Waverley train station at the eastern end. On the Royal Mile, there are toilets at the top of Castle Wynd stairs (open 10am to 8pm daily, summer only), just outside the castle esplanade, and in Hunter Square (open 10am to 10pm daily) at the junction with North Bridge. Some busy public toilets, such as the ones at Waverley train station and inside Edinburgh Castle charge 20p.

Some disabled toilets can only be opened with a special key that can be obtained from the TIC or by sending a cheque or postal order for £2.50 to RADAR (see Information & Organisations under Disabled Travellers later in the chapter), together with a brief description of your disability.

LEFT LUGGAGE

There is a left-luggage office at Waverley train station, beside Platform 1/19. The charge per item is £3.50 for up to three hours, £4 for three to 12 hours, £4.50 for 12 to 24 hours, and £4.50 per subsequent 24-hour period. It opens 7am to 11pm daily.

While the new bus station at St Andrew Square is under construction (see Bus in the Getting There & Away chapter), there are temporary luggage lockers in the southwestern corner of St Andrew Square.

HEALTH

Travel health largely depends on predeparture preparations, day-to-day health care while travelling and how you handle any medical problem or emergency that may develop. In reality, few travellers experience anything worse than an upset stomach.

Tap water in Edinburgh is safe to drink so there's no need to pay the high prices restaurants ask for bottled water.

No jabs are required for Scotland, though it's recommended that everyone keeps up-to-date with diphtheria, tetanus and polio vaccinations.

Medical Services

Medical treatment under the UK's National Health Service is free to citizens of EU countries, and to citizens of countries that have a reciprocal agreement with the UK (check with your health service before you leave). Emergency ambulance transport and initial treatment in a hospital Accident and Emergency department is free to everyone.

Long-term visitors with the proper documentation will receive care under the NHS by registering with a specific practice near where they live. Again check the phone book for one close to you. EU nationals can obtain free emergency treatment on presentation of an E111 form, validated in their home country.

Travel insurance, however, is advisable as it offers greater flexibility over where and how you're treated and covers expenses for an ambulance and repatriation that won't be picked up by the NHS (see the Travel Insurance section under Documents earlier in the chapter). Regardless of nationality, anyone will receive free emergency treatment if it's a simple matter like bandaging a cut.

Hospital The main general hospital in the city is the Royal Infirmary of Edinburgh (Map 5; ☎ 536 4000) at 1 Lauriston Place. It has a 24-hour accident and emergency department.

Dental Services The Edinburgh Dental Institute (☎ 536 4900), also part of the Royal Infirmary, has an emergency dental clinic, open 9am to 3pm Monday to Friday, closed weekends.

Chemists (Pharmacies) All chemists are open 9am to 5.30pm Monday to Saturday and can advise you on minor ailments. The addresses of duty chemists, where prescriptions can be dispensed after hours, are displayed on the door or window of all chemist shops. Alternatively, look in the local newspaper or in the *Yellow Pages*. Boots (Map 2; ☎ 225 6757), 48 Shandwick Place (the extension of Princes St in the West End), opens 8am to 9pm Monday to Friday, to 7pm Saturday, and 10am to 5pm on Sunday. Medications are readily available either over the counter or on prescription, so there's no need to stock up. All prescription drugs cost a flat rate of £6.10.

Hypothermia

Hypothermia can occur when the body loses heat faster than it can produce it, resulting in the body's core temperature falling. It's surprisingly easy to progress from very cold to dangerously cold through a combination of wind, wet clothing, fatigue and hunger, even if the air temperature is above freezing.

Walkers in Scotland should always be prepared for difficult conditions. It's best to dress in layers and a hat is important since a lot of heat is lost through the head. A strong, waterproof outer layer is essential. Carry basic supplies, including food that contains simple sugars to generate heat quickly.

Symptoms of hypothermia are exhaustion, numb skin (particularly toes and fingers), shivering, slurred speech, irrational or violent behaviour, lethargy, stumbling, dizzy spells, muscle cramps and violent bursts of energy.

To treat mild hypothermia, get the person out of the wind and rain, remove wet clothing and replace it with dry, warm clothing. Give them hot liquids – not alcohol – and some high-calorie, easily digestible food. Do not rub victims; instead, allow them to slowly warm themselves. This should be enough to treat the early stages of hypothermia and prevent the onset of critical hypothermia.

HIV & AIDS

Infection with the human immunodeficiency virus (HIV) may lead to acquired immune deficiency syndrome (AIDS), which is fatal. Any exposure to blood, blood products or body fluids may put the individual at risk. The disease is often transmitted through sexual contact or dirty needles – vaccinations, acupuncture, tattooing and body piercing can be potentially as dangerous as intravenous drug use. HIV/AIDS can be spread through infected blood transfusions but in Scotland these are screened and safe.

Organisations For those with HIV/AIDS, advice and support are available from the National AIDS Helpline (☎ 0800-567123, 24 hours).

WOMEN TRAVELLERS

Women are unlikely to have any problems in Edinburgh, although common-sense caution should be observed, especially after dark. The tide of alcohol and testosterone that washes through the city's pubs on Friday and Saturday nights spills out onto the streets from 11pm onwards. Places you might want to avoid at these times include the western end of Princes St, Lothian Rd, Dalry Rd, Leith Walk and Cowgate.

Avoid crossing The Meadows (the park that lies between Old Town and Marchmont) alone after dark – several women have been attacked here. And be aware that Coburg St in Leith is a notorious red-light district – lone women here at any time of day might be approached by kerb crawlers.

Condoms are usually available in women's toilets in bars. Otherwise, chemists and many service stations stock them. The contraceptive pill is available only on prescription, as is the 'morning-after' pill (effective for up to 72 hours after unprotected sexual intercourse).

Organisations

Edinburgh's Well Woman Services (☎ 343 1282) is at 18 Dean Terrace, Stockbridge. This is the place to come to for advice on general health issues, contraception and pregnancy.

For information on the Edinburgh Rape Crisis Centre see under Emergencies later in the chapter

GAY & LESBIAN TRAVELLERS

Edinburgh has a small but flourishing gay scene (see Gay & Lesbian Venues in the Entertainment chapter). In general, the city has a fairly tolerant attitude towards homosexuality but overt displays of affection aren't wise away from acknowledged gay venues. The age of consent for homosexual sex in the UK is 16.

The main centre for information on gay, lesbian, bisexual and transgender issues is the LGBT Centre (Map 3; ☎ 557 2625) at 58a Broughton St. This is also the base for Pride Scotland (☎ 556 8822, e info@pridescotland.org), which organises the annual Pride parade and festival (for details see The Festival City special section).

The Lothian Gay & Lesbian Switchboard (☎ 556 4049, e mail@lgls.org) is available 7.30pm to 10pm every evening. The Lothian

Lesbian Line (☎ 557 0751), open 7.30pm to 10pm Monday and Thursday, can help with general enquiries, counselling and advice.

The magazine *Scotsgay* (**W** www.scots gay.com) is a useful source of information – you can find copies at most gay venues in Edinburgh. In even months it publishes an '80/-' (heavy) edition, discussing serious issues, and in odd months it puts out a '60/' (light) edition, covering the gay scene in Scotland. *Gay Scotland* (**W** www.gayscot land.com) was established in 1982 and ceased publication in April 1999, but there are plans to resurrect it as a free monthly mag – check the Web site for the latest.

For details on the Pride Scotland parade see The Festival City special section.

DISABLED TRAVELLERS

Edinburgh's Old Town, with its steep hills, narrow closes, flights of stairs and cobbled streets, is something of a challenge for wheelchair users. By law, new buildings must be made accessible to wheelchair users, so large, new hotels and modern tourist attractions are usually fine. However, most B&Bs and guesthouses are in hard-to-adapt older buildings.

It's a similar story with public transport. Newer buses sometimes have steps or suspension that lowers for easier access, as do trains, but it's always wise to check before setting out. Tourist attractions sometimes reserve parking spaces near the entrance for disabled drivers.

Many ticket offices and banks are fitted with induction loops to assist the hearing impaired. A few tourist attractions, such as cathedrals, have Braille guides or scented gardens for the visually impaired.

Information & Organisations

Get in touch with your national support organisation (preferably the travel officer if there is one) before leaving home. These often have complete libraries devoted to travel and can put you in touch with travel agents, who specialise in tours for people with special needs.

The STB produces a guide, *Accessible Scotland*, for disabled travellers and the tourist information office has accessibility details for Edinburgh and the Lothians. For more advice, including specialist tour operators, contact Disability Scotland (☎ 229 8632, **W** www.disabilityscotland.org.uk) at Princes House, 5 Shandwick Place, Edinburgh EH2 4RG.

Historic Scotland and the National Trust for Scotland (see Useful Organisations later in the chapter) provide details on disabled access and facilities at their properties.

The Royal Association for Disability & Rehabilitation (RADAR) publishes a guide on travelling in the UK that gives a good overview of facilities. Contact RADAR (☎ 020-7250 3222, **W** www.radar.org.uk), Information Dept, 12 City Forum, 250 City Rd, London EC1V 8AF.

The Holiday Care Service (☎ 01293-774535, **W** www.holidaycare.org.uk), 2nd Floor, Imperial Buildings, Victoria Rd, Horley, Surrey RH6 7PZ, publishes a guide (£7.50) to accessible travel and accommodation in Britain and can offer advice.

SENIOR TRAVELLERS

Senior citizens are entitled to discounts on things such as public transport and admission fees to tourist attractions, provided you can show proof of your age. Sometimes you need a special bus pass. The minimum qualifying age is generally 60 to 65 for men, 55 to 65 for women.

In your home country, a lower age may entitle you to special travel packages and discounts (on car hire, for instance) through organisations and travel agents that cater to senior travellers. Start hunting at your local senior citizens advice bureau.

In Scotland, rail companies offer a Senior Citizens Railcard for those aged 60 and over, giving 33% discounts.

EDINBURGH FOR CHILDREN

Edinburgh has a multitude of attractions for kids, and most things to see and do are child-friendly. Kids under five travel for free on Edinburgh buses, and those aged five to 15 pay a flat fare of 50p.

The ESIC (see Tourist Offices earlier in the chapter) has lots of info on children's events, and the handy guidebook *Edinburgh for Under Fives* can be found in most bookshops. *The List* (see Newspapers & Magazines earlier in the chapter) has a special Kids section listing children's activities and events in and around Edinburgh.

There are good, safe playgrounds in most Edinburgh parks, including Princes St Gardens, The Meadows and Bruntsfield Links. Scotland Yard, in Scotland St (north-eastern corner of New Town), is an adventure playground.

Ideas for outdoor activities include: going to see the animals at Edinburgh Zoo or Gorgie City Farm; taking snowboarding lessons on the dry slope at Midlothian Ski Centre or hiring rollerblades from BG Cycles (☎ 657 5832), 48 Portobello High St near Portobello beach (£6 for four hours) and skating in the nearby park; and feeding the swans and playing on the beach at Cramond.

If it's raining, you could visit the Discovery Centre, a hands-on activity zone in the Museum of Scotland; play on the flumes at the Commonwealth Pool; try out the earthquake simulator at Dynamic Earth; shop for kites, rockets and other flying toys at Another Planet; or join a kids' art workshop at the City Art Centre.

Emergency Mums (☎ 447 7744, mobile ☎ 07748-964144, e emergencymums@hotmail.com), 23 Hope Terrace, offers babysitting services for children of all ages.

USEFUL ORGANISATIONS

Membership of Historic Scotland (HS) and the National Trust for Scotland (NTS) is worth considering, especially if you're going to be in Scotland for a while. Both are non-profit organisations dedicated to the preservation of the environment and both care for hundreds of spectacular sites.

Historic Scotland

Historic Scotland (HS; Map 5; ☎ 668 8800, w www.historic-scotland.net), Longmore House, Salisbury Place, Edinburgh EH9 1SH, manages more than 330 historic sites in Scotland, including top attractions such as Edinburgh and Stirling castles. A year's membership of Friends of Historic Scotland

(☎ 668 8999) costs £28 for an adult and £21 for senior citizens and students, giving free entry to HS sites and half-price entry to English Heritage properties in England and Cadw properties in Wales. It also offers short-term 'Explorer' membership – the full/reduced rate for seven days is £17/12.50, for 14 days £22/16.50. The reduced rate applies to people over 60 and children up to 15.

National Trust for Scotland

National Trust for Scotland (NTS; Map 3; ☎ 243 9555 for Membership Services, w www.nts.org.uk), Wemyss House, 28 Charlotte Square, Edinburgh EH2 4ET, is separate from the National Trust (England, Wales and Northern Ireland), although there are reciprocal membership agreements. The NTS cares for over 100 properties and 185,000 acres of countryside.

A year's membership of the NTS costing £28 (£19 for the over-60s, £12 for those aged under 26) offers free access to all NTS and NT properties. HI/SYHA members and student-card holders get half-price entry to NTS properties.

LIBRARIES

The Edinburgh Central Library (Map 8; ☎ 242 4800) on George IV Bridge has a room devoted to Edinburgh (one floor down), another to all things Scottish (in the basement) and a Reference Department on the top floor with Internet access, a wide range of magazines and newspapers, and newspaper archives. It opens 10am to 8pm Monday to Thursday, to 5pm Friday, and 9am to 1pm on Saturday. Next to the Central Library is the Children's Library (Map 8; ☎ 242 8027), open 1pm to 8pm Monday and Wednesday, 10am to 5pm Tuesday, Thursday and 9am to 1pm on Saturday.

Opposite the Central Library is the National Library of Scotland (Map 8; ☎ 226 4531, w www.nls.uk), which houses a reference-only, general reading room. It opens 9.30am to 8.30pm weekdays (from 10am Wednesday) and 9.30am to 1pm on Saturday. There's a branch south of the city in Newington (Map 5), at 33 Salisbury

The Festival City

MARTIN MOOS

Edinburgh International Science Festival

The Science Festival runs over ten days in the first two weeks of April.

First held in 1987, the Science Festival hosts a wide range of events, including talks, lectures, exhibitions, demonstrations, guided tours and interactive experiments designed to stimulate, inspire and challenge. From dinosaurs and ghosts to alien life forms, there's something to interest everyone.

☎ 530 2001, fax 530 2002
e esf@scifest.demon.co.uk,
w www.sciencefestival.co.uk
✉ Roxburgh's Court, 323 High St, Edinburgh EH1 1PW

Beltane

Held annually on the night of 30 April into the early hours of 1 May.

Beltane is a pagan fire festival that marks the end of winter and the rebirth of spring. It was resurrected in its modern form in 1988 and is now celebrated annually on the summit of Calton Hill. The spectacular rituals involve lots of fire, drumming, body paint and sexual innuendo (well, it's a fertility rite, after all). Bring your sparklers.

☎ 228 5353
e scribe@beltane.org
w www.beltane.org
✉ The Beltane Fire Society, 19 Leven St, Edinburgh EH3 9LH

Scottish International Children's Festival

The Children's Festival takes place annually in the last week of May.

This is Britain's biggest festival of performing arts for children, with events suitable for kids aged from three to 12. Groups from around the world perform classic tales such as Hansel and Gretel, as well as new material written especially for youngsters.

☎ 225 8050, fax 225 6440,
e info@imaginate.org.uk
w www.imaginate.org.uk
✉ 45a George St, Edinburgh EH2 2HT

Title Page: Christmas festivities to put you in a spin (photograph: Ne Wilson)

Above left: What a hoo Nosing around at the International Science Festival

Caledonian Brewery Traditional Beer Festival

The Beer Festival is held on the first weekend in June.

A celebration of all things fermented and yeasty, Scotland's biggest beerfest is hosted by Edinburgh's leading brewer of cask-conditioned ales. You can also sample a wide range of traditionally brewed beers from around the world, while enjoying live jazz and blues and snacking on pies and barbecued fare. Froth-topped bliss.

☎ 623 8066
w www.caledonian-events.co.uk
✉ Caledonian Brewery, 42 Slateford Rd, Edinburgh EH11 1PH

Pride Scotland

The Pride Scotland parade and festival takes place in odd years in Edinburgh, even years in Glasgow, on the last Saturday in June.

This annual celebration of Scotland's gay, lesbian and transgender community begins with a colourful parade along The Mound, Princes St, Leith St and Broughton St, followed by lots of eating, drinking and dancing at various venues in the Pink Triangle, Edinburgh's 'gay village'.

☎ 556 8822
e info@pridescotland.org
w www.pridescotland.org
✉ 58a Broughton St, Edinburgh EH1 3SA

Right: White warrior women at Beltane, the pagan festival

NEIL WILSON

Edinburgh International Jazz & Blues Festival

The Jazz Festival runs for nine days, beginning on the last Friday in July (ie the week before the Fringe and Tattoo begin).

Held annually since 1978, the Jazz and Blues Festival pulls in the top talent from all over the world. The first weekend sees a Mardi Gras street parade on Saturday from the City Chambers, up the Royal Mile and down into Grassmarket, for an afternoon of free, open-air music. On the Sunday there's a series of free concerts at the Ross Bandstand in Princes St Gardens.

☎ 225 2202
W www.jazzmusic.co.uk
✉ 29 St Stephens St, Edinburgh EH3 5AN

Edinburgh International Games

The Games are held on the last Saturday in August.

A one-day international athletics event, with teams from Scotland, England, Wales, Ireland and the USA plus individual athletes from Europe, complemented by a programme of traditional Scottish Highland Games (tossing the caber, throwing the hammer, putting the shot), demonstrations of Highland dancing and performances by pipe bands appearing at the Military Tattoo.

☎ (ticket booking) 228 8616
☎ (venue) 661 5351
✉ (ticket booking) Usher Hall, Lothian Rd EH1 2EA
✉ (venue) Meadowbank Sports Centre

MANFRED GOTTSCHALK

Left: The Military Tattoo has dazzled audiences with stunning musical displays for over 50 years.

GARETH MCCORMACK

Edinburgh Military Tattoo

The Tattoo takes place over the first three weeks of August (from a Friday to a Saturday); there's one show at 9pm Monday to Friday, and two (at 7.30pm and 10.30pm) on Saturday, but no performance on Sunday.

The Military Tattoo is a spectacular display of military marching bands, massed pipes and drums, acrobats, cheerleaders and motorcycle display teams, all played out in front of the magnificent backdrop of the floodlit castle. Each show traditionally finishes with a lone piper, dramatically lit, playing a lament on the battlements.

☎ 225 1188, fax 225 8627
e edintattoo@edintattoo.co.uk,
w www.edintattoo.co.uk
✉ The Tattoo Office, 32 Market St, Edinburgh EH1 1QB

Edinburgh Festival Fringe

The Fringe take place over three and a half weeks in August, the last two weeks overlapping with the first two of the Edinburgh International Festival.

When the first Edinburgh Festival was held in 1947, there were eight theatre companies who didn't make it onto the main programme. Undetered, they grouped together and held their own mini-festival, on the fringe... and an Edinburgh institution was born. Today the Fringe is *the* biggest festival of the performing arts anywhere in the world.

Since 1990 the Fringe has been dominated by stand-up comedy, but the sheer variety of shows on offer is staggering – everything from chainsaw juggling to performance poetry to Tibetan yak-milk gargling. So how do you decide what to see? There are daily reviews in *The Scotsman*

Above right: All fired up for the Edinburgh Festival

newspaper – one good *Scotsman* review and a show sells out in hours – but the best recommendation is word of mouth. If you have the time, go to at least one unknown show – it may be crap but at least you'll have your obligatory 'worst show I ever saw' story to bandy about in the pub.

The big names play at the mega-venues such as the Assembly Rooms, the Gilded Balloon and the Pleasance, and charge mega-prices (£8 per ticket and more). However, there are plenty of good shows for under a fiver and, best of all, lots of free stuff. Fringe Sunday – usually the second Sunday – is a smorgasbord of free performances, traditionally held in Holyrood Park (but there is talk of moving it to the Meadows).

☎ 226 5257, fax 220 4205
e admin@edfringe.com
w www.edfringe.com
✉ The Fringe Office, 180 High St, Edinburgh EH1 1QS

Edinburgh International Festival

Edinburgh's annual culture-fest takes place over the three weeks ending on the first Saturday in September; the programme is usually available from April.

First held in 1947 to mark a return to peace after the ordeal of WWII, the Edinburgh International Festival is festooned with superlatives – the oldest, the biggest, the most famous, the best in the world. The original was a modest affair but today hundreds of the world's top musicians and performers congregate in Edinburgh for three weeks of diverse and inspirational music, opera, theatre and dance.

The famous Fireworks Concert, held on the final Saturday of the Festival, is one of the most spectacular events of the year. A concert performed at the Ross Bandstand in Princes St Gardens (and broadcast live on radio) is accompanied by the carefully choreographed detonation of around 40 tons of artistically arranged gunpowder. Tickets for the band-

GARETH McCORMACK

Left: Fiddler on the rock
Edinburgh Festival
attracts artistes and
audiences from
around the globe.

stand and gardens sell out early but some are held back for personal callers at The Hub – these go on sale from the previous Sunday. If you don't manage to get a ticket, bring along a radio and join the crowds of locals on Princes St, North Bridge, Calton Hill and Inverleith Park.

Tickets for popular events – especially music and opera – sell out quickly, so it's best to book as far in advance as possible. You can buy tickets in person at The Hub or by phone, fax or Internet.

☎ 473 2000, fax 473 2002
e eif@eif.co.uk
w www.eif.co.uk
✉ The Hub, Castlehill, Edinburgh EH1 2NE

Edinburgh International Book Festival

The Book Festival lasts for two weeks in August (usually the first two weeks of the Edinburgh International Festival).

Held in a little village of marquees in the middle of Charlotte Square, the Book Festival is a fun fortnight of talks, readings, debates, lectures, book signings and meet-the-author events, with a cafe and tented bookshop thrown in.

☎ 228 5444, fax 228 4333
e admin@edbookfest.co.uk
w www.edbookfest.co.uk
✉ Scottish Book Centre, 137 Dundee St, Edinburgh EH11 1BG

Edinburgh International Film Festival

The Film Festival last for two weeks in August (usually the first two weeks of the Edinburgh International Festival).

The Film Festival is one of the original Edinburgh Festival trinity, having first been staged in 1947 along with the International Festival and the Fringe. It is a major international event, serving as a showcase for new British and European films, and staging the European premieres of one or two Hollywood blockbusters.

☎ 229 2550, fax 229 5501
e info@edfilmfest.org.uk,
w www.edfilmfest.org.uk
✉ Filmhouse, 88 Lothian Rd, Edinburgh EH3 9BZ

Scottish International Storytelling Festival

The Storytelling Festival runs over ten days, ending on the first Sunday in November.

The Storytelling Centre was established in 1996 and now organises this annual celebration of the art of spinning a yarn. Events for all ages are staged at a variety of indoor and outdoor venues, leavened with traditional music and crafts workshops.

☎ 557 5724, fax 557 5224
e netherbowstorytelling@dial.pipex.com
w www.storytellingcentre.org.uk
✉ Scottish Storytelling Centre, The Netherbow, 43–45 High St, Edinburgh EH1 1SR

Edinburgh's Capital Christmas

The celebrations are held over the three weeks before Christmas.

The newest of the Scottish capital's festivals, first held in 2000, the Christmas bash includes a big street parade, a fairground and Ferris wheel, and an open-air ice rink in Princes St Gardens.

☎ 529 4310
ⓔ p.philip@edin-city-dev.demon.co.uk
ⓦ www.edinburghscapitalchristmas.org
✉ City of Edinburgh Council, City Chambers, High St, Edinburgh EH1 1HQ

Edinburgh's Hogmanay

New Year events run from 29 December to 1 January.

Traditionally, the New Year has always been a more important celebration for Scots than Christmas. In towns, cities and villages all over the country, people fill the streets at midnight on 31 December to wish each other a Guid New Year and, yes, to knock back a dram or six to keep the cold at bay.

In 1993, Edinburgh's city council had the excellent idea of spicing up Hogmanay by organising some events, laying on some live music in Princes St and issuing an open invitation to the rest of the world. Most of them turned up, or so it seemed, and had such a good time that they told all their pals and came back again the following year. Now Edinburgh's Hogmanay is the biggest winter festival in Europe, regularly pulling in over 250,000 partying punters.

To get into the main party area in the city centre after 8pm on 31 December you'll need a ticket – book well in advance.

☎ 529 4461
ⓔ hogmanay@edinburgh.gov.uk
ⓦ www.edinburghshogmanay.org
✉ Hogmanay Box Office, The Hub, Castlehill, Edinburgh EH1 2NE

NEIL WILSON

Left: Winter wonderlan the ice rink in Princes St Gardens is just one of the city's Christmas attractions.

Place on the corner of Causewayside, which contains the Scottish Science Library, open 9.30am to 5pm Monday, Tuesday, Thursday and Friday, and 10am to 8.30pm Wednesday. In the same building is the Map Library, open 9.30am (from 10am Wednesday) to 5pm Monday to Saturday.

UNIVERSITIES

Edinburgh has three universities. The oldest, biggest and most prestigious is the University of Edinburgh, with over 15,000 undergraduates. Its information centre (Map 8; ☎ 650 1000, W www.ed.ac.uk) on Nicolson St, next to the Edinburgh Festival Theatre, opens 9.15am to 5pm weekdays.

Heriot-Watt University (☎ 449 5111, W www.hw.ac.uk) has its main campus south-west of the city at Riccarton, near Currie. Napier University (☎ 444 2266, W www.napier.ac.uk) has its main campuses at 10 Colinton Rd in Merchiston and at 219 Colinton Rd in Craiglockhart.

CULTURAL CENTRES

The British Council promotes cultural, educational and technical cooperation between Britain and other countries. Its Scottish headquarters (Map 5; ☎ 447 4716, fax 452 8487) is at 3 Bruntsfield Crescent, Bruntsfield.

The Institut Français d'Écosse (Map 2; ☎ 225 5366, fax 220 0648), 13 Randolph Crescent, offers French language lessons and courses in aspects of French culture, as well as having an excellent French restaurant and cafe.

The Italian Cultural Institute (Map 8; ☎ 668 2232, fax 668 2777) 82 Nicolson St, organises Italian language courses and events promoting Italian culture.

DANGERS & ANNOYANCES

Lothian Rd, Dalry Rd, Rose St and the western end of Princes St, at the junction with Shandwick Place and Queensberry and Hope Sts, can get a bit rowdy on Friday and Saturday nights after people have been out drinking. Calton Hill offers good views during the day but is probably best avoided at night.

See under Women Travellers earlier for more safety advice.

Crime

Edinburgh is safer than most cities of a similar size but it has its share of crime (often drug related), so the normal big-city precautions apply. Pickpockets and bag-snatchers operate in crowded public places, although this isn't a big problem. To make it harder for them, place your wallet in a front pocket or carry your bag in front of you.

Carry valuables next to your skin or in a sturdy pouch on your belt. Carry your own padlock for hostel lockers. Be cautious, even in hotels, and don't leave your valuables lying around. *Never* leave valuables in a car and remove all luggage overnight. Report thefts to the police and ask for a statement, or your travel insurance won't pay out; thefts from cars are often excluded anyway.

Beggars

The flip side of Edinburgh's image as a wealthy, prosperous city is the number of homeless people you will see begging in the streets. If you don't want to give money but would like to help the homeless and long-term unemployed, you can buy a copy of the magazine *Big Issue* (£1) from homeless street vendors, who benefit directly from sales. Also, consider giving a donation to Shelter Scotland (☎ 473 7170), 4th floor, Scotia Bank House, 6 South Charlotte St, a charity that helps the homeless.

Lost Property

If you lose anything or leave something behind in a pub or restaurant, check first with the establishment concerned, then with the lost property department (Map 2; ☎ 311 3141) at the police headquarters on Fettes Ave, north of the centre near the Western General Hospital. It opens 8am to 5pm Monday to Friday. Anything lost in the street or left behind in a city taxi should also end up here.

The lost property office (Map 3; ☎ 554 4494) of the Lothian Buses bus company, at 1–4 Shrub Place on Leith Walk. It opens 10am to 1.30pm Monday to Friday.

EMERGENCIES

In an emergency, dial ☎ 999 (no money needed at public phones) and ask for police, ambulance, fire brigade or coastguard.

The Edinburgh Rape Crisis Centre (☎ 556 9437) can offer advice and support after an attack.

See Medical Services earlier in the chapter for information on hospitals, dentists and chemists.

LEGAL MATTERS

The 1707 Act of Union preserved the Scottish legal system as separate from the law in England and Wales. Although there has been considerable convergence since then, Scots Law remains distinct.

Police have the power to detain anyone suspected of having committed an offence punishable by imprisonment (including any drugs offences) for up to six hours. They can search you, take photographs and fingerprints, and question you. You are legally required to provide your correct name and address – not doing so, or giving false details, is an offence – but you are not obliged to answer any other police questions. After six hours, the police must either formally charge you or let you go. If you are detained and/or arrested, you have the right to inform a solicitor and one other person, though you have no right to actually see the solicitor or to make a telephone call. If you don't know a solicitor, the police will inform the duty solicitor on your behalf.

If you need legal assistance contact Scottish Legal Aid (☎ 226 7061, fax 220 4878), 40–44 Drumsheugh Gardens, Edinburgh EH3 7SY.

Drugs

Possession of a small amount of cannabis is an offence punishable by a fine but possession of a larger amount of cannabis – which will be construed as having intent to supply – or any amount of harder drugs is much more serious, with punishments of up to 14 years in prison. Police have the right to search anyone who they suspect of possessing drugs.

Alcohol

The legal drinking age is 18. Anyone under the age of 16 cannot be served in a pub, even with a soft drink, unless the pub has a restaurant licence. The legal blood-alcohol limit for driving is 35mg/100ml (equivalent to drinking a pint of beer or two small glasses of wine) but the safest approach is not to drink at all.

BUSINESS HOURS

Offices generally open 9am to 5pm Monday to Friday. Shops may open longer hours and most are open 9am to 5pm on Saturday. An increasing number of shops also open 10am to 4pm on Sunday. There are many small grocery stores that stay open until 10pm daily and a few that open 24 hours.

Post offices are open 9am to 5.30pm Monday to Friday and 9am to 12.30pm Saturday. Bank hours vary but they generally open 9.30am to 4pm Monday to Friday. Some banks open later on Wednesday and Thursday, and 9.30am to 12.30pm on Saturday.

PUBLIC HOLIDAYS & SPECIAL EVENTS
Public Holidays

On public holidays and bank holidays banks, post offices and government offices will be closed and public transport may run a reduced service. Many shops stay open however, except on Christmas and New Year's days.

The following days are public holidays in Scotland:

New Year's Day 1 January
New Year Bank Holiday 2 January
Spring Bank Holiday 2nd Monday in April
Good Friday Friday before Easter Sunday
May Day Holiday 1st Monday in May
Victoria Day 3rd Monday in May
Autumn Holiday 3rd Monday in September
Christmas Day 25 December
Boxing Day 26 December

Edinburgh also has its own local holiday on the third Monday in May and the third Monday in September.

Special Events

Edinburgh hosts a wide range of events throughout the year but August is far and away the busiest month. Check with the ESIC (see Tourist Offices earlier in the chapter) for details. The main festivals are listed in The Festival City special section but here are a few others:

December/January
Burns Night
25 January: Special dinners (Burns Suppers) are held all over Scotland celebrating the birthday of poet Robert Burns.

April
Edinburgh Folk Festival
This festival specialises in Scottish music but also attracts international performers; held for one week early in the month.

June
Royal Highland Show
A huge agricultural fair showcasing Scottish farming produce, with craft and antique fairs, showjumping and so on; held on the last weekend in June at the Royal Highland Showground in Ingliston, near Edinburgh airport.

Mid-September
Festival of the Environment
One week of displays and workshops that starts in the Meadows.

DOING BUSINESS

Edinburgh is the second most important business centre in the UK after London and one of the largest financial centres in the European Union (EU). Two Scottish banks, several insurance companies and a few other financial bodies are headquartered here. The city has a highly developed public transport network and is easily accessible by air, rail and road. With three universities and five colleges, the city has a highly educated professional workforce. Many of the educational institutions themselves have business divisions to provide better communication between business and education.

The annual *Edinburgh Business Directory,* published jointly by the City of Edinburgh Council and the Edinburgh Chamber of Commerce & Enterprise, has useful information on the city and its business economy.

The directory can be viewed in the Edinburgh Room of the Central Library. The Newington branch of the National Library has an information service on business in Scotland (see Libraries earlier in the chapter).

The pink-coloured daily *Financial Times* and *The Economist*, published weekly, are the foremost publications on business and finance in the UK.

Most of Edinburgh's top and mid-range hotels provide business facilities including conference rooms, secretarial services, fax and photocopying services, ISDN lines and use of computer and private office space.

Some language schools provide translation and interpreting services as well as training in English and other languages (see Courses in the Things to See & Do chapter for listings).

Conferences

Edinburgh is high in the world league table of cities hosting business conferences. Conference Edinburgh (☎ 921 3636, fax 921 3333, W www.conferenceedinburgh.co.uk), 27 Princes St, Edinburgh EH1 6TY, is responsible for promoting Edinburgh as a conference destination and offers information and support in planning. There's a range of conference venues but the main one is the Edinburgh International Conference Centre (EICC; Map 2; ☎ 300 3000, fax 519 4060, W www.eicc.co.uk), The Exchange, Morrison St, Edinburgh EH3 8EE, which can hold up to 1200 people. Conference Edinburgh can advise on smaller, more intimate locations.

Useful Organisations

Edinburgh has a number of development and business support organisations.

The City of Edinburgh Council's Economic Development Department (Map 8; ☎ 529 4625, fax 529 3215) at 1 Cockburn St, Edinburgh EH1 1BP, is responsible for integrating economic development, transport and town planning. It also promotes local economic regeneration, investment and vocational training.

The Edinburgh Chamber of Commerce & Enterprise (☎ 477 7000, fax 477 7002,

 www.ecce.org) is at Conference House, 152 Morrison St, Edinburgh EH3 8EB. It provides a wide range of business support services including information technology, start-up and development advice and financial help.

Scottish Enterprise Edinburgh & Lothian (Map 2; ☎ 313 4000, fax 313 4231,  www.scottish-enterprise.com/edinburghandlothian) at Apex House, 99 Haymarket Terrace, Edinburgh EH12 5HD, is part of the Scottish Enterprise Network (SEN). Its role is to promote economic development in Edinburgh and the Lothians. It provides support to new and existing business and improves access to jobs.

WORK

Edinburgh's job market is booming – in summer 2001 there were around 35,000 unfilled job vacancies in the city.

EU citizens do not need a work permit. Citizens of Commonwealth countries aged 17 to 27 can apply for a Working Holiday Entry Certificate that allows up to two years in the UK, during which you can take work that is 'incidental' to a holiday. Commonwealth citizens with a UK-born parent may be eligible for a Certificate of Entitlement to the Right of Abode, which allows you to live and work in the UK.

Commonwealth citizens with a UK-born grandparent, or a grandparent born before 31 March 1922 in what's now the Republic of Ireland, may qualify for a UK Ancestry-Employment Certificate, allowing you to work full time for up to four years in the UK.

Visiting full-time US students aged 18 and over can apply for a six-month work permit through the Council on International Educational Exchange (☎ 212-822 2600,  www.ciee.org), 205 East 42nd St, New York, NY 10017. British Universities North America Club (BUNAC; ☎ 203-264 0901,  www.bunac.org), PO Box 49, South Britain, CT 06487, can also help organise a permit and find work.

Seasonal work is available in the tourist industry, in hotels, restaurants and bars. Hostel noticeboards advertise casual work and hostels themselves sometimes employ travellers to staff the reception, clean up and so on. Bars and restaurants also advertise jobs in their windows.

Those with IT skills will find themselves in demand. There are also opportunities for secretaries, receptionists, book-keepers and accountants. Other possibilities include call centre and telesales work, nursing and nursery care. A wide range of full and part-time jobs are advertised in the Recruitment section of Friday's edition of *The Scotsman* newspaper, and online at  www.scottishappointments.com.

The minimum wage in the UK is £3.70 per hour but there is a loophole that allows employers to include tips in this figure; be warned, some restaurants pay as little as £2 per hour plus tips. However, other places can pay as much as £5 per hour for bar work, so have a shop around. Call-centre and telesales work pays around £6 per hour and office work is mostly in the range of £5 to £10 per hour.

Whatever your skills, it's worth registering with a number of employment agencies. There are dozens of agencies so check the the Edinburgh Guide Web site at  www.edinburghguide.com/business/recruitment.htm or the *Yellow Pages*.

Getting There & Away

The recent expansion of Edinburgh Airport, the continued upgrading of the main railway line between London and Edinburgh, and the proposed opening of a car-ferry link between Rosyth and mainland Europe in 2002 mean that the options for travel to and from Scotland's capital are improving all the time.

AIR

Edinburgh is served directly by Edinburgh Airport, 8 miles west of the city centre. Glasgow Airport, 60 miles to the west and a ½-hour journey away by bus, train or taxi, has a wider range of international flights.

Buying Tickets

World aviation has never been so competitive, making air travel better value than ever. But you have to research the options carefully to make sure you get the best deal. The Internet is an increasingly useful resource for checking air fares.

Full-time students and those aged under 26 (under 30 in some countries) have access to better deals than other travellers. You have to show a document proving your date of birth or a valid International Student Identity Card (ISIC) when buying your ticket.

Generally, there is nothing to be gained by buying a ticket direct from the airline. Discounted tickets are released to selected travel agents and specialist discount agencies, and these are usually the cheapest deals going.

One exception is the expanding number of no-frills carriers, which mostly only sell direct to travellers. Unlike the full-service airlines, no-frills carriers often make one-way tickets available at around half the return fare, meaning that it is easy to put together an open-jaw ticket when you fly to one place but leave from another.

Many airlines, full service and no frills, offer some excellent fares to Web surfers. They may sell seats by auction or simply cut prices to reflect the reduced cost of electronic selling.

Many travel agencies have Web sites, which can make the Internet a quick and easy way to compare prices. There is also an increasing number of online agents such as [W] www.travelocity.co.uk and [W] www.deckchair.com, which operate only on the Internet. Online ticket sales work well if you are doing a simple one-way or return trip on specified dates. However, online superfast fare generators are no substitute for a travel agent who knows all about special deals, has strategies for avoiding layovers and can offer advice on everything from which airline has the best vegetarian food to the best travel insurance to bundle with your ticket.

You may find the cheapest flights are advertised by obscure agencies. Most such firms are honest and solvent but there are some rogue fly-by-night outfits around.

Paying by credit card generally offers protection, as most card issuers provide refunds if you can prove you didn't get what you paid for. Similar protection can be obtained by buying a ticket from a bonded agent, such as one covered by the Air Travel Organiser's Licence (ATOL) scheme in the UK. Agents who only accept cash should hand over the tickets straight away and not tell you to 'come back tomorrow'.

After you've made a booking or paid your deposit, call the airline and confirm that the booking was made. It's generally not advisable to send money (even cheques) through the post unless the agent is very well established – some travellers have reported being ripped off by fly-by-night mail-order ticket agents.

Many travellers change their routes halfway through their trips, so think before you buy a ticket that is not easily refunded.

Travellers with Specific Needs

If they're warned early enough, airlines can often make special arrangements for travellers, including wheelchair assistance at airports or vegetarian meals on the flight. Children aged under two travel for 10% of the standard fare (or free on some airlines) as long as they don't occupy a seat. They don't get a baggage allowance. 'Skycots', baby food and nappies should be provided by the airline if requested in advance. Children aged between two and 12 can usually occupy a seat for half to two-thirds of the full fare, and do get a baggage allowance.

The disability-friendly Web site, **w** www.everybody.co.uk, has an airline directory that provides information on the facilities offered by various airlines.

Departure Tax

All UK domestic flights and those from Britain to destinations within the EU carry a £10 departure tax. For flights to other destinations abroad the tax is £20. This is usually included in the price of your ticket.

Other Parts of Scotland

Flying is a pricey way of travelling around Scotland but is certainly the fastest and easiest way of reaching the islands of the north and west. There are daily flights from Edinburgh to Inverness, Wick, Kirkwall (Orkney), Sumburgh (Shetland) and Stornoway (Isle of Lewis). The main domestic carrier is British Airways.

The cheapest return flight from Edinburgh to Shetland costs around £140; a return flight to Kirkwall or Stornoway via Inverness costs from £120.

England & Wales

There are a couple of dozen daily flights between London and Edinburgh, and several daily from other UK airports. British Airways has flights to Edinburgh from London's Heathrow, Gatwick and Stansted and from Bristol, Birmingham, Manchester and Cardiff. British Midland flies from Heathrow, Manchester, East Midlands, Leeds/Bradford and Nottingham. KLM UK and Go fly from London Stansted, and easyJet flies from London's Luton airport. British European (under the name Jersey European) flies from London City.

Prices vary enormously. A standard economy return ticket from London to Edinburgh costs around £265 from British Midland, while Jersey European, easyJet and Go offer return flights, travelling midweek or on a Saturday and booking a month or two in advance, from as little as £45.

Ireland

The Union of Students in Ireland (USI **☎** 01-679 8833, 677 8117, **w** www.usi.ie) 19 Aston Quay, O'Connell Bridge, Dublin 2, the Irish youth and student travel association, has offices in major cities in Ireland.

Aer Lingus and British Airways fly direct from Dublin to Edinburgh; the lowest return fares start at around £70. British Airways, Go and easyJet have direct flights from Belfast. The no-frills airlines offer Belfast–Edinburgh return flights from £35.

Continental Europe

The major airlines operate several direct daily flights to Edinburgh from Amsterdam, Brussels, Frankfurt and Paris, and one or two daily from Copenhagen, Düsseldorf

Munich. In addition, it's possible to reach Edinburgh via London Stansted from European cities using Go and easyJet, including Athens, Barcelona, Copenhagen, Geneva, Madrid, Munich, Naples, Nice, Prague, Reykjavik, Rome, Venice and Zurich.

The best fare from continental Europe is with easyJet, which offers direct flights from Amsterdam to Edinburgh from around €55 return.

Travelling via London, there is not much variation in air-fare prices for departures from the main European cities. All the major airlines usually offer some sort of deal, and travel agencies generally have a number of offers, so shop around.

Expect to pay the equivalent of about £120 to £200 on major airlines for discounted return tickets to Edinburgh. Flying from Brussels to Edinburgh with Sabena will cost from €210 return. A return flight from Munich to Brussels costs from around €290. Flying from Munich to Edinburgh via London Stansted with Go costs from around €190.

Across Europe many travel agencies have ties with STA Travel, where cheap tickets can be purchased. Outlets in major cities include: STA Travel in Berlin (☎ 030-311 0950), Goethesttrasse 73, 10625 Berlin; Voyage Wasteels in Paris (☎ 0803 88 70 04 – this number can only be dialled from within France – fax 01 43 25 46 25), 11 rue Dupuytren, 756006 Paris; and Passaggi in Rome (☎ 06-474 0923, fax 482 7436), Staione Termini FS, Galleria di Tesla, Rome.

In Belgium, Connections (☎ 02-550 01 0), 19–21 rue du Midi, 1000 Brussels, and Nouvelles Frontières (☎ 02-547 44 44), 2 blvd Maurice Lemmonier, 1000 Brussels, re recommended agencies.

NBBS Reizen (☎ 020-620 5071), 66 Rokin, Amsterdam, is the official student ravel agency in the Netherlands. Another ood agency in Amsterdam is Malibu Travel (☎ 020-626 3230), Prinsengracht 230.

he USA

here are no direct flights from the USA to dinburgh Airport but a couple land at Glasgow – Continental Airlines from New York, and American Airlines from Chicago. Flight time from New York to Glasgow is around 7½ hours and return fares start from around US$650.

Due to a system – currently being challenged – in which the landing fees for airlines are considerably higher at Scottish airports than at Heathrow, the majority of transatlantic flights to the UK still arrive at London. This also means that flights from US cities to Scotland via London are cheaper – from around US$560 – but the flight time is two to three hours longer.

Rather than fly via London, it's worth considering flying via Iceland. Icelandair have direct flights from New York, Boston, Baltimore/Washington, Minneapolis and Orlando (during fall and winter) to Reykjavik, where you can connect with a flight to Glasgow. Fares start at around US$530.

Discount travel agents in the USA are known as consolidators. San Francisco is the ticket-consolidator capital of America, although some good deals can be found in Los Angeles, New York and other big cities. Consolidators can be found through the *Yellow Pages* or major daily newspapers. *The New York Times,* the *Los Angeles Times,* the *Chicago Tribune* and *The San Francisco Examiner* all produce weekly travel sections in which you will find a number of travel-agency ads. Ticket Planet is a leading ticket consolidator in the USA and is recommended. Visit its Web site at W www.ticketplanet.com.

Council Travel, America's largest student travel organisation, has around 60 offices in the USA; its head office (☎ 800 226 8624) is at 205 E 42 St, New York, NY 10017. Call it for the office nearest you or visit its Web site at W www.ciee.org. STA Travel (☎ 800 777 0112) has offices in Boston, Chicago, Miami, New York, Philadelphia, San Francisco and other major cities. Call the toll-free 800 number for office locations or visit its Web site at W www.statravel.com.

Canada

The charter operator Air Transat has one direct flight per week from Toronto to Edinburgh, while between them Air Canada,

Air Transat and Canada 3000 have two to four flights per day to Glasgow. There are also two flights a week from Calgary and one a week from Vancouver to Glasgow. Return fares from Toronto to Edinburgh start at around C$550.

Canadian discount air-ticket sellers are also known as consolidators and their air fares tend to be about 10% higher than those sold in the USA. *The Globe & Mail, The Toronto Star*, the *Montreal Gazette* and the *Vancouver Sun* carry travel-agents ads and are a good place to look for cheap fares.

Travel CUTS (☎ 800 667 2887) is Canada's national student travel agency and has offices in all major cities. Its Web address is 🔲 www.travelcuts.com.

Australia

For flights between the UK and Australia, there are a lot of competing airlines and a wide variety of air fares. Flying to Edinburgh, travellers can either take a flight via London or another European capital. Expect to pay from A$1650 in the low season to A$2350 in the high season for return tickets from Australia to Edinburgh.

Cheap flights from Australia to Europe generally go via South-East Asian capitals, involving stopovers at Kuala Lumpur, Bangkok or Singapore. If a long stopover between connections is necessary, transit accommodation is sometimes included in the price of the ticket. If it's at your own expense, it may be worth considering a more expensive ticket.

Quite a few travel offices specialise in discount air tickets. Some travel agents, particularly smaller ones, advertise cheap air fares in the travel sections of weekend newspapers, such as *The Age* in Melbourne and *The Sydney Morning Herald*.

Two well-known agents for cheap fares are STA Travel and Flight Centre. STA Travel (☎ 03-9349 2411) has its main office at 224 Faraday St, Carlton, VIC 3053, and offices in all major cities and on many university campuses. Call ☎ 131 776 Australiawide for the location of your nearest branch or visit its Web site at 🔲 www.statravel .com.au. Flight Centre (☎ 131 600 Australia-

wide) has a central office at 82 Elizabeth St, Sydney, and there are dozens of offices throughout Australia. Its Web address is 🔲 www.flightcen tre.com.au.

New Zealand

From New Zealand, flights go via one of the South-East Asian capitals or the western coast of the USA before arriving in Europe. There are no direct flights to Edinburgh so you will need to change in London or another European capital.

Prices are similar to those from Australia but the trip is even longer – two 12-hour flights minimum. Return low-/high-season fares start from NZ$2299/NZ$2699.

The New Zealand Herald has a travel section in which travel agents advertise fares. Flight Centre (☎ 09-309 6171) has a large central office in Auckland at National Bank Towers (corner of Queen and Darby Sts) and many branches throughout the country. STA Travel (☎ 09-309 0458) has its main office at 10 High St, Auckland, and has other offices in Auckland as well as in Hamilton, Palmerston North, Wellington, Christchurch and Dunedin. Visit online at 🔲 www.sta.travel.com.nz.

Asia

There are no direct flights from Asia to Scottish airports. Travelling via London, return flight from Hong Kong to Edinburgh will cost from around HK$7500, and from Singapore around S$1170.

Although most Asian countries are now offering fairly competitive air-fare deals, Bangkok, Singapore and Hong Kong are still the best places to shop around for discount tickets. Hong Kong's travel market can be unpredictable, but some excellent bargains are available if you are lucky.

Hong Kong has a number of excellent reliable travel agencies and some not-so-reliable ones. A good way to check on a travel agent is to look it up in the phone book: fly-by-night operators don't usually stay around long enough to get listed. Many travellers use the Hong Kong Student Travel Bureau (☎ 2730 3269), 8th floor, Star House, Tsimshatsui. You could also try

Air Travel Glossary

Alliances Many of the world's leading airlines are now intimately involved with each other, sharing everything from reservations systems and check-in to aircraft and frequent-flyer schemes. Opponents say that alliances restrict competition. Whatever the arguments, there is no doubt that big alliances are the way of the future.

Cancelling or Changing Tickets If you have to cancel or change a ticket, you need to contact the original travel agent who sold you the ticket. Airlines only issue refunds to the purchaser of a ticket – usually the travel agent who bought the ticket on your behalf. There are often heavy penalties involved; insurance can sometimes be taken out against these penalties.

Courier Fares Businesses often need to send urgent documents or freight securely and quickly. Courier companies hire people to accompany the package through customs and, in return, offer a discount ticket which is sometimes a bargain. However, you may have to surrender all your baggage allowance and take only carry-on luggage.

Fares Airlines traditionally offer 1st-class (coded F), business-class (coded J) and economy-class (coded Y) tickets. These days there are so many promotional and discounted fares available that few passengers pay full fare.

Lost Tickets If you lose your airline ticket an airline will usually treat it like a travellers cheque and, after enquiries, issue you with another one. Legally, however, an airline is entitled to treat it like cash and if you lose it then it's gone forever. Take good care of your tickets.

Onward Tickets An entry requirement for many countries is that you have a ticket out of the country. If you're unsure of your next move, the easiest solution is to buy the cheapest onward ticket to a neighbouring country or a ticket from a reliable airline that can later be refunded if you do not use it.

Open-Jaw Tickets These are return tickets where you fly out to one place but return from another. If available, this can save you backtracking to your arrival point.

Overbooking Since every flight has some passengers who fail to show up, airlines often book more passengers than they have seats. Usually excess passengers make up for the no-shows but occasionally somebody gets 'bumped' onto the next available flight. Guess who it is most likely to be? The passengers who check in late. If you do get 'bumped' you are normally offered some form of compensation.

Reconfirmation Some airlines require you to reconfirm your flight at least 72 hours prior to departure. Check your travel documents to see if this is the case.

Restrictions Discounted tickets often have various restrictions on them – such as needing to be paid for in advance and incurring a penalty to be altered or cancelled. Others are restrictions on the minimum and maximum period you must be away.

Round-the-World Tickets RTW tickets give you a limited period (usually a year) in which to circumnavigate the globe. You can go anywhere the carrying airlines go, as long as you don't backtrack. The number of stopovers or total number of separate flights is decided before you set off and they usually cost a bit more than a basic return flight.

Ticketless Travel Airlines are gradually waking up to the realisation that paper tickets are unnecessary encumbrances. On simple one-way or return trips, reservations details can be held on computer and the passenger merely shows ID to claim his or her seat.

Transferred Tickets Airline tickets cannot be transferred from one person to another. Travellers sometimes try to sell the return half of their ticket but officials can ask you to prove that you are the person named on the ticket. On an international flight tickets are compared with passports.

Phoenix Services (☎ 2722 7378) at 7th floor, Milton Mansion, 96 Nathan Rd, Tsimshatsui.

In Singapore, STA Travel (☎ 65-737 7188, W www.statravel.com.sg) is at 35a Cuppage Rd, Cuppage Terrace.

Africa

There are no direct flights from Africa to Scotland. Travelling via London, return fares from Johannesburg to Edinburgh start at around R4300.

Nairobi and Johannesburg are probably the best places in East and South Africa to buy tickets. Some major airlines have offices in Nairobi, which is a good place to determine the standard fare before you make the rounds of the travel agencies. Getting several quotes is a good idea as prices are always changing. Flight Centres (☎ 02-210024) in Lakhamshi House, Biashara St, has been in business for many years.

In Johannesburg, the South African Student's Travel Services (☎ 011-716 3045) has an office at the University of the Witwatersrand. STA Travel (☎ 011- 447 5551) has an office in Johannesburg on Tyrwhitt Ave in Rosebank.

Airlines

The main airlines serving Edinburgh Airport are British Airways (☎ 0845 773 3377, W www.britishairways.co.uk), British Midland (☎ 0870 607 0555, W www.flybmi .com) and KLM UK (☎ 0870 507 4074, W www.klmuk.com). Other airlines can be contacted on the following numbers:

Aer Lingus	☎ 0845 973 7747
Air Canada	☎ 0870 524 7226
Air France	☎ 0845 084 5111
American Airlines	☎ 0345 789789
British European	☎ 0870 567 6676
Continental Airlines	☎ 0800 776464
Lufthansa	☎ 0845 773 7747
Sabena	☎ 0845 601 0933
ScotAirways	☎ 0870 606 0707

There are also several discount, no-frills airlines whose flights do not appear on the computerised reservations systems used by travel agents and Web sites such as W www .travelocity.com and W www.expedia.com. To check their fares you have to call their reservations numbers or check their Web sites (which often offer extra discounts for tickets bought on the Internet).

easyJet (☎ 0870 600 0000, W www.easyjet .com) A feisty carrier with bright-orange aircraft, easyJet has direct flights into Edinburgh from London Luton, Amsterdam and Belfast.

Go (☎ 0845 605 4321, W www.go-fly.com) Originally a spin-off of British Airways but now independent, Go flies into Edinburgh from London Stansted and Belfast.

Ryanair (☎ 0870 156 9569, W www.ryanair .com) An Ireland-based airline, Ryanair flies direct to Glasgow Prestwick (about two hours by bus or train from Edinburgh) from London Stansted, Dublin, Paris and Frankfurt.

BUS
Other Parts of Britain

Long-distance buses (coaches) are usually the cheapest method of getting to Edinburgh. The main operators are National Express (☎ 0870 580 8080, W www.goby coach.com) and its subsidiary Scottish Citylink (☎ 0870 550 5050, W www.citylink.co .uk).

At the time of writing, buses and coaches arrive and depart from various temporary stops on St Andrew Square and Waterloo Place (Map 3); a new bus station on the eastern side of the square is due to open in late 2002. The Scottish Citylink ticket office is in the Edinburgh and Scotland Information Centre, on top of Princes Mall at the eastern end of Princes St.

Fares & Journey Times

Standard return fares and journey times to Edinburgh from other parts of Scotland include:

destination	return fare	best time (hrs)
Aberdeen	£25	3½
Dundee	£13	1¾
Fort William	£28	4
Glasgow	£5	1¼
Inverness	£24	4
Stirling	£10.50	1¼

Standard return fares and journey times to Edinburgh from England and Wales include:

destination	return fare	best time (hrs)
Birmingham	£47.50	7½
Bristol	£59.50	10
Cardiff	£58	10½
Leeds	£41	7
London	£36	9½
Manchester	£29.50	7
Newcastle	£25	2¾
Oxford	£57	10
Plymouth	£69.50	13½
Swansea	£60	11¾
York	£33.50	6

Ireland

Scottish Citylink runs a daily bus service from Edinburgh to various destinations in Ireland, including Belfast (£42 return, 7½ hours) and Dublin (£52, 10½ hours) via Glasgow and the high-speed ferry link between Stranraer and Belfast.

Bus Passes & Discounts

The Scottish Citylink Explorer Pass gives unlimited free travel on all Citylink services within Scotland, and discounted travel on other Scottish bus networks and ferry services. It costs £33 for three consecutive days of travel; £55 for five days' travel out of 10; and £85 for eight days' travel out of 16.

National Express also offer travel passes – check their Web site for details.

TRAIN

The main terminus in Edinburgh is Waverley train station, located in the heart of the city in the valley between Old and New Towns. Trains arriving at and departing from the west also stop at Haymarket train station, which is more convenient for the West End. The Edinburgh Rail Travel Centre in Waverley station opens 8am to 11pm Monday to Saturday and 9am to 8pm on Sunday. For fare and timetable enquires, phone the National Rail Enquiry Service (☎ 0845 748 4950 or ☎ 44 1332-387601 outside the UK) or check the timetable on Railtrack's Web site w www.railtrack.co.uk.

Buying Tickets

If the Byzantine Empire had designed a railway system, it could not have come up with anything more impenetrably complex than the labyrinthine structure created by the privatisation of British Rail in the mid-1990s. Rail services are provided by 25 different train operating companies (TOCs), while the rails themselves, along with the stations and signalling systems, are owned and operated by a completely separate company called Railtrack.

There's a bewildering range of ticket types with various restrictions attached, depending on when you book and when you're travelling. You can check timetables and fares with the National Rail Enquiry Service (☎ 0845 748 4950), who will then give you the phone number of one of the TOCs where you can make a credit-card booking.

ScotRail operates most train services within Scotland, as well as the Caledonian Sleeper service to London; you can book tickets on ☎ 0845 755 0033 or online at w www.scotrail.co.uk. Great North Eastern Railways (GNER; ☎ 0845 722 5225, w www.gner.co.uk) operates the main, east-coast London-Edinburgh route, and Virgin Trains (☎ 0845 722 2333, w www.virgin trains.co.uk) runs services from Wales and northern, central-southern and south-western England to Glasgow and Edinburgh.

For most journeys it's easy enough to buy a ticket at the station just before departure, but as the London-Edinburgh route is very popular it's safer to make a seat reservation.

Other Parts of Scotland

There's a regular shuttle service (departures every 15 minutes) between Edinburgh and Glasgow (£14.30, 50 minutes), and frequent daily services to all Scottish cities, including Aberdeen (£44.90, 2½ hours), Dundee (£17.40, 1½ hours) and Inverness (£37.10, 3¼ hours).

England & Wales

GNER operates a fast and frequent rail service between London (four hours) and Edinburgh, passing through Peterborough, York and Newcastle, with around 20 daily departures between 7am and 7pm. Standard returns costs around £85 but special-offer fares can be as low as £39.

The Caledonian Sleeper service between Edinburgh and London is operated by Scot-Rail and runs nightly from Sunday to Friday. Northbound, it departs London Euston around 11.40pm and arrives in Edinburgh about 7.20am. Southbound, it leaves Edinburgh at 11.55pm and arrives in London at 7am (Sunday departures are about 20 minutes earlier). A standard return (sharing a two-bunk compartment) costs £119, and a first-class return (single-bunk compartment) costs £165; the seven-day advance purchase Apex fare is £89. You also have the option of travelling on the sleeper in a first-class coach with a reclining seat, rather than a bunk; this costs £35/65 for an Apex/standard return.

Services to Edinburgh from other parts of England and Wales usually require changing trains at some point. Typical discount return fares and journey times include: Bristol (£105, seven hours), Cardiff (£105, 7½ hours), Leeds (£54, three hours) and Manchester (£46.60, four hours).

Ireland

ScotRail offers various 'Rail and Sail' deals between Edinburgh and Belfast via the ferry crossings at Stranraer and Troon. Off-peak returns cost from £45 and the journey time is about five hours.

Continental Europe

You can travel from Paris or Brussels to Edinburgh using the Eurostar service as far as London Waterloo station, but you'll have to take the underground from Waterloo to Kings Cross station to connect with the Edinburgh train. The total journey time from Paris is about eight hours and the standard return fare from Paris to London is around €500. Even with discount fares to London of around €120, flying is usually faster and cheaper.

Rail Passes

Unfortunately, Eurail passes are not recognised in Britain. There are local equivalents but they in turn aren't recognised in the rest of Europe. The BritRail pass, which includes travel in Scotland, must be bought outside Britain.

ScotRail's Freedom of Scotland Travelpass is excellent value, covering all rail travel in Scotland, all CalMac ferry services and certain bus routes, plus giving discounts on the Caledonian Sleeper and on Guide Friday bus tours of Edinburgh. In high/low season it costs £79/69 for four days' travel out of eight, and £99/89 for eight days' travel out of 15, and can be bought from the British Travel Centre in London, train stations throughout Britain, BritRail outlets in Europe and North America and from ScotRail telesales (☎ 0845 755 0033).

The Central Scotland Rover ticket costs £29 for three days' travel out of seven and covers rail travel between Edinburgh and Glasgow, North Berwick, Stirling, Falkirk and Fife, plus unlimited travel on Glasgow underground.

CAR & MOTORCYCLE

The main routes into Edinburgh from the west and north are the M8 motorway from Glasgow (46 miles), and the M90/A9 across the Forth Road Bridge from Perth (42 miles) and Inverness (158 miles).

The fastest driving route from London (401 miles) is via the M1 and M6 to Carlisle, and then the M74 as far as Abington, where you fork right on the A702 for the final leg to Edinburgh. From Leeds (200 miles) and Newcastle (107 miles), the M1/A1 along the east coast and the A68 via Jedburgh are the main routes to the Scottish capital.

From Ireland, the main car-ferry links to Scotland are the Belfast–Stranraer and Larne–Cairnryan crossings, operated by Stena Line (☎ 028 90 747 747 from Northern Ireland, W www.stenaline.com) and P&O Irish Sea (☎ 0870 242 4777, W www .poirishsea.com) respectively. There are standard- and high-speed ferries on both routes; Larne–Cairnryan is slightly shorter (2¼ hours/one hour). Fares vary widely depending on season and there are special deals worth looking out for. An Apex return on the Larne–Cairnryan fast ferry for one car and two adults in July costs around £226. The drive from Cairnryan/Stranraer to Edinburgh is 132 miles.

Drivers of vehicles registered in other EU countries will find bringing a car or motorcycle into Britain fairly straightforward. The vehicle must have registration papers and a nationality plate, and the driver must have insurance. Although the International Insurance Certificate (Green Card) is no longer compulsory, it still provides excellent proof that you are covered. Driving to Edinburgh from mainland Europe via the Channel Tunnel or ferry ports, head for London and follow the busy M25 orbital road to the M1 motorway, then follow the route as described from London.

Arriving in or leaving Edinburgh by car during the morning and evening rush hours (7.30am to 9.30am and 4.30pm to 6.30pm Monday to Friday) is an experience you can live without. Try to time your journey to avoid these periods.

BICYCLE
Edinburgh is included in the UK's National Cycle Network, a 6500-mile network of cycle paths created and maintained by the nonprofit group Sustrans. For further information, contact Sustrans (☎ 0117-929 0888, e info@nationalcyclenetwork.org .uk, w www.sustrans.org.uk), 35 King St, Bristol BS1 4DZ.

Bicycles can be transported by bus provided there's enough room in the luggage compartment and that they're folded or dismantled and boxed. On most long-distance rail routes it's necessary to make a reservation for your bike (free on ScotRail services). Some trains carry only one or two bikes so make your reservation and get your ticket at least 24 hours before travelling.

HITCHING
Hitching is never entirely safe in any country in the world and we don't recommend it. Travellers who decide to hitch should understand that they are taking a small but potentially serious risk. People who do choose to hitch will be safer if they travel in pairs and let someone know their plans.

BOAT
Starting in spring 2002, Superfast Ferries (w www.superfastscotland.com) will run a roll-on roll-off car ferry between Rosyth, 12 miles north-west of Edinburgh, and Zeebrugge, Belgium. One daily crossing is planned, and the journey time is expected to be around 16 hours. Superfast's sales agent in the UK is Viamare Travel (☎ 020-7431 4560, fax 7431 5456), Graphic House, 2 Sumatra Rd, London NW6 1PU.

ORGANISED TOURS
There are hundreds of companies around the world offering package tours of Scotland that include Edinburgh. Ask a travel agent, or contact the Scottish Tourist Board/ visitscotland or the British Tourist Authority (see Tourist Offices in the Facts for the Visitor chapter for details).

Ancestral Journeys
(☎ 01383-720522, e ancestralconnections@ compuserve.com), 105 St Margaret St, Dunfermline KY12 7PH. This company will research your Scottish ancestry and organise a personalised tour, accompanied by a professional genealogist and historian, that combines sightseeing with visiting the places where your ancestors lived.

Footprints
(☎ 01683-221592, e enquiries@footprints-scotland.co.uk), Moffat, Dumfriesshire DG10 9BN. Take a small, personalised tour beginning in Edinburgh or Glasgow and explore Scotland's prehistoric past in the company of an archaeological expert. Highlights include visits to Pictish symbol stones, Iron Age forts and stone circles.

Saltire Tours
(☎ 0131-442 2324, e chris@saltiretours.co .uk), 3 Baberton Mains Cottage, Edinburgh EH14 5AB. This small company provides imaginative tours on a wide range of subjects from art and architecture to castles, whisky and Sir Walter Scott.

Taste of Scotland
(☎ 01592-260101, fax 261333, e admin@ robertthebruce.com), 9 Nicol St, Kirkcaldy KY1 1NY. Unwind with a bespoke luxury tour. Stay in top hotel, eat at the best restaurants and travel in a Rolls-Royce with a qualified guide and driver.

From the USA

There are a number of good organised tours operating from the USA, including:

About Travel
(☎ 605-362 1741, ⓔ cheryl@abouttravel.com), 3548 S Gateway Blvd 302, Sioux Falls SD 57106 – This company offers eight-day trips to the Edinburgh Festival, including tickets to two major shows, Fringe performances and the Military Tattoo.

Celebrity Tours Inc
(☎ 914-244 1300 or ☎ 1-800-663 5578, ⓔ info@celebritytours.net), 2 Ascot Circle, Mount Kisco NY 10459 – These tours combine a visit to Edinburgh with golf at the Old Course in St Andrews and other famous Scottish courses.

From New Zealand

Organised tours from New Zealand include:

Scottish Heritage Travel
(☎ 03-318 8066, fax 318 8464 ⓔ travel@scottish-heritage.co.nz), Kinnairdy, Coal Track Rd, R.D. 1, Christchurch 8021. Find something to suit among a wide range of special-interest tours offered by Scottish Heritage Travel, including trips to whisky distilleries and clan gatherings.

Getting Around

THE AIRPORT

Edinburgh Airport (☎ 333 1000) is 8 miles west of the city centre on the A8 Edinburgh–Glasgow road. It has recently undergone a £100-million-pound expansion and redevelopment, which will help to cope with an expected 5.5 million passengers per year in 2002.

The arrivals hall, on the ground floor, contains an information desk run by the Edinburgh and Lothians Tourist Board (☎ 333 2167), a Thomas Cook travel and accommodation booking office (☎ 333 5119) and several car-hire agencies including Alamo (☎ 333 5100), Avis (☎ 333 1866), Europcar (☎ 333 2588), Hertz (☎ 333 1019) and National (☎ 333 0900). Upstairs, in the departure hall, there are currency exchanges, cash machines, shops, a pub and a restaurant. There's a left-luggage and lost-property office outside the terminal, next to the UK arrivals area.

TO/FROM THE AIRPORT

The Lothian Buses Airlink service runs from Waverley Bridge, just outside the train station, to Haymarket and the airport (£3.30/5 one-way/return, 30 minutes). Buses run between 4.50am and 12.20am, with departures every 10 minutes from 7am to 9.30pm. The Airsaver ticket (adult/child tickets cost £4.20/2.50) can be purchased on the bus and gives a one-way trip on the Airlink bus plus unlimited travel for one day on all Lothian Bus services in the city.

An airport taxi to the city centre costs around £13 and takes about 20 minutes. Both buses and taxis depart from just outside the arrivals hall at stand Nos 17 and 18.

BUS

Edinburgh is covered by a good network of bus services run by two companies, Lothian Buses and First Edinburgh. There are timetables, route maps and fare guides posted at all main bus stops, and you can pick up the free *Edinburgh Travelmap*, showing all the city's bus routes, from the city council's Traveline office (Map 8; ☎ 225 3858, 0800 232323), 2 Cockburn St, which has details on all of Edinburgh's public transport. It opens 8.30am to 5pm Monday to Friday.

Adult fares range from 50p to £1; children aged under 5 travel free and those aged 5 to 15 pay a flat fare of 50p. On Lothian Buses you must pay the driver the exact fare but First Edinburgh buses will give change. Lothian Bus drivers also sell a Daysaver ticket (adult/child tickets cost £2.20/1.50) that gives unlimited travel on Lothian buses for a day. Night-service buses, which run hourly between midnight and 5am, charge a flat fare of £1.60.

Ridacards, which cost £10.50/6.50 for a week's unlimited bus travel and £30.50/18 for four weeks, are available from the Lothian Bus Travelshops (Map 8; ☎ 555 6363). The Travelshop on Waverley Bridge opens 8.30am to 6pm Monday to Saturday; the branch at 27 Hanover St opens 8am to 7.15pm Monday to Saturday, 9am to 4.30pm Sunday (Easter to October) and 9am to 4.30pm Tuesday to Saturday (November to Easter). Ridacards are also available from newsagents and grocery stores throughout the city.

First Edinburgh, whose route network extends to nearby towns in East and West Lothian, has a Bus Shop (Map 3; ☎ 663 9233) on the site of the new St Andrew Square bus station, open 9am to 5pm Monday to Saturday. It also has discount schemes, including a Day Explorer ticket for £2/1 and a Capital Card, which gives a week's unlimited travel within Edinburgh for £7.

Information on timetables and fares is available online at W www.lothianbuses.co.uk and W www.firstedinburgh.co.uk.

TRAIN

Edinburgh suburban train services link Waverley and Haymarket stations to Musselburgh in the east and to Slateford, Kingsknowe, Wester Hailes and Curriehill

Edinburgh's Amazing Technicolour Roadways

Many of Edinburgh's main streets are paved not in gold but in green. The city's celebrated Greenways – loved by bus passengers, loathed by motorists – are priority lanes reserved exclusively for buses, taxis and bicycles. At times when the Greenways are in force (generally 7.30am to 6.30pm Monday to Friday and 8.30am to 6.30pm Saturday), private cars are not allowed to drive in them, nor to park, nor even stop for a minute to drop someone off (unless they are registered as disabled). In the first six months following their introduction in 1996, Greenways cut bus journey times by up to 25% and attracted around 250,000 extra passengers onto the buses.

Other road markings you will see include double red lines along the edges of streets (no stopping at any time) and double yellow lines (no waiting at any time, though you can stop to drop someone off). Many other streets are decorated with brick-red bicycle lanes and advanced stop lines. If you are caught parked on a Greenway or a double red line, your car will be towed away and you will be charged a minimum of £105 to get it back. You have been warned!

Greenway regulations are enforced by a team of traffic wardens with yellow hat-bands, known colloquially as 'The Yellow Peril'. In 1998, the city council hired a private contractor to provide extra wardens for the policing of on-street parking regulations; with their blue hat-bands and the unenviable job of dishing out parking tickets to unfortunate motorists, they inevitably became known as 'The Blue Meanies'. And as if that wasn't enough in the way of colourful nicknames, the council responded to complaints about changes in parking regulations by suggesting a team of on-street advisors to explain to confused drivers where they were able to park legally. To make them easily recognisable they would wear orange jackets... and were immediately dubbed 'Orange Smarties'.

---

stations in the south-west. Trains run about once an hour, and a return ticket to Waverley from the outskirts costs under £3. For timetable and fares information call ☎ 0845 748 4950.

CAR & MOTORCYCLE

Though useful for day trips beyond the city, a car in central Edinburgh is more of a liability than a convenience. There is restricted access on Princes St, George St and Charlotte Square, many streets are one-way, and finding a parking place in the city centre is like striking gold. Queen's Drive around Holyrood Park is closed to motorised traffic on Sunday.

Road Rules

Anyone unfamiliar with driving in the UK should get hold of the *Highway Code* (£1.49), which is available from bookshops and some TICs. A foreign driving licence is valid in Britain for up to 12 months from the time of your last entry into the country. If you're bringing a car from Europe make sure you're adequately insured.

Briefly, vehicles drive on the left-hand side of the road; front seat belts are compulsory and if seat belts are fitted in the back they must be worn; the speed limit is 30mph (48kph) in built-up areas, 60mph (96kph) on single carriageways, and 70mph (112kph) on dual or triple carriageways; you give way to your right at roundabouts (traffic already on the roundabout has right of way); and motorcyclists must wear helmets.

See Legal Matters in Facts for the Visitor for information on blood-alcohol limits for driving.

Parking

There's no parking on main roads into the city from 7.30am to 6.30pm Monday to Saturday. On-street parking in the city centre is controlled by parking meters and self-service ticket machines from 8.30am to 6.30pm Monday to Friday and 8.30am to 1.30pm Saturday and costs £1 per hour, with a two-hour maximum. If you break the rules, you'll get a parking ticket – the fine is £40, reduced to £20 if you pay up within 14 days. Cars parked illegally will be towed away.

There are large, long-stay car parks at the St James Centre, Greenside Place, New St, Castle Terrace and Morrison St. Motorcycles can be parked for free at designated areas in the city centre.

Yellow or red lines painted along the edge of a street indicate that there are parking restrictions. The only way to establish the exact restrictions is to find the nearby sign that spells them out. See also the boxed text 'Edinburgh's Amazing Technicolour Roadways'.

Rental

All the big, international car-rental agencies have offices in Edinburgh, including Avis (Map 4; ☎ 337 6363), Budget (☎ 551 3322), 394 Ferry Rd and 3 West Park Place, Dalry Rd; Europcar (Map 3; ☎ 557 3456), 24 East London St; Hertz (☎ 557 5272), Waverley train station; and Thrifty (Map 2; ☎ 337 1319), 42 Haymarket Terrace.

There are many smaller, local agencies that offer better rates. One of the best is Arnold Clark (Map 5; ☎ 228 4747) at 1–13 Lochrin Place in Tollcross, which charges from £18 per day/£90 per week, including VAT and insurance, for a Fiat Seicento. The daily rate includes 250 miles per day; excess is charged at 4p per mile. For periods of four days and more, mileage is unlimited.

Most agencies require that a driver be aged between 23 and 75, with at least two years' driving experience.

TAXI

Edinburgh's taxis – or 'fast blacks', as they are called locally – can be hailed in the street, ordered by phone, or picked up at one of the many central ranks. Taxis are fairly expensive – the flag fall starts at £1.20 for the first 340 yards, then 20p for every subsequent 240 yards – a 2-mile trip will cost around £4. The main local companies are Capital Taxis (☎ 228 2555), Central Radio Taxis (☎ 229 2468), City Cabs (☎ 228 1211) and Radiocabs (☎ 225 9000).

BICYCLE

See the boxed text 'Cycling Edinburgh' later for details of routes and bike rental.

ORGANISED TOURS
Walking Tours

There are lots of organised walks around Edinburgh, many of them related to ghosts, murders and witches. For starting times, phone or check the Web sites listed below.

Auld Reekie Tours
(☎ 557 4700, W www.auldreekietours.co.uk) Cost £5. More interested in the blood-and-guts aspects of medieval torture than in real history, Auld Reekie can boast a 'working pagan temple' complete with witches' coven.

Black Hart Storytellers
(☎ 221 1249, W www.blackhart.uk.com) Cost £5. Many people who take their 'City of the Dead' tour of Greyfriars Kirkyard have reported encounters with the 'MacKenzie Poltergeist'.

Cadies & Witchery Tours
(☎ 225 6745, W www.witcherytours.com) Adult/child £7/4. The becloaked and pasty-faced Adam Lyal leads a 'Murder & Mystery' tour of Old Town's darker corners. These tours are famous for their 'jumper-ooters' – costumed actors who 'jump oot' when you least expect it. Ooooh, scary.

Celtic Trails
(☎ 672 3888, W www.celtictrails.co.uk) Adult/child £20/10. Offers half-day tours of Edinburgh's ancient pilgrimage wells, Templar stones and religious and Celtic sites. Bookings are necessary.

Geowalks
(☎ 555 5488, W www.geowalks.demon.co.uk) Adult/concession £8/6. For those interested in history that goes back millions, rather than hundreds of years, geologist Dr Angus Miller leads walks that explore the geological history of Edinburgh's very own extinct volcano, Arthur's Seat.

McEwan's 80/- – Literary Pub Tour
(☎ 226 6665, W www.scot-lit-tour.co.uk) Adult/concession £7/5. An enlightening two-hour trawl through Edinburgh's literary history – and its associated howffs – in the entertaining company of Messrs Clart and McBrain. One of the best of Edinburgh's walking tours.

Mercat Tours
(☎ 557 6464, W www.mercat-tours.com) Adult/child £5/3. Mercat offers a wide range of tours, including history walks in Old Town and Leith, 'Ghosts & Ghouls', and visits to haunted Mary King's Close, hidden underground vaults and darkened graveyards. Their latest offering is a tour of sites linked with the fictional detective John Rebus, featured in the novels of Ian Rankin.

GETTING AROUND

Cycling Edinburgh

ASA ANDERSSON

Despite its many hills and cobbled streets, Edinburgh is a seriously cycle-friendly city. This is largely due to the efforts of the cycle campaign group Spokes (Map 4; ☎ 313 2114, W www.spokes.org.uk), St Martins Church, 232 Dalry Rd, and a city council that has pledged to reduce car use.

The city and its surrounding countryside are covered by a wide-reaching network of signposted cycle routes. Many of these are traffic-free and shared by cyclists and pedestrians, but some are simply cycle lanes marked on ordinary roads; the latter are often blocked by parked cars. The main cycle paths follow the routes of former railway lines, and are thus delightfully free of any serious hills. The *Edinburgh Cycle Map* (£4.95), published by Spokes and available from bike shops, shows all the cycle routes in and around the city. Spokes also publish cycle maps for Midlothian and West Lothian.

The main off-road routes from the city centre out to the countryside follow the Union Canal towpath and the Water of Leith Walkway from Tollcross south-west to Balerno (7½ miles) on the edge of the Pentland Hills, and the Innocent Railway Cycle Path from the southern side of Arthur's Seat eastwards to Musselburgh (5 miles) and on to Ormiston and Pencaitland. There are several routes through the Pentland Hills that are suitable for mountain bikes – for details ask at any bike shop or contact the Pentland Hills Ranger Service (☎ 445 3383). There's even a dedicated downhill mountain-biking trail at the Midlothian Ski Centre at Hillend.

Visiting cyclists should be aware that the increased popularity of cycling in Edinburgh – and, it has to be said, the inconsiderate behaviour of a selfish minority of cyclists – has caused a backlash and an increase in hostility towards bike riders from both pedestrians and motorists. Follow the Good Cycling Code – be courteous and considerate to others, obey the rules of the road and always give way to walkers, remembering that some people may have impaired hearing or sight. Police have the power to issue on-the-spot fines of up to £40 for offences such as cycling on the pavement, jumping a red light, going the wrong way down a one-way street and cycling after dark without proper lights.

Bicycle Hire

Biketrax (Map 5; ☎ 228 6633, W www.biketrax.co.uk, 11 Lochrin Place) Open 9.30am-6pm Mon-Fri, 9.30am-5.30pm Sat, noon-5pm Sun. Biketrax rent out a wide range of cycles and equipment, including kids' bikes, tandems, recumbents, pannier bags, child seats – even unicycles! If you phone a day or two ahead with your measurements, they'll have a correctly sized and adjusted bike set up and waiting for you. A mountain bike costs £15 for one day (24 hours), £10 for extra days, and £60 for one week, £40 for extra weeks. You'll need a £100 cash or credit-card deposit and some form of ID.

Edinburgh Cycle Hire & Scottish Cycle Safaris (Map 8; ☎/fax 556 5560, W www.cyclescotland.co.uk, 29 Blackfriars St) Open 10am-6pm Mon-Sun. This friendly and helpful agency rents top-quality bikes for £10 to £15 per day, £50 to £70 per week, including helmet, lock and repair kit; there are occasionally older bikes available for £5 per day. You can hire tents and touring equipment too. They also organise cycle tours in Edinburgh and all over Scotland – check the Web site for details.

Both the above shops offer a repair service. You can also get repairs done and buy spares and accessories at Edinburgh Bicycle Cooperative (Map 5; ☎ 228 1368), 8 Alvanley Terrace, Whitehouse Loan, and City Cycles (Map 3; ☎ 557 2801), 30 Rodney St.

Bus Tours

Open-topped buses leave from Waverley Bridge outside the main train station and offer hop-on, hop-off tours of the main sights, taking in New Town, Grassmarket and the Royal Mile. They're a good way of getting your bearings – although with a bus map and a Day Saver bus ticket (£2.20) you could do much the same thing but without the commentary. Guide Friday (☎ 556 2244) charges £8.50/7/2.50 for adults/concessions/children, and Lothian Buses' (☎ 555 6363) bright-red Edinburgh Tour buses cost £7.50/6/2.50; tours depart every 10 minutes from Waverley Bridge. Mac Tours (☎ 220 0770) has a similar offering, but in a vintage bus, with departures every 20 minutes (£7.50/6/2.50).

Helicopter Tours

Lothian Helicopters (☎ 01875-320032, W www.lothianhelicopters.co.uk), Suite 1, Vineyard Business Centre, Tynehead, Pathhead, offers sightseeing flights over Edinburgh and the Forth Bridges in a seven-seat Bell 206L-4. Prices range from £35 per person for a 10-minute flight, to £125 for 45 minutes.

GETTING AROUND

Things to See & Do

SUGGESTED ITINERARIES

If you only have a day to spare, visit Edinburgh Castle in the morning and then take a leisurely stroll down the Royal Mile, stopping off at any of the museums or attractions that take your fancy – but be sure to take a look inside St Giles Cathedral. In the afternoon, spend an hour or two in the Museum of Scotland on Chambers St and then, if the weather's fine, take a walk up Calton Hill or Arthur's Seat.

If you're in town for the weekend, head down to Ocean Terminal in Leith on the second day for a tour of the former Royal Yacht *Britannia*, and enjoy a leisurely lunch in one of Leith's many excellent restaurants. In the afternoon, depending on your tastes (and the weather), take a tour of the Palace of Holyroodhouse, visit the Botanic Gardens, cruise the shops on Princes St, take a walk along the Water of Leith or find a pub with outdoor tables and sit in the sun and drink beer.

If you're lucky enough to have a week in Edinburgh, you can do all the walks described in this book, and add the following to

the list above: visit the Museum of Edinburgh in Huntly House and the Scottish National Gallery of Modern Art; explore Duddingston, Cramond and Swanston; and make a day trip to St Andrews.

Old Town

EDINBURGH CASTLE (Map 7)

The brooding, black crags of the Castle Rock, shouldering above Princes St Gardens, are the very reason for Edinburgh's existence. This rocky hill – the glacier-worn stump of an ancient volcano – was the most easily defended hilltop on the invasion route between England and central Scotland, a route followed by countless armies from the Roman legions of the 1st and 2nd centuries AD to the Jacobite troops of Bonnie Prince Charlie in 1745. No-one knows when the rock was first fortified but archaeological excavations have uncovered evidence of habitation from as early as 900 BC.

The castle has played a pivotal role in Scottish history, both as a royal residence – King Malcolm Canmore (reigned 1057–93) and Queen Margaret made their home here in the 11th century – and as a military stronghold. From the 16th century the royal family favoured more comfortable domestic accommodation at places such as Holyrood and Linlithgow, and the castle became more a seat of government and military power. However, in 1566 Mary Queen of Scots underlined its continuing symbolic importance when she chose to give birth to her son, King James VI, in the castle.

The castle suffered extensive damage during the Lang Siege, between 1571 and 1573, when supporters of Mary Queen of Scots held out against the forces of James Douglas, earl of Morton. It was occupied by English soldiers from 1650 to 1660 during Oliver Cromwell's invasion of Scotland and by Jacobites during the siege of 1689, when the duke of Gordon faced off against William of Orange.

But when the army of Bonnie Prince Charlie passed through Edinburgh in 1745, they made only a cursory attempt to take the castle before moving quickly on. That was the last time the castle saw military action, and from then until the 1920s it served as the British army's main base in Scotland.

Edinburgh Castle (☎ 225 9846; adult/concession/child £7.50/5.50/2 including audioguide; open 9.30am-6pm daily Apr-Sept, 9.30am-5pm daily Oct-Mar, closed 25-26 Dec, last ticket sold 45 mins before closing) is now Scotland's most popular pay-to-enter tourist attraction, pulling in over 1.2 million visitors in 2000. The **Esplanade**, a parade ground dating from 1820, is now a car park with superb views south over the city towards the Pentland Hills. On the northern side is an equestrian **statue of Field Marshall Earl Haig** (1861–1928). Haig was commander-in-chief of British forces during WWI and was responsible for the policy of attrition and trench warfare that killed thousands of troops.

The **Entrance Gateway** dates from between 1886 and 1888, and is flanked by statues of Robert the Bruce and William Wallace. Above the gate is the Royal Standard of Scotland – a red lion rampant on a gold field – and the Scottish Royal motto in Latin, 'NEMO ME IMPUNE LACESSIT'. This is translated into Scots as 'wha daur meddle wi' me', and into English as 'watch it, pal' (OK, it literally means 'no one messes with me with impunity'). Inside, a cobbled lane leads up beneath the 16th-century **Portcullis Gate**, topped by the 19th-century **Argyle Tower**, and past the cannon of the Argyle and Mills Mount batteries. The battlements here have great views over New Town to the Firth of Forth.

At the far end of Mills Mount Battery, to the right of the Cart Shed (which houses a cafe and restaurant), is the **One O'Clock Gun**, a gleaming WWII 25-pounder that fires an ear-splitting time signal at exactly 1pm every day (except Sunday, Christmas Day and Good Friday). A staircase leads down to a little exhibition explaining the

The Daily Bang

On Princes St, you can tell locals and visitors apart by their reaction to the sudden explosion that rips through the air each day at one o'clock. Locals check their watches, while visitors shy like startled ponies. It's the One O'-Clock Gun, fired from Mills Mount Battery on the castle battlements at 1pm sharp every day except Sunday.

The gun's origins date from the mid-19th century, when the accurate setting of a ship's chronometer was essential for safe navigation (finding your longitude at sea depended on knowing the exact time in your home port). The city authorities installed a time-signal on top of the Nelson Monument on Calton Hill – a ball that was hoist to the top of a flagstaff and dropped exactly on the stroke of one o'clock – that was visible to ships anchored in the Firth of Forth. The gun was added as an audible signal that could be used when rain or mist obscured the ball.

Of course, the ship-bound navigators – and the Edinburgh public – had to make an allowance for the time it took for the sound of the gun (travelling at 330m/s) to reach them. The Edinburgh Post Office Directory used to publish maps showing the time delay for various places – two seconds for New Town, 11 seconds for Leith and up to 15 seconds for vessels anchored offshore. An interesting little exhibition in Edinburgh Castle details the history and workings of the One O'Clock Gun.

history of the gun, and beyond lie the **Western Ramparts**, a battlement walk with grand views over Edinburgh's West End.

To the left of the Cart Shed, a road leads down to the **National War Museum of Scotland** (☎ 225 7534, Edinburgh Castle; admission included in Edinburgh Castle ticket; open 9.45am-5.30pm daily Apr-Nov, 9.45am-4.30pm daily Dec-Mar). Opened in 2000, this museum brings Scotland's military history vividly to life. The exhibits have been personalised by telling the stories of the original owners of the objects on

Trunk and Disorderly

One of the most unusual exhibits in the National War Museum of Scotland is a set of sawn-off elephant's toenails. They belonged to a beast that was adopted as a regimental mascot by the 78th Regiment of Foot (the Ross-shire Buffs), while they were serving in Ceylon (now Sri Lanka) in the 1830s, and travelled back to Edinburgh with them on their return to Scotland. The elephant lived in stables at Edinburgh Castle and was trained to march at the head of the regiment during parades. It was looked after by Private James McIntosh, a bibulous Highlander who regularly retired to the canteen in the evenings to partake of alcoholic refreshment.

The elephant, no doubt feeling lonely and a little disoriented, would follow him to the canteen and loiter with intent, regularly extending its trunk through the window where the amused clientele would serve it large quantities of beer. Legend has it that both McIntosh and the elephant would then retire to the stable and sleep it off together.

ASA ANDERSSON

display, making it easier to empathise with the experiences of war than any dry display of dusty weaponry ever could. You'll see more than one person brushing away a tear as they pass through.

South of Mills Mount, the road curls up leftwards through **Foog's Gate** to the highest part of the Castle Rock, crowned by the tiny **St Margaret's Chapel**, the oldest surviving building in Edinburgh. It's a simple Romanesque structure that was probably built by David I or Alexander I in memory of their mother Queen Margaret sometime around 1130 (she was canonised in 1250). Following Cromwell's capture of the castle in 1650 it was used to store ammunition until it was restored at the order of Queen Victoria; it was rededicated in 1934. The tiny stained-glass windows – depicting Margaret, St Andrew, St Columba, St Ninian and William Wallace – date from the 1920s. Immediately north of the chapel is **Mons Meg**, a giant 15th-century siege gun built at Mons in Belgium in 1449. The gun was last fired in 1681, as a birthday salute for the future King James VII/II, when its barrel burst. Take a peek over the wall to the north of the chapel and you'll see a charming little garden that was used as a **pet cemetery** for officer's dogs.

Beyond is the Half Moon Battery, which was built around and over the ruins of **David's Tower** – the royal residence of David II (1329–71) – after it was destroyed in the Lang Siege of 1571–73; you can visit the ruined vaults of the tower via a stairway beneath the battery.

The main group of buildings on the summit of the castle rock are arranged around Crown Square, dominated by the hushed shrine of the **Scottish National War Memorial**. Opposite is the **Great Hall**, built for James IV (reigned 1488–1513) as a ceremonial hall and used as a meeting place for the Scottish Parliament until 1639. It most remarkable feature is the original 16th-century hammer-beam roof.

On the eastern end of the square is the **Royal Palace**, built during the 15th and 16th centuries, where a series of historical tableaux leads to a strongroom housing the

Honours of Scotland (the Scottish crown jewels), the oldest surviving crown jewels in Europe. Locked away in a chest following the Act of Union in 1707, the crown (made in 1540 from the gold of Robert the Bruce's 14th-century coronet), sword and sceptre lay forgotten until they were unearthed at the instigation of the novelist Walter Scott in 1818. Also on display here is the Stone of Destiny (see the boxed text).

Among the neighbouring Royal Apartments is the bedchamber where Mary Queen of Scots gave birth to her son James VI, who was to unite the crowns of Scotland and England in 1603.

The Castle Vaults beneath the Great Hall were used at various times as storerooms, bakeries and prisons – French prisoners in the 18th century carved the graffiti on the walls.

THE ROYAL MILE

Edinburgh's Old Town stretches along a ridge to the east of the castle, a jagged, jumbled pile of masonry riddled with closes, wynds, vaults and tunnels, and cleft along its spine by the cobbled ravine of the Royal Mile. The mile-long street earned its regal appellation in the 16th century because it was used by the king to travel between the castle and the Palace of Holyroodhouse. There are four sections – Castlehill, Lawnmarket, High St and Canongate – whose names reflect their historical origins.

Until the founding of New Town in the 18th century, old Edinburgh was remarkable for its incredible concentration of humanity. Constrained between the boggy ground of the Nor' Loch to the north, and the city walls to the south and east, the only way for the town to expand was upwards. The five- and six-storey tenements that were raised along the Royal Mile in the 16th and 17th centuries were the skyscrapers of their day, remarked upon with wonder by visitors. All classes of society, from beggars to magistrates, lived cheek by jowl in these urban ants' nests, the wealthy occupying the middle floors – high enough to be above the

The Stone of Destiny

On St Andrew's Day 1996, with much pomp and ceremony, a block of sandstone – 26½ inches by 16½ inches by 11 inches in size, with rusted iron hoops at either end – was installed in Edinburgh Castle. For the previous 700 years it had lain in London, beneath the Coronation Chair in Westminster Abbey. Almost every English, and later British, monarch from Edward II in 1307 to Elizabeth II in 1953 had parked their backside firmly over this stone during their coronation ceremony.

The legendary Stone of Destiny – said to have originated in the Holy Land, and on which Scottish kings placed their feet during their coronation (not their bums; the English got that bit wrong) – was stolen from Scone Abbey near Perth by King Edward I of England in 1296. It was taken to London and there it remained for seven centuries – except for a brief removal to Gloucester during WWII air raids, and a three-month sojourn in Scotland after it was stolen by Scottish students at Christmas in 1950 – an enduring symbol of Scotland's subjugation by England.

The Stone of Destiny returned to the political limelight in 1996, when the then Scottish Secretary and Conservative Party MP, Michael Forsyth, arranged for the return of the sandstone block to Scotland. A blatant attempt to boost the flagging popularity of the Conservative Party in Scotland prior to a general election, Forsyth's publicity stunt failed miserably. The Scots said thanks very much for the stone and then, in May 1997, voted every Conservative MP in Scotland into oblivion.

Many people, however, believe that Edward I was fobbed off with a shoddy imitation in 1296 and that the true Stone of Destiny remains safely hidden somewhere in Scotland. This is not impossible – some descriptions of the original state that it was made of black marble and decorated with elaborate carvings. Interested parties should read Stone of Destiny (1997), by Pat Gerber, which details the history of Scotland's most famous lump of rock.

noise and stink of the streets, but not so high that climbing the stairs would be too tiring – while the poor squeezed into attics, basements, cellars and vaults amid the rats, rubbish and raw sewage.

The Old Town tenements still support a thriving city-centre community, but today the street level is crammed with tourists and tacky souvenir shops. Most people stick to the main High St but it's worth taking a little time to duck up the countless closes (narrow alleys) that lead off into quiet courtyards with unexpected views of sea and hills.

Castlehill (Map 8)

A short distance downhill from the Castle Esplanade, a former school house the **Scotch Whisky Heritage Centre** (☎ 220 0441, 354 Castlehill; adult/child £6.50/3.25 including tour & tasting; open 9.30am-5.30pm daily). The centre explains the making of whisky from barley to bottle, in a series of exhibits that combine sight, sound and smell. The first, and more interesting, part is led by a guide, while the second part consists of riding a 'barrel car' past several tableaux depicting the history of the 'water of life' – Johnnie Walker meets Walt Disney. As a reward, you get a wee taste of the real thing, before being channelled into a shop full of whisky (though it's cheaper at Oddbins off-licence five minutes down the road).

The quaint building across the street is the **Outlook Tower and Camera Obscura** (☎ 226 3709, Castlehill; family/adult/child £12/4.25/2.10; open 9.30am-6pm Mon-Fri, 10am-6pm Sat & Sun Apr-Oct, 10am-5pm daily Nov-Mar). The 'camera' itself is a curious device (originally dating from the 1850s, although improved in 1945) a bit like a periscope, which uses lenses and mirrors to throw a live image of the city onto a large horizontal screen. The accompanying commentary is entertaining and the whole exercise has a quirky charm. The Outlook Tower offers great views over the city.

With Edinburgh's tallest spire (71.7m), the **Highland Tolbooth Kirk** is a prominent feature of the Old Town skyline. It was built in the 1840s by James Graham and Augustus Pugin (architect of London's Houses of

Parliament) and takes its name from the Gaelic services that were held here in the 19th century for Edinburgh's Highland congregations. The interior has been refurbished and it now houses **The Hub** (☎ 473 2000, ⓦ www.eif.co.uk/thehub, Castlehill; admission free; ticket centre open 10am-5pm Mon-Sat), the ticket office and information centre for the Edinburgh Festival. There's also a good cafe here (see the Places to Eat chapter).

Opposite the kirk are the Assembly Rooms of the Church of Scotland, which are the temporary home of the debating chamber of the new **Scottish Parliament** (the visitors entrance is in Milne's Court, beside the Ensign Ewart pub). See the entry for the Scottish Parliament Visitor Centre under High St later in this section.

Lawnmarket (Map 8)

A corruption of 'Landmarket', Lawnmarket takes its name from the large cloth market that flourished here until the 18th century (selling goods from the land outside the city); this was the poshest part of Old Town, where many of its most distinguished citizens made their homes.

One of these was Thomas Gledstanes, a 17th-century merchant – and ancestor of the 19th-century British prime minister William Gladstone – who in 1617 bought the tenement later known as **Gladstone's Land** (☎ 226 5856, 477 Lawnmarket; adult/child £3.50/2.50; open 10am-5pm Mon-Sat & 2pm-5pm Sun Apr-Oct). Built in the mid-16th century and extended in the 17th, it gives a fascinating glimpse of the Old Town's past. The comfortable interior contains fine painted ceilings, walls and beams and some splendid furniture from the 17th and 18th centuries. The volunteer guides provide a wealth of stories and detailed history.

Tucked down a close just east of Gladstone's Land you'll come across **The Writers' Museum** (☎ 529 4901, Lady Stairs Close, Lawnmarket; admission free; open 10am-5pm Mon-Sat year-round, plus 2pm-5pm Sun during Edinburgh Festival). Located in Lady Stair's House (built in 1622)

it contains manuscripts and memorabilia belonging to Robert Burns, Sir Walter Scott and Robert Louis Stevenson.

High St (Map 8)

High St, which stretches from George IV Bridge down to the Netherbow at St Mary's St, is the heart and soul of Old Town, home to the city's main church, the Law Courts, the city council and – until 1707 – the Scottish Parliament.

On the corner of the Royal Mile and George IV Bridge is the **Scottish Parliament Visitor Centre** (☎ 348 5000, [w] www.scottish.parliament.uk, George IV Bridge; admission free; open 10am-5pm Mon-Fri, earlier when parliament is sitting). The centre explains the workings of the new parliament, which was officially opened on 1 July 1999 – the first Scottish Parliament for almost 300 years. You can visit the debating chamber when parliament is not sitting (usually 10am-noon and 2pm to 4pm Monday and Friday), or phone ahead (☎ 348 5411, no more than a week in advance) to arrange free tickets for the public gallery while parliament is sitting.

Dominating High St is the great grey bulk of **St Giles Cathedral** (☎ 225 9442, High St; admission free but donations welcome; open 9am-7pm Mon-Fri, 9am-5pm Sat & 1pm-5pm Sun Easter-Sept, 9am-5pm Mon-Sat & 1pm-5pm Sun Oct-Easter). Properly called the High Kirk of Edinburgh it was only a true cathedral – ie the seat of a bishop – from 1633 to 1638 and from 1661 to 1689), St Giles was named after the patron saint of cripples and beggars. There has been a church on this site since the 9th century. A Norman-style church was built in 1126 but was destroyed by English invaders in 1385; the only substantial remains are the central piers that support the tower. The present church dates largely from the 15th century – the beautiful crown spire was completed in 1495 – but much of it was restored in the 19th century.

St Giles was at the heart of the Scottish Reformation. John Knox served as minister here from 1559 to 1572, preaching his uncompromising Calvinist message, and when Charles I attempted to re-establish episcopacy in Scotland in 1637 by imposing a new liturgy, he only hardened the Scots' attitude against him. As the service from Charles I's *Book of Common Prayer* was read out for the first time in St Giles, a local woman called Jenny Geddes hurled her stool at the Dean and called out, 'De'il colic the wame o' thee – wouldst thou say Mass at ma lug?' (The devil buckle your belly – would you say Mass in my ear?) – and ignited a riot whose aftermath led to the signing of the National Covenant at Greyfriars the following year. A plaque marks the spot where Jenny launched her protest and a copy of the National Covenant is displayed on the wall.

There are several ornate monuments in the church, including the tombs of James Graham, marquis of Montrose, who led Charles I's forces in Scotland and was hanged in 1650 at the Mercat Cross; and his Covenanter opponent Archibald Campbell, marquis of Argyll, who was decapitated in 1661 after the Restoration of Charles II. One of the most interesting corners of the church is the **Thistle Chapel**, built between 1909 and 1911 for the Knights of the Most Ancient & Most Noble Order of the Thistle. The elaborately carved Gothic-style stalls have canopies topped with the helms and arms of the 16 knights.

Around St Giles is the cobbled expanse of **Parliament Square**, flanked to the south by **Parliament House**, the meeting place of the Scottish Parliament from 1639 to 1707 (the neoclassical facade was added in the early 19th century). After the Act of Union the building became the centre of the Scottish legal system, housing the Court of Session and the High Court, a function which it still serves today. The most interesting feature is the 17th-century **Parliament Hall**, where the parliament actually met. Now used by lawyers and their clients as a meeting place, it boasts its original oak hammerbeam roof and magnificent 19th-century stained-glass windows.

By the side of the street outside the western door of St Giles, a cobblestone **Heart of Midlothian** is set in the paving. Passers-by traditionally spit on it for luck (don't stand

Underground Edinburgh

As Edinburgh expanded in the late 18th and early 19th centuries, many old tenements were demolished and new bridges were built to link Old Town to the newly built areas to its north and south. South Bridge (built between 1785 and 1788) and George IV Bridge (built between 1829 and 1834) lead southwards from the Royal Mile over the deep valley of Cowgate, but since their construction so many buildings have been built closely around them that you can hardly tell they are bridges – George IV Bridge has a total of nine arches but only two are visible; South Bridge has no less than 18 hidden arches.

These subterranean vaults were originally used as storerooms, workshops and drinking dens. But as early-19th-century Edinburgh's population was swelled by an influx of penniless Highlanders cleared from their lands and Irish refugees from the potato famine, the dark, dripping chambers were given over to slum accommodation and abandoned to poverty, filth and crime.

The vaults were eventually cleared in the late 19th century, then lay forgotten until 1994 when the South Bridge vaults were opened to guided tours (see Organised Tours in the Getting Around chapter). Certain chambers are said to be haunted and one particular vault was investigated by paranormal researchers in 2001 (see the boxed text 'The Mackenzie Poltergeist' later in the chapter).

Nevertheless, the most ghoulish aspect of Edinburgh's hidden history dates from much earlier – from the plague that struck the city in 1645. Legend has it that the disease-ridden inhabitants of Mary King's Close (a lane on the northern side of the Royal Mile on the site of the City Chambers – you can still see its blocked-off northern end from Cockburn St) were walled up in their houses and left to perish. When the lifeless bodies were eventually cleared from the houses, they were so stiff that workmen had to hack off limbs to get them through the small doorways and narrow, twisting stairs.

From that day on the close was said to be haunted by the spirits of the plague victims. The few people who were prepared to live there reported seeing apparitions of severed heads and limbs, and the largely abandoned close fell into ruin. When the Royal Exchange (now the City Chambers) was constructed between 1753 and 1761, it was built over the lower levels of Mary King's Close, which were left, intact and sealed off, beneath the building.

Interest in the close revived in the 20th century when Edinburgh's city council began to allow occasional guided tours to enter. Then in the late 1990s, Mercat Tours was given permission to take tour groups into the close. Since then, visitors have reported many supernatural experiences – the most famous ghost is 'Sarah', a little girl, whose sad tale has prompted people to leave gifts of dolls in a corner of one of the rooms.

downwind!). This was the site of the Tolbooth, originally built to collect tolls, but subsequently a meeting place for parliament, the town council and the General Assembly of the Reformed Kirk, then law courts and, finally, a notorious prison and place of execution. The Tolbooth was immortalised in Sir Walter Scott's novel *The Heart of Midlothian*.

At the other end of St Giles is the **Mercat Cross**, a 19th-century copy of the 1365 original, where merchants and traders met to transact business and Royal Proclama-

tions were read. In a revival of this ancient tradition, the dissolution of the Westminster Parliament prior to the 2001 general election was proclaimed here by costumed officials, much to the bemusement of tourists and locals alike.

Across the street from the Cross is the **City Chambers**, originally built by John Adam (brother of Robert) in 1761 to serve as the Royal Exchange – a covered meeting place for city merchants, to replace the Mercat Cross. However, the merchants continued to prefer their old stamping grounds in the street and the building became the offices of the city council in 1811. Though only four storeys high on this side, the building plummets 11 storeys on the northern side, overlooking Cockburn St. Part of it was built over the sealed-off remains of Mary King's Close (see the boxed text 'Underground Edinburgh').

At the south-western corner of the intersection with South Bridge is the **Tron Kirk**; it owes its name to a *tron*, or public weighbridge, that once stood on the site. It was built in 1637 on top of Marlin's Wynd, which has been excavated to reveal a cobbled street with cellars and shops on either side.

Halfway down the next block is 'the noisiest museum in the world' – the **Museum of Childhood** (*☎ 529 4142, 42 High St; admission free; open 10am-5pm Mon-Sat year-round plus 2pm-5pm Sun in July & Aug*). Often overrun with screaming kids, it covers serious issues related to childhood – health, education, upbringing and so on – but also has an enormous collection of toys, games and books: everything from Victorian dolls to a video history of the 1960s' Gerry Anderson TV puppet series *Thunderbirds*.

Across the street from the Museum of Childhood, Chalmers Close leads down to Trinity Apse, the only surviving part of the 15th-century Trinity College Church. The Gothic apse now houses a **Brass Rubbing Centre** (*☎ 556 4364, Chalmers Close, High St; admission free, cost per rubbing from £1; open 10am-5pm Mon-Sat year-round plus noon-5pm Sun during Edinburgh Festival*). Here you can learn how to take rubbings from the centre's collection of medieval brasses and replicas of Pictish and Celtic stones.

The Royal Mile narrows at the foot of the High St beside the jutting facade of **John Knox House** (*☎ 556 9579, 43-45 High St; adult/child £2.25/75p; open 10am-5pm Mon-Sat*). It is the oldest surviving tenement in Edinburgh, dating from around 490, and the outside staircase, overhanging upper floors and crow-stepped gables are all typical of a 15th-century town house. John Knox is thought to have occupied the 2nd floor from 1561 to 1572. The labyrinthine interior has some beautiful painted

timber ceilings and an interesting display on Knox's life and work.

High St ends at the intersection with St Mary's and Jeffrey Sts, where Old Town's eastern gate, the **Netherbow Port** (part of the Flodden Wall) once stood. Though it no longer exists, its former outline is marked by brass strips set in the road.

Canongate (Map 3)

Canongate – the stretch of the Royal Mile from the Netherbow to Holyrood – takes its name from the Augustinian canons (monks) of Holyrood Abbey. From the 16th century it was home to aristocrats attracted to the Palace of Holyroodhouse. Originally governed by the monks, Canongate was an independent burgh until 1856.

One of the surviving symbols of Canongate's former independence is **Canongate Tolbooth** (*☎ 529 4057, 163 Canongate; admission free; open 10am-5pm Mon-Sat year-round plus 2pm-5pm Sun during Edinburgh Festival*). Built in 1591, it served successively as a collection point for tolls (taxes), a council house, a courtroom and a jail. With its picturesque turrets and projecting clock, it's a splendid example of 16th-century architecture. It now houses a fascinating museum, **The People's Story**, recording the life, work and pastimes of ordinary Edinburgh folk from the 18th century to the present day.

Across the street from the Tolbooth is **Huntly House**. Built in 1570, it is a good example of the luxurious accommodation that aristocrats built for themselves along Canongate – the projecting upper floors of plastered timber are typical of the period. It now houses the **Museum of Edinburgh** (*☎ 529 4143, 142 Canongate; admission free; open 10am-5pm Mon-Sat year-round plus 2pm-5pm Sun during Edinburgh Festival*). The exhibits cover the history of the city from prehistory to the present. Exhibits of national importance include an original copy of the National Covenant of 1638, but the big crowd-pleaser is the dog collar and feeding bowl that belonged to Greyfriars Bobby, the city's most famous canine citizen.

Downhill on the left is the attractive curved gable of **Canongate Kirk**, built in

1688. In 1745 Charles Edward Stuart (Bonnie Prince Charlie) used it to hold prisoners taken at the Battle of Prestonpans. The kirkyard contains the graves of several famous people, including the economist Adam Smith (1723–90), author of *The Wealth of Nations*, who lived nearby in Panmure Close, and Mrs Agnes MacLehose (the 'Clarinda' of Robert Burns's love poems). Walk down the left-hand side of the kirk to a tree and turn left – the grave with the low iron railing belongs to the 18th-century poet Robert Fergusson (1750–74). He was much admired by Robert Burns – take a look at the inscription on the back – who paid for the gravestone and penned the epitaph.

HOLYROOD

The district at the foot of the Royal Mile is undergoing a major upheaval during the construction of the new Scottish Parliament Building (due for completion in late 2003).

Palace of Holyroodhouse & Holyrood Abbey (Map 3)

The **Palace of Holyroodhouse** (☎ 556 1096, Canongate; family/adult/child 30/6.50/3.30; open 9.30am-6pm daily Apr-Oct, 9.30am-4.30pm daily Nov-Mar) is the Queen's official residence in Scotland. It is closed to the public when the Royal Family is visiting and during state functions (usually in mid-May and from mid-June to around early July; telephone first to check).

The palace developed from a guesthouse attached to Holyrood Abbey, which was extended by King James IV in 1501 to create more comfortable living quarters than were possible in the exposed and windy hill-top castle. The oldest surviving section of the building, the north-western tower, was built in 1529 as a royal apartment for James V and his wife, Mary of Guise. Mary Queen of Scots spent six eventful years living here, during which time she married Darnley (in the abbey) and Bothwell (in what is now the Picture Gallery), and it was here that she debated with John Knox and witnessed the murder of her secretary Rizzio.

Although Holyrood was never again used as a permanent royal residence after James

VI departed for London in 1603, it was further extended during Charles II's reign, completing the great quadrangle you see today. It lay neglected through much of the 18th century – though Bonnie Prince Charlie briefly held court here in 1745 on his way south to Derby – but was gradually renovated as royal interest in Scotland revived following George IV's visit in 1822.

The guided tour leads you through a series of impressive royal apartments, ending in the **Great Gallery**. The 89 portraits of Scottish kings, commissioned by Charles II, supposedly record his unbroken lineage from Scota, the Egyptian pharaoh's daughter who discovered the infant Moses in a reed basket on the banks of the Nile.

The highlight of the tour is **Mary Queen of Scots' Bed Chamber** in the 16th-century tower house. This bedroom – with its low, painted ceilings and secret staircase connecting to her husband Lord Darnley's bedroom – was home to the unfortunate Mary from 1561 to 1567. It was here that her jealous husband restrained the pregnant queen while his henchmen murdered her secretary – and favourite – David Rizzio. In her own words, they '...dragged David forth with great cruelty from our cabinet and at the entrance of our chamber dealt him 56 dagger blows'. A plaque in the next room marks the spot where he bled to death. The exit from the palace leads into Holyrood Abbey.

King David I founded **Holyrood Abbey** here in the shadow of Salisbury Crags in 1128. It was probably named after a fragment of the True Cross (*rood* is an old Scots word for cross) said to have been brought to Scotland by his mother St Margaret. As it lay outside the city walls it suffered repeated attacks by English invaders, and the great abbey church was demolished in 1570, except for the nave, which remained in use as Canongate parish church until it collapsed in 1768. Most of the surviving ruins date from the 12th and 13th centuries, although a doorway in the far south-eastern corner has survived from the original Norman church. The bay on the right, as you look at the huge, arched, eastern window, is the royal burial vault, which holds the renains of kings David II, James II and James V, and of Mary's husband Lord Darnley.

In the gardens to the north of the palace s the tiny, turreted lodge known as **Queen Mary's Bath House**. According to legend, Mary Queen of Scots used to bathe in white wine here. It is more likely to have been a dovecote or summer house.

Scottish Parliament Building (Map 3)

The new Scottish Parliament Building (see he boxed text 'The Bottomless Pit?') is being built on the site of a former brewery and is due to open by early 2003. The temporary **Parliament Building Visitor Centre** *(Holyrood Rd; admission free; open 10am-4pm daily)* records the development of the project from the initial architectural design competition to the current state of construction. The competition to design the new building was won in July 1998 by the late Catalan architect Enric Miralles, who envisaged a group of lenticular buildings with curved roofs inspired by upturned boats seen on a beach in northern Scotland.

The Bottomless Pit?

It has been called Scotland's answer to the Sydney Opera House and 'the most jinxed public building in Scottish history' – a flagship architectural project that has gone way over budget, way over schedule and is dogged by contention at every step.

The large hole in the ground at the foot of Edinburgh's Royal Mile will one day be filled by the new Scottish Parliament Building. It had long been thought that if Scotland was ever granted a devolved parliament it would be housed in the former Royal High School on Calton Hill, which had already been restored and fitted with a debating chamber in anticipation of such an event. The option of siting the new parliament in Leith was also discussed.

Instead, the Labour government in Westminster chose Holyrood – because, they claimed, it was the least expensive, best-value alternative. But it has been suggested that the siting of the Parliament Building was a political, not an economic, decision, and that the Labour Party – whose main opposition in Scotland is from the Scottish National Party (SNP) – decided against the Calton Hill site because it was favoured by the nationalists and had become associated in the public mind with full independence rather than devolution.

When a new home for the Scottish Parliament was first discussed in London in 1997, price estimates ranged from £10 million to £40 million, and it was expected to be ready by 2001. By the time the Scottish Parliament had convened for the first time in 1999, the cost estimate had been revised to £109 million. Following an official enquiry into the project, a price cap of £195 million was agreed in April 2000, with a completion date set at December 2002. Then in June 2001, parliament was asked to ratify a new figure of £230 million, amid claims that the cost of inflation had not been taken into account. The author David Black, whose book *All the First Minister's Men – The Truth Behind Holyrood* (2001) reveals the political machinations surrounding the project, claims that the final cost could be over £300 million.

What rankles with many people and politicians is that all the main financial decisions on the Parliament Building – the site, the design, the architect, the construction contracts – were taken by Labour cabinet ministers in London before the Scottish Parliament had even been elected, and yet the ever-increasing cost of the project has to be met entirely out of Scottish Parliament funds.

In the meantime, light-hearted claims that the project was jinxed took on a darker aspect when the architect Enric Miralles died of a brain tumour in July 2000. This tragedy was followed only three months later by the death of Scotland's First Minister Donald Dewar, who had initiated the project.

Sir David Steel, the first presiding officer of the new parliament, said that 'this building is the most important to be built in Scotland for some 300 years'. It also promises to be the most controversial.

Queensberry House, a 17th-century mansion once owned by the dukes of Queensberry, occupies the northern part of the site. It has been restored inside and out and will be incorporated as part of the parliament complex. Ironically, James, the second duke of Queensberry, was Commissioner to Parliament for King William and was instrumental in securing the passage of the Act of Union that brought about the end of the Scottish Parliament in 1707.

Our Dynamic Earth (Map 3)

The modernistic white marquee pitched beneath Salisbury Crags marks Edinburgh's newest tourist attraction, Our Dynamic Earth (☎ 550 7800, Holyrood Rd; family/ adult/child £20/7.95/4.50; open 10am-6pm daily Apr-Oct, 10am-5pm Wed-Sun Nov-Mar). Advertised with the slogan 'Live 4500 million years in one day!', it's billed as an interactive, multimedia 'journey of discovery' through Earth history from the Big Bang to the present day. Hugely popular with kids of all ages, it's a slick extravaganza of whizz-bang special effects cleverly designed to fire up young minds with curiosity about all things geological and environmental. Its true purpose, of course, is to disgorge you into a gift shop where you can buy model dinosaurs and souvenir T-shirts.

Holyrood Park & Arthur's Seat (Maps 3 & 5)

In Holyrood Park, Edinburgh is blessed with a little bit of wilderness in the heart of the city. The former hunting ground of Scottish monarchs, the park covers 650 acres of varied landscape, including crags, moorland and loch. The highest point is the 251m summit of **Arthur's Seat**, the deeply eroded remnant of a long-extinct volcano. The park can be circumnavigated by car or bike along Queen's Drive (closed to motorised traffic on Sunday). See Walk 3 in the Walking Tours section for details of walks in the area.

NORTH OF THE ROYAL MILE (Map 8)

Cockburn St, lined with trendy fashion, jewellery and music shops, leads down from the Royal Mile to Waverley Bridge. Halfway down on the left is the **Collective Gallery** (☎ 220 1260, 22-28 Cockburn St; admission free; open 11am-5.30pm Tues-Sat), an artist-run gallery with exhibitions by contemporary Scottish artists and others.

Across the street is **Stills Gallery** (☎ 622 6200, 23 Cockburn St; admission free; open 10am-5pm Tues-Sat). Scotland's top photographic gallery, it exhibits the best of international contemporary photography.

Near the foot of Cockburn St is **The Edinburgh Dungeon** (☎ 556 6700, 1 Market St; adult/child £6.95/4.95; open 10am-6pm daily). This manufactured attraction combines gruesome tableaux of torture and degradation with live actors who perform scary little sketches along the way. Mildly amusing in a large group, mildly embarrassing in a small one and genuinely terrifying for small children. Not recommended for kids under eight.

Also on Market St is the **Fruitmarket Gallery** (☎ 225 2383, 45 Market St; admission free; open 11am-5pm Mon-Sat, noon-5pm Sun). One of the city's most innovative and popular galleries, the Fruitmarket showcases contemporary Scottish and international artists; it also has an excellent arts bookshop and cafe.

Across the street is the **City Art Centre** (☎ 529 3993, 2 Market St; admission free; open 10am-5pm Mon-Sat year-round plus noon-5pm Sun July & Aug). The largest of Edinburgh's smaller galleries, it comprises six floors of exhibitions with a variety of themes, including Scottish art.

SOUTH OF THE ROYAL MILE Grassmarket (Map 8)

The site of a market from the 15th century until the start of the 20th, Grassmarket has always been a focal point of Old Town. As well as being a cattle market, this was the main place of execution in the city, and over 100 martyred Covenanters are commemorated by a monument at the eastern end, where the gallows used to stand. The notorious murderers Burke and Hare operated from a now vanished close off the west end. In 1827 they enticed at least 18 victims to

Half-Hangit Maggie

The Grassmarket pub called Maggie Dickson's (Map 8), just opposite the point where the gallows used to stand, commemorates a Musselburgh woman who was hanged in 1724 for the crime of concealing the death of her prematurely born, illegitimate child. Her corpse was taken down from the gallows, placed in a casket and put on a cart for the journey back to Musselburgh. On the way, an argument erupted between Maggie's friends, who wanted to give her a Christian burial, and a group of medical students from Edinburgh University, who wanted the corpse for dissection. (At that time, executed criminals provided the only legal source of bodies for medical research.)

The argument was settled by the corpse itself, as noises were heard coming from within the coffin. The rope had not done its job properly and Maggie had revived – much to the consternation of both friends and students. Maggie Dickson made a full recovery and legal opinion was that someone who had already been pronounced dead could not be hanged again. She lived for another 30 years, and was ever after known in the town as 'Half-Hangit Maggie'.

their boarding house, suffocated them and sold the bodies to Edinburgh's medical schools.

Nowadays, the broad, open square edged by tall tenements and dominated by the looming castle has many lively pubs and restaurants, including the White Hart Inn which was once patronised by Robert Burns. Cowgate – the long, dark ravine leading eastwards from Grassmarket – was once the road along which cattle were driven from the pastures around Arthur's Seat to the safety of the city walls. Today it is the heart of Edinburgh's nightlife, with a few dozen clubs and bars within five minutes' walk of each other (see the Entertainment chapter).

At the western end of Grassmarket, a narrow close called The Vennel leads steeply up to one of the few surviving fragments of the

Flodden Wall, the city wall that was built in the early 16th century as protection against a feared English invasion. Beyond it is the Telfer Wall, a later extension that continues to Lauriston Place. East of the wall is George Heriot's School (☎ 229 7263, Lauriston Place; admission free; open during summer holidays, June, July & first 2 weeks in Aug), one of the most impressive buildings in Old Town. Built in the 17th century with funds bequeathed by George Heriot (goldsmith and banker to King James VI, and popularly known as Jinglin' Geordie), it was originally a school and home for orphaned children, but became a fee-paying public school in 1886. Senior pupils conduct guided tours – phone ahead to book.

Greyfriars (Map 8)

Candlemaker Row leads up from the eastern end of Grassmarket towards one of Edinburgh's most famous churches. Greyfriars Kirk was built on the site of a Franciscan friary and opened for worship on Christmas Day 1620. In 1638 the National Covenant was signed, rejecting Charles I's attempts to impose episcopacy and a new English prayer book, and affirming the independence of the Scottish Church. Many who signed were later executed in Grassmarket and, in 1679, 1200 Covenanters were held prisoner in terrible conditions in an enclosure in the kirkyard. There's a small exhibition inside.

Hemmed in by high walls and overlooked by the brooding presence of the castle, Greyfriars Kirkyard is one of Edinburgh's most evocative spots, a peaceful green oasis dotted with elaborate monuments. Many famous Edinburgh names are buried here, including poet Allan Ramsay (1686–1758), architect William Adam (1689–1748) and William Smellie (1740–95), editor of the first edition of Encyclopaedia Britannica.

However, the memorial that draws the biggest crowds is the tiny statue of Greyfriars Bobby, in front of the pub beside the kirkyard gate. Bobby was a Skye terrier who maintained a vigil over the grave of his master, an Edinburgh police officer, from 1858 to 1872. The story was immortalised (and romanticised) by Eleanor Atkinson in

The MacKenzie Poltergeist

Two centuries ago, boys from George Heriot's School would climb over the wall from the school grounds into Greyfriars Kirkyard to dodge lessons. One of their schoolboy dares was to go up to the mausoleum of Sir George MacKenzie, and yell through the keyhole, 'Bluidy Mackingie come out if ye daur, Lift the sneck and draw the bar', before running away giggling and screaming. The tomb was described as long ago as 1824 as 'a place of peculiar horror, as it was supposed to be haunted by the spirit of the bloody persecutor'.

Sir George MacKenzie (1636–91) was the King's Advocate (the chief law officer in Scotland) and was responsible for the persecution of the Covenanters, sending many of them to the gallows – hence his popular nickname, 'Bloody MacKenzie'. Just around the corner from his tomb is the Covenanters Prison, a long, narrow corner of Greyfriars Kirkyard where around 1200 Covenanters were incarcerated for five months in appalling conditions, while awaiting trial after the Battle of Bothwell Brig (1679).

In 1999 a homeless man, looking for shelter in the kirkyard on a cold and rainy night, wandered into Bloody MacKenzie's mausoleum. Perhaps fortified by some Buckfast tonic wine, he lifted the metal grating in the floor and descended into the vault. There he found a second, smaller grating in the floor and lifted it too... then accidentally tumbled into the dark hole. The story goes that he found himself sprawled in a mossy heap of human bones, grinning skulls and long-decayed flesh.

Just at that moment, the Greyfriars caretaker passed by, and noticed the door to MacKenzie's tomb was open. He edged inside with his torch, only to be faced with a deranged figure charging up from the vault, wailing and screaming like a madman. Paranormal investigators have theorised that it was the incredible bolt of fear given off by these two men that awakened what has come to be known as the MacKenzie Poltergeist.

Since 1999, the guides who lead ghost tours around Edinburgh's vaults and graveyards have logged around 200 cases of high-level poltergeist activity, including punching, bruising, scratching, hair-pulling and ankle-grabbing, both in the South Bridge vaults (near the former home of Sir George MacKenzie) and in the Covenanters Prison. There have been around 30 incidents where people have actually been rendered unconscious.

The MacKenzie Poltergeist is now the best-documented case of poltergeist activity ever studied. During the Science Festival in April 2001, the well-known psychologist and paranormal investigator Dr Richard Wiseman conducted a large-scale experiment in the 'haunted vaults' beneath South Bridge, and concluded that there was a measurable phenomenon that was worthy of further scientific investigation.

Whether that phenomenon is truly paranormal, or just some sort of psychological effect, remains to be seen. Meanwhile, ghost-tour customers are queuing up to scare themselves silly by repeating that ancient schoolboy dare. Bloody MacKenzie come out if ye daur...

her 1912 novel, and in 1963 was made into a movie by – who else? – Walt Disney. In the kirk you can buy *Greyfriars Bobby – The Real Story at Last* (£3.95), Forbes Macgregor's debunking of some of the myths. Bobby's grave – marked by a small, pink granite stone – is just inside the entrance to the kirkyard. His original collar and bowl are in the Museum of Edinburgh (see the Canongate section earlier in the chapter).

Chambers St (Map 8)

Broad and elegant Chambers St stretche eastwards from Greyfriars Bobby and i dominated by the long facade of the **Roya Museum and Museum of Scotland** (☎ 24: 4219, W www.nms.ac.uk, Chambers St; ad mission free, fee for special exhibitions open 10am-5pm Mon & Wed-Fri, 10am 8pm Tues, noon-5pm Sun, closed 25 Dec) The golden stone and striking modern ar

Robert and William guard the Entrance Gateway.

Keeping an eye on the Honours of Scotland

Scotland's Lion Rampant in a stained-glass crest

The lofty castle is more than a historic stronghold; it is a working military establishment.

A dusting of snow on Arthur's Seat gives it a magical air, making it just right for a winter walk.

Fit for a queen: the Palace of Holyroodhouse has been a royal residence since the 16th century.

chitecture of the Museum of Scotland – opened in 1998 – is one of the city's most distinctive new landmarks. The five floors of the museum trace the history of Scotland from geological beginnings to the 1990s, with many imaginative and stimulating exhibits – audioguides are available in several languages – and the interior design is an attraction in itself. It would take several visits to do justice to the museum; highlights include the Monymusk Reliquary, a tiny silver casket dating from AD 750, which is said to have been carried into battle with Robert the Bruce at Bannockburn in 1314; and a set of charming, 12th-century chess pieces made from walrus ivory. At the other end of the cultural spectrum is a 20th-century gallery devoted to objects that were nominated by celebrities and members of the general public as representing their life and times; Prime Minister Tony Blair chose a Fender Stratocaster electric guitar – make of that what you will. Don't forget to take the lift to the Roof Terrace for a fantastic view of the castle.

The modern Museum of Scotland connects with the original, Victorian Royal Museum, dating from 1861, whose stolid, grey exterior gives way to a bright and airy, glass-roofed entrance hall. The museum houses an eclectic collection covering the natural world (evolution, natural history, minerals, fossils and so on), archaeology, scientific and industrial technology, and the decorative arts of ancient Egypt, Islam, China, Japan, Korea and the west. One of the prize exhibits is the *Wylam Dilly* 1813), the world's oldest steam locomotive. Volunteers give free, 45-minute guided tours of the Royal Museum (at 3pm daily except Tuesday and Thursday) and Museum of Scotland (at 2pm daily and also at 6pm on Tuesday).

At the eastern end of Chambers St, beyond College Wynd, is Edinburgh University's **Old College** (also called Old Quad; it now houses the Law Faculty), a neoclassical masterpiece designed by Robert Adam in 1789 but not completed till 1834. Inside the Old College, at the College Wynd end, is the **Talbot Rice Art Gallery** (☎ 650 2210, *Old College, South*

Bridge; admission free; open 10am-5pm Tues-Sat year-round, 10am-5pm daily during Edinburgh Festival), which houses a small, permanent collection of old masters, plus regular exhibitions of new work.

New Town

New Town lies north of the Old, on a ridge running parallel to the Royal Mile and separated from it by the valley of Princes St Gardens. Its regular grid of elegant, Georgian terraces is a complete contrast to the chaotic tangle of tenements and wynds that characterise Old Town.

Between the end of the 14th century and the start of the 18th, the population of Edinburgh – still confined within the walls of Old Town – increased from 2000 to 50,000. The tottering tenements were unsafe and occasionally collapsed, fire was an ever-present danger and the overcrowding and squalor became unbearable. There was no sewer system and household waste was disposed of by flinging it from the window into the street with a euphemistic shout of 'Gardyloo!' (from the French *gardez l'eau* – beware of the water). Passers-by replied with 'Haud yer haun'!' (Hold your hand) but were often too late. The stink that rose from the streets was ironically referred to as 'the floo'rs o' Edinburgh' (the flowers of Edinburgh).

So when the Act of Union in 1707 brought the prospect of long-term stability, the upper classes were keen to find healthier, more spacious living quarters, and in 1766 the Lord Provost of Edinburgh announced an architectural competition to design an extension to the city. It was won by an unknown 23-year-old, James Craig, a self-taught architect whose simple and elegant plan envisaged the main axis of George St following the crest of the ridge to the north of Old Town, with grand squares at either end. Building would also be restricted to one side of Princes and Queen Sts, so that the houses enjoyed views over the Firth of Forth to the north, and to the castle and Old Town to the south.

During the 18th and 19th centuries, New Town continued to sprout squares, circuses, parks and terraces, with some of its finest neoclassical architecture designed by Robert Adam. Today, New Town remains the world's most complete and unspoilt example of Georgian architecture and town planning. Along with Old Town, it was declared a UNESCO World Heritage Site in 1995.

PRINCES ST

Princes St is one of the world's most spectacular shopping streets. Built up on one side only – the northern side – it catches the sun in summer and allows expansive views across Princes St Gardens to the castle and the crowded skyline of Old Town.

The western end of Princes St is dominated by the red-sandstone edifice of the Caledonian Hotel and the tower of **St John's Church**, worth visiting for its fine Gothic Revival interior. It overlooks **St Cuthbert's Parish Church**, built in the 1890s on a site of great antiquity – there has been a church here since at least the 12th century, and perhaps since the 7th century. There is a circular **watch tower** in the graveyard – a reminder of the Burke and Hare days when graves had to be guarded against robbers.

At the eastern end is the prominent clock tower – traditionally three minutes fast so that you don't miss your train – of the Balmoral Hotel, and the beautiful **Register House** (1788), designed by Robert Adam, with a statue of the Duke of Wellington on horseback in front. It houses the National Archives of Scotland.

Princes St Gardens (Map 3)

These beautiful gardens lie in a valley that was once occupied by the Nor' Loch (North Loch), a boggy depression that was drained in the early 19th century. They are split in the middle by **The Mound** – around two million cart-loads of earth dumped here during the construction of New Town, to provide a road link across the valley to Old Town. It was completed in 1830.

In the middle of the western part of the gardens is the **Ross Bandstand**, a venue for open-air summer concerts and the stage for

the famous Fireworks Concert during the Edinburgh Festival. At the gate beside The Mound is the **Floral Clock**, a working clock laid out in flowers; it was first created in 1903, but the design changes every year.

The eastern half of the gardens is dominated by the massive Gothic spire of the **Scott Monument** (☎ *529 4068, East Princes St Gardens; admission £2.50; open 9am-8pm Mon-Sat & 10am-6pm Sun June-Sept, 9am-6pm Mon-Sat & 10am-6pm Sun Mar-May & Oct, 9am-4pm Mon-Sat & 10am-4pm Sun Nov-Feb)*. Built by public subscription in memory of Sir Walter Scott after his death in 1832, it testifies to a popularity largely inspired by his role in rebuilding pride in Scottish identity. You can climb the 287 steps to the top for a superb view of the city; the stone figures that decorate the niches on the monument represent characters from Scott's novels. The statue of Scott at the base of the monument, with his favourite deerhound Maida, was carved from a single, 30-tonne block of white Italian marble.

Royal Scottish Academy (Map 3)

The distinguished Greek Doric temple at the corner of The Mound and Princes St, its northern pediment crowned by a seated figure of Queen Victoria, is the home of the Royal Scottish Academy *(RSA; ☎ 558 7097, The Mound; admission free, £2-5 for special exhibitions; open 10am-5pm Mon-Sat, 2pm-5pm Sun)*. Designed by William Playfair and built between 1823 and 1836, it was originally called the Royal Institution; the RSA took over the building in 1910. The galleries display a collection of paintings, sculptures and architectural drawings by academy members dating from 1831. It also hosts temporary exhibitions throughout the year.

National Gallery of Scotland (Map 8)

Immediately south of the RSA is the National Gallery of Scotland *(☎ 624 6200, The Mound; admission free, £2-5 for special exhibitions; open 10am-5pm Mon-Sat &*

2pm-5pm Sun year-round, 10am-6pm Mon-Sat & 11am-6pm Sun during Edinburgh Festival). Also designed by William Playfair, this imposing classical building with its Ionic porticoes dates from the 1850s. It houses an important collection of European art from the Renaissance to post-impressionism. There are paintings by Verrocchio (Leonardo da Vinci's teacher), Tintoretto, Titian, Holbein, Rubens, van Dyck, Vermeer, El Greco, Poussin, Rembrandt, Gainsborough, Turner, Constable, Monet, Pissaro, Gauguin and Cezanne.

The USA is also represented by the works of Frederick Church, John Singer Sargent and Benjamin West. The section dedicated to Scottish art includes portraits by Allan Ramsay and Sir Henry Raeburn, rural scenes by Sir David Wilkie and impressionistic landscapes by William MacTaggart. Annually in January the gallery exhibits its collection of Turner watercolours, bequested by Henry Vaughan in 1900.

Antonio Canova's statue of the Three Graces (in Room 10) is owned jointly with London's Victoria & Albert Museum. In Greek mythology the Three Graces – Aglaia (Brightness), Euphrosyne (Joyfulness) and Thalia (Bloom) – were the daughters of Zeus and Euryonome, and embodied beauty, grace and youth.

At the time of research, the RSA and National Gallery were undergoing major refurbishment that will see the two buildings linked by an underground mall and their gallery space increased by 4500 sq m, giving them twice the temporary exhibition space of the Prado in Madrid, and three times that of the Royal Academy in London. The work is due for completion in summer 2002.

GEORGE ST

Until recently, George St – the major axis of New Town – was the centre of Edinburgh's financial industry and Scotland's equivalent of Wall St. Now many of the big financial firms have moved to premises in the new office district west of Lothian Rd, and George St's banks and offices are being turned into shops, pubs and restaurants.

Charlotte Square (Map 3)

At the western end of George St is Charlotte Square, the architectural jewel of New Town, designed by Robert Adam shortly before his death in 1791. The northern side of the square is Adam's masterpiece and one of the finest examples of Georgian architecture anywhere. **Bute House**, in the centre at No 6, is the official residence of Scotland's first minister.

Next door is the **Georgian House** (☎ 226 3318, 7 Charlotte Square; adult/child £5/4; open 10am-5pm Mon-Sat & 2pm-5pm Sun Mar-Oct, 11am-4pm Mon-Sat & 2pm-4pm Sun Nov-24 Dec). Owned by the National Trust for Scotland (NTS), it has been beautifully restored and refurnished to show how Edinburgh's wealthy elite lived at the end of the 18th century. The walls are decorated with paintings by Allan Ramsay, Henry Raeburn and Sir Joshua Reynolds. A 35-minute video brings it to life rather well.

The headquarters of the **National Trust for Scotland** (NTS; ☎ 243 9300, w www .nts.org.uk, 28 Charlotte Square; admission free; open 10am-5pm Mon-Sat, noon-5pm Sun) is on the southern side of the square. As well as a shop, cafe, restaurant and information desk, the building contains a restored 1820s drawing room with Regency furniture and a collection of 20th-century Scottish paintings. Around the corner, at 16 South Charlotte St, a plaque marks the house where Alexander Graham Bell, the inventor of the telephone, was born in 1847.

On the western side of Charlotte Square, the former St George's Church (1811) is now **West Register House**, an annexe to Register House in Princes St. It houses maps and plans owned by the National Archives of Scotland and mounts occasional exhibitions in the entrance hall.

St Andrew Square (Map 3)

St Andrew Square is not as distinguished architecturally as its sister at the opposite end of George St. Dominating the square is the fluted column of the **Melville Monument**, commemorating Henry Dundas, first viscount Melville (1742–1811), who was the most powerful Scottish politician of his time, often referred to when alive as the

'Uncrowned King of Scotland'. The impressive Palladian mansion of **Dundas House** (built between 1772 and 1774) on the eastern side of the square was built for Sir Laurence Dundas. It has been the head office of The Royal Bank of Scotland since 1825 and has a spectacular iron dome (you can go into the banking hall for a look).

A short distance along George St is the **Church of St Andrew & St George**, built in 1784, with an unusual oval nave. It was the scene of the Disruption of 1843, when 451 dissenting ministers left the Church of Scotland to form the Free Church.

Just north of the square, at the junction with Queen St, is the Venetian Gothic palace of the **Scottish National Portrait Gallery** (☎ 624 6200, 1 Queen St; admission free; open 10am-5pm Mon-Sat, noon-5pm Sun, hours extended during Edinburgh Festival). Its galleries depict Scottish history through portraits and sculptures of famous Scottish personalities, from Robert Burns and Bonnie Prince Charlie to Sean Connery and Billy Connolly. It also houses the National Photography Collection, which includes works by David Octavius Hill and Robert Adamson, 19th-century Scottish pioneers of portrait photography.

CALTON HILL (Map 3)

Calton Hill (100m), which rises dramatically above the eastern end of Princes St, is Edinburgh's acropolis, its summit scattered with grandiose memorials, mostly dating from the first half of the 19th century. It is also one of the best viewpoints in Edinburgh, with a panorama that takes in the castle, Holyrood, Arthur's Seat, the Firth of Forth, New Town and the full length of Princes St. See Walk 3 in the Walking Tours section for details.

Approaching from Princes St along Waterloo Place, you pass over **Regent Bridge**, built across the chasm of Calton St between 1816 and 1819 to give access to Calton Hill and allowing the development of the exclusive Georgian terraces on its northern and south-eastern sides. (Fans of the film *Trainspotting* might recognise Calton St – it is where Renton spreadeagles himself across a car in the opening sequence of the movie.)

Old Calton Burying Ground, on the southern side of Waterloo Place, is one of Edinburgh's many atmospheric old cemeteries. It is dominated by the tall black obelisk of the Political Martyrs' Monument, which commemorates those who suffered in the fight for electoral reform in the 1790s. In the southern corner is the massive, cylindrical grey stone tomb of David Hume (1711–76), Scotland's most prominent philosopher. Hume was a noted atheist, prompting rumours that he had made a Faustian pact with the devil; after his death his friends held a vigil at the tomb for eight nights, burning candles and firing pistols into the darkness lest evil spirits should come to bear away his soul. Near the tomb is a statue of Abraham Lincoln, commemorating Scots-Americans who died in the American Civil War.

Beyond Waterloo Place, on Regent Rd, is the modernist facade of **St Andrew's House** (built between 1936 and 1939), which housed the civil servants of the Westminster government's Scottish Office until they were moved to the new Scottish Executive building in Leith in 1996. It was built on the site of Calton Gaol, the successor to the much-despised Tolbooth in the High St, and once the biggest prison in Scotland. All that remains is the distinctive turreted building just west of St Andrew's House, and well seen from North Bridge – this was the **Governor's House** built in 1817.

Just beyond St Andrew's House, on the opposite side of the road, is the imposing **Royal High School** building, dating from 1829 and modelled on the Temple of Theseus in Athens. Former pupils include Robert Adam, Alexander Graham Bell and Sir Walter Scott. The building was at one time cited as a potential home for the new Scottish parliament but now stands empty. To its east, on the other side of Regent Rd, is the **Burns Monument** (1830), a Greek-style memorial to Robert Burns. It was designed by Thomas Hamilton, another former pupil of the school.

You can reach the summit of Calton Hill by the road beside the Royal High School or via the stairs at the eastern end of

Waterloo Place. The largest structure on the summit is the **National Monument**, a rather over-ambitious attempt to replicate the Parthenon and intended to honour Scotland's dead in the Napoleonic Wars. Construction – paid for by public subscription – began in 1822 but funds ran dry when only 12 columns were complete. It became known locally as 'Edinburgh's Disgrace'.

Looking a bit like an upturned telescope – the similarity is intentional – and offering even better views, the **Nelson Monument** (☎ 556 2716, Calton Hill; admission £2.50; open 1pm-6pm Mon & 10am-6pm Tues-Sat Apr-Sept, 10am-3pm Mon-Sat Oct-Mar) was built to commemorate Admiral Lord Nelson's victory at Trafalgar in 1805. In 1852 a time-ball was added as a time signal for ships anchored in the Firth of Forth (see the boxed text 'The Daily Bang' earlier in the chapter).

The design of the **City Observatory** (☎ 556 4365, Calton Hill; admission free; open 8pm-10pm Fri only), built in 1818, was based on the ancient Greek Temple of the Winds in Athens. Its original function was to provide a precise, astronomical time-keeping service for marine navigators. Smoke from Waverley train station forced the astronomers to move to Blackford Hill (see that section later in the chapter) in 1895, but the City Observatory's telescopes are still operated (when the sky is clear) by the Astronomical Society of Edinburgh (☎ 556 4365, W www.roe.ac.uk/asewww).

Just downhill from the observatory is the small, circular **Monument to Dugald Stewart** (1753–1828), who was Professor of Mathematics and of Moral Philosophy at Edinburgh University.

Edinburgh's Villages

The inexorable expansion of Edinburgh throughout the 19th and 20th centuries saw it swallow up what were previously separate villages, many of which still preserve a distinct identity within the city.

The Cramond Lioness

In November 1996, ferryman Robert Graham, who operates the rowing-boat ferry across the River Almond at Cramond, noticed part of a carved stone sticking out of the mud at low tide. He started to dig it out, thinking it might make a nice ornament for his garden, but when he realised that he was uncovering a five-foot long Roman sculpture of a lioness gripping a man's head in its teeth, he informed the local authorities who oversaw its safe recovery and preservation.

Archaeologists have dated the white, sandstone sculpture to the late 2nd or early 3rd century AD, and have conjectured that it was a funerary monument. The 1800-year-old lioness is the only Roman statue of its kind ever found in Britain and is now on display in the Museum of Scotland on Chambers St.

CRAMOND

With its moored yachts, stately swans and whitewashed houses spilling down a hillside at the mouth of the River Almond, Cramond is Edinburgh's most picturesque village. It is also rich in history – it has long been known that the Romans built a fort here in the 2nd century AD (the village's name comes from Caer Amon, 'the fort on the River Almond'), but recent archaeological excavations have revealed evidence of a Bronze-Age settlement as long ago as 8500 BC, the oldest known site in the whole of Scotland.

Cramond, which was originally a mill village, has an historic, 17th-century church, a 15th-century tower house and some rather unimpressive Roman remains, but most visitors come to enjoy walking along the river to the ruined mills and taking the rowing-boat ferry across the river to Dalmeny Estate. A bit farther downstream from the ferry landing is **The Maltings** (☎ 312 6034, Cramond Village; admission free; open 2pm-5pm Sat & Sun June-Sept, daily during Edinburgh Festival), which hosts a small exhibition on Cramond's history.

About a mile from the mouth of the river lies **Cramond Island**, uninhabited except for nesting seabirds. The gap between the island and the shore is spiked with a row of concrete teeth – a WWII barrier designed to prevent miniature submarines creeping upstream to Rosyth naval base. You can walk out to the island at low tide – there are some small sandy beaches that make pleasant summer picnic sites. The walk takes about 20 minutes and the safe period for crossing lasts from two hours before to two hours after the time of low water. To check on tide times call Forth Coastguard (☎ 01333-450666). Do *not* cross unless you are sure of the tides – every year dozens of people get caught out and have to be rescued.

A leisurely 30-minute walk through the wooded grounds of the Dalmeny Estate, on the far bank of the river from Cramond, leads to the stately home of **Dalmeny House** (☎ 331 1888, *South Queensferry; adult/ child £4/2; open 2pm-5.30pm Sun-Tues July & Aug*). Dalmeny is the seat of the earls of Rosebery, and a guided tour of the house – often conducted by the present Lord and Lady Rosebery themselves – takes in beautiful 18th-century furniture, tapestries, porcelain and paintings by Millais, Gainsborough, Reynolds and Raeburn, and a fascinating collection of Napoleon Bonaparte memorabilia assembled by the fifth earl of Rosebery. You can also reach Dalmeny House by car from Edinburgh – head westwards on the A90, following signs for the Forth Road Bridge, then leave the main road on the B924 to Dalmeny and South Queensferry. The entrance to the house is signposted on the right, half a mile after leaving the A90.

There are a couple of good places in Cramond to stop for a drink, or even a meal. See the Places to Eat chapter for full Edinburgh listings.

Cramond Inn (☎ 336 2035, *30 Cramond Glebe Rd*) Soup £2.25, mains from £6.50. Open 11am-11pm Mon-Thur, 11am-midnight Fri & Sat, 12.30pm-11pm Sun. The Cramond Inn is a welcoming, traditional pub with wood-panelled rooms and cosy fireplaces. It serves good food from 11am

to 2.30pm and 6pm to 9.30pm on weekdays, and all day until 9.30pm at weekends.

Cramond Gallery Bistro (☎ 312 6555, *5 Cramond Village*) 2-course lunch £6.95. Open 10am-6pm daily in summer, 10am-5pm in winter. The bistro has a delightful setting beside the river and serves good fish dishes as well as coffee, cakes and pastries.

Getting There & Away

Take bus No 40 or 41 from The Mound, Hanover St (northbound) or Charlotte Square to Cramond Glebe Rd, then walk 400m northwards.

The Cramond Ferry operates on demand from 9am to 1pm and 2pm to 7pm Saturday to Thursday from April to September, and from 10am to 1pm and 2pm to 4pm Saturday to Thursday from October to March, except for Christmas Day and New Year's Day. The fare is 50/10p for adults/children. Prams are carried but bikes and dogs are not allowed.

DEAN VILLAGE

If you follow Queensferry St northwards from the western end of Princes St, you come to the **Dean Bridge**, designed by Thomas Telford and built between 1829 and 1832. Vaulting gracefully over the narrow, steep-sided valley of the Water of Leith, it was built to allow New Town to expand to the north-west. It became notorious as a suicide spot – it soars 27m above the river – and in 1912 the parapets were raised to deter jumpers.

Down in the valley, just west of the bridge, is Dean Village (*dene* is a Scots word for valley); to get there, descend the steep, cobbled lane of Bell's Brae at the southern end of Dean Bridge. The village was founded as a milling community by the canons of Holyrood Abbey in the 12th century and by 1700 there were 11 water-mills here, which were operated by the Incorporation of Baxters (the bakers' trade guild). One of the old mill buildings has been converted into flats, and the village is now an attractive residential area.

Several 17th-century houses and carved stones remain. On the parapet of the old

Art Galleries

You shouldn't miss the National Gallery of Scotland, the Royal Scottish Academy (RSA), the Scottish National Portrait Gallery or the Scottish National Gallery of Modern Art, but look out for many other smaller galleries. *The Edinburgh Gallery Guide* is a free monthly booklet available around town containing an index of current exhibitions and venues. *The List* magazine and *The Scotsman* also provide a list of what's on.

Admission is free to all the galleries listed here.

Calton Gallery (Map 3) (☎ *556 1010, 10 Royal Terrace; open 10am-6pm Mon-Fri, 10am-1pm Sat)* This gallery displays paintings, watercolours and sculptures by British and European artists from 1750 to 1940.

Edinburgh Printmakers' Workshop & Gallery (Map 3) (☎ *557 2479, 23 Union St; open 10am-6pm Tues-Sat)* Here you'll find workshops and courses on the ground floor, exhibitions of lithographs, screenprints and so on by local artists on the 1st floor.

The Leith Gallery (Map 6) (☎ *553 5255, 65 The Shore, Leith; open 11am-5pm Tues-Fri, 11am-4pm Sat)* This gallery exhibits work by young Scottish artists.

Portfolio Gallery (Map 8) (☎ *220 1911, 43 Candlemaker Row; open noon-5.30pm Tues-Sat)* A photographic gallery with the emphasis on local and Scottish themes.

The Scottish Gallery (Map 3) (☎ *558 1200,* W *www.scottish-gallery.co.uk, 16 Dundas St; 10am-6pm Mon-Fri, 10am-4pm Sat)* Exhibits here include paintings and crafts by contemporary artists and past masters.

bridge (18th-century) at the foot of Bell's Brae, there is a carving showing crossed peels' – long shovels for putting loaves into ovens – and the inscription 'Blesit be God for al His giftis'. On the door lintel of the house opposite is another carving of crossed peels with three loaves of bread, and the words 'God bless the Baxters of Edinbrugh uho bult this hous 1675'.

From the old bridge, you can follow the Water of Leith Walkway downstream to Stockbridge (10 minutes – see Walk 2 in the Walking Tours special section), or follow the signs upstream to the Scottish National Gallery of Modern Art (15 minutes).

Scottish National Gallery of Modern Art & Dean Gallery (Map 2)

Set in an impressive neoclassical building surrounded by a sculpture park, 500m west of Dean Village, is the **Scottish National Gallery of Modern Art** (☎ *624 6200, 75 Belford Rd; admission free, fee for special exhibitions; open 10am-5pm Mon-Sat, 2pm-5pm Sun).*

The collection – housed in bright, modern galleries that belie the building's austere facade – concentrates on 20th-century art, with various European art movements represented by the likes of Matisse, Picasso, Kirchner, Magritte, Miro, Mondrian and Giacometti. American and English artists are also represented, but most space is given to Scottish painters – from the Scottish colourists of the early 20th century to contemporary artists, such as Peter Howson and Ken Currie. There's an excellent cafe downstairs and the surrounding park features sculptures by Henry Moore, Sir Eduardo Paolozzi and Barbara Hepworth among others.

Directly across Belford Rd from the National Gallery of Modern Art, another neoclassical mansion houses its adjunct, the **Dean Gallery** *(☎ 624 6200, 73 Belford Rd; admission free, fee for special exhibitions; open 10am-5pm Mon-Sat, 2pm-5pm Sun).* The Dean holds the Gallery of Modern Art's collection of Dada and surrealist art, including works by Dali, Giacometti and Picasso, and a large collection of sculpture and graphic art created by the Edinburgh-born sculptor Sir Eduardo Paolozzi.

DUDDINGSTON (Map 1)

Nestling beneath the south-eastern slopes of Arthur's Seat, the picturesque little village of Duddingston is a place of great antiquity – archaeologists have unearthed Bronze Age remains here. The village itself dates from the 12th century, though all that remains from that date are parts of **Duddingston Parish Church**, which sits on a promontory overlooking Duddingston Loch. The western door of the church is Norman, decorated with chevron patterns and carvings of Christ on the Cross and a soldier with a sword and axe. There are some interesting medieval relics at the kirkyard gate – the **Joug**, a metal collar that was used, like the stocks, to tether criminals and sinners; and the **Loupin-On Stane**, a stone step to help gouty and corpulent worshippers mount their horses. The early-19th-century **watch tower** inside the gate was built to deter body snatchers.

The village itself consists of only two streets – Old Church Lane and The Causeway. At the western end of the latter stands an 18th-century pub, **The Sheep Heid Inn** (see the boxed text 'Trad vs Trendy' in the Entertainment chapter), and at the eastern end is **Prince Charlie's Cottage**, where the Young Pretender held a council of war before the Battle of Prestonpans in 1745.

To climb **Arthur's Seat** (251m) from Duddingston, head westwards from the church to the parking area just inside the gate to Holyrood Park, then turn right and climb up the steep stairs known as Jacob's Ladder to another road. Turn right, and when you reach another parking area (200m), leave the road and take the path on the left to the summit (20 to 30 minutes total).

LEITH (Map 6)

Leith – 2 miles (3km) north-east of the city centre – has been Edinburgh's seaport since the 14th century, and remained an independent burgh with its own town council until it was incorporated by the city in the 1920s. Like many of Britain's dockland areas, it fell into decay in the decades following WWII but has been undergoing a revival since the late 1980s. Old warehouses have been turned into luxury flats and a lush crop of trendy bars and restaurants has sprouted along the waterfront. The area was given an additional boost in the late 1990s when the Scottish Office (a government department, now renamed the Scottish Executive) moved to a new building on Leith docks. The city council has now formulated a major redevelopment plan for the entire Edinburgh waterfront from Leith to Granton, the first phase of which is Ocean Terminal (due to open in October 2001), a shopping and leisure complex that includes the former Royal Yacht *Britannia* and a berth for visiting cruise liners. Parts of Leith are still a bit rough – Coburg St, for example, is a notorious red-light district – but it's a distinctive corner of the city and well worth exploring.

The Shore

The most attractive part of old Leith is The Shore, where the Water of Leith runs into Leith Docks. Before the docks were built in the 19th century, this was Leith's original wharf. An iron plaque set into the quay in front of No 30 The Shore marks the **King's Landing** – the spot where King George IV (the first reigning British monarch to visit Scotland since Charles II in 1650) stepped ashore in 1822.

North of the bridge across the river is the circular **Signal Tower**, built in 1686, and originally a windmill; it now houses the excellent Fisher's seafood restaurant (see the Places to Eat chapter). Beyond is the 19th-century baronial facade and clock tower of the old Sailor's Home, now the Malmaison Hotel (see the Places to Stay chapter).

Four hundred yards (364m) south of the bridge, hidden away in the Kirkgate, is

Romanesque and radiant: St Margaret's Chapel

MARTIN MOOS

Heraldic panel at the entrance to Holyroodhouse

MARTIN MOOS

View of the Monument to Dugald Stewart on Calton Hill as the sun descends over Edinburgh

JONATHAN SMITH

MARTIN MOOS

Time for a sit-down and a cuppa: coffee culture hits the Royal Mile.

NEIL SETCHFIELD

A Jock for all seasons

The beer might be deer in her

BETHUNE CARMICHAEL

BETHUNE CARMICHAEL

A haunt to get you buzzing!

MARTIN MOOS

With your beer goggles on, you may find one of these three tast

Trinity House, a neoclassical building dating from 1816. It was the headquarters of the Incorporation of Masters and Mariners (founded in 1380), the nautical equivalent of a tradesmen's guild, and is a treasure house of old ship models, navigation instruments and artefacts relating to Leith's maritime history. The management of Trinity House was taken over by the Historic Scotland agency in 2001, and it may well be open to the public by the time you read this.

Leith Links

This public park, in the eastern part of Leith, was originally common grazing land, but is more famous as the home of golf. Although golf has not been played on the links since the 19th century, the game has a long history in Leith. The kirk Session Records of 1610 for the parish church of South Leith note that the Session agreed that there should be no 'public playing suffered on the Sabbath dayes. As playing else, the Ball so stop'd, at the penny stane, archery, gowfe etc'.

Although St Andrews claims seniority in having the oldest golf course in the world, it was at Leith Links in 1744 that the first official rules of the game were formulated by the Honorable Company of Edinburgh Golfers – these 13 rules formed the basis of the modern game. Rule No 9 gives some insight into the 18th-century game – 'If a ball be stop'd by any person, Horse, Dog or anything else, the Ball so stop'd must be played where it lyes'. The original document is in the National Library of Scotland and the Honorable Company is now the famous Muirfield Golf Club. A stone cairn on the western side of the links bears a plaque that describes how the game was played over five holes, each being around 400 yards. There are plans to re-create one of the original holes, along with a permanent exhibition.

Royal Yacht *Britannia*

One of Edinburgh's biggest tourist attractions is the former Royal Yacht *Britannia* (☎ 555 5566, W *www.royalyachtbritannia.co.uk, Ocean Drive, Leith; family/adult/child £20/7.75/3.75; open 10am-3.30pm Mon-Fri Oct-Mar, 9.30am-4pm Mon-Fri Apr-May, 9.30am-4.30pm Mon-Fri June-Sept, 9.30am-4.30pm Sat & Sun year-round, closed 1 Jan & 25 Dec*). She was the Royal Family's floating home during their foreign travels from her launch in 1953 until her decommissioning in 1997, and is now moored permanently in front of Ocean Terminal.

The tour, which you take at your own pace with an audioguide (also available in French, German, Italian and Spanish), gives an intriguing insight into the Queen's private tastes – *Britannia* was one of the few places where the Royal Family could enjoy true privacy. The entire ship is a monument to 1950s' decor and technology, and the accommodation reveals Her Majesty's preference for simple, unfussy surroundings – the Queen's own bed is surprisingly tiny and plain. In fact, the initial interior design was rejected by the Queen for being too flashy.

There was nothing simple or unfussy about the running of the ship, though. When the Queen travelled, along with her went 45 members of the Royal Household, five tons of luggage and a Rolls-Royce that was carefully squeezed into a specially built garage on the deck. The ship's company consisted of an admiral, 20 officers and 220 yachtsmen. The decks (of Burmese teak) were scrubbed daily, but all work near the royal accommodation was carried out in complete silence and had to be finished by 8am. A thermometer was kept in the Queen's bathroom to make sure that the water was the correct temperature, and when in harbour one yachtsman was charged with ensuring that the angle of the gangway never exceeded 12 degrees. And note the mahogany windbreak that was added to the balcony deck in front of the bridge – it was put there to stop wayward breezes from blowing up skirts and inadvertently revealing the Royal Undies.

Buses run from Waverley Bridge to the ship every 20 minutes during opening times.

NEWHAVEN (Map 1)

Immediately to the west of Leith, Newhaven was once a distinctive fishing community whose fishwives tramped the streets of Edinburgh's New Town selling 'caller herrin' (fresh herring) from wicker creels on their backs. The old fish-market building beside the harbour now houses the **New-haven Heritage Museum** (*☎ 551 4165, 24 Pier Place; admission free; open noon-5pm daily).* A 15-minute video illustrates the hard-working lifestyle that survived here until the 1950s when overfishing put paid to the traditional source of income.

During the summer you can take a tour around the Firth of Forth on a high-speed RIB (semi-rigid inflatable boat). *Sea.fari Adventures (☎ 331 5000)* runs cruises from Newhaven, weather permitting, to visit seal and seabird colonies around the islands of Inchkeith and Inchcolm. A one-hour cruise costs £15/12 for adults/children and a two-hour cruise costs £20/15 – telephone Sea.fari to check cruise times and book tickets. Waterproofs and lifejackets are provided but dress warmly too.

To get to Newhaven, take bus No 10, 11 or 16 (eastbound) from Princes St.

STOCKBRIDGE (MAP 2)

New Town's Georgian architecture extends north into Stockbridge, a trendy district with its own distinct identity, some interesting shops and a good choice of pubs and restaurants. Originally a milling community, Stockbridge was developed in the early 19th century on lands owned largely by the painter, Sir Henry Raeburn. The garden villas along **Ann St**, named after Raeburn's wife and dating from 1817, are among the most beautiful and desirable houses in Edinburgh, while the giant Doric columns that line **St Bernard's Crescent** are the most grandiose decoration on any private residence in the city.

A 10-minute walk northwards from Stockbridge, along St Bernard's Row, Arboretum Ave and Arboretum Place, leads to the Royal Botanic Garden (see the Greater Edinburgh section later in the chapter).

SWANSTON

Huddled in the shadow of the Pentland Hills on the southern fringe of the city, the tiny hamlet of Swanston is an unlikely survivor – a village green, an old schoolhouse and a

square of whitewashed cottages with reed-thatched roofs barely 500m from the roaring traffic of Edinburgh's ring-road. This picturesque spot is a favourite starting point for walks into the Pentland Hills, but is most famous as the childhood summer retreat of Robert Louis Stevenson. Stevenson's father leased the nearby 18th-century villa, **Swanston Cottage**, as a summer home from 1867 to 1880, hoping that the clean air would improve the health of his sickly son.

To get to Swanston, take bus No 4 (westbound) from Princes St and get off at Oxgangs Rd, just past Hunter's Tryst, then walk 750m southwards on Swanston Rd.

Greater Edinburgh

ROYAL BOTANIC GARDEN (MAP 1)

Just north of Stockbridge is the lovely **Royal Botanic Garden** (*☎ 552 7171,* W *www.rbge .org.uk, 20a Inverleith Row; admission free; open 9.30am-4pm daily Nov-Jan, 9.30am-5pm daily Feb & Oct, 9.30am-6pm Mon-Sun Mar & Sept, 9.30am-7pm daily Apr-Aug).* Founded near Holyrood in 1670 and moved to its present location in 1823, Edinburgh's Botanic Garden is the second oldest institution of its kind in Britain (after Oxford), and one of the most respected in the world. Seventy beautifully landscaped acres include splendid Victorian palm houses, colourful swathes of rhododendron and azalea, and a world-famous rock garden. The Terrace Cafe offers good views towards the city centre.

To get to the Royal Botanic Garden take bus No 8, 17, 23, 27 or 37 to East Gate.

EDINBURGH ZOO (MAP 1)

Opened in 1913, and located 2½ miles west of the city centre, Edinburgh Zoo (*☎ 334 9171,* W *www.edinburghzoo.org.uk, 134 Corstorphine Rd; adult/child £7/4; open 9am-6pm daily Apr-Sept, 9am-5pm daily Oct & Mar, 9am-4.30pm daily Nov-Feb)* is one of the world's leading conservation zoos. Edinburgh's captive breeding programme has saved many endangered species, including Siberian tigers, pygmy hippos and red pandas. The main attractions are the four species of penguin, kept in the world's biggest penguin pool, the sea lion and red panda feeding times, the animal handling sessions and the new Lifelinks 'hands on' zoology centre.

To get to the zoo take bus No 12, 16, 26, 31, 86 or 100 (the Airlink airport bus) westbound from Princes St.

BLACKFORD HILL (MAP 1)

Lying 1½ miles (2.5km) directly south of the centre, Blackford Hill (164m) offers a splendid panorama of the castle, Old Town and Arthur's Seat. It is also home to the **Royal Observatory of Edinburgh** *(☎ 668 8405,* **w** *www.roe.ac.uk, Blackford Hill; adult/child £3.50/2.50; open 10am-5pm Mon-Sat, noon-5pm Sun).* The visitor centre offers a multimedia gallery with computers and CD-ROMs on astronomy and the chance to see the 36-inch telescope housed in the original 1894 dome.

To get to the observatory take bus No 41 southbound from Hanover St or The Mound.

PORTOBELLO (MAP 1)

Located 4 miles (6.5km) east of the city centre, the suburb of Portobello was a fashionable 19th-century seaside resort, known as 'the Brighton of the North'. Although its heyday has long since passed, its promenade and sandy beach still attract crowds on warm summer days. From 1995 to 1998 swimming at Portobello was banned due to pollution, but a new waste-treatment plant has resulted in cleaner water. The beach and prom are undergoing redevelopment, with the hope of winning a 'Clean Beach Guide' award. The famous music-hall entertainer Sir Harry Lauder (1870–1950) was born on Bridge St in Portobello.

To get to Portobello, take Lothian bus No 15 or 26 (eastbound) from Princes St or No 46 from St Andrew Square.

ROSLIN

On the eastern edge of the village of Roslin, 7 miles south of Edinburgh city centre, is one of Scotland's most beautiful and enig-matic churches – **Rosslyn Chapel** *(Collegiate Church of St Matthew;* ☎ *440 2159,* **w** *www.rosslyn-chapel.com, Roslin, Midlothian; admission £4; open 10am-5pm daily Mar-Oct, 10am-4.30pm daily Nov-Mar).* Built in the mid-15th century for William St Clair, third earl of Orkney, the chapel does not conform to the architectural fashion of its time. The ornately carved interior is a monument to the mason's art and is rich in symbolic imagery. As well as flowers, vines, angels and biblical figures, the carved stones include many examples of the pagan 'Green Man'; other figures are associated with Freemasonry and the Knights Templar. Intriguingly, there are also carvings of plants from the Americas that predate Columbus' voyage of discovery. The symbolism of these images has led some researchers to conclude that Rosslyn is some kind of secret Templar repository, and it has been claimed that hidden vaults beneath the chapel could conceal anything from the Holy Grail to the head of John the Baptist to the body of Christ himself. The chapel is owned by the Episcopal Church of Scotland and services are still held here on Sunday mornings.

A 200m walk south of the chapel, on a promontory overlooking the River North Esk, are the dramatic ruins of **Roslin Castle**, the former home of the St Clair family.

Lothian Buses bus No 37 (90p, 50 minutes) runs every 30 minutes from Frederick St and North Bridge (southbound).

SOUTH QUEENSFERRY

South Queensferry lies on the southern bank of the Firth of Forth, 8 miles (13km) west of Edinburgh city centre. Located at the narrowest part of the firth, ferries plied across the water to Fife from the earliest times, ceasing only in 1964 when the graceful **Forth Road Bridge** – now the fifth longest in Europe – was opened.

Predating the Forth Road Bridge by 74 years, the magnificent **Forth Bridge** – only outsiders ever call it the Forth Rail Bridge – is one of the finest engineering achievements of the 19th century. Completed in 1890 after seven years' work, its three huge cantilevers span 1447m and took 59,000 tonnes of steel, 8 million rivets and the lives of 58 men.

On the pretty, terraced High St in South Queensferry is the small **Queensferry Museum** *(☎ 331 5545, 53 High St, South Queensferry; admission free; open 10am-1pm & 2.15pm-5pm Mon & Thur-Sat, noon-5pm Sun)*. It contains some interesting information on the bridges and a model of the 'Burry Man', part of the summer gala festivities. On the first Friday of August, some hapless local male spends nine hours roaming the streets covered from head to toe in burrs and clutching two floral staves in honour of a medieval tradition.

There are several good pubs along the High St. One of them is the ***Hawes Inn*** *(☎ 331 1990, Newhalls Rd, South Queensferry)*, famously mentioned in Robert Louis Stevenson's novel *Kidnapped*, serves food from noon to 10pm daily; it's opposite the Inchcolm ferry, right beside the railway bridge.

To get to South Queensferry, take First bus No 88 (25 minutes) westbound from Princes St (eastern end) or Charlotte Square; there's a bus (90p) every 20 minutes. It's a 10-minute walk eastwards from the bus stop to the Hawes Inn and the Inchcolm ferry.

There are also frequent trains (15 minutes) from Edinburgh Waverley and Haymarket to Dalmeny station. From the station exit, the Hawes Inn is only a five-minute walk along a footpath (across the road, behind the bus stop) that leads north beside the railway and under the bridge.

Inchcolm

The island of Inchcolm lies east of the Forth bridges, less than a mile off the coast of Fife. Only 800m long, it is home to the ruins of **Inchcolm Abbey** *(☎ 01383-823332, Inchcolm, Fife; adult/child £2.80/1; open 9.30am-6.30pm daily Apr-Sept)*. Inchcolm is one of Scotland's best-preserved medieval abbeys, founded by Augustinian priors in 1123. In the well-tended grounds stand the remains of a 13th-century church and a remarkably well-preserved octagonal chapter house with a stone roof.

The ferry boat **Maid of the Forth** *(☎ 331 4857)* sails from Hawes Pier in South Queensferry to Inchcolm. There are daily sailings mid-July to early September, and weekends only April to June and October. The return fare costs £9.75/4 for adults/children; the prices includes entry to Inchcolm Abbey. In summer, evening cruises with jazz or folk music cost £9.50 per head. It's a half-hour sail to Inchcolm and you're allowed 1½ hours ashore. As well as the abbey, the trip gives you the chance to see the island's grey seals, puffins and other seabirds.

Hopetoun House

Two miles west of South Queensferry lies one of Scotland's finest stately homes, Hopetoun House *(☎ 331 2451; adult/child £5.30/2.70; open 10am-5.30pm daily Apr-Sept, 10am-5.30pm Sat & Sun Oct)*. It has a superb location in lovely grounds beside the Firth of Forth. There are two parts, the older built to Sir William Bruce's plans between 1699 and 1702 and dominated by a splendid stairwell, the newer designed between 1720 and 1750 by three members of the Adam family, William and sons Robert and John. The rooms have splendid furnishings and staff are on hand to make sure you don't miss details such as the revolving oyster stand for two people to share.

The Hope family supplied a viceroy of India and a governor-general of Australia so the upstairs museum displays interesting reminders of the colonial life of the ruling class. Even farther up there's a viewing point on the roof, ideal for photos.

Hopetoun House can be approached along the coastal road from South Queensferry or, from Edinburgh, turn off the A90 onto the A904 just before the Forth Bridge and follow the signs.

WATER OF LEITH

Edinburgh's river is a modest stream, flowing only 20 miles (32km) from the northwestern slopes of the Pentland Hills through western and northern Edinburgh to enter the Firth of Forth at Leith. Rarely more than 10 yards (10m) across, it cuts a surprisingly rural swathe through the city, offering the chance to stroll along wooded riverbanks only 500m from Princes St.

Through history the river has served as a source of power for water-mills (see Dean Village in the Edinburgh Villages section earlier in the chapter) and a convenient waste-disposal system, but it has now been cleaned up and provides an important wildlife habitat (you can see otters and kingfishers) and recreation resource for walkers and anglers. The **Water of Leith Walkway**, a project that started in the 1970s, is now nearing completion, offering an almost uninterrupted walking and cycling route along the river from Leith to the village of Balerno, on the south-western edge of the city. There are access points and signposts throughout its length.

The **Water of Leith Visitor Centre (Map 1)** ☎ 455 7367, [W] www.wateroflleith.edin org, 24 Lanark Rd; adult/child £1.90/1.20; open 10am-4pm daily Apr-Sept, 10am-4pm Wed-Sun Oct-Mar) has interactive displays on the river's wildlife and ecology, and underwater video cameras that allow you to watch aquatic creatures live.

To get to the visitors centre take bus No 28, 35, 44 or 66.

ACTIVITIES
Bird-Watching
There are several good bird-watching areas in and around Edinburgh. Within the city is **Bawsinch Nature Reserve (Map 1)**, on the reedy southern edge of Duddingston Loch, where you can see great crested grebe, heron, ruddy duck and flocks of wintering wildfowl; the Scottish Wildlife Trust has set up a number of hides here. Waders congregate at low tide on the mud flats at **Cramond** and in **Granton Harbour**. For woodland birds, including woodpeckers and owls, try the **Hermitage of Braid** (Map 1) near Blackford Hill. An unusual development in the past few years has been the appearance of nesting fulmars on the north end of Salisbury Crags.

Aberlady Bay Nature Reserve, 15 miles (25km) east of Edinburgh, is famous for the vast flocks of pink-footed geese that visit in winter. The **islands** in the Firth of Forth – notably Inchkeith, Inchmickery, Bass Rock and the Isle of May – support large colonies of breeding seabirds. All can be visited by tour boat. See the Scottish Seabird Centre, North Berwick, in the Excursions chapter.

Climbing
Unfortunately, local bye-laws make it illegal to climb on Salisbury Crags. **Alien Rock (Map 1)** (☎ 552 7211, 8 Pier Place, Newhaven; adult/child £5/3, off-peak adult rate before 4pm weekdays & after 5pm weekends £3.50; open noon-11pm Mon-Fri, 10am-9pm Sat & Sun) provides excellent indoor climbing facilities in a converted church.

The new **National Rock Climbing Centre of Scotland** ([W] www.nrcc.co.uk, South Plate Hill, Ratho; admission £4-5 per day, beginners lessons from £15) is the largest covered climbing hall in the world, offering both natural rock and artificial walls. The centre is located in a former quarry on the banks of the Union Canal, 8 miles (13km) west of Edinburgh.

The nearest natural rock-climbing crags are at Traprain Law, near Haddington (20 miles east of Edinburgh) and at Aberdour on the Fife coast (15 miles north).

Cycling
Edinburgh and surroundings offer many excellent opportunities for cycling. See the boxed text 'Cycling Edinburgh' in the Getting Around chapter.

Golf
There are 19 golf courses in Edinburgh, and another 70 within 20 miles of the city. Two of the best city courses are the challenging **Braid Hills Golf Course (Map 1)** (☎ 452 9408, Braid Hills Approach; green fees weekdays/weekends £10/12.50) and the scenic **Lothianburn Golf Course** (☎ 445 5067, 106a Biggar Rd, Fairmilehead; green fees £16.50/22.50 weekdays/weekends).

Melville Golf Centre (☎ 654 8038, Lasswade, Midlothian; green fee for nine holes £8-10; open 9am-10pm Mon-Fri & 9am-8pm Sat & Sun), on the southern edge of the

Playing the Old Course

Golf has been played at St Andrews since the 15th century and by 1457 was apparently so popular that James II had to ban it because it was interfering with his troops' archery practice. Everyone knows that St Andrews is the home of golf but few people realise that anyone can play the Old Course, the world's most famous golf course. Although it lies beside the exclusive, all-male Royal and Ancient Golf Club, the Old Course is a public course and is not owned by the club.

However, getting a tee-off time is – literally – something of a lottery. Unless you book a year or two in advance, the only chance you have of playing here is by entering the daily ballot. You must enter a minimum of two players by 2pm on the day before you wish to play; the results are shown by 4pm at the clubhouse, the starter's box, and on the Web at W www.golfagent.com/ballot. You can enter names in the ballot in person or by phone. Be warned that applications by ballot are normally heavily oversubscribed, and green fees are a mere £85 (£56 in winter). There's no play on Sunday.

Single golfers can sometimes get lucky by turning up at the starter's box as early as possible in the morning – the starter will try to join you up with the first available two- or three-ball.

If your number doesn't come up, there are five other public courses in the area, none with quite the cachet of the Old Course, but all of them significantly cheaper.

Advance bookings for the Old Course can be made by letter, phone, fax or email to the Reservations Office, St Andrews Links Trust (☎ 01334-466666, fax 477036, e reservations@standrews.org.uk), Pilmour House, St Andrews KY16 9SF. It's advisable to book at least a year in advance and you must present a handicap certificate or letter of introduction from your club.

JANE SMITH

city, offers a nine-hole course, floodlit driving range, putting green, equipment hire, professional tuition and golf shop.

Some of the most famous links courses in the world lie within an hour's drive of Edinburgh, including **Muirfield** (☎ 01620-842123, Gullane; green fees per round £85; open to visitors Tues & Thur only), **Gullane No 1** (☎ 01620-842255, West Links Rd, Gullane; green fees £60; open to visitors 10.30am-noon & 2.30pm-4pm Mon-Fri) in East Lothian, and **St Andrews Old Course** (☎ 01334-476666, W www.standrews.org.uk, Pilmour House, St Andrews; green fees in high/low season £85/56; open to visitors Mon-Sat) in Fife. To play on these courses you will have to book at least a month in advance. For details of other courses in and around Edinburgh, check out the Web site W www.scotlands-golf-courses.com.

Horse-Riding

There are many scenic bridle paths in the countryside around Edinburgh, and a few riding schools offer two- and three-hour treks as well as tuition. Try **Pentland Hill Icelandics** (☎ 01968-661095, W www.phicelandics.co.uk, Windy Gowl Farm, Carlops, Midlothian) or the **Edinburgh & Lasswade Riding Centre** (☎ 663 7676, Kevock Rd, Lasswade).

Sailing

The Firth of Forth provides sheltered water for all kinds of sailing. **Port Edgar Marina & Sailing School** (☎ 331 3330, W www.portedgar.co.uk, Shore Rd, South Queensferry; boat rental sessions 10am-noon & 2pm-4pm daily, plus 7pm-9pm Mon-Fri Apr-Oct) rents out Topper/420/Wayfarer sailing dinghies at £9.80/18.20/25.40 for two-hour session. It also offers canoeing, power-boating and sailing courses.

Skiing & Snowboarding

Skiing in Edinburgh? Yup – Europe's longest dry ski slope disfigures the northern slopes of the Pentland Hills at the southern edge of the city. You can punish your thighs in preparation for winter at **Midlothian Ski Centre** *(☎ 445 4433, Biggar Rd, Hillend; adult/child £8.50/5.60 for two hours; open 9.30am-9pm Mon-Sat & 9.30am-7pm Sun)*. There are two button tows and a chairlift. Admission includes ski hire but snowboard and boot rental costs £2 extra for two hours.

Swimming

The Firth of Forth is a bit on the chilly – and polluted – side for enjoyable swimming but there are several indoor alternatives. The city's main facility is the **Royal Commonwealth Pool (Map 5)** *(☎ 667 7211, 21 Dalkeith Rd; adult/child £2.70/1.40; open 9am-9pm Mon, Tues, Thur & Fri, 10am-9pm Wed, 10am-4pm Sat & Sun)*, which has a 50m pool, diving pool, children's pool, flumes and fitness centre, and there are smaller pools at **Warrender Swim Centre (Map 5)** *(☎ 447 0052, 55 Thirlestane Rd)*, **Glenogle Swim Centre (Map 3)** *(☎ 343 6376, Glenogle Rd)* and **Dalry Swim Centre** *(☎ 313 3964, 25-29 Caledonian Crescent)*. Admission charges for the latter are £1.70/1 for adults/children, and opening times are variable, generally from 8am to 8pm on weekdays, and from 9am to 4pm on Saturday and Sunday – phone to confirm.

Walking

Edinburgh is lucky to have several good walking areas within the city boundary, including Arthur's Seat, Calton Hill, Blackford Hill, Hermitage of Braid, Corstorphine Hill and the coast and river at Cramond. The Pentland Hills, which rise to over 500m, stretch south-westwards from the city for 15 miles (25km), offering excellent high- and low-level walking.

You can follow the Water of Leith Walkway from the city centre to Balerno (8 miles), and continue across the Pentlands to Silverburn (6½ miles) or Carlops (8 miles), and return to Edinburgh by bus. Another good option is to walk along the towpath of the Union Canal, which begins in Fountainbridge (Map 4), and runs all the way to Falkirk (31 miles). You can return to Edinburgh by bus at Ratho (8½ miles) and Broxburn (12 miles), and by bus or train from Linlithgow (21 miles).

COURSES

The University of Edinburgh's **Centre for Continuing Education** *(Map 5; ☎ 650 3073, fax 667 6097, W www.cce.ed.ac.uk/summer, 11 Buccleuch St, Edinburgh EH8 9LW)* runs summer courses for adults on a wide range of subjects, including Scottish archaeology, Scottish literature, Scottish history and Gaelic language. A one-week course on Scottish Poetry costs £155, while the three-week Elementary Gaelic course costs £265.

Edinburgh is a popular place to learn English as a second language, and is home to many establishments offering a range of intensive courses, summer schools, weekend workshops and specialised-English courses (eg for medicine, business or tourism). Check the *Yellow Pages* under 'Language Courses & Schools' or make enquiries at the following schools:

Edinburgh Language Centre (☎/fax 343 6596, W www.elc.mcmail.com) 10b Oxford Terrace, Edinburgh EH4
Edinburgh School of English (☎ 557 9200, fax 557 9192, W www.edinburghschool.ac.uk) 271 Canongate, Edinburgh EH8 8BQ
English Language Institute (☎ 447 2398, fax 447 7131, W www.eli.co.uk) 69 Nile Grove, Edinburgh EH10 4SN
International Language Academy (☎ 220 4278, fax 220 1107, W www.language-academies .com) 11 Great Stuart St, Edinburgh EH3 7TP
Institute for Applied Language Studies (☎ 650 6200, fax 667 5927, W www.ials.ed.ac.uk) University of Edinburgh, 21 Hill Place, Edinburgh EH8 9DP

If you're interested in studying French language and culture, contact the **Institut Français d'Écosse (Map 2)** *(☎ 225 5366, fax 220 0648, W www.ifecosse.org.uk, 13 Randolph Crescent)* at the French Consulate.

Walking Tours

Walk 1: Old Town
(Map 8)

Edinburgh's Old Town spreads down the Royal Mile to the east of the castle and southwards to Grassmarket and Cowgate. This walk explores a few of Old Town's many interesting nooks and crannies, and involves a fair bit of climbing up and down steep stairs and closes. Allow one to two hours.

Begin on the Castle Esplanade, which provides a grandstand view southwards over Grassmarket. The prominent quadrangular building with all the turrets is **George Heriot's School** (see the Things to See & Do chapter). Head towards Castlehill and the start of the Royal Mile. The 17th-century house on the right, above the steps of North Castle Wynd, is known as **Cannonball House** because of the iron ball lodged in the wall (look between, and slightly below, the two largest windows). It was not fired in anger, but instead marks the gravitation height to which water would flow naturally from the city's first piped water supply.

The low, rectangular building across the street (now a touristy tartan-weaving mill) was originally the reservoir that held Old Town's water supply. On its western wall is the **Witches Well**, where a modern bronze fountain commemorates around 4000 people (mostly women) who were burnt or strangled in Edinburgh between 1479 and 1722 for suspicion of witchcraft.

Go past the reservoir and turn left down Ramsay Lane, and take a look at **Ramsay Garden** – one of the most desirable addresses in Edinburgh – where late-19th-century apartments were built around the nucleus of the octagonal Ramsay Lodge, once home to poet Allan Ramsay. The cobbled street continues around to the right below student residences to the twin towers of the **New College** – home to Edinburgh University's Faculty of Divinity. Nip into the courtyard to see the **statue of John Knox**.

Just past New College turn right and climb up the stairs into **Milne's Court**, a student residence that houses the public entrance to the temporary home of the Scottish Parliament. Exit into Lawnmarket, cross the street (bearing slightly left) and duck into **Riddell's Court** at No 322–8, a typical Old Town close. You'll find yourself in a small courtyard but the house in front of you (built in 1590) was originally the edge of the street (the building you just walked under was added in 1726 – check the doorway on the right). The arch (with the inscription 'VIVENDO DISCIMUS' – 'we live and learn') leads into the original 16th-century courtyard.

Go back into the street, turn right, and then right again down Fisher's Close, which ejects you into the delightful **Victoria Terrace**, strung above the cobbled curve of Victoria St. Wander right, enjoying the view, then descend the stairs at the foot of Upper Bow and continue downhill to Grassmarket. Turn left along the gloomy defile of Cowgate. The first bridge you come to is **George IV Bridge** (built between 1829 and 1834). Although you can see only one arch here, there are nine in total – one more is visible a block south at Merchant St. The rest are hidden beneath and between the surrounding buildings, such as the haunted vaults of South Bridge, farther westwards along Cowgate (see the boxed text 'Underground Edinburgh' in the Things to See & Do chapter).

Pass under the bridge – the buildings to your right are the new **Law Courts**, while high up to the left you can see the projecting, stained-glass windows of **Parliament Hall** (see the Things to See & Do chapter). Past the courts on the right is **Tailors Hall** (built in 1621 and extended in 1757), now a hotel and bar (see the Places to Stay and Entertainment chapters) but formerly the meeting place of the 'Companie of Tailzeours' (Tailors' Guild).

Turn left and climb up **Old Fishmarket Close**, and perhaps stop for lunch at the little brasserie of Le Sept (see the Places to Eat chapter). Emerge once more into the Royal Mile – across the street and slightly downhill is **Anchor Close**, named after a tavern that once stood here. It hosted the Crochallan Fencibles, an 18th-century drinking club that provided its patrons with an agreeable blend of intellectual debate and intoxicating liquor. Founded by William Smellie, editor of the 1st edition of the *Encyclopaedia Britannica*, its best-known member was Robert Burns, the poet.

Should you wish to wet your own whistle, more than a dozen hostelries lie between here and Holyrood. And it's downhill all the way...

Walk 2: New Town to Stockbridge
(Maps 2 & 3)
This perambulation probes the more interesting parts of New Town and ends with a pleasant stroll along a wooded river valley. Allow one to two hours.

Begin in St Andrew Square (Map 3). Looking westwards along George St, you can see the dome of **West Register House** (see the Things to See & Do chapter). The original plans for New Town envisaged a matching church of St Andrew on the eastern side of St Andrew Square, but the rich and ambitious Sir Lawrence Dundas had other plans – he bought up the land, and had his own elaborate mansion (now the Royal Bank of Scotland) built on the site.

Walk westwards along George St, noting the ostentatious temple to Mammon on your left that was once a bank and is now a restaurant and bar (The Dome; see the Places to Eat chapter). Turn right at Hanover St, where a **statue of George IV** commemorates his royal visit in 1822, and then left along Thistle St. This and its companion Rose St were built to house the servants, tradesmen and stables that catered to the needs of New Town gentry; today it continues to serve a similar purpose, with its expensive restaurants and antique shops.

Turn right on Frederick St and continue downhill past Queen St and its gardens, and turn right into Heriot Row. A few doors along at No 17 a plaque marks the house where Robert Louis Stevenson lived from 1857 to 1880. Retrace your steps and continue westwards along Heriot Row, a typical Georgian terrace. Turn left at Wemyss Place (pronounced 'weems'), then go right and first left into North Charlotte St, which leads to **Charlotte Square** (see the Things to See & Do chapter).

After looking around the square, exit via Glenfinlas St in the northwestern corner, and bear left into Ainslie Place (Map 2). This elegant oval space, with its octagonal neighbour Moray Place on one side and semicircular Randolph Crescent on the other, constitute the **Moray Estate** (built between 1822 and 1850), the most beautiful part of New Town.

Go left along Great Stuart St, bear right through Randolph Crescent and cross busy Queensferry St, before turning right towards **Dean Bridge**. Go out onto the middle of the bridge for a view of Dean Village, then return and descend the steep cobbled lane of Bells' Brae to Dean Village itself. By the old bridge, turn right along Miller Row and follow the footpath along the Water of Leith.

The buildings high up on the cliff above the private gardens on the right are the backs of the ones you saw earlier on Ainslie Place. Five minutes' walk brings you to **St Bernard's Well** (1789), a circular temple with a statue of Hygeia, the goddess of health. The footpath continues under a bridge and into Saunders St, which deposits you at Deanhaugh St in Stockbridge, where various bars, cafes and restaurants await. You can return to George St by turning right and climbing up the steep hill of Gloucester St and its continuation Gloucester Lane, or by catching any bus heading uphill on Circus Place.

Walk 3: Calton Hill & Arthur's Seat
(Maps 1, 3 & 5)
Edinburgh's city-centre hills provide superb views over the city and countryside. This walk is fairly strenuous, taking in both summits and covering around 4 miles. Allow 1½ to 2½ hours.

Start at the eastern end of Princes St (Map 3). Walk eastwards along Waterloo Place, past the **Old Calton Burial Ground** (see the Things to See & Do chapter), and climb up the stairs on the left (just after Howie's restaurant). At the top of the steps, on the left, is an iron gate marked 'Rock House'. This was once the home of David Octavius Hill, an early pioneer of portrait photography. Beyond the gate, turn right up another flight of steps and continue up the path to the monuments at the summit of **Calton Hill**.

On the northern side, the view extends from the Forth Bridges in the west to the distant conical hill of North Berwick Law in the east. Walk eastwards from the summit, and follow the road curving right and dropping down to Regent Rd. Cross the road and go left until you're opposite the **Greek temple** of the former Royal High School. Once intended to house a Scottish Parliament, it now overlooks the new Scottish Parliament building site at Holyrood.

Take a quick look at the nearby **Burns Monument**, then descend the footpath that drops down on the southern side of Regent Rd and double-back left to reach Calton Rd. Follow Calton Rd east to the **Palace of Holyroodhouse** (see the Things to See & Do chapter), and finish the walk here if you're tired. Otherwise turn right on Horse Wynd, then go left and right on Queen's Drive, cross the road and follow the footpath that angles leftwards up the hill. At the top of the rise, the main path turns southwards into the flat-bottomed valley of Hunter's Bog; bear left on an unsurfaced footpath that climbs gently along the foot of the crags called Long Row. Where the path forks, keep to the higher, left fork that eventually climbs steeply up some steps to a saddle; turn right, and make the final short climb to the rocky summit of **Arthur's Seat** (251m).

After taking in the view, descend easily eastwards to the road at Dunsapie Loch (Map 1). Turn right and follow Queen's Drive around the southern side of the hill, above Duddingston Loch, to a point just below the southern end of Salisbury Crags (Map 5); from here, you can return to Holyrood by crossing the little saddle northwards into Hunter's Bog, or climbing up left and following the Radical Road along the foot of Salisbury Crags.

Walk 4: Cramond to Queensferry

This delightful 6½-mile hike takes you along riverbank and seashore and through the attractive parkland of Dalmeny Estate. Allow half a day.

Take bus No 40 or 41 northbound from The Mound or Hanover St, or westbound from the western part of George St or Charlotte Square; ask the driver to let you off at the bus stop near Brae Park Rd in Cramond. From the bus stop walk back the way you came and turn right on Brae Park Rd (there's a cycle route signpost marked 'Queensferry 4 miles'). Five minutes of gentle downhill walking leads to a fork beside the River Almond. A left turn leads in a few metres to the **Old Cramond Brig** (c.1500) – the white cottage at the far end was formerly the toll house. Retrace your steps and take the right fork, Dowie's Mill Lane, which becomes a footpath along the bank of the river.

The riverside walk continues for 1¼ miles to the village of **Cramond** (see Edinburgh's Villages in the Things to See & Do chapter), at one point climbing high above the river via a long flight of steps. At Cramond, take the rowing-boat ferry across the mouth of the River Almond – there has been a ferry here since at least 1556 – and follow the signposted coastal path through Dalmeny Estate. About five minutes' walk from the ferry is **Eagle Rock**, a sandstone crag jutting out from the shore; on it sits the carved figure of an eagle, which dates from Roman times. Another 20 minutes of walking takes you to Dalmeny House, from which it's an hour's hike to the Hawes Inn in **South Queensferry** (see the Things to See & Do chapter).

At the Hawes Inn, you can walk up a path directly under the Forth Bridge (it starts from the main road, just east of the pub) to Dalmeny train station in less than 10 minutes; from here there are frequent trains back to Edinburgh (15 minutes).

Places to Stay

A boom in hotel building has seen Edinburgh's tourist capacity swell markedly in recent years, but you can guarantee that the city will still be packed to the gills during the Festival and Fringe period (August) and over Hogmanay/New Year. If you want a room during these periods, book as far in advance as possible. In general, it's best to book ahead at Easter and between mid-May and mid-September. Accommodation might also be in short supply during the Royal Highland Show (late June) and at weekends when international rugby matches are being played at Murrayfield (two or three weekends from January to March).

If you are having trouble finding a vacant room for the Festival period, try Festival Beds (☎ 225 1101, w www.festivalbeds .co.uk), which specialises in matching visitors with B&Bs during August only.

If you arrive in the city without a room, there are several agencies that can help. The Edinburgh and Scotland Information Centre's booking service (☎ 473 3800) will try and find a room to suit, and will charge you a £4 fee if successful. If you have the time, get hold of its free accommodation brochure, the *Edinburgh Holiday Guide*, and ring round yourself.

For a £5 fee, three branches of Thomas Cook will make hotel reservations: the Edinburgh airport office (☎ 333 5119); the office (☎ 557 0905) in Waverley Steps near the TIC; and the office (☎ 557 0034) on Platform 1 of Waverley train station.

In the following sections, the price breakdown is based on the cost per person for bed and breakfast, sharing a double room. Budget is less than £25; Mid-Range is between £25 and £50; and Top End is more than £50.

PLACE TO STAY – BUDGET
Camping
Edinburgh has two well-equipped camp sites reasonably close to the city centre.

Edinburgh Caravan Club Site (☎ 312 6874, Marine Drive) Bus: 8A from North Bridge or Broughton St. Pitches £2-3 plus £3.75-4.75 per person. Overlooking the Firth of Forth, 5 miles north-west of the city centre, this site opens year-round.

Mortonhall Caravan Park (☎ 664 1533, fax 664 5387, w www.meadowhead.co.uk mortonhall, 38 Mortonhall Gate, Frogston Rd East) Map 1 Bus: No 11 from Princes St (west bound). Pitches £9-13.25. Located in attractive parkland 5 miles south-east of the centre, Mortonhall has an on-site shop, bar and restaurant and opens March to October.

SYHA Hostels
The Scottish Youth Hostels Association (SYHA; ☎ 01786-891400, reservations ☎ 0870-155 3255, fax 891333, w www.syha .org.uk, 7 Glebe Crescent, Stirling FK8 2JA) runs around 80 hostels throughout Scotland, including four in Edinburgh.

You need to be a member of SYHA or Hostelling International (HI) – if not, you can join on the spot at any SYHA hostel. Senior membership (for those aged 18 and over) costs £6 and junior membership (for those aged 17 and under) costs £2.50 (under-5s are not allowed). Breakfast is included in the prices given below.

Bruntsfield Youth Hostel (☎ 447 2994, 7 Bruntsfield Crescent) Map 5 Bus: No 11 or 16 from Princes St (get off at Forbes Rd) Seniors £9.75-11, juniors £8.50-9.75. Situated in an attractive location overlooking a park, the hostel was renovated in June 2000. New facilities include email access and computer games. It's about 2½ miles from Waverley train station.

Eglinton Youth Hostel (☎ 337 1120, 18 Eglinton Crescent) Map 2 Seniors £12-14, juniors £10.50-12.50. This hostel is a mile west of Waverley train station. It's a pleasant place, but can get a bit crowded and noisy, and the kitchen and bathroom facilities have trouble coping with a full house.

The *Central Youth Hostel (☎ 556 5566, 11-2 Robertson's Close, Cowgate)* Map 8 and the *Pleasance Youth Hostel (☎ 668*

3423, New Arthur Place) **Map 3** are both open in July and August only and charge the same prices as the Bruntsfield Youth Hostel.

Independent Hostels

There's a growing number of independent backpackers hostels, many of them right in the town centre. Most have 24-hour access and no curfew.

Near Waverley Station The following places are within five minutes' walk of Edinburgh's main train station.

City Centre Tourist Hostel (☎ 556 8070, fax 220 5141, **w** *www.edinburghhostels .com, 3rd floor, 5 West Register St)* **Map 3** Beds £10-18. The City Centre is a small (40-odd beds), clean and bright hostel, with pine-wood bunks and comfortable mattresses in four-, six-, eight- and 10-bed dorms. There's a small kitchen, a TV lounge and a laundry (£3 per load).

St Christopher's Inn (☎ 020-7407 1856, fax 7403 7715, **w** *www.st-christophers.co .uk, 9-13 Market St)* **Map 8** Dorm beds from £12. The closest hostel to Waverley train station, 108-bed St Christopher's is just across the street from the Market St entrance. The price includes a continental breakfast.

Edinburgh Backpackers Hostel (☎ 220 1717, fax 539 8695, **w** *www.hoppo.com, Cockburn St)* **Map 8** Dorm beds/doubles £11.50/35. Just up the hill from St Christopher's, Edinburgh Backpackers is another clean and bright hostel.

Old Town These hostels are right in the heart of things, and close to pubs and clubs.

Brodie's Backpacker Hostel (☎/fax 556 6770, **w** *www.brodieshostels.co.uk, 12 High St)* **Map 8** Dorm beds weekday/weekend July-Sept £13.90/15.90, Dec-Apr £9.90/ 11.90, rest of year £11.90/13.90. Brodie's is a small (50 beds), friendly place ten minutes' walk from Waverley train station. It has four dorms (three mixed and one women-only) with hotel-quality mattresses and duvets, a kitchen and a cosy lounge area with a fireplace. There is no telly, which makes for good socialising. They'll wash, dry and fold your laundry for £3.50 per load.

The following three places are all run by Scotland's Top Hostels (**w** www.scotlands-top-hostels.com). All hostels charge £10.50 to £12.50 for a dorm bed, depending on the season.

High Street Hostel (☎ 557 3984, fax 556 2981, **e** *high-street@scotlands-top-hostels .com, 8 Blackfriars St)* **Map 8** This long-established and well-equipped hostel is housed in a 17th-century building. It has a reputation as a party place, so if you're not in the party mood you might find it noisy.

Royal Mile Backpackers (☎ 557 6120, fax 556 3999, **e** *rmb@scotlands-top-hostels.com, 105 High St)* **Map 8** This is a small and cosy place that shares its facilities with nearby High Street Hostel.

Castle Rock Hostel (☎ 225 9666, fax 226 5078, **e** *castlerock@scotlands-top-hostels .com, 15 Johnston Terrace)* **Map 8** With its bright, spacious, single-sex dorms, superb views and friendly staff, the 200-bed Castle Rock has prompted plenty of positive feedback from travellers. It has a great location only a minute's walk from the castle, Internet access for £1 per hour, laundry for £2.50 per load, and big-screen video nights.

West End The following are 20 minutes' walk west of Waverley train station – if you're arriving by train from Glasgow, get off at Haymarket station; it is much closer.

Belford Hostel (☎ 225 6209, fax 539 8695, 6 Douglas Gardens) **Map 2** Dorm beds £11.50-14. Housed in a converted church, the Belford is under the same management as Edinburgh Backpackers. Although some people have complained of noise – there are only thin partitions between rooms, and no ceilings – it's well run and cheerful with good facilities.

Palmerston Lodge (☎/fax 220 5141, **w** *www.rooms-in-edinburgh.co.uk, 25 Palmerston Place)* **Map 2** Dorm beds £10-15, private rooms £25-50. Situated in a listed building on the corner of Chester St, this quiet hostel-cum-B&B has no bunks, only single beds, and there are showers and toilets on every floor. The rates include a continental breakfast – there are no kitchen facilities for guests.

Marchmont Although Marchmont is a bit of a hike from Waverley (25 minutes) it's a very pleasant neighbourhood, away from the bustle of the Royal Mile.

Argyle Backpackers (☎ 667 9991, fax 662 0002, W www.argyle-backpackers.co .uk, 14 Argyle Place) **Map 5** Dorm beds £10-15, doubles £15-20. The Argyle is a hostel with a slightly upmarket feel; the dorms and doubles are well kept, and there is a comfortable lounge, a conservatory and a pleasant garden.

University Accommodation

Edinburgh has a large student population and during vacations universities and colleges offer accommodation in student halls of residence. The majority are a fair way from the centre and cost as much as lower-end, more central B&Bs. Most offer comfortable, functional single bedrooms with shared bathroom facilities. Increasingly, however, there are rooms with private bathroom, twin and family units, self-contained flats and shared houses. Full-board, half-board, B&B and self-catering options are available. Rooms are usually available from late June to late September.

Pollock Halls of Residence (☎ 0800-028 7118, fax 667 7271, W www.edinburgh first.com, 18 Holyrood Park Rd) **Map 5** Singles (with breakfast) from £23.90. This is a modern complex belonging to Edinburgh University, with 1200 rooms (500 en suite). Busy and often noisy, but close to the city centre, Pollock Halls has Arthur's Seat as a backdrop.

Heriot-Watt University (☎ 451 3669, fax 451 3199, W www.ecc.scot.net, Riccarton) B&B £23-30 per person. The Heriot-Watt campus is set in attractive parkland 6 miles west of Edinburgh. There are 200 beds with en-suite facilities available during term time, augmented by 1000 more rooms during summer vacation.

Napier University (☎ 455 4331, fax 455 4411, W www.napier.ac.uk, 219 Colinton Rd) **Map 4** Flats £300-460 per week. Napier lets out self-catering flats for four to five people year-round. Some have disabled access and all have free car parking.

Queen Margaret College (☎ 317 3310, fax 317 3256, W www.qmced.ac.uk/ conference, 36 Clerwood Terrace, Corstorphine) Beds from £17.50. QMC – located 3 miles west of the centre near Edinburgh Zoo – offers 300 bedrooms (with shared bathrooms) and 37 flats from late May to August.

B&Bs & Hotels

Old Town Apart from backpacker hostels, the only budget accommodation in Old Town is in chain hotels.

Edinburgh (City Centre) Premier Lodge (☎ 0870-700 1370, fax 700 1371, W www .premierlodge.com, 94 Grassmarket) **Map 8** Rooms from £49.95. The Premier Lodge is a budget chain hotel with a great Old Town location. Rooms are small but comfy, and can sleep up to two adults and two children. Breakfast is not included.

Travelodge (☎ 557 6281, fax 557 3681, 33 St Mary's St) **Map 8** Rooms £49.95. Yet another centrally located budget hotel, convenient for the Royal Mile and Cowgate's pubs and clubs, the Travelodge's twin rooms accommodate up to two adults and two kids.

New Town There are a couple of reasonably priced guesthouses on the northern edge of New Town.

Marrakech Guest House (☎ 556 4444, fax 557 3615, e marr@rapidial.co.uk, 30 London St) **Map 3** B&B £20-30. The friendly, family-run Marrakech is handy for New Town and for Broughton St's nightlife. There's an excellent Moroccan restaurant in the basement.

Dene Guest House (☎ 556 2700, fax 557 9876, e deneguesthouse@yahoo.com, 7 Eyre Place) **Map 3** B&B from £19.50. The Dene is a friendly and informal guesthouse set in a charming Georgian town house.

Haymarket This is a convenient area for the West End and Princes St.

Edinburgh City Travel Inn (☎ 228 9819, fax 228 9836, W www.travelinn.co.uk, 1 Morrison Link) **Map 2** Rooms £49.95. Part of the Travel Inn budget chain, this place is sleek, modern and comfortable, and is only three minutes' walk from Haymarket train station. Rooms take up to two adults and two children but breakfast is not included.

Newington There are lots of budget B&Bs in Newington, about a mile and a half south of Prince St.

Avondale Guest House (☎/fax 667 6779, e *isabel.fraser@breathemail.net, 10 South Gray St)* **Map 5** B&B £18-30. The friendly, family-run Avondale is in a quiet, residential street with private parking, close to a main bus route into town.

Grange Guest House (☎/fax 667 2125, e *ash252@email.msn.com, 2 Minto St)* **Map 5** B&B £18-40. Near the corner of Salisbury Rd and convenient for the centre, this is a two-storey terrace house with TV in all rooms.

Kenvie Guest House (☎ 668 1964, fax 668 1926, w *www.kenvie.co.uk, 16 Kilmaurs Rd)* **Map 5** B&B £20-32. Situated in a quiet side street but close to a main bus route, the Kenvie is bright and welcoming, with TV and coffee in all rooms.

Pilrig Guesthouses abound along Pilrig St, about 20 minutes' walk north-eastwards from Princes St.

Balmoral Guest House (☎ 554 1857, fax 553 5712, e *mpimbert@aol.com, 32 Pilrig St)* **Map 6** B&B £20-30. Travellers have recommended this comfortable B&B located in an elegant Georgian terrace.

The seven-bedroom *Barrosa Guest House* (☎ 554 3700, 21 Pilrig St), the lovely Victorian *Balquhidder Guest House* (☎ 554 3377, 94 Pilrig St) and the larger *Balfour House* (☎ 554 2106, fax 478 2600, 92 Pilrig St) have similar room rates to the Balmoral.

Leith Several new hotels have been built in Leith in recent years.

Travel Inn (☎ 555 1570, fax 554 5994, w *www.travelinn.co.uk, 51-3 Newhaven Place)* **Map 1** Rooms £40.95. Part of the Travel Inn budget hotel chain, this branch overlooks Newhaven Harbour, about 20 minutes by bus from the city centre. It has good parking facilities.

PLACES TO STAY – MID-RANGE
Old Town

Ibis Hotel (☎ 240 7000, fax 240 7007, w *www.ibishotel.com, 6 Hunter Square)* **Map 8** Rooms £60. A spruce, modern chain hotel just off the Royal Mile, the Ibis offers a flat room rate that includes a self-service breakfast buffet.

New Town

rick's (☎ 622 7800, fax 622 7801, w *www.ricksedinburgh.co.uk, 55a Frederick St)* **Map 3** Rooms £105.75. Describing itself as 'not a hotel', just a restaurant with rooms (10 of them), rick's was voted one of the world's coolest places to stay by *Condé Nast Traveller* magazine. All walnut and designer fabrics – niiiiccccce...

Sibbet House (☎ 556 1078, fax 557 9445, w *www.sibbet-house.co.uk, 26 Northumberland St)* **Map 3** Doubles £90-110. With five tastefully decorated rooms in a range of styles and a magnificent breakfast menu, Sibbet House is more personal and homely than most B&Bs – you might even be treated to an impromptu bagpipe recital by your host.

Calton Hill

Ailsa Craig Hotel (☎ 556 1022, ☎/fax 556 6055, w *www.townhousehotels.co.uk, 24 Royal Terrace)* **Map 3** B&B £25-45. Many of the elegantly furnished rooms in the Ailsa Craig – an 1820 Georgian town house – have grand views towards the Firth of Forth.

Carlton Greens Hotel (☎ 556 6570, fax 557 6680, e *carltongreens@british-trust-hotels.com, 2 Carlton Terrace)* **Map 3** Singles £35-60, doubles £70-90. Set at the leafy, eastern end of Calton Hill, the flower-bedecked Carlton Greens is a quiet, relaxing place with views of Arthur's Seat.

Greenside Hotel (☎ 557 0121, ☎/fax 557 0022, w *www.townhousehotels.co.uk, 9 Royal Terrace)* **Map 3** B&B £22.50-50. The 15 huge rooms here are each furnished differently, and all have en-suite facilities.

West End & Haymarket

Dunstane House Hotel (☎/fax 337 6169, w *www.dunstanehousehotel.co.uk, 4 West*

Hotels with a History

A number of Edinburgh's most atmospheric hotels are housed in interesting historic buildings.

Bank Hotel (☎ 622 6800, fax 622 6822, ⓔ bank@festival-inns.co.uk, 1 South Bridge) **Map 8** Singles/doubles from £85/100. The Bank Hotel, on the corner of the Royal Mile, is in an imposing, neoclassical building dating from 1923. Formerly a bank (surprise, surprise), it has nine elegant rooms themed around famous Scots, including Robert Burns, RL Stevenson and Charles Rennie Mackintosh.

Malmaison Hotel (☎ 468 5000, fax 468 5002, ⓔ edinburgh@malmaison.com, 1 Tower Place, Leith) **Map 6** Singles/doubles from £130. This stylish, award-winning hotel, located in a 19th-century Seaman's Mission in Leith, has an attractive waterfront location and an excellent French brasserie (see the Places to Eat chapter).

The Point Hotel (☎ 221 5555, fax 221 9929, Ⓦ www.point-hotel.co.uk, 34 Bread St) **Map 3** Singles/doubles from £95. Housed in the beautiful former showrooms of the St Cuthbert Co-operative Association (built in 1937), The Point is famous for its striking contemporary interior design.

The Scotsman Hotel (☎ 556 5565, fax 652 3652, Ⓦ www.thescotsmanhotelgroup.co.uk, 20 North Bridge) **Map 8** Singles/doubles from £150. The former offices of The Scotsman – opened in 1904 and hailed as 'the most magnificent newspaper building in the world' – are now home to Edinburgh's newest luxury hotel. The rooms on the northern side enjoy superb views over New Town and Calton Hill.

Simpsons Hotel (☎ 622 7979, fax 622 7900, Ⓦ www.simpsons-hotel.com, 79 Lauriston Place) **Map 5** Singles/doubles from £80/90. Nope, nothing to do with Bart and Homer. Dating from 1879, and now tastefully restored and redecorated, Simpsons was originally the Edinburgh Royal Maternity Hospital, and is named after James Young Simpson (1811–70), a pioneer in the use of anaesthetics. It's good value but there's no bar or restaurant.

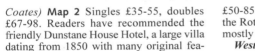

Coates) **Map 2** Singles £35-55, doubles £67-98. Readers have recommended the friendly Dunstane House Hotel, a large villa dating from 1850 with many original features including beautiful rooms with four-poster beds. Parking is available.

Greens Hotel (☎ 337 1565, fax 346 2990, 24 Eglinton Crescent) **Map 2** Singles/doubles from £55/90. This hotel occupies four terrace houses and caters mostly to business people, but it's reasonably priced.

The Original Raj (☎ 346 1333, fax 337 6688, ⓔ originalrajhotel@aol.com, 6 West Coates) **Map 2** Rooms £35-55 per person. Enjoy some oriental splendour at the Raj – Edinburgh's only Indian-themed hotel. It has 17 colourfully decorated rooms and must be the only hotel in the city where you can get samosas for breakfast.

Rothesay Hotel (☎ 225 4125, fax 220 4350, Ⓦ www.rothesay-hotel.com, 8 Rothesay Place) **Map 2** Singles £45-65, doubles

£50-85. Located in a quiet, central street, the Rothesay has pleasant, spacious rooms, mostly en suite, and fantastic breakfasts.

West End Hotel (☎ 225 3656, fax 220 5141, Ⓦ www.rooms-in-edinburgh.co.uk, 35 Palmerston Place) **Map 2** Singles/doubles from £40/60. Renowned as a home-from-home for city-bound Highlanders, the West End has eight good-value rooms above a lively lounge bar.

Stockbridge

Christopher North House Hotel (☎ 225 2720, fax 220 4706, Ⓦ www.christophernorth.co.uk, 6 Gloucester Place) **Map 3** B&B £30-70. This is a small, elegant boutique hotel set in a lovely Georgian building, handy for the shops and restaurants in Stockbridge and walks along the Water of Leith.

Six Mary's Place Guest House (☎ 332 8965, fax 468 2661, Ⓦ www.sixmarysplace.co.uk, 6 Mary's Place, Raeburn

Place) **Map 2** B&B £28-35. Six Mary's Place is an attractive Georgian town house that was fully refurbished in 2001. It caters to vegetarians and has some nice touches, such as free coffee and newspapers in the lounge and Internet data points in the rooms

Wayfarer Guest House (☎/fax 556 3025, **w** *www.wayfarergh.co.uk, 5 Eyre Place)* **Map 3** Singles £30-35, doubles £50-60, triples £65-75. A newly renovated Georgian town house with 10 rooms (all with en suite and TV), the Wayfarer does great breakfasts and is only 10 minutes' walk from Princes St.

Lothian Rd & Tollcross

Amaryllis Guest House (☎/fax 229 3293, **e** *ghamaryllis@aol.com, 21 Upper Gilmore Place)* **Map 5** Singles/doubles £25-35/36-60. The gay-friendly Amaryllis has five rooms, all with TV and some with en-suite facilities. There's private parking out front, and Princes St is only 10 to 15 minutes' walk away.

Ballarat Guest House (☎ 229 7024, fax 622 1265, 14 Gilmore Place) **Map 5** B&B from £28. Named after a former gold-mining town in Australia, the Ballarat is a small (five rooms) and friendly family guesthouse with a no-smoking policy.

Herald House Hotel (☎ 228 2323, fax 228 3101, **w** *www.heraldhousehotel.co.uk, 70 Grove St)* **Map 4** Singles £52-57, doubles £60-88. This place has good-value double rooms, all with TV and en suite, close to Haymarket and the theatre district and only 10 minutes' walk from Grassmarket.

Bruntsfield

Aaron Guest House (☎ 229 6459, fax 228 5807, **w** *www.aaron-guesthouse.com, 16 Hartington Gardens)* **Map 4** Singles £35-50, doubles £55-85. Located at the end of the street, this comfortable and friendly place is handy for drivers as it has a private car park. It is nonsmoking and caters to vegetarians.

The Greenhouse (☎ 622 7634, **e** *greenhouse_edin@hotmail.com, 14 Hartington Gardens)* **Map 4** B&B £25-40. The Greenhouse is a nonsmoking, wholly vegetarian and vegan guesthouse, and uses organic and

GM-free foods as much as possible. Even the soap and shampoo are free of animal products.

Menzies Guest House (☎/fax 229 4629, **e** *hazim@cableinet.co.uk, 33 Leamington Terrace)* **Map 5** Singles £20-40, doubles £28-60. This is a clean, friendly and well-run place, with seven rooms spread over three floors.

Nova Hotel (☎ 447 6437, fax 452 8126, 5 Bruntsfield Crescent) **Map 5** Singles/ doubles from £58/75. The Nova is in a quiet, three-storey Victorian terrace, with views over Bruntsfield Links at the front and to the Pentland Hills at the back.

Robertson Guest House (☎ 229 2652, fax 221 0130, **w** *www.robertson-guesthouse .com, 5 Hartington Gardens)* **Map 4** B&B £23-50. Tucked away down a quiet back street, the Robertson offers a good range of food in the mornings including yoghurt, fresh fruit and a cooked vegetarian breakfast.

Newington

Fairholme Guest House (☎ 667 8645, fax 668 2435, **w** *www.fairholme.co.uk, 13 Moston Terrace)* **Map 5** Doubles £25-40. A pleasant, quiet Victorian villa with four rooms and free parking, the gay-friendly Fairholme has been recommended by several readers.

Linden House (☎ 667 9050, **e** *linden housegh@aol.com, 13 Mayfield Rd)* **Map 5** Singles/doubles £20-35 per person. Readers have recommended the Linden for its well-appointed rooms (with en suite, TV and coffee-making kit) and friendly, helpful owners.

Salisbury Guest House (☎/fax 667 1264, **e** *brenda.wright@btinternet.com, 45 Salisbury Rd)* **Map 5** B&B £23-35. A semi-detached Georgian villa with 12 rooms, large gardens and private parking, the Salisbury is quiet, comfortable and nonsmoking. It's closed over Christmas and New Year.

Sherwood Guest House (☎/fax 667 1200, fax 667 2344, **e** *sherwood@fastfacts.net, 42 Minto St)* **Map 5** Singles £40-60, doubles £50-70. One of the better B&B guesthouses on Minto St, the Sherwood is a refurbished Georgian villa with some limited off-road parking. It is wholly nonsmoking and has TV in all rooms.

Southside Guest House (☎ *668 4422, fax 667 7771,* W *www.southside guesthouse.co .uk, 8 Newington Rd)* **Map 5** Singles/ £40-50, doubles £70-100. Forget traditional guesthouses – the Southside is deeply trendy and has seven, stylish rooms that just ooze interior design. There's a good cafe too.

Pilrig

Ardmor House (☎*/fax 554 4944,* E *robin@ ardmorhouse.freeserve.co.uk, 74 Pilrig St)* **Map 6** Singles/doubles from £35/50. The gay-friendly Ardmor is a stylishly renovated Victorian house with five en-suite rooms.

Portobello

Robert Burns Guest House (☎ *669 5678,* E *robertburnshotel@aol.com, 41 Abercorn Terrace)* **Map 1** Rooms £18-40. An attractive, twin-gabled villa near Portobello Beach run by a New York couple, the Robert Burns has bright, comfortable rooms with pine furniture; most are en suite.

Leith

Express by Holiday Inn (☎ *555 4422, fax 555 4646,* E *info@hiex-edinburgh .com, Britannia Way, Ocean Drive)* **Map 6** Rooms £59.95. Close to Ocean Terminal and the Scottish Executive, the Express is a big, modern, comfortable hotel with ample free parking. Rooms accommodate up to two adults and two children (aged up to 18).

The Thirty Nine Steps Guest House (☎ *552 1349,* W *www.thirtyninesteps.co .uk, 62 South Trinity Rd)* **Map 1** B&B £22-35. The Thirty Nine Steps is a bright and cheerful, nonsmoking guesthouse, only five minutes' walk from the Botanical Garden and the waterfront. It has ample parking.

PLACES TO STAY – TOP END
Old Town

Apex International Hotel (☎ *300 3456, fax 220 5345,* W *www.apexhotels.co.uk, 31- 35 Grassmarket)* **Map 8** Doubles/twins £120-160. Centrally located and with good business facilities, the modern, 175-room

Apex has a rooftop restaurant and off-street parking.

Crowne Plaza (☎ *0800-027 1022* W *www.crowneplazaed.co.uk, 80 High St)* **Map 8** Singles/doubles from £155/180. This luxury hotel was built in the 1990s but blends well with the Royal Mile's 17th-century architecture. The interior is, nonetheless, as modern as you would expect. Check the Web site for cheaper deals on rooms.

Macdonald Holyrood Hotel (☎ *550 4500, fax 550 4545,* W *www.macdonaldho tels.co.uk, Holyrood Rd)* **Map 3** Doubles £90-166. A new luxury hotel built alongside the site of the new Scottish Parliament, the Macdonald has a 14m indoor pool. Check the Web site for special offers.

Tailor's Hall Hotel (☎*/fax 622 6800,* W *www.festival-inns.co.uk, 139 Cowgate)* **Map 8** Singles/doubles/triples £85/105/130. Tailor's Hall, with bright, modern rooms decorated in blue, pink and natural pine, is located bang in the middle of Edinburgh's clubland, and has three big bars of its own downstairs. Good for partying but not a place for the quiet life.

New Town

Balmoral Hotel (☎ *556 2414, fax 557 3747,* E *reservations@thebalmoralhotel.com, 1 Princes St)* **Map 3** Singles/doubles from £130/150. This 188-room hotel has some of the best accommodation in Edinburgh, including suites with 18th-century decor and superb views of the city. Rooms have two phone lines, a modem point and satellite TV.

Caledonian Hilton Hotel (☎ *459 9988, fax 225 6632,* W *www.caledonianhotel.co .uk, 4 Princes St)* **Map 3** B&B £125-195. An Edinburgh institution, the century-old 'Caley' is a vast, red-sandstone palace of Edwardian pomp and splendour. It has a spa, swimming pool and gym, and full business and conference facilities.

Carlton Hotel (☎ *472 3000, fax 556 2691,* W *www.paramount-hotels.co.uk, 19 North Bridge)* **Map 8** B&B £50-90 per person. Complete with swimming pool and leisure complex, the Carlton has undergone a £7-million renovation and is now one of the city's most luxurious hotels.

George Inter-Continental Hotel (☎ 225 1251, fax 226 5644, W www.edinburgh interconti.com, 19-21 George St) **Map 3** B&B £95-120. With its elegant, Robert Adam facade and sophisticated Le Chambertin restaurant, the George is a very traditional hotel in the heart of New Town.

Hanover Hotel (☎ 226 7576, fax 226 3260, 40 Rose St) **Map 3** Singles/doubles from £90/130. The 96-room Hanover is a modern, welcoming hotel right in the middle of Edinburgh's shopping district.

Old Waverley Hotel (☎ 556 4648, fax 557 6316, W www.paramount-hotels .co.uk, 43 Princes St) **Map 3** Singles/ £60-121, doubles £70-160. This hotel has a prime location opposite the Scott Monument and only two minutes' walk from Waverley train station. Many rooms have castle views.

Roxburghe Hotel (☎ 240 5500, fax 240 5555, 38 Charlotte Square) **Map 3** B&B £48-75. What with one of Edinburgh's most prestigious locations, a recent £12-million facelift (including a new 12-metre pool, sauna and steam room), the very elegant, Georgian-era Roxburghe is simply *the* place to stay, dahhling.

Calton Hill

Royal Terrace Hotel (☎ 557 3222, fax 557 5334, 18 Royal Terrace) **Map 3** B&B £55-65. This is one of the swishest hotels in Edinburgh – in a frilly, valanced sort of way – with rooms full of fine furnishings. It also has an indoor pool and sauna.

A Scotsman's Home is...

...his castle but a Scottish castle can also be your home – at least for a couple of days. There are a number of castles around Edinburgh that offer accommodation to visitors.

Borthwick Castle (☎ 01875-820514, fax 821702, North Middleton, Gorebridge EH23 4QY) Singles/doubles from £80/120. Fifteenth-century Borthwick Castle stands foursquare on a hillside overlooking the Gore Water. At 110-foot tall, it is one of the tallest and most impressive tower-houses in Britain. Mary Queen of Scots sought refuge here in 1567, and the castle walls still bear the scars of cannon fire from the time in 1650 when it was beseiged by Oliver Cromwell's forces. Today it is a luxury hotel with ten 'bedchambers', five of them with four-poster beds. Dinner in the vast, vaulted Great Hall is a memorable experience. Borthwick Castle is 12 miles south-east of Edinburgh, near North Middleton on the A7 road to Galashiels.

Dalhousie Castle (☎ 01875-820153, fax 821936, W www.dalhousiecastle.co.uk, Bonnyrigg, Edinburgh EH19 3JB) Standard singles £105-130, doubles £130-165. Situated on the bank of the River South Esk just 7 miles south-east of Edinburgh city centre, Dalhousie Castle was built in the 15th century for the Ramsay family; it was converted to a hotel in 1972. The castle's 29 rooms include 10 with historical themes – the De Ramseia Suite (double £200-260) has an 18th-century carved oak bed, a stone alcove containing the 500-year-old castle well, and an oak-panelled bathroom with a (considerably more recent) double Jacuzzi. The hotel also has a luxurious spa.

Dundas Castle (☎ 0131-319 2039, fax 319 2068, W www.dundascastle.co.uk, South Queensferry, Edinburgh EH30 9SP) Built in 1818 to the design of William Burn, and incorporating a 15th-century keep, Dundas Castle was originally the seat of the Dundas family. Now the home of Sir Jack Stewart-Clark and his family, you can rent out the castle for a wedding or the ultimate dinner party. There are nine luxurious twin/double rooms with en-suite bathrooms, but you have to take a minimum of four at once – for £1600 per night all in, including free run of the castle for a day. A gourmet dinner will cost from £35 per guest. Alternatively, you can rent the double room in the Boathouse for a romantic hideaway at £300 per night. Dundas Castle is 6 miles west of Edinburgh city centre, just south of South Queensferry.

Parliament House Hotel (☎ *478 4000, fax 478 4001,* [e] *phadams@aol.com, 15 Calton Hill)* **Map 3** Singles/doubles from £90/130. Tucked away on a quiet corner of Calton Hill, the cosily traditional Parliament House is only five minutes' walk from Princes St.

West End
Channings (☎ *315 2226, fax 332 9631,* [w] *www.channings.co.uk, 12-16 South Learmonth Gardens)* **Map 2** Singles/doubles from £125/170. Channings is a charming, Edwardian-style hotel with the feel of a gentleman's club.

Lothian Rd
Sheraton Grand Hotel (☎ *229 9131, fax 229 6254,* [w] *www.sheraton.com, 1 Festival Square)* **Map 3** Rooms £120-170. Rising glumly opposite the Usher Hall on Lothian Rd, the Sheraton is bland on the outside but all elegance and finery within.

Bruntsfield
Bruntsfield Hotel (☎ *229 1393, fax 229 5634,* [w] *www.thebruntsfield.co.uk, 69 Bruntsfield Place)* **Map 5** Singles/doubles £82-95/85-155. The spacious and elegant Bruntsfield, overlooking the Links, has an excellent restaurant (called The Potting Shed), a lively bar and free private parking.

SELF-CATERING
There's plenty of self-catering accommodation in Edinburgh. The minimum stay is usually one week in the summer peak season, three nights or less at other times.

The Scottish Tourist Board and the Edinburgh and Scotland Information Centre (see Tourist Offices in the Facts for the Visitor chapter) can provide listings of self-catering accommodation in Edinburgh and the Lothians. Depending on facilities, location and time of year, prices range from £150 to £750 plus per week. The following prices are for a one-bedroom apartment (sleeping two or three).

Edinburgh Central Apartments (☎ *622 7840, fax 622 7841,* [e] *enquiries@edinburgh-central-apartments.co.uk, Home St)* **Map 5** Apartments £225-325 per week. ECA provides basic but comfortable flats in centrally located Tollcross.

Glen House Apartments (☎ *228 4043, fax 229 8873,* [w] *www.edinburgh-apartments.co.uk, 101 Lauriston Place)* **Map 5** Apartments £290-500 per week. This is a large agency that can provide flats of all sizes and categories throughout Edinburgh.

At the more expensive end of the market are serviced apartments, which can be let by the night and include a daily maid service and house manager. The following prices are for one-bedroom flats.

Royal Garden Apartments (☎ *621 8000, fax 621 8008,* [w] *www.royal-garden.co.uk, York Buildings, Queen St)* **Map 3** Apartments £135-180 per night. These luxurious, central apartments have business facilities, a private garden and access to a nearby health club.

The Knight Residence (☎ *622 8120, fax 622 7363,* [w] *www.theknightresidence.co .uk, 12 Lauriston St)* **Map 3** Apartments £70-130 per night. The Knight has a good central location only a few minutes' walk from Grassmarket. You can even order specific CDs and videos to be waiting in your rooms when you arrive.

Fountain Court Apartments (☎ *622 6677, fax 622 6679,* [w] *www.fountaincourtapartments.com, 123 Grove St)* **Map 4** Apartments £70-85 per night. These places close to Haymarket come with well-equipped kitchens (microwave, dishwasher, washing machine) and free private parking.

LONG-TERM RENTALS
The Edinburgh rental market has boomed in recent years and there is no shortage of rooms, apartments and houses to let. Rates for a single or double room in a shared flat start at around £220 per calendar month in districts such as Tollcross and Marchmont, though £250 to £350 is more common. A one-bedroom flat in the highly desirable New Town would cost at least £500 per month, but you can get a flat with two double bedrooms in Bruntsfield for around £750. If you don't mind travelling into the city, it's possible to find a two-bedroom

house or cottage within an hour's drive of Edinburgh for £500 per month.

The minimum lease on places such as these is usually six months, but there are also many short-term lettings available (usual minimum three nights), especially during the summer and the festival period. Most landlords will demand a security deposit (normally one month's rent) plus a month's rent in advance; some will also ask for some sort of reference.

There are many letting agencies that will find accommodation for you and act as your agent in dealings with landlords. Most have Web sites where you can search for available properties by cost, number of bedrooms and location, including:

Clouds Accommodation Agency (☎ 550 3808, fax 550 3807, W www.clouds.co.uk) 26 Forth St, EH1 3LH

Edinburgh Property Management (☎ 623 2100, fax 623 2101, W www.e-p-m.com) 104 Marchmont Crescent, EH9 1HD

James Gibb Property Management (☎ 229 3481, fax 229 3771, W www.jamesgibb.co.uk) 4 Atholl Place, EH3 8HT

Ryden Lettings (☎ 226 2545, fax 226 2472, W www.rydenlettings.co.uk) 100 Hanover St, EH2 1DR

If you want to find accommodation yourself, check out the property section in the Thursday edition of The Scotsman, or the Flatshare section in The List magazine (see Newspapers & Magazines in the Facts for the Visitor chapter). Hostel noticeboards area also a good place to look.

When you inspect a flat it's wise to take someone else with you, both for safety reasons and for help in spotting any shortcomings. A few things to check before signing a tenancy agreement include: the cost of gas, electricity, phone, TV and how they're to be paid for; whether there's street parking and/or how close the flat is to public transport; the arrangements for cleaning the house or flat; whether you can have friends to stay.

PLACES TO STAY

Places to Eat

FOOD

Traditional Scottish cookery centres around hearty, working-class fare – food cooked by crofters, farmers, fisherfolk and factory workers to provide fuel for a working day and comfort in a cold climate. Herring, oatmeal and potatoes in the Highlands, bread, butter and tea in the city tenements – these were the staples of the working-class diet until well into the 20th century.

Scotland can boast of having some of the finest natural produce in the world, including top-quality beef, lamb, venison, game, salmon, seafood, cheese, potatoes, oats, barley and raspberries. But until as recently as the 1980s, professional chefs in big hotels and 'gourmet' restaurants traditionally looked to France for culinary inspiration. It is only in the last decade that there has been a real upsurge of interest and pride in Scottish produce, and the emergence of a new wave of restaurants promoting it to the public.

It is this top-quality produce that forms the basis of what is now called 'modern Scottish' cuisine. 'Fusion' is the buzz-word and most Edinburgh restaurants calling themselves 'Scottish' take fresh Scottish ingredients and prepare them with a French, Mediterranean or even Asian twist. And as farmhouse cooking and 'peasant cuisine' have gained increasing popularity and respect, many of the old, traditional Scots dishes are getting onto top-end restaurant menus. Haggis has finally become haute cuisine.

Breakfast

Surprisingly few Scots eat porridge, and even fewer eat it in the traditional way – with salt instead of sugar. A typical hotel breakfast will offer a choice of fruit juice, cereal, muesli, yoghurt and fruit, and a fried breakfast, which may include bacon, sausage, egg, black pudding (a sausage made with blood and oatmeal), tomato, mushrooms and potato scones. More upmarket hotels may add kedgeree and grilled kippers (smoked herrings) to the menu. As well as toast, there may be oatcakes to spread your marmalade on.

Cafe breakfasts offer a similar menu plus a choice of filled rolls (bacon or fried egg) and maybe croissants and muffins.

Fast Food

As in England, the traditional provider of take-away food in Scotland is the chip shop. The purveyor of all things deep-fried, the local chippie offers everything from fish and chips (known in Scotland as a fish supper) to deep-fried pies, deep-fried pizza, and (yes, it's true) deep-fried Mars Bars.

Savoury pies include the *bridie* (a pie filled with meat, potatoes and onion) and the Scotch pie (minced mutton with black pepper in a plain round pastry casing – best eaten hot). A *toastie* is a toasted sandwich.

Soups

Scotch broth, made with mutton stock, barley, lentils and peas, is highly nutritious and very tasty, while cock-a-leekie is a hearty soup made with chicken and leeks. Warming vegetable soups include leek and potato soup and lentil soup (traditionally made using ham stock – vegetarians beware!).

Seafood soups include the delicious *cullen skink*, made with smoked haddock, potato, onion and milk, and *partan bree* (crab soup).

Meat & Game

Connoisseurs of steak will salivate at the sight of a thick, tender fillet of world-famous Aberdeen Angus beef, served plain or with a pepper or cream-and-whisky sauce. Dark, gamey venison, often served with a tart sauce of redcurrant or rowan berries, appears on many menus.

Game includes pheasant, grouse (traditionally roasted and served with game chips and fried breadcrumbs), rabbit and hare.

Fish & Seafood

Scottish salmon is famous worldwide but there's a big difference between farmed

Oat Cuisine

oats: a grain, which in England is generally given to horses, but in Scotland appears to support the people.

A Dictionary of the English Language by Samuel Johnson (1709–84)

The most distinctive feature of traditional Scottish cookery is the abundant use of oatmeal. Oats (*Avena sativa*) grow well in the cool, wet climate of Scotland and have been cultivated here for at least two-thousand years. Up to the 19th century, oatmeal was the main source of calories for the rural Scottish population. The farmer in his field, the cattle drover on the road to market, the soldier on the march, all would carry with them a bag of meal that could be mixed with water and baked on a girdle (a flat metal plate) or on hot stones beside a fire.

Long-despised as an inferior foodstuff (see Johnson's sneering description above), oatmeal is enjoying a return to popularity as recent research has proved it to be highly nutritious (high in iron, calcium and B vitamins) and healthy (rich in soluble fibre, which helps to reduce cholesterol).

The best-known Scottish oatmeal dish is, of course, porridge, which is simply oatmeal boiled with water. A lot of nonsense has been written about porridge and whether it should be eaten with salt or with sugar. It should be eaten however you like it – as a child in the 1850s, Robert Louis Stevenson had golden syrup with his – and you can bet that if 18th-century crofters had had any sugar they would have used it.

Oatcakes are another traditional dish that you will certainly come across during a visit to Scotland, usually as an accompaniment to cheese and fruit at the end of a meal. A *mealie pudding* is a sausage-skin stuffed with oatmeal and onion and boiled for an hour or so. Add blood to the mixture and you have a black pudding. *Skirlie* is simply chopped onions and oatmeal fried in beef dripping and seasoned with salt and pepper; it's usually served as a side dish. Trout and herring can be dipped in oatmeal before frying, and it can be added to soups and stews as a thickening agent. It's even used in desserts – toasted oatmeal is a vital flavouring in *cranachan*, a delicious mixture of whipped cream, whisky and raspberries.

almon and the leaner, more expensive, wild fish. Smoked salmon is traditionally dressed with squeezed lemon juice and eaten with fresh brown bread and butter. Trout, the salmon's smaller cousins – whether wild, rod-caught brown trout, or farmed rainbow trout – are delicious fried in oatmeal.

As an alternative to kippers (smoked herrings) you may be offered Arbroath smokies (lightly smoked fresh haddock), traditionally eaten cold. Herring fillets fried in oatmeal are good, if you don't mind picking out a few bones. Mackerel paté and smoked or peppered mackerel (both served cold) are also popular.

Juicy langoustines (also called Dublin Bay prawns), crabs, lobsters, oysters, mussels and scallops are also widely available in Edinburgh.

Cheeses

Processed cheddar is the Scottish cheese industry's main output but there are also many speciality cheese-makers whose products are definitely worth sampling. Many are based on the islands, particularly Arran, Bute, Gigha, Islay, Mull and Orkney. Brodick Blue is a ewes' milk blue cheese made on Arran. Lanark Blue is rather like Roquefort. There are several varieties of cream cheese (Caboc, St Finan, Howgate), which are usually rolled in oatmeal.

Scottish oatcakes make a perfect accompaniment to the cheese board.

Puddings

Traditional Scottish puddings are irresistibly creamy, calorie-enriched concoctions. *Cranachan* is whipped cream, flavoured with whisky and mixed with toasted oatmeal and raspberries. *Atholl brose* is a mixture of cream, whisky and honey flavoured with oatmeal. *Clootie dumpling* is a delicious, rich, steamed pudding filled with currants and raisins.

DRINKS
Nonalcoholic Drinks
In terms of consumption, coffee has recently overtaken tea as Scotland's most popular beverage. In the last five or six years, Edinburgh has been swamped by a gurgling tide of espresso machines as cafes and coffee shops have opened on almost every street corner, dispensing cappuccinos and lattes to a caffeine-craving public. Fortunately, a few old-style tearooms survive where you can still get a decent pot of orange pekoe with which to wash down your shortbread.

Despite having some of the purest tap water in the world, Scotland has been quick to jump aboard the bottled-water bandwagon, with several brands of Scottish mineral water (notably Highland Spring) available in shops, bars and restaurants.

And then there's Irn-Bru (see the boxed text 'The Other National Drink').

Alcoholic Drinks
The legal minimum age for buying alcoholic drinks in Scotland is 18.

Wine, beer and spirits for home consumption are sold in supermarkets and neighbourhood off-licences (liquor stores) rather than bars. Opening hours are generally 10am to 10pm Monday to Saturday and 12.30pm to 8pm on Sunday.

Most restaurants are licensed to sell alcoholic drinks. Those that are not are often advertised as BYO (Bring Your Own) – buy a bottle of wine at an off-licence and take it with you to the restaurant, which usually charges £1 to £3 corkage.

Whisky Scotch whisky (always spelt *without* an 'e' – whiskey *with* an 'e' is Irish or American) is Scotland's best-known product and biggest export. The spirit has been distilled in Scotland since at least the 15th century. See the boxed text 'How to Be

The Other National Drink...

What do Scotland and Peru have in common?

Answer: they are the only countries in the world where a locally manufactured soft drink outsells Coca Cola. In Peru it's Inca Cola but in Scotland it's Barr's Irn-Bru, which commands 25% of the Scottish fizzy-drinks market (Coke has 24%). A Barr's advertising campaign in the 1980s promoted Irn-Bru as 'Scotland's other national drink'.

Barr's have been making soft drinks in Scotland since 1880 but it was in 1901 that they launched a new beverage called 'Iron-Brew' (labelling regulations forced a change of spelling to 'Irn-Bru' in 1946). As with Coke, the recipe (32 ingredients, including caffeine and ammonium ferric citrate – the source of the iron in the name) remains a closely guarded secret known by only two people. Scots swear by its efficacy as a cure for hangovers, which may account for its massive sales. You can even get Irn-Bru along with your Big Mac in Scottish branches of McDonald's.

In recent years Barr's have begun to build their brand overseas, exporting the quirky, humorous and award-winning advertising campaign that positions Irn-Bru drinkers as mischievous and rascally. Irn-Bru is hugely popular in Russia, where it is the third-favourite soft drink after Coke and Pepsi (maybe it's that hangover thing again), and in the Middle East, but it has yet to challenge Coke and Pepsi in the USA. Big Red, beware!

Tasting notes: Colour is a rusty, radioactive orange. Nosing reveals a bouquet of bubble gum, barley sugar and something vaguely citrussy, maybe tangerine? Carbonation is medium, and mouth-feel... well, you can almost feel the enamel dissolving on your teeth.

an Instant Malt Whisky Buff' in the Entertainment chapter.

As well as whiskies, there are whisky-based liqueurs such as Drambuie. If you must mix your whisky with anything other than water try a whisky-mac (whisky with ginger wine). After a long walk in the rain there's nothing better to warm you up.

At a bar, older Scots may order a 'half' or 'nip' of whisky as a chaser to a pint or half-pint of beer (a 'hauf and a hauf'). Only tourists ask for 'Scotch' – what else would you be served in Scotland? The standard measure in pubs is either 25mL or 35mL.

Beer Edinburgh has long been an important centre for brewing, and on many a day you can detect the malty aroma of boiling wort wafting over the city. The Fountain Brewery in Fountainbridge is the biggest in town, turning out passable beers under the McEwan's label, but the Caledonian Brewery in Slateford Rd is the one that is most appreciated by fans of real ale.

The best beers are hand-pumped from the cask and usually served at cellar temperature, which may come as a shock to drinkers used to chilled lager. They have subtle flavours that a cold, chemical lager can't match. Most popular is what the Scots call 'heavy', a dark beer similar to English bitter, though in recent years Deuchars IPA has grown to be one of Edinburgh's most popular pints. Most Scottish brews are graded in shillings so you can tell their strength, the usual range being 60 to 80 shillings (written 0/-). The higher the number – originally the amount of money that was paid in tax on each barrel – the stronger the beer.

Beer is served by the pint (average price in Edinburgh £1.90 to £2.20) or half-pint. Most beers contain from 3% to 5% alcohol by volume.

Wine Good wines from around the world are widely available in shops and restaurants. In supermarkets and off-licences you can expect to pay around £4 to £6 for a bottle of decent wine. In a restaurant the same bottle would cost from £12 to £18.

PLACES TO EAT

In the last few years there has been a huge boom in the number of restaurants and cafes in Edinburgh and there is a wide range of cuisines to choose from. In addition, most pubs serve food, offering either bar meals or a more formal restaurant or both, but be aware that pubs without a restaurant licence are not allowed to serve children under the age of 16. Lunch is generally served from 12.30pm to 2.30pm, dinner from 7pm to 10pm.

The excellent *Edinburgh & Glasgow Eating & Drinking Guide* (£4.95), published annually by *The List* magazine, contains reviews of restaurants, cafes and bars. An interesting new development is the '5pm' Web site (**W** www.5pm.co.uk), which lists last-minute offers from restaurants with tables to spare that evening. Using this service you can find a three-course meal at one of Edinburgh's better restaurants for as little as £10 if you're prepared to eat early or late.

The price gradings in this section are based on the average cost of a two-course dinner for one, excluding drinks – Budget means less than £10, Mid-Range means £10 to £20, and Top End means over £20. Note that many Mid-Range and Top End places offer good-value set lunches that would be graded as Budget or Mid-Range respectively. Some of these are listed in the boxed text 'Lunch for Less' later in the chapter.

PLACES TO EAT – BUDGET
Cafes

Cafe culture has swept through Edinburgh in the last decade and it's as easy to get your daily caffeine fix here as it is in New York or Paris. Most cafes offer some kind of food, from cakes and sandwiches to full-on meals.

Café Barcode (☎ 466 8168, 32 Argyle Place) **Map 5** Open 8am-6pm Mon-Fri, 10am-6pm Sat, 10am-3pm Sun. Cafe Barcode is a little, white corner of coffee heaven tucked in beside an architect's office on this increasingly trendy street. The Italian coffee is the best for miles around, and there are sandwiches, muffins and fresh fruit and yoghurt if you want something to eat. There's Internet access too – on Macs, of course.

Elephant House (☎ 220 5355, 21 George IV Bridge) **Map 8** Open 8am-11pm daily. Counters at the front, tables and views of the castle at the back, and little effigies and

PLACES TO EAT

Best Breakfasts

Edinburgh has lots of cafes where you can kick-start the morning with a shot of caffeine, but the following places provide more substantial fare with which to fortify yourself for a day's clambering among Old Town's closes or a hard schedule of festival-bashing.

Blue Moon Café (☎ 557 0911, 1 Barony St) **Map 3** Breakfast served 11am-4pm Mon-Fri, 9.30am-4pm Sat & Sun. For £5 the Blue Moon will ply you with a full Scottish breakfast including bacon, sausage, egg, mushrooms, tattie scones and baked beans, or its tasty vegetarian equivalent (including veggie sausages).

Café Mediterraneo (☎ 557 6900, 73 Broughton St) **Map 3** Breakfast served 8.30am-11.30am Mon-Fri, 10am-11.30am Sat, 9.30am-4.30pm Sun. The Med serves a full Scottish fry-up for £5.95 or lighter meals, such as a smoked salmon and scrambled-egg croissant, for £3.95.

Elephant's Sufficiency (☎ 220 0666, 170 High St) **Map 8** Breakfast served 8am-noon Mon-Fri, 9am-noon Sat & Sun. A lively, old-style caff with comfy booths and window tables looking onto the Royal Mile, the Elephant offers porridge and cream for £1.85, scrambled egg on toast for £3.50, a continental breakfast (croissant, scone, orange juice and coffee or tea) for £3.95 or the full-fat fry-up for £5.50.

Hadrian's (☎ 557 5000, Balmoral Hotel, 1 Princes St) **Map 3** Breakfast served 7am-10.30am Mon-Sat, 7.30am-11am Sun; brunch served 12.30pm-2.30pm Sun. The regular breakfast menu (£5.95) includes everything from croissants to bacon and egg to eggs Benedict, while the slap-up three-course Sunday brunch (£14.95) is accompanied by live jazz until 4pm.

Montpeliers (☎ 229 3115, 159-161 Bruntsfield Place) **Map 4** Breakfast served 9am-6pm daily. Monty's is a popular hang-out, offering good food all day. Breakfast offerings (£3.25-6.95) include pancakes and maple syrup, French toast, scrambled eggs and a full Scottish fry-up (meat or veggie).

Stir (☎ 221 1155, 248 Morrison St) **Map 2** Open 7.30am-6pm Mon-Fri, 9am-5pm Sat. At Stir you can buy gourmet soups to take away, or sit and slurp at the counter. At breakfast time, they also offer porridge with various flavourings such as honey or maple syrup. Breakfasts cost from £1.25.

Valvona & Crolla Caffè Bar (☎ 556 6066, 19 Elm Row, Leith Walk) **Map 3** Breakfast served 8am-11.30am Mon-Sat. A bright and cheerful cafe tucked upstairs at the back of the famous deli, V&C offers brekkie with an Italian flavour – full *paesano* (meat) or *verdure* (veggie) fry-ups (both £5.95), or deliciously light and crisp *panettone in carrozza* (sweet brioche dipped in egg and fried; £3.75). There are also almond croissants, muesli, yoghurt and fruit, and freshly squeezed orange juice.

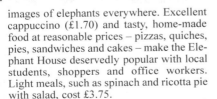

images of elephants everywhere. Excellent cappuccino (£1.70) and tasty, home-made food at reasonable prices – pizzas, quiches, pies, sandwiches and cakes – make the Elephant House deservedly popular with local students, shoppers and office workers. Light meals, such as spinach and ricotta pie with salad, cost £3.75.

Filmhouse Cafe Bar (☎ 229 5932, 88 Lothian Rd) **Map 3** Open 10am-11.30pm Sun-Thur, 10am-12.30am Fri & Sat. Located inside the Filmhouse cinema, the main drawback to this cafe is its lack of windows.

But the coffee (£1.20) and hot chocolate (lots of cream and flaky chocolate topping) are good, as are the cakes, sandwiches and soup of the day. The Filmhouse is quiet in the mornings but gets very busy in the evenings just before a screening.

The Garden Cafe (☎ 624 8624, 17 Rose St) **Map 3** Open 9am-5.30pm Mon-Sat. This attractive, outdoor cafe is in a sunken courtyard at the back of The Dome (see Top End – New Town & Around later). Littered with potted palms strewn beneath the towering stained-glass windows of The Dome' dining room, it becomes a midday sun-trap in summer. A cappuccino costs £1.90 and sandwiches cost £5-5.50.

Kariba Coffee (☎ 220 1818, 160 High St) Map 8 Open 8am-7pm daily. A bright, new addition to the Royal Mile, Kariba offers special deals on its excellent coffee 8am to 10am and 4.30pm to 6pm, Monday to Friday – a regular latte, cappuccino or Americano costs £1.20. Their large cappuccino (£1.70) is big enough to bathe in. Also on the menu are freshly squeezed juices, fruit smoothies and sandwiches.

The Lower Aisle (☎ 225 5147, St Giles Cathedral, High St, Royal Mile) Map 8 Open 8.30am-4.30pm Mon-Fri, 9am-2pm Sun. Hidden in a vault beneath St Giles Cathedral (entrance on the side opposite the Royal Mile), the Lower Aisle is a good place to escape the crowds, except at lunchtime when it's packed with lawyers and secretaries from the nearby courts.

Made In Italy (☎ 622 7328, 42 Grass-market) Map 8 Open 8am-11pm Mon-Thur, 8am-1.30am Fri & Sat, 10am-11pm Sun. Look out for this traditional-style cafe where you can sit inside at the counters or outside at the pavement tables and enjoy real Italian coffee (large cappuccinos cost £1.75) and real Italian ice cream. If you're hungry, they do good pizzas and panini sandwiches too.

Ndebele (☎ 221 1141, 57 Home St) Map Open 10am-10pm daily. This South African cafe is hidden deep in darkest Tollcross, but it is worth seeking out for the changing menu of unusual African dishes (including at least one veggie option), such as a boere-ors sandwich (sausage made with pork, beef and coriander).

Starbuck's (☎ 226 5881, 120b Princes) Map 3 Open 7.30am-8pm Mon-Sat, 8.30am-6pm Sun. You may not approve of their plans for world domination but there's no denying that Starbuck's Princes St flag-ship – reputedly the largest coffee shop in Scotland – enjoys what is probably the best view in the city. Settle down with a large cappuccino (£2.15) and take in the breath-taking panorama of the castle and gardens across the street.

Self-Catering
There are grocery stores and food shops all over the city, many of them open 9am to 10pm daily. Many petrol stations also have shops that sell groceries. *Day & Night* (☎ 221 9059, 141 Lauriston Place) Map 5, *Alldays* (☎ 667 7481, 91-93 Nicolson St) and *Spar* (☎ 346 4493, 37a-39 Dalry Rd) are all open 24 hours a day.

There are several large supermarkets spread throughout the city too. The most central ones are *Safeway* (☎ 556 1190, St James Centre) and *Tesco* (☎ 456 2400, 94 Nicolson St). *Sainsbury's* (☎ 332 0704, 185 Craigleith Rd) has an ATM and stays open until 10pm on Friday and Saturday. The food hall in *Marks & Spencer* (☎ 225 2301, 54 Princes St) Map 3 sells high-quality, ready-cooked meals.

There are also many excellent delicatessens where you can buy fresh produce from all over the world (see the Food & Drink section in the Shopping chapter).

Old Town & Around
Bar Italia (☎ 228 6379, 100 Lothian Rd) Map 3 Pizzas & pastas £6-7.75. Open noon-midnight Mon-Thur, noon-1am Fri & Sat, 5pm-midnight Sun. A classic Italian restaurant of the old school, Bar Italia comes complete with red-and-white check tablecloths, candles in Chianti bottles and smartly dressed, wise-cracking waiters who occasionally burst into song. Good-value Italian nosh and a lively atmosphere make it a popular venue for birthdays and office parties.

Café Odile (☎ 225 1333, 23 Cockburn St) Map 8 Mains £4.95-5.45. Open 10am-5pm Tues-Sat. This attractive white room, tucked away upstairs at the back of the Stills Gallery, provides a cool escape from the bustle of the Royal Mile. Home-cooked French treats include mouth-watering soups, savoury tarts and a chocoholic's paradise of desserts. The set lunch (£6.50-7.90) is available from noon to 2.30pm.

Chinese Home Cooking (☎ 668 4946, 34 West Preston St) Map 5 Mains £3.50-7. Open noon-2pm & 5.30pm-11pm Mon-Fri, 5.30pm-11.30pm Sat & Sun. This long-established, no-nonsense eatery has been serving up good-value, authentic Chinese food for around 25 years now. Menus in Chinese and Japanese, as well as English, show that the place is favoured by people who really know oriental food.

Favorit (☎ 220 6880, 19-20 Teviot Place) **Map 3** Sandwiches £3.65-3.95, salads £4.65-4.95. Open 8am-3am daily. A stylish cafe-bar with a slightly retro feel, Favorit caters for everyone from workers grabbing breakfast on the way to the office, to coffee-slurping students skiving off afternoon lectures, to late-night clubbers with an attack of the munchies. They also do the best bacon butties in town. There's a second branch at 30-32 Leven St in Tollcross.

Khushi's Lothian Restaurant (☎ 556 8996, 16 Drummond St) **Map 8** Mains £3-5. Open noon-3pm & 5pm-9pm Mon-Thur, noon-3pm & 5pm-9.30pm Fri & Sat. Established in 1947, Khushi's is an authentic Punjabi canteen and something of an Edinburgh institution. Its speciality is basic Indian dishes cooked in the traditional way, served with no frills at very low prices. It's not licensed but you can bring your own booze (no corkage) or get a jug of beer from the pub next door.

The Human Be-In (☎ 662 8860, 2-8 West Crosscauseway) **Map 5** Mains £6.50-7.85. Open 11am-1am daily. A stylish cafe-bar with a choice of tables, comfy booths or chill-out sofas, the Be-In has a fancy fusion menu (how about venison sausage with wasabi mash, browned onion and madeira gravy?) with good veggie options. The weekend brunch menu, served 11am to 4pm (£3.95-4.25), includes eggs Benedict and crepes with black pudding and lardons.

Petit Paris (☎ 226 2442, 38-40 Grassmarket) **Map 8** Mains £4.75-8.95. Open noon-3pm & 5.30pm-11pm daily. Closed Sun Oct-Easter. Like the name says, this is a little piece of Paris, complete with check tablecloths, friendly waiters and good value grub – the *moules et frites* (mussels and chips) are excellent. There's a lunch and pre-theatre deal of the plat du jour and a coffee for £5, and from Sunday to Thursday you can bring your own wine (£2 corkage).

New Town & Around

Blue Moon Café (☎ 557 0911, 1 Barony St) **Map 3** Starters £1.95-4.95, mains £4-5.95. Open 11am-10pm Mon-Fri, 9.30am-10pm Sat & Sun. The Blue Moon is the focus of Broughton Street's gay social life, always busy, always friendly, and serving up delicious nachos, salads, sandwiches and baked potatoes. It's famous for its brilliant, home-made hamburgers, which come plain or topped with cheese or chilli sauce, and delicious daily specials such as smoked haddock mornay.

Gurkha Brigade (☎ 557 8855, 9a Antigua St) **Map 3** Starters £1.50-2.95, mains £5.50-9.95. Open noon-2pm & 5pm-11pm Tues-Thur, noon-2pm & 5pm-midnight Fri & Sat, 5pm-11pm Sun. You'll get a warm welcome at the Gurkha, a new Nepalese restaurant near the top of Leith Walk. Sample dishes such as *solukhumbu bheda* (long slices of spiced lamb cooked with ginger, garlic, onion and tomato), from the Everest region in north-eastern Nepal, and Tibetan specialities such as *momo* (steamed dumplings filled with minced pork and served with spicy pickle). The set three-course lunch is only £4.95.

Marrakech (☎ 556 4444, 30 London St) **Map 3** Dinner £11. Open 6pm-10pm Mon-Sat. A friendly and homely little Moroccan restaurant in the basement of the guesthouse of the same name, the Marrakech dishes up delicious *tajines* (a slow-cooked casserole of lamb with almonds and dried fruit, often prunes or apricots) accompanied by home-baked, caraway-scented bread. Round off the meal with a pot of mint tea.

Tampopo (☎ 220 5254, 25a Thistle St) **Map 3** Mains £6.20-7.50. Open noon-2.30pm & 6pm-9pm Tues-Fri, noon-3pm & 6pm-9pm Sat. This tiny, no-frills, one-man-operated Japanese restaurant serves filling noodle dishes for £6.20 to £6.80, and a sushi platter with green tea for £7.50.

Haymarket & Dalry

Guru Balti (☎ 221 1281, 9 Dundee Terrace) **Map 4** Mains £5.95-8.95. Open 5pm-midnight Tues-Sun. The small and friendly Guru Balti provides its leagues of loyal fans

Lunch for Less

In the mid-1980s, a restaurant called Pierre Victoire opened in Victoria St and made a name for itself by serving excellent, three-course lunches for under five pounds. Fifteen years later, after many trials and tribulations, it's still doing just that. In the meantime, many other places have joined it in offering good-value lunches.

The Basement (☎ 557 0097, 10a-12a Broughton St) **Map 3** Food served noon-10.30pm daily. The Basement is a groovy bar with a separate restaurant area. It offers a two-course lunch for only £5.95, from noon to 3pm Monday to Friday. The grub is sort of international – *bruschetta*, nachos, spaghetti, chicken in orange and ginger sauce – but goes Thai on Wednesdays and Mexican at the weekend.

Britannia Spice (☎ 555 2255, 150 Commercial St, Britannia Way) **Map 6** Lunch served noon-2.15pm daily. No, not Geri Halliwell's latest incarnation, but an award-winning curry house with ocean-liner decor, serving a wide range of dishes from northern India, Bangladesh, Nepal, Thailand and Sri Lanka. The waist-widening, all-you-can-eat buffet lunch costs £7.95.

Chinese Home Cooking (☎ 668 4946, 34 West Preston St) **Map 5** Lunch served noon-2pm Mon-Fri. You'll be pushed to find better value than the good, down-to-earth Chinese food served in this basic, no-nonsense restaurant where the three-course set lunch only costs £4.50.

Daniel's Bistro (☎ 553 5933, 88 Commercial St, Leith) **Map 6** Lunch served noon-2.30pm daily. The conservatory at the back often gets packed out on weekdays with suits from the Scottish Executive across the way, so book a table. The cuisine is country French and the set lunch costs £4.95/5.95 for two/three courses.

La P'tite Folie (☎ 225 7983, 61 Frederick St) **Map 3** Lunch served noon-3pm Mon-Sat. This is a delightful little French place whose menu includes the classics – French onion soup, *moules marinières*, coquilles St Jacques – and a range of *plats du jour*. The two-/three-course lunch is a bargain at £5.90/6.90.

The Old Chain Pier (☎ 552 1233, 1 Trinity Crescent) **Map 1** Food served noon-8pm daily. The Old Chain Pier is a lovely little pub overlooking – nay, overhanging – the Firth of Forth on the waterfront near Granton Harbour. The excellent bar menu includes soup of the day for £1.60, a creamy and filling mussel and smoked haddock stew for only £3.95 and a succulent steak and onion baguette with chips for £4.95. The menu of real ales is no less enticing than the food.

Pierre Victoire (☎ 225 1721, 10 Victoria St) **Map 8** Lunch served noon-3pm. The place that launched a thousand cheap-eats, and still one of the best-value restaurants in town, Pierre's three-course set lunch (£4.95) includes a basket of French bread, but potatoes, vegetables and drinks are all extra. A glass of house wine costs £2.30, so ask for a jug of water if you're counting the pennies.

ASA ANDERSSON

with some of the best Pakistani food in Scotland. Delicious *chana puri* (chick-pea curry in fried, unleavened bread) and fiery chicken jalfrezie are favourites. It's small, so book ahead if you want a table at the weekend. If you're ordering a takeaway, better bring a wheelbarrow – the portions are big enough to keep you going for a week.

Taste Good (☎ 313 5588, 67-69 Slateford Rd) **Map 4** Mains £5-8. Open 4.30pm-midnight daily. The Taste Good's downstairs dining area, with its clean lines in pale wood and stainless steel, makes a refreshing change from the usual Chinese restaurant decor. The food matches the interior design in style and taste – the aromatic crispy duck is meltingly sweet, and the beef in black bean sauce has just enough chilli to be pleasantly hot.

PLACES TO EAT – MID-RANGE
Old Town & Around

The Apartment (☎ 228 6456, 7-13 Barclay Place) **Map 5** Mains £5.25-8.95. Open 5.45pm-11pm Mon-Fri, noon-3pm & 5.45pm-11pm Sat & Sun. Cool, classy and almost always full, The Apartment is just too popular for its own good. Fantastic bistro food and a buzzy, busy atmosphere make it hard to get a table. Book in advance – by at least three weeks, preferably – and don't be surprised if you still have to wait. But it's worth being patient for treats such as marinated lamb meatballs with merguez and basil-wrapped goat's cheese, roasted monkfish marinated in yoghurt with sweet red chilli, new potato and spring onion, or deliciously sweet grilled scallops with a smoked salmon and hazelnut butter.

Beluga Canteen & Bar (☎ 624 4545, 30a Chambers St) **Map 8** Starters £3.75-4.50, mains £11.25-15.95. Open noon-3pm & 6pm-10pm daily. New and hip, Beluga caters to the 20-something clubbing crowd, and is correspondingly stylish – all brown leather, slate and steel – and loud. The downstairs bar offers booze-absorbing grub such as nachos (£4.95) or leek and mustard sausages with garlic mash (£5.95), while the sophisticated restaurant has intricate,

culinary confections that take longer to read from the menu than to eat.

blue bar cafe (☎ 221 1222, 10 Cambridge St) **Map 3** Mains £11-13.50. Open noon-3pm & 6pm-11pm Mon-Sat. Set above the foyer of the Traverse Theatre, bright, white blue is a lighter and less formal version of The Atrium (see Places to Eat – Top End later). The food is simple, but perfectly cooked and presented – try rump of lamb with pureed peas and bubble and squeak – and the atmosphere loud and chatty – all those luvvies from the theatre downstairs.

Buffalo Grill (☎ 667 7427, 12-14 Chapel St) **Map 5** Mains £6.95-12.95. Open noon-2pm & 6pm-10.15pm Mon-Fri, 6pm-10.15pm Sat, 5pm-10pm Sun. The BG is cramped, noisy, fun and always busy, so book ahead. An American-style menu offers burgers, steaks and side orders of fries and onion rings, along with fish and chicken dishes, prawn tempura and the vegetarian Andybub burger. But steaks are the main event – from eight to 16 ounces – cooked perfectly to order. You can have your steak plain or marinated (lemon pepper or teriyaki) and served as it is or with a choice of extras from jalapeno chillis to oysters. You can buy booze in the restaurant or bring your own wine (£1 corkage).

Café Hub (☎ 473 2067, Castlehill, Royal Mile) **Map 3** 2-/3-course lunch £8/10. Open 9.30am-10pm Tues-Sat, 9.30am-6pm Sun & Mon. A Gothic hall beneath the Tolbooth Kirk – now home to the Edinburgh Festival offices – has been transformed with some zingy yellow paint, cobalt blue furniture and lots of imagination into this bright and breezy bistro. Drop in for some cake and cappuccino, or try something more filling sweetcorn and smoked sausage chowder (£2.85) or a hummus and roast veg sandwich (£3.65) – or linger over the good value set lunch.

Le Sept (☎ 225 5428, 7 Fishmarket Close, High St) **Map 8** Mains £6.50-12.95. Open noon-2pm, 6pm-10.30pm Mon-Thu, noon-11.30pm Fri, noon-11pm Sat, noon-10pm Sun. French bistro Le Sept is a hidden gem, stashed away down a steep cobbled alley off the Royal Mile. Enjoy xcellent crepes, daily seafood specials and lovely little suntrap of a terrace.

Metro (☎ 474 3466, 31-35 Grassmarket) Map 8 Starters £2.95-4.95, mains £7.50-4.50. Open noon-3pm & 6pm-10pm daily. ¹epending on your tastes, Metro is either esperately stylish or looks a bit like a :hool canteen. Either way, the international ¹enu is way better than anything you had at :hool – jalfrezie-marinated chicken, monk-sh satay, sweet and sour deep-fried tofu – ¹d the view of the castle is fantastic.

Mother's Mexican Grill (☎ 662 0772, ⁷7-109 St Leonard's St) Map 5 Starters ¹.25, mains £12.25. Open 6pm-10pm Sun Tues-Thur, 6pm-10.30pm Fri & Sat. ¹other's is a cool Mexican restaurant, with ¹ripped-pine furniture and petrol-blue walls. s well as the usual Mexican offerings of the ¹chilada and quesadilla variety there are ¹me surprises on the menu – how about ¹icken breast stuffed with onion and chori-¹n mousse, or Mexican paella? Expect huge ¹lpings, and very moreish margaritas.

Pancho Villa's (☎ 557 4416, 240 Canon-¹te) Map 8 Mains £5.95-8.95. Open noon-¹30pm & 6pm-10pm Mon-Thur, noon-¹.30pm Fri & Sat, 6pm-10.30pm Sun. ¹ith a Mexican manager and lots of Latin-¹nerican staff, it's not surprising that Pan-¹o's is one of the most authentic-feeling ¹exican places in town. It's also the city's ¹st-value Mexican, with a set lunch for £5. ¹e dinner menu includes delicious steak ¹itas and great vegetarian spinach enchi-¹las. It's often busy, so book ahead.

The Point Hotel (☎ 221 5555, 34 Bread Map 3 Lunch £7.90, dinner £12.90. ¹en noon-2pm & 6pm-10pm Mon-Wed, ¹on-2pm & 6pm-10pm Thur & Fri, 6pm-¹pm Sat. The Point's, now legendary, ¹o-course lunch and three-course dinner ¹nus offer exceptional value – delicious ¹ottish/international cuisine served in an ¹gant room with crisp, white linen and ¹entive service. They must make their ¹fit on the drinks, though the house wine ¹ts only £10.95 per bottle. Reservations ¹ strongly recommended.

Rainbow Arch (☎ 221 1288, 8-16 Mor-¹n St) Map 3 Mains £6.50-10.50. Open noon-11.30pm daily. It's always a sign of a good Chinese restaurant when you see members of the local Chinese community eating there, and you'll see them eating regularly at the Arch. The menu is more adventurous than most and even the standard dishes, such as lemon chicken, are a cut above the usual.

Ho Ho Mei Noodle Shack (☎ 221 1288, 8-16 Morrison St) Map 3 Mains £4.50-8.50. Open 5.30pm-1.30am Mon-Sat. The Ho Ho Mei, upstairs from the Rainbow Arch and under the same management, serves big bowls of noodles and tasty Chinese hot-pot dishes to eat in or take away.

Songkran (☎ 225 7889, 24a Stafford St) Map 2 Mains £5.25-8.95. Open noon-2.30pm & 5.30pm-11pm Mon-Sat, 5.30pm-11pm Sun. Better book a table and be ready for a squeeze to get in to this tiny New Town basement. The reason for the crush is some of the best Thai food in town – try the tender *yang* (marinated and barbecued beef, chicken or prawn), the crisp and tart orange chicken, or the chilli-loaded warm beef salad. This place serves the real thing.

Sukhothai (☎ 229 1537, 23 Brougham Place) Map 5 Starters £4.15-6.95, mains £6.95-7.70. Open noon-2.30pm & 6pm-11pm daily. This unassuming but attractive Tollcross restaurant serves up authentic, good-value Thai food, including a fiery *tom yum goong* (hot and sour soup with prawns) and a creamy, coconutty *gaeng phed* (mild, red curry). The Sunday lunchtime buffet – all you can eat for £9.95 – is excellent value.

Suruchi (☎ 556 6583, 14a Nicolson St) Map 8 Mains £6.95-12.95. Open noon-2pm & 5.30pm-11.30pm daily, closed Sun lunch. A laid-back Indian eatery with warm buff walls, hand-made turquoise tiles, lazy ceiling fans and chilled out jazz guitar, the Suruchi offers a range of exotic dishes as well a traditional tandoori fare. Try *shakuti* from Goa (lamb or chicken with coconut, poppy seeds, nutmeg and chilli) or vegetarian *kumbhi narial* (mushrooms, coconut and coriander). An amusing touch is provided by the menu descriptions – they're translated into broad Scots ('a beezer o' a curry this... gey nippie oan the tongue').

The Tower (☎ 225 3003, Museum of Scotland, Chambers St) **Map 8** Starters £4.95-9.95, mains £8.95-18.95. Open noon-11pm daily. Chic and sleek, with a keek at the castle oot the windae, the trendy Tower, set atop the new museum building, offers grand views and a menu of quality Scottish food simply prepared – try half a dozen Loch Fyne oysters followed by an Aberdeen Angus steak. The theatre-supper menu costs only £12 for two courses.

New Town & Around

Café Marlayne (☎ 226 2230, 76 Thistle St) **Map 3** Starters £1.50-5.90, mains £8.60-11.90. Open noon-2pm & 6pm-10pm Tues-Sat. All weathered wood and warm yellow walls, little Café Marlayne is a cosy nook offering French farmhouse cooking – *escargots* with garlic and parsley, oysters with lemon and tabasco, *boudin noir* (black pudding) with sauteed apples, peppered duck breast with balsamic vinegar – at very reasonable prices.

Café Mediterraneo (☎ 557 6900, 73 Broughton St) **Map 3** Starters £4, mains £8. Open 8am-10pm Mon-Sat, 9.30am-4.30pm Sun. Closes at 6pm Mon-Thur from Oct-Mar. Blond-wood furniture in a bright, busy dining room behind the deli counter makes the Med a favourite hang-out for local residents. The food, mostly inspired by Italy and the south of France, is good value and tasty too.

Channings (☎ 315 2226, 12-16 South Learmonth Gardens) **Map 4** 2-/3-course dinner £19.50/24.50. Open 12.30pm-2pm & 6.30pm-9.30pm Mon-Thur, 12.30pm-2pm & 6.30-10pm Fri & Sat, 6.30pm-9.30pm Sun. Channings has a bit of a split personality. The main dining room at the front, with its dark wood, striped wallpaper and station waiting-room clock, is an elegant, Edwardian gentleman of vaguely military bearing, but the conservatory out the back – pale and interesting – is a 1990s trendy intellectual. The Scottish-Mediterranean food is strong on seafood and game and similarly blends the traditional with the modern. Try this place for something unerringly superb.

Howie's Stockbridge (☎ 225 5553, 4-6 Glanville Place) **Map 3** Lunch £7.50, dinner £14.95. Open noon-2.30pm & 6pm-10pm daily. This· branch of Howie's – all chrome, blond wood and feng-shui – is a trendier incarnation of their no-nonsense Dalry and Bruntsfield restaurants, designed to pander to the fashionable New Town crowd. But the 'Scottish fusion' food is as good, and as good value, as ever. And who can resist a place with quaffable house wine at £6.10 per bottle?

Modern India (☎ 556 4547, 20 Union Place, Leith Walk) **Map 3** Starters £2.95-6.95, mains £7.95-14.95. Open 11am-2pm & 5pm-midnight Mon-Thur, 5pm-1am Fri & Sat, 4pm-midnight Sun. Stylish and.. well, modern, this restaurant marks a radical departure from the standard Scottish curry house. 'Modern Indian' cuisine includes things such as roast monkfish tail with an achari marinade, and chicken tikka salsa – a superb Indian-Mexican fusion. Well worth a visit.

Mussel Inn (☎ 225 5979, 61-65 Rose St **Map 3** Lunch £8.50, dinner £14. Open noon-10pm Mon-Sat, 1.30pm-10pm Sun. Owned by shellfish farmers on the western coast, the Mussel Inn provides a direct outlet for fresh Scottish seafood. The busy restaurant is all bright beech wood, and tables spill out onto the pavement in summer. A kilogram pot of mussels with choice of sauces – try leek, bacon, white wine and cream – costs £8.95, while smaller platter of queen scallops is £5.45.

Nargile (☎ 225 5755, 73 Hanover St **Map 3** Lunch £7.50, dinner £13.50. Open noon-3pm & 5.30pm-10.30pm Mon-Thur, noon-3pm & 5.30pm-11pm Fri & Sat. Throw away any preconceptions about kebab shops – this Turkish restaurant is a class act. Enjoy a spread of delicious *mezele* (think Turkish tapas) followed by sweet marinated lamb chargrilled to crispy perfection. Finish off with *baklava* (nut-filled pastry soaked in syrup) and a Turkish coffee. If it wasn't for the prices, you could almost be in Turkey.

No 3 Royal Terrace (☎ 477 4747, Royal Terrace) **Map 3** Starters £2.95-5.2

mains £8-18.95. Open noon-2.30pm & 5pm-11pm (dinner served till 10pm) daily. Set in a spacious Georgian town house, No 3 has a homely bar and bistro, complete with open fireplace, at street level and a more formal restaurant upstairs. Traditional Scottish produce – beef, lamb, salmon and seafood – is complemented by more unusual offerings such as filo parcels of vegetarian haggis with oriental vegetables and teriyaki sauce, and chargrilled fillet of Scottish ostrich (yes, they *are* farmed here) with pavé potatoes and stir-fried pak choi.

No 27 (☎ 243 9339, 27 Charlotte Square) Map 3 Starters £4.95, mains £12.25-15.75. Open 6pm-10pm Tues-Sat. Owned by the National Trust, No 27 is a starkly elegant Georgian dining room decorated with period portraits and an incongruously modern colour scheme. The menu is starkly elegant modern Scottish, with the emphasis on seafood, beef, lamb and game.

Rhodes & Co (☎ 220 9190, 3 Rose St) Map 3 Dinner £16.50. Open noon-3pm & 5pm-10pm Mon-Sat, noon-3pm Sun. This place, housed in the former Jenners tearooms, was set up by the TV chef Gary Rhodes – though he doesn't actually cook here – and offers solid, top-quality British cuisine with an inventive touch. Traditional roast pork with apple sauce becomes soft knuckle of ham with caramelised apple and cider jus, and the fish in the fish and chips is actually monkfish tail, delicately fried in the lightest and crispest of batters.

rick's (☎ 622 7800, 55a Frederick St) Map 3 Evening starters £2.85-4.95, mains £7.25-14.80. Open 7am-11pm daily. Hidden in a labyrinthine New Town basement, rick's is hip to the power *n*. The daytime menu includes breakfast dishes, salads, sandwiches and pastas (£5.50-6.10) as well as grills and seafood, coffee and cakes. The eclectic evening menu (from 6pm) offers simple but tasty dishes with international influences, such as marinated wild mushrooms on bruschetta, and *chorizo* and cajun chicken fettucine.

Stac Polly (☎ 556 2231, 29-33 Dublin St) Map 3 Lunch £10-13, dinner £20-23. Open noon-2.30pm & 6pm-11pm Mon-Fri, 6pm-11pm Sat & Sun. Named after a mountain in north-western Scotland, Stac Polly's kitchen adds sophisticated twists to fresh Highland produce. Meals such as garden pea and fresh mint soup with garlic cream and parmesan crouton, followed by pan-fried saddle of venison with orange, tarragon and green peppercorn sauce, keep the punters coming back for more. The restaurant's famous baked filo-pastry parcels of haggis, served with plum sauce, are so popular they've almost become a national dish. What would Burns think?

wok wok (☎ 220 4340, 137 George St) Map 3 Starters £3.75-4.95, mains £6.50-8.95. Open noon-11pm Mon-Wed, noon-midnight Thur-Sat, 12.30pm-10.30pm Sun. wok wok is the first Scottish branch of the chain of funky London restaurants serving South-East Asian cuisine. Choose from Thai fishcakes, Vietnamese aromatic beef stew, Indonesian *nasi goreng* and Chinese beef in black-bean sauce. In summer, wok wok has the added attraction of outdoor tables.

Haymarket & Dalry
Howie's Dalry (☎ 313 3334, 63 Dalry Rd) Map 4 Lunch £7.50, dinner £14.95. Open noon-2pm & 6pm-10pm Tues-Sun. The Dalry branch of Howie's is a small and laid-back restaurant serving affordable modern Scottish cuisine, with dishes such as crispy-skinned salmon fillet and poached vegetables with a Thai fish broth. House wine is a bargain at £6.10 per bottle. Alternatively you can bring your own wine (£3 corkage).

McKirdy's Steakhouse (☎ 229 6660, 151 Morrison St) Map 2 Mains £10.95-16.95. Open 10.30am-2.30pm & 5pm-10.30pm Mon-Sat. In 1999 the McKirdy brothers – owners of a butcher's business established in 1895 – decided to cut out the middle-man and open their own restaurant. The result is one of Edinburgh's best steakhouses, with friendly staff serving starters such as haggis with Drambuie sauce, and juicy, perfectly cooked steaks from rump (£10.95) to T-bone (£16.95), accompanied by mustard mash or crispy fries.

Leith

Fishers (☎ 554 5666, 1 The Shore, Leith)
Map 6 Mains £11.50-16.95. Open noon-
10.30pm daily. This cosy little bar-turned-
restaurant, tucked beneath a 17th-century
signal tower, is one of the city's best
seafood places. Fishers' fishcakes (£4.50)
are almost an Edinburgh institution, and the
rest of the hand-written menu (you might
need a calligrapher to decipher it) rarely
disappoints. Booking is recommended – if
you can't get a table here, try their new
branch, **Fishers in the City** (☎ 225 5109, 58
Thistle St) **Map 3**.

Daniel's Bistro (☎ 553 5933, 88 Commercial St, Leith) **Map 6** Pasta dishes £5.85-
6.25, mains £7.95-10.95, set menu lunch/
dinner from £4.95/11.45. Open 10am-10pm
daily. The eponymous Daniel comes from
Alsace, and his all-French kitchen staff combine top Scottish and French produce with
Gallic know-how to create a wide range of
delicious dishes. The fish soup is excellent
and main courses range from seafood crepes
to Alpine raclette (grilled cheese with baked
potatoes). It's open all day so you can nip in
for a snack and a coffee in the afternoon.

Khublai Khan (☎ 555 0005, 43 Assembly
St, Leith) **Map 6** Dinner £15.50. Open 6pm-
11pm Mon-Sat, noon-2.30pm & 6.30pm-
10.30pm Sun. How many cities outside
Ulan Baator can boast a Mongolian restaurant? OK, the authenticity may be ques-
tionable but it certainly makes a change
from curry or pizza. Choose from a buffet
of raw meat, seafood and vegetables, and
have it cooked to order on a Mongolian-
style barbecue (veggies have their own
grills). The cost of dinner includes three
courses and all you can eat from the grill.

Brasserie de Malmaison (☎ 468 5001, 1
Tower Place, Leith) **Map 6** Starters £4.50-
6.50, mains £8.95-13.95. Open 7am-10am,
noon-2.30pm & 6pm-11pm Mon-Fri;
8am-11am, noon-2.30pm & 6pm-10.30pm
Sat; 8am-10.30am, noon-2.30pm & 6pm-
10.30pm Sun. Art Nouveau decor and
wholesome French cooking are the distin-
guishing features of the Malmaison. The
a la carte menu includes dishes such as
citrus-cured salmon with fennel remoulade,

roasted artichoke and black-eyed bean stew,
and roast lamb niçoise with a tapenade jus,
while the prix fixe dinner menu (from
£10.95) and express lunch (from £9.95) are
good value.

The Raj (☎ 553 3980, 91 Henderson St,
The Shore, Leith) **Map 6** Mains £5.95-
11.95. Open noon-2.30pm & 5.30pm-11pm
Sun-Thur, noon-2.30pm & 5.30pm-midnight
Fri & Sat. Run by celebrity chef Tommy
Miah (author of True Taste of Asia), The Raj
is an atmospheric curry house overlooking
the Water of Leith and serving Indian,
Bangladeshi and Goan cuisine. Specialities
include the tongue-tingling green Bengal
chicken (marinated with lime juice, mint
and chilli) and spicy Goan lamb garam fry.
If you want to eat at home or in your hotel
room, try their Curry-in-a-Hurry delivery
service (toll-free ☎ 0800 073 1983) 5.30pm
to 11pm daily.

PLACES TO EAT – TOP END
Old Town & Around

The Atrium (☎ 228 8882, 10 Cambridge St)
Map 3 Set 3-course dinner £38.50. Open
noon-2pm & 6.30pm-10pm Mon-Fri,
6.30pm-10pm Sat. Elegantly dressed in
wood and white linen, The Atrium is one of
Edinburgh's most fashionable restaurants,
counting Mick Jagger and Jack Nicholson
among its past guests. The cuisine is modern Scottish with a Mediterranean twist,
with the emphasis on the finest of fresh
seasonal produce – fillet of sea bream with
mussels and white-bean stew, pan-fried
Gressingham duck with bok choi or
caramelised pork and a lentil and coriander
sauce. The entrance is off from the foyer of
the Traverse Theatre.

Igg's (☎ 557 8184, 15 Jeffrey St) **Map 8**
Starters £5.75, mains £15.75. Open noon-
2.30pm & 6pm-10.30pm Mon-Sat. A sumptuous dining room with crisp, white linen
and rich, yellow walls makes Igg's a good
choice for a special night out. The menu is
mostly Spanish, with tapas-style starters and
interesting main courses including pan-fried
fillet of barracuda on a spicy plum risotto
with spinach and red-pepper coulis. Lunches
are much cheaper, with mains around £7.

Late-Night Munchies

Edinburgh has more than a few places where it's possible to chow down after 10.30pm. Many of them are Italian, Indian and Chinese restaurants that accept sit-down customers until 11pm on weekdays and midnight on Fridays and Saturdays. The following places stay open into the small hours.

Bann UK (☎ 226 1112, *5 Hunter Square*) **Map 8** Starters £3.90, mains £9.80. Open 11am-1am Sun-Thur, 11am-3am Fri & Sat. From 11pm to 3am on Friday and Saturday, Bann's gourmet vegetarian restaurant metamorphoses into the 'urban hang suite', a hip bar serving tapas-style grub along with your drinks, with music provided by resident DJs.

Dario's (☎ 229 9625, *85-87 Lothian Rd*) **Map 3** Pizzas & pastas £5.40-7.20. Open noon-5am daily. Ah, Dario's – table for five, food for 10, wine for 20. You get the idea. After midnight in this frantic Italian noshery no-one is sober except the waiters – and they heartily wish they weren't. Noisy but nice, and best appreciated slightly out of focus.

Favorit (☎ 221 1800, *30-32 Leven St*) **Map 5** Sandwiches £3.65-3.95, salads £4.65-4.95. Open 8am-3am daily. This is a cool cafe where you can chill with a cappuccino and a chocolate-fudge brownie, or fend off a serious attack of the munchies with a 'Favorit melt' (cheese sandwich dipped in beaten egg and fried).

Gordon's Trattoria (☎ 225 7992, *231 High St*) **Map 8** Pizzas £5-7, mains £8-16.50. Open noon-midnight Sun-Thur, noon-3am Fri & Sat. The aroma of garlic bread wafting into the street will guide you into this snug haven of chattering diners, wise-cracking waiters and hearty Italian comfort food. Gordon's often develops something of a party atmosphere after midnight on Friday and Saturday.

Kebab Mahal (☎ 667 5214, *7 Nicolson Square*) **Map 8** Kebabs £3.25-5.50. Open noon-midnight Sun-Thur, noon-2am Fri & Sat. Sophisticated it ain't but this is the Holy Grail of kebab shops – quality shish kebab and tandoori chicken washed down with chilled *lassi* for less than a fiver. Forget the stainless-steel counter and glaring fluorescent lights – the Mahal is kebab nirvana.

Lazio (☎ 229 7788, *95 Lothian Rd*) **Map 3** Pizzas & pastas £5.95-7.70. Open 5pm-1.30am Mon-Thur, noon-3am Fri-Sun. This Italian joint is a little bit upmarket and just a little bit uphill from Dario's (see earlier). For the (slightly) more sober Lothian Rd late-night diner.

Negociants (☎ 225 6313, *45-47 Lothian St*) **Map 8** Open 9am-3am Mon-Sat, 10am-3am Sun. A student stalwart that's been around for 20 years, Negociants is a bar-bistro that keeps the food coming till well into the wee hours of the morning. Nachos, burgers and fajitas are the best-value choices.

The Witchery by the Castle (☎ 225 5613, *Castlehill, Royal Mile*) **Map 8** Starters £4.95-9.95, mains £13.95-18.95. Open noon-4pm, 5.30pm-11.30pm daily. At first, the Witchery looks a little like a tourist trap, with its oak-panelled walls, low ceilings, opulent wall-hangings and red-leather upholstery. But a brief glance at the menu – from the roast quail with tarragon, tomato and chanterelles to the honey-roast Gressingham duck with savoy cabbage, bacon and sweet potato rosti – and especially at the wine list – there are almost 1000 bins – shows that this is a serious gastronomic enterprise. Dinner can be expensive but you can sample the Witchery's delights without risking bankruptcy – their bargain two-course light lunches (noon to 4pm) and pre- or post-theatre dinners (5.30pm-6.30pm and 10.30pm-11.30pm) cost only £9.95.

New Town & Around
Caffé D.O.C. (☎ 220 6846, *49a Thistle St*) **Map 3** Mains £12-16. Open 10.30am-3pm

& 7pm-10pm Tues-Sat. As the name suggests – D.O.C. stands for 'Denominazione d'Origina Controllata', the Italian equivalent of the French 'appellation contrôllée' – this simple and elegant little restaurant, ideal for a quiet dinner for two, offers a range of excellent Italian wines. Wash down sea-bass baked with herbs (£14.80) with a bottle of Vernaccia di San Gimignano (£14).

Café Royal Oyster Bar (☎ 556 4124, 17a West Register St) **Map 3** Mains £14.75-24.70. Open noon-2pm & 7pm-10pm daily. Pass through the revolving doors on the corner of West Register St, and you're transported back to Victorian times – a palace of mahogany, polished brass, marble floors, stained glass, Doulton tiles, gilded cornices and table linen so thick that it creaks when you fold it. The Oyster Bar is a place for a very special occasion. The menu is mostly seafood, from oysters on ice, to coquilles St Jacques Parisienne, to lobster thermidor, augmented by a handful of beef and game dishes.

The Dome (☎ 624 8624, 14 George St) **Map 3** Starters £3.50-7.50, mains £8.50-18.50. Open noon-10.30pm Sun-Thur, noon-11pm Fri & Sat. Housed in the former headquarters of a bank, The Dome boasts one of the city's most impressive dining rooms. The lofty, domed ceiling and ornate decoration keep dragging your eyes away from your plate, which is probably just as well – the food, though decent, does not quite measure up to the surroundings, or to the prices. It's best to go there for lunch, when you can ogle the fittings without breaking the bank, as it were.

Number One (☎ 557 6727, Balmoral Hotel, 1 Princes St) **Map 3** Dinner £35-50. Open noon-2pm & 7pm-10pm Mon-Thur, noon-2pm & 7pm-10.30pm Fri, 7pm-10.30pm Sat, 7pm-10pm Sun. If the Pompadour is a grand old dame, then Number One – at the opposite end of Princes St – is stylish and sophisticated chatelaine, all gold and elegance. The food is top-notch Scottish – a three-course dinner for £35, or six courses for £50 – and the service is just the right side of fawning. You'll need two of the waiters to pull you out of the opulent sofas where you peruse the menu.

The Pompadour (☎ 200 9912, Caledonian Hilton Hotel, Princes St) **Map 3** Set dinner menu £25. Open 6.30pm-10.30pm Tues, Wed & Sat, 12.30-2pm & 6.30pm-10.30pm Thur & Fri. On the go since 1925, the Pompadour is the classy old lady of Edinburgh restaurants. The palatial decor includes red carpets (of course), delicate oriental murals and glittering mirrors, and there's a view of the castle. The food is French, the wine expensive, the service attentive but discreet – just sit back and be pampered.

Leith

(fitz) Henry (☎ 555 6625, 19 Shore Place, Leith) **Map 6** Starters £4-8, mains £13-16. Open noon-2.30pm & 6.30pm-10.30pm Mon-Fri, 6.30pm-10.30pm Sat. A deeply trendy brasserie tucked away in a warehouse in deepest Leith, (fitz) Henry exudes an atmosphere of wicked decadence. The menu is full-on French, allowing you to choose a politically incorrect, but thoroughly delicious, dinner of foie gras followed by roasted veal. Other delights on the menu include roasted calf's liver, rabbit *en cocotte à la Provençal* and rare grilled tuna with puy lentil salad and mustard vinaigrette.

Martin Wishart (☎ 553 3557, 54 The Shore, Leith) **Map 6** Starters £6.50-9, mains £13.50-18. Open noon-2pm & 7pm-10pm Tues-Fri, 7pm-10pm Sat. In 2001 this restaurant became the only one in Edinburgh to win a Michelin star. The eponymous chef has worked with Albert Roux, Marco Pierre White and Nick Nairn, and brings a modern-French approach to the best Scottish produce – lobster and truffle ravioli with buttered Savoy cabbage and shellfish cream, fillet of Scottish beef with artichoke and French beans and a red wine and shallot jus. Book as far ahead as possible.

PLACES TO EAT – VEGETARIAN

Many restaurants, of all descriptions, offer vegetarian options on the menu, some good, some bad, some indifferent. The places listed here are all 100% veggie, and all fall into the 'good' category.

Ann Purna (☎ 662 1807, 45 St Patrick Square) **Map 5** Mains £4.75-7.95. Open noon-2pm & 5.30pm-11pm Mon-Fri, 5.30pm-11pm Sat & Sun. This little gem of an Indian restaurant serves exclusively vegetarian dishes from southern India. If you're new to this kind of food, opt for a *thali* – a self-contained platter that consists of half a dozen different dishes, including a dessert.

Bann UK (☎ 226 1112, 5 Hunter Square) **Map 8** Starters £3.90, mains £9.80. Open 11am-1am Sun-Thur, 11am-3am Fri & Sat. If you want to convince a carnivorous friend that cuisine a la veg can be every bit as tasty and inventive as a meat-muncher's menu, take them to Bann, a darkly stylish restaurant with chunky furniture and burgundy and pale-cream walls. Dishes such as Thai potato fritters with coconut and coriander relish, and veggie-haggis and leek sausages with red-onion gravy are guaranteed to win converts. They also do an all-day veggie breakfast for £6.50.

Black Bo's (☎ 557 6136, 57-61 Blackfriars St) **Map 8** Mains £5.50-8.50. Open 6pm-10.30pm Sun-Thur, noon-2pm & 6pm-10.30pm Fri & Sat. You can't accuse the chef at Black Bo's, a popular vegetarian eatery just off the Royal Mile, of being unadventurous. The menu is always interesting, though some dishes – deep-fried potato and coconut balls stuffed with brie, served with a fig, rum and chilli chutney, for example – don't quite work. There's a lively bar next door, which often has live music.

Henderson's (☎ 225 2131, 94 Hanover St) **Map 3** Mains £3.75-4.50. Open 8am-10.45pm Mon-Sat (open Sun during the Edinburgh Festival). Established in 1963, Henderson's is the grandmother of Edinburgh's vegetarian restaurants. The food is mostly organic, guaranteed GM-free, and special dietary requirements can be catered for. The place still has something of a '70s

feel to it (but in a good way), and the daily salads and hot dishes are as popular as ever. Favourite dishes include vegetable haggis with neeps and tatties, and a ratatouille of roasted vegetables. A three-course dinner with coffee costs £13.50.

It's Organic (☎ 228 9444, 15 Bread St) **Map 3** Soups & juices £2-4. Open 8am-6pm Mon-Fri, 9am-5pm Sat, 11am-5pm Sun. This is the place to go for freshly juiced organic fruit and vegetables, filling vegetable soups, big coffees and a range of wraps and sandwiches. For 50p extra you can add a shot of various nutritional supplements such as ginseng and guarana to your coffee.

Kalpna (☎ 667 9890, 2-3 St Patrick Square) **Map 5** Mains £4.25-6.50. Open noon-2pm & 5.30pm-11pm Mon-Fri, 5.30pm-11pm Sat. Another long-standing Edinburgh favourite, Kalpna is one of the best Indian restaurants in the country, vegetarian or otherwise. The cuisine is mostly Gujarat, with a smattering of dishes from other parts of India – try the *khoya kaju* (vegetables, cashew nuts, sultanas and pistachios in a cream sauce with coriander and nutmeg, served with coconut rice and puri). The Kalpna thali (set meal; £8.50) includes samosas, two curry dishes, rice, puri and a dessert.

Susie's Diner (☎ 667 8729, 51-53 West Nicolson St) **Map 5** Mains £3-6. Open 9am-8pm Mon, 9am-9pm Tues-Sat. Susie's is a down-to-earth, self-service, vegetarian restaurant with scrubbed wood tables, rickety chairs and a friendly atmosphere. The menu changes daily but includes things such as tofu, aubergine and pepper casserole, stuffed roast tomatoes, and Susie's famous falafel plates – reputedly 'the best falafel in the western world'.

PLACES TO EAT

Entertainment

Glasgow folk have a colourful expression – 'all fur coat and nae knickers' – that they occasionally apply to Edinburgh, suggesting that it projects an air of middle-class respectability on the surface but is down and dirty underneath. There's an element of truth there – the city that inspired the story of Jekyll and Hyde certainly has its seamier side – and the high culture epitomised in the Edinburgh Festival finds its counterpoint in the city's lively club scene and its reputation as a pub-crawler's paradise.

The city has a number of fine theatres and concert halls, and there are independent art-house cinemas as well as mainstream movie theatres. Many pubs offer entertainment ranging from live Scottish folk music to pop, rock and jazz to karaoke and quiz nights, while the new generation of style bars purvey house, dance and hip hop to the pre-clubbing crowd.

Edinburgh's most comprehensive source of what's-on information is *The List* (£1.95; w www.list.co.uk), an excellent, fortnightly listings and reviews magazine (also covering Glasgow), available from most newsagents. *Gig Guide* (w www.gigguide.co.uk) is a free, monthly leaflet that advertises regular music gigs under the headings Rock, Pop & Blues, Jazz, and Folk & World; you can pick it up in bars, cafes and music venues. The free, monthly booklet *What's On Edinburgh & Lothians* (w www.whatson-scotland.co.uk) is produced by the Edinburgh and Lothians Tourist Board. It covers a wide range of events and exhibitions, including art galleries and museums. *The Edinburgh Evening News* newspaper has daily reviews and listings of cinema, music, theatre, clubs, comedy and arts events.

PUBS & BARS

Edinburgh has always been a drinker's city. The 18th-century poets Robert Fergusson and Robert Burns spent much of their time in – and drew inspiration from – Edinburgh's public houses, and rather than attend his law lectures at Edinburgh University, the young Robert Louis Stevenson preferred to haunt the city's many howffs (drinking dens) – a practice perpetuated by many Edinburgh students to this day.

Although many city-centre pubs have been 'themed' or converted into vast drinking halls catering to office workers unwinding at the end of the day, the local, neighbourhood bar is still a social centre, where you can meet friends, watch the football on TV, listen to live music or take part in the Tuesday night quiz. Edinburgh has over 700 bars that are as varied as the population... everything from Victorian palaces to rough-and-ready drinking dens, and from real-ale howffs to trendy cocktail bars.

Bars generally open from 11am to 11pm Monday to Saturday and 12.30pm to 11pm on Sunday. Many have a late licence on Friday and Saturday, when they stay open till midnight or 1am, while a few party on until 3am. The bell for last orders rings about 15 minutes before closing time and you're allowed 15 minutes' drinking-up time after the bar closes.

Royal Mile & Around (Map 8)

The pubs on the Royal Mile are – not surprisingly – aimed mainly at the tourist market but there are some good places hidden up the closes and along the side streets.

Ensign Ewart (☎ 225 7440, 225 Lawnmarket) The nearest pub to the castle, the Ensign Ewart trades on its historic setting and military associations. A mix of tourists, students from the university residences in Milne's Court and journalists, covering events at the Scottish Parliament's temporary home next door, drop in to enjoy real ale and good bar food.

The Jolly Judge (☎ 225 2669, 7a James Court) A snug little howff tucked away down a close, the Judge exudes a cosy 17th century character (low, painted ceilings) and has the added attraction of a cheering fire in cold weather.

The Malt Shovel (☎ *225 6843, 11-15 Cockburn St*) A traditional-looking pub, with dark wood and subdued tartanry, offering a good range of real ales and over 100 malt whiskies, the Malt Shovel is famed for its regular Tuesday night jazz from Swing 2001.

The Tron (☎ *220 1500, Hunter Square*) A popular place with the student crowd, the lower floors of The Tron (called It's A Scream) form a horror-theme pub (oooh, scary) with wild discos on Friday and Saturday only. The street-level bar is open the rest of the week.

The Hebrides Bar (☎ *220 4213, 17 Market St*) Friendly, welcoming and handy for Waverley train station, the Hebrides offers a taste of Highland hospitality in the heart of the city. There's live Scottish folk music on Thursday to Sunday evenings.

Logie Baird's Bar (☎ *556 9043, 1 South Bridge*) Yet another former bank that has been converted into a bar, the Logie Baird offers good bar meals and has outdoor tables in summer.

Royal Mile Tavern (☎ *557 9681, 127 High St*) An elegant, traditional bar lined with polished wood, mirrors and brass, the Royal Mile serves real ale, good wines and fine food – *moules marinières* and crusty bread is a lunchtime speciality.

The World's End (☎ *556 3628, 4 High St*) So named because this part of High St once lay next to the Old Town limit – part of the 16th-century Flodden Wall can still be seen in the basement – the World's End is an old local pub, with plenty of regulars as well as tourists. They do good bar food, including excellent fish and chips.

Grassmarket & Around

Grassmarket pubs have outdoor tables on sunny summer afternoons, but in the evenings they are favoured by boozed-up lads on the pull. Cowgate – Grassmarket's extension to the east – is Edinburgh's clubland. Unless otherwise indicated all the following places are on Map 8.

Fiddlers Arms (☎ *229 2665, 9-11 Grassmarket*) In contrast to the mostly student and touristy bars that characterise Grass-

market, the Fiddlers is an unpretentious, traditional pub with old fiddles lining the walls and a well-used pool table in the back room. It's famous for its wild, Monday-night folk-music sessions.

The Three-Quarter (☎ *622 1622, 4 Grassmarket*) Sited in a converted church, the Three-Quarter is a vast and lively sports bar and cafe where the faithful can worship at the altar of the large-screen satellite TVs. Altogether now, *In nomine* rugby, *et* footie, *et* spirituous liquors...

The Beehive (☎ *225 7171, 18-20 Grassmarket*) Formerly a real-ale haven, the Beehive has changed tack and is now a big, buzzing party pub, with cheesy disco music on Friday and Saturday nights. You can get reasonable grub during the day, and out the back is Grassmarket's only beer garden, with grand views up to the castle.

The Last Drop (☎ *225 4851, 74 Grassmarket*) The name commemorates the gallows that used to stand nearby, but the Last Drop is now a swinging party pub, popular with students and backpackers.

Bow Bar (☎ *226 7667, 80 West Bow*) A busy, traditional pub serving a range of excellent real ales and a vast selection of malt whiskies, it's often standing-room only at the Bow Bar on Friday and Saturday evenings.

The Three Sisters (☎ *622 6800, 39 Cowgate*) This huge pub is actually three bars – one American, one Irish and one Gothic – with a big cobbled courtyard for outdoor drinking in summer. It's a bit of a mad party place but you can come back the morning after and soothe your hangover with a big, fried breakfast – and a free Bloody Mary if you order before 11am.

Bannerman's (☎ *556 3254, 212 Cowgate*) A long-established favourite, Bannerman's straggles through a warren of old vaults, and pulls in crowds of students, locals and backpackers. The beer is good, but their weekend breakfasts are best avoided.

Greyfriars Bobby's Bar (☎ *225 8328, 34 Candlemaker Row*) The Bobby is a pretty average Edinburgh bar but it's popular with students (it serves inexpensive food and is on the way to the fleshpots of Cowgate) and tourists sheltering from the rain after trying

ENTERTAINMENT

Trad vs Trendy

At one end of Edinburgh's broad spectrum of hostelries lies the traditional 19th-century bar, which has preserved much of its original Victorian decoration and generally serves cask-conditioned real ales and a staggering range of malt whiskies. At the other end is the modern 'style bar', with a cool clientele and styling so sharp you could cut yourself on it. The bar staff here are more likely to be serving schnapps, shooters and absinthe cocktails. Here are some suggestions from each end of the range:

Top 5 Traditional Bars

The Athletic Arms (The Diggers) (☎ 337 3822, 1-3 Angle Park Terrace) **Map 4** Named for the cemetery across the street – the grave-diggers used to nip in and slake their thirst after a hard day's interring – the Diggers dates from the 1890s. Its heyday as a real-ale drinker's mecca has passed but it's still staunchly traditional – the decor has barely changed in 100 years – and it's packed to the gills with football and rugby fans on match days.

The Abbotsford (☎ 225 5276, 3 Rose St) **Map 3** One of the few pubs in Rose St that has retained its Edwardian splendour, the Abbotsford has long been a hang-out for writers, actors, journalists and media people and has many loyal regulars. Dating from 1902 and named after Sir Walter Scott's country house, the pub's centrepiece is a splendid, mahogany island bar.

Bennet's Bar (☎ 229 5143, 8 Leven St) **Map 5** Situated beside the King's Theatre, Bennet's has managed to retain almost all of its beautiful Victorian fittings, from the leaded, stained-glass windows and ornate mirrors to the wooden gantry and brass water taps on the bar (if whisky is your particular poison, there are over 100 malts to choose from).

Café Royal Circle Bar (☎ 556 1884, 17 West Register St) **Map 3** Perhaps *the* classic Edinburgh bar, the Café Royal's main claims to fame are its magnificent oval bar and the series of Doulton tile portraits of famous Victorian inventors. Check out the bottles on the gantry – staff line them up to look as if there's a mirror there, and many a drink-befuddled customer has been seen squinting and wondering why he can't see his reflection.

The Sheep Heid (☎ 656 6951, 43-45 The Causeway, Duddingston) **Map 1** Possibly the oldest inn in Edinburgh – with a licence dating back to 1360 – the Sheep Heid feels more like a country pub than an Edinburgh bar. Set in the semi-rural shadow of Arthur's Seat, it's famous for its 19th-century skittles alley and lovely little beer garden.

to photograph the statue of the eponymous pup outside.

Bar Kohl (☎ 225 6939, 54 George IV Bridge) One of the city's original style bars, Kohl is all wood and vodka – it stocks some 250 different vodkas from around the world, including 54 flavoured Finlandias, from bubblegum to red hot chilli pepper.

Pear Tree House (☎ 667 7533, 38 West Nicolson St) **Map 5** The Pear Tree is another student favourite, with comfy sofas and board games inside plus the biggest beer garden in the city centre. There's live music in the garden on Sunday afternoons in summer.

Rose St & Around (Map 3)

Rose St was once a famous pub crawl where generations of students, sailors and rugby fans would try to visit every pub on the street (around 17 of them) and down a pint of beer in each one. These days shopping, not boozing, is Rose St's *raison d'être* but there are still a few pubs worth visiting

The Kenilworth (☎ 226 4385, 152-154 Rose St) A gorgeous, Edwardian drinking palace, complete with original fittings – from the tile floors, mahogany circle bar and gantry, to the ornate mirrors and gas lamps – the Kenilworth was Edinburgh's original gay bar back in the 1970s. Today it attract

Trad vs Trendy

Top 5 Trendy Bars

Baracoa (☎ 225 5846, 7 Victoria St)
Map 8 This is the place to come for Latin sounds, Cuban cocktails and Havana cigars. There's a two-for-one happy hour 5pm to 7pm, and salsa classes (£3.50) from 7pm on Tuesday and Thursday.

Iguana (☎ 220 4288, 41 Lothian St)
Map 8 Iguana opened in 1996, making it positively prehistoric for a style bar, but a combination of timeless decor, cool sounds and good value have kept it popular. The crowd is mostly students, nurses and medics during the day, and clubbers in the evening.

Oxygen (☎ 557 9997, 3 Infirmary St)
Map 8 Czech beer and Morgans Spiced aren't the only things that come in bottles here. This place is so breathtakingly cool that they serve bottled oxygen to keep you from passing out.

ASA ANDERSSON

Pivo Caffé (☎ 557 2925, 2-6 Calton Rd)
Map 3 Aiming to add a little taste of Bohemia to Edinburgh's bar scene, Pivo (the Czech word for beer) serves goulash and dumplings, bottled and draught Czech beers and two-pint cocktails – try a 'long absinthe' (absinthe with lemonade and lime).

Tonic (☎ 225 6431, 34a North Castle St) **Map 3** As cool and classy as a perfectly mixed martini, Tonic prides itself on the authenticity of its cocktails, of which there are many – the menu goes on forever. Check out the Phillipe Starck bar stools – do you sit on them or use them as ashtrays?

a mixed crowd of all ages and serves a good range of real ales and malt whiskies.

Robertsons 37 (☎ 225 6185, 37 Rose St) No 37 is to malt whisky connoisseurs what The Diggers once was to real-ale fans. Its long gantry sports a choice of more than 100 single malts, and the bar provides a quiet and elegant environment in which to sample them. It is not far from the Hanover Hotel.

Guildford Arms (☎ 556 4312, 1 West Register St) Located next door to the Café Royal (see the boxed text 'Trad vs Trendy'), the Guildford is another classic Victorian pub full of polished mahogany, brass and ornate cornices.

George St & Around (Map 3)

George St, once the city's most prestigious business address, is changing. Many of the offices are now shops and all the grand old bank buildings have been turned into bars, allowing city wags to make lots of lame jokes about liquid assets, standing orders and export markets.

Bar 38 (☎ 220 6180, 126-128 George St) Unisex toilets with a sofa and a fountain? In Bar 38, trendiness extends right into the plumbing. This is a big, busy bar with an excellent range of snack food, from breakfast kebabs of coconut chicken to dim sum and crispy whitebait.

ENTERTAINMENT

The Standing Order (☎ *225 4460, 62-66 George St)* One of several converted banks on George St, the Standing Order is a cavernous beer hall with a fantastic vaulted ceiling and some cosy rooms off to the right – look for the one with the original 27-tonne safe. Despite its size, it can be standing-room only at the weekend.

Frazer's (☎ *624 8624, 14 George St)* Frazer's is the bar at The Dome (see the Places to Eat chapter), formerly a temple to Mammon (OK then, a bank – but it looks like a temple) and now a shrine to Dionysius – stand in the foyer for a moment and be impressed. The gleaming bar is a beautiful Art Deco masterpiece and serves fine real ales as well as pukka cocktails.

Tiles Bar-Bistro (☎ *558 1507, 1 St Andrew Square)* A regular haunt of city lawyers and accountants, Tiles is a smart and stylish bar in yet another converted bank. It takes its name from the lovely Victorian tiles inside.

The Oxford Bar (☎ *539 7119, 8 Young St)* The Oxford is that rarest of things these days – a real pub for real people, with no 'theme', no music, no frills and no pretensions. Immortalised by regular Ian Rankin, author of the Inspector Rebus novels, the Ox is a place to meet people and have genuine conversations.

The West End

Bert's Bar (☎ *225 5748, 29-31 William St)* **Map 2** A classic re-creation of a 1930s-style pub – complete with a jar of pickled eggs on the bar – Bert's is a good place to sample real ale and down-to-earth pub grub such as Scotch pies and bangers and mash.

Ryan's (☎ *226 6669, 2 Hope St)* **Map 3** Housed in a former fruit market, Ryan's has retained its original vaulted ceiling but is best known as a loud and lively bar where New Town office workers gather for a drink at the end of the day. In summer there are outdoor tables and good food is served all day.

Indigo Yard (☎ *220 5603, 7 Charlotte Lane)* **Map 2** Set around an airy, glass-roofed courtyard, Indigo is a *trés* fashionable West End watering hole that has been patronised by the likes of Liam Gallagher, Pierce Brosnan and Kylie Minogue. Good food – including open-air barbecues in summer – just adds to the attraction.

New Town & Broughton St (Map 3)

Clark's Bar (☎ *556 1067, 142 Dundas St)* A century old and still going strong, Clark's caters to a clientele of real-ale aficionados and regulars, who appreciate an old-fashioned, no frills pub.

The Cumberland Bar (☎ *558 3134, 1-3 Cumberland St)* Under the same management as the Bow Bar in Victoria St (see Grassmarket & Around earlier), the Cumberland pays the same attention to serving well-looked-after, cask-conditioned ales. Though relatively new, the bar has an authentic, traditional wood-brass-and-mirrors look and there's a nice little beer garden outside.

Kay's Bar (☎ *225 1858, 39 Jamaica St)* **Map 3** Housed in a former wine-merchant's office, tiny Kay's Bar is a cosy haven with a coal fire and a fine range of real ales. Good food is served in the back room at lunchtime but you'll have to book a table – Kay's is a popular spot.

The Basement (☎ *557 0097, 10a Broughton St)* With a relaxed and friendly atmosphere, this is one of Broughton St's most popular bars. Music in the evenings includes hip hop, house and funk.

Mathers (☎ *556 6754, 25 Broughton St)* Mathers is the 40-something generation's equivalent of the 20-something's Basement bar across the street – a friendly, relaxed pub with Edwardian decor serving real ale and good pub grub.

The Cask & Barrel (☎ *556 3132, 115 Broughton St)* At the foot of Broughton St the Cask is a beer-drinker's delight, with a selection of up to ten real ales, as well as Czech and German beers.

Stockbridge

The Antiquary (☎ *225 2858, 72-78 S Stephen St)* **Map 3** The long-established Antiquary has lively folk-music sessions on Thursday night, when all comers are welcome to perform.

How to Be a Malt Whisky Buff

'Love makes the world go round? Not at all! Whisky makes it go round twice as fast.'
From *Whisky Galore,* by Compton MacKenzie (1883–1972)

Whisky-tasting today is almost as popular as wine-tasting was in the yuppie heyday of the late 1980s. Being able to tell your Ardbeg from your Edradour is *de rigeur* among the whisky-nosing set, so here are some pointers to help you impress your friends.

What's the difference between malt and grain whiskies? Malts are distilled from malted barley – that is, barley that has been soaked in water, then allowed to germinate for around 10 days until the starch has turned into sugar – while grain whiskies are distilled from other cereals, usually wheat, corn or unmalted barley.

So what is a single malt? A single malt is a whisky that has been distilled from malted barley and is the product of a single distillery. A pure (vatted) malt is a mixture of single malts from several distilleries, and a blended whisky is a mixture of various grain whiskies (about 60%) and malt whiskies (about 40%) from many different distilleries.

Why are single malts more desirable than blends? A single malt, like a fine wine, somehow captures the essence of where it was made and matured – a combination of the water, the barley, the peat smoke, the oak barrels in which it was aged, and (in the case of certain coastal distilleries) the sea air and salt spray. Each distillation varies from the one before, like different vintages from the same vineyard.

How should a single malt be drunk? Either neat, or preferably with a little water added. To appreciate the aroma and flavour to the utmost, a measure of malt whisky should be cut (diluted) with one-third to two-thirds as much spring water (still, bottled spring water will do). Ice, tap water and (God forbid) mixers are for philistines. Would you add lemonade or ice to a glass of Chablis?

Give me some tasting tips! Go into a bar – maybe Robertsons 37 on Rose St or Bennet's on Tollcross – and order a Lagavulin (Islay) and a Glenfiddich (Speyside). Cut each one with half as much again of still, bottled spring water. Taking each one in turn, hold the glass up to the light to check the colour; stick your nose in the glass and take two or three short, sharp sniffs. For the Lagavulin you should be thinking: amber colour, peat-smoke, iodine, seaweed. For the Glenfiddich: pale, white-wine colour, malt, pear drops, acetone, citrus. Then taste them. Then try some others. Either you'll be hooked, or you'll never touch whisky again.

Where's the cheapest place to buy Scotch whisky? A French supermarket, unfortunately. In the UK, a bottle of single malt typically costs £20 to £30 – taxes account for around 72% of the price, making Scotland one of the most expensive places in Europe to enjoy its own national drink.

If you're serious about spirits, the ***Scotch Malt Whisky Society*** (☎ 554 3451, Ⓦ *www.smws.com, The Vaults, 87 Giles St, Edinburgh EH6 6BZ*) **Map 3** runs an intensive one-day Whisky School that covers the basics of whisky-tasting and evaluation. The cost is £210, including lunch, canapes and drinks. Membership of the society costs from £75 per year and includes use of members' rooms in Edinburgh and London.

The nearest distillery to Edinburgh is the Glenkinchie Distillery at Pencaitland, which produces the excellent Glenkinchie 10-year-old single malt. It's 15 miles (25km) east of the city, and has a Visitor Centre (☎ 01875-342004) that opens 9.30am to 5pm Monday to Saturday and noon to 5pm Sunday June to September; 9.30am to 5pm Monday to Friday and noon to 5pm Saturday and Sunday in October; 10am to 5pm weekdays March to May; and 10am to 4pm weekdays November to February.

Bert's Bar (☎ *332 6345, 2 Raeburn Place*) **Map 2** Under the same management as its namesake in the West End, Bert's is the place to enjoy a pint of real ale and a decent pie.

The Bailie (☎ *225 4673, 2 St Stephen St*) **Map 3** Down in a basement, the Bailie is an old Stockbridge stalwart, a dark, warm and welcoming nook where you can enjoy good coffee as well as real ales and malts.

Hector's (☎ *332 5328, 47 Deanhaugh St*) **Map 2** A trendy cafe-bar with good food and an excellent range of wines, Hector's is a popular meeting place, whether for breakfast, afternoon coffee or an evening meal and a drink.

Tollcross, Bruntsfield & Morningside

Cloisters (☎ *221 9997, 26 Brougham St*) **Map 5** Housed in a converted manse, Cloisters now ministers to a mixed congregation of students, locals and real-ale connoisseurs. It has decent grub and a nice, warm fireplace in winter.

The Auld Toll (☎ *229 1010, 39 Leven St*) **Map 5** This is an old and pleasantly unpretentious local boozer, with the public bar to the left and a narrow lounge to the right as you go in.

The Golf Tavern (☎ *229 5040, 30 Wright's Houses*) **Map 5** Overlooking the pitch-and-putt course on Bruntsfield Links, the Golf is housed in a 19th-century building, though there have been licensed premises on this spot since the 15th century. Its an attractive place, with luxurious leather sofas, that pulls in a young, studenty crowd at the weekends.

The Golden Rule (☎ *622 7112, 30 Yeaman Place*) **Map 4** Hard to find but worth the hunt, the Golden Rule is a great wee local with a lively atmosphere and up to eight real ales on tap.

Montpeliers (☎ *229 3115, 159-161 Bruntsfield Place*) **Map 4** The 'in' place to down a pint in Morningside, Monty's is packed at weekends with rugby-playing, public-school-educated financial analysts chasing sun-tanned, blonde Emmas and Carolines just back from skiing in St Moritz

or villa-hunting in Tuscany. The food and the beer are good though.

The Canny Man's (☎ *447 1484, 237 Morningside Rd*) **Map 4** A lovably eccentric pub, the Canny Man's is a crowded warren of tiny rooms crammed with a bizarre collection of antiques and curiosities – a description that applies to some of the regulars – where the landlord regularly refuses entry to anyone who looks scruffy, inebriated or vaguely pinko/commie/subversive. If you can get in, you'll find it serves excellent real ale, vintage port and Cuban cigars.

Caley Sample Room (☎ *337 7204, 58 Angle Park Terrace*) **Map 4** Owned by the nearby Caledonian Brewery, the Sample Room is a big, lively pub with a wide range of excellent real ales. It's popular with sports fans too, and football and rugby matches are shown on the large-screen TVs.

Leith & Granton

Port o'Leith (☎ *554 3568, 58 Constitution St*) **Map 6** A good, old-fashioned, friendly local boozer, the Port is swathed with flags and cap bands left behind by visiting sailors – the harbour is just down the road. Pop in for a pint and you'll probably stay till closing time.

Carriers Quarters (☎ *554 4122, 42 Bernard St*) **Map 6** With a low, wooden ceiling, stone walls and a fine old fireplace, the Carriers has all the historic atmosphere that its 18th-century origins would imply. It serves real ales and malt whiskies, and has folk sessions on Thursday nights.

The King's Wark (☎ *554 9260, 36 The Shore*) **Map 6** Set in a fine old 17th-century building, the King's Wark is a very cosy, candlelight-and-fireplace sort of a pub, with an upmarket clientele and excellent food and wine.

The Starbank Inn (☎ *552 4141, 64 Laverockbank Rd*) **Map 1** Along with the Old Chain Pier (see the boxed text 'Lunch for Less' in the Places to Eat chapter), the Starbank is an oasis of fine ales and good home-made food on Edinburgh's windswept waterfront. In summer there's a sunny conservatory and in winter there's a blazing fire to toast your toes in front of.

PRE-CLUB BARS

Edinburgh's club scene has engendered a rash of hip pre-club bars, complete with drinks promos, decks and resident DJs, where you can begin the process of metamorphosis from weekday wage slave to dance-floor diva.

Bam Bou (☎ *556 0200, 67 South Bridge*) **Map 8** Bam Bou is all – you've guessed it – bamboo and mock-oriental. You can get tanked on Japanese *sake* cocktails here, and snack on sushi and dim sum. There's drum' n'bass on Friday and hip hop on Saturday.

City Cafe (☎ *220 0125, 19 Blair St*) **Map 8** Dating from the 1980s, the City Cafe is Edinburgh's original pre-club bar, with a 1950s-American-diner retro look, excellent munchies, and a downstairs DJ spinning hip hop, R'n'B, ragga and funk.

Cuba Norte (☎ *221 1430, 192 Morrison St*) **Map 2** Swagger in, order a cuba libra and prepare to salsa. Cuba Norte provides a little touch of Latino levity in the cold, northern winters, dishing up good Cuban tapas, Havana cigars and hip-swaying salsa beats. You can hone your technique at one of the regular salsa classes.

Po Na Na (☎ *226 2224, 43b Frederick St*) **Map 3** This bar is one of a UK-wide chain, which makes the North African souk-style decor seem more contrived than imaginative. Still, the DJs play great party music and the place opens till 3am every night, so... rock the casbah, rock the casbah...

PopRokit (☎ *556 4272, 2 Picardy Place*) **Map 3** A shrine to chrome, steel and glass – even part of the floor is glass – PopRokit is style with a capital yessss. Full-length glass walls mean you can ogle the passers-by outside, that is if you can tear your eyes away from the beautiful people inside. Resident DJs pump out groove, funk and disco for the pre-club crowds.

CLUBS

Edinburgh's club scene has got some fine DJ talent and is well worth exploring. Most of the venues are concentrated in and around the twin sumps of Cowgate and Calton Rd – so it's downhill all the way...

For details of club nights and venues check the latest issue of *The List* and look for flyers in pre-club bars and music shops – Underground Solush'n in Cockburn St is a good place for information. The Edinburger Web site (W www.edinburger.com) also has a good guide to Edinburgh club nights.

La Belle Angele (☎ *225 7536, 11 Hastie's Close, Cowgate*) **Map 8** Home to Manga, Edinburgh's unmissable drum'n'bass club, and jazz-funk session Big Beat (both monthly, Friday), the Belle also has a great house and garage night in Ultragroove (held on Saturday, monthly).

The Bongo Club (☎ *558 7604, 14 New St*) **Map 8** Famous for the hip hop clubs El Segundo and Headspin, at the time of writing the word was that the Bongo may have to move out of its New St premises. Check the location in *The List*.

Ego (☎ *478 7434, 14 Picardy Place*) **Map 3** A glitzy two-floor venue in a former casino, Ego dishes up everything from the wild electronic jazz of Keep It Unreal to the glam cheese-fest of Disco Inferno.

The Honeycomb (☎ *530 5540, 15-17 Niddry St*) **Map 8** Tucked in the vaults beneath South Bridge, Honeycomb is one of the city's hottest clubs. Try to catch the cutting edge It (held on Saturday, fortnightly) or the gay-friendly garage and house night Taste (held on Sunday, weekly).

The Mambo Club (☎ *228 3252, 3 West Tollcross*) **Map 5** Just upstairs and yet a thousand miles away from the Cavendish (see Discos later in the chapter), the long-established Mambo provides a Saturday fix of reggae, ragga, R'n'B and hip hop.

Club Mercado (☎ *226 4224, 36-39 Market St*) **Map 8** At Club Mercado's house night Eye Candy (held on Saturday, fortnightly) the dress code is 'dress glam or scram', while the Time Tunnel (held on Friday, weekly) carries jaded office workers back to the 1960s, '70s and '80s.

Studio 24 (☎ *558 3758, 24 Calton Rd*) **Map 3** The programme at Studio 24 covers all bases, from house to goth to nu metal. The big night for serious clubbers, though, is the hard-house club Oxygen (held on Saturday, fortnightly).

ENTERTAINMENT

The Venue *(☎ 557 3073, 17-23 Calton Rd)* **Map 3** Spread over three floors and hosting live gigs as well as clubs, The Venue is a top nightspot. Try Cerotonin (held on Friday, monthly) for techno and trance, Scratch (held on Saturday, monthly) for hip hop, or Rhombus (held on Saturday, monthly) for jazz, funk, reggae and soul.

DISCOS

The Cavendish *(☎ 228 3252, 3 West Tollcross)* **Map 5** It's been around for decades, and has a reputation as a bit of a meat market, but the Cavendish still packs them in with a policy of over-25s only, smart dress code and 1970s disco music. (See also the Mambo Club in the Clubs section earlier in the chapter.)

Gaia *(☎ 229 9438, 28 Kings Stables Rd)* **Map 3** Gaia pulls in a pissed-up, studenty, dance-till-you-puke crowd, gamely thrashing away to a soundtrack of pop, funk, disco and house while trying not to barf up the gallon of cheap promo drinks they just downed. Grand fun.

Why Not? *(☎ 624 8633, 14 George St)* **Map 3** Located downstairs at The Dome (see the Places to Eat chapter), Why Not? is a sophisticated club playing mainstream chart sounds to a well-heeled, 30-something, New Town crowd. Dress smart and raid a cash machine on the way.

GAY & LESBIAN VENUES

Edinburgh has a small – but perfectly formed – gay and lesbian scene, centred on the area around Broughton St (known affectionately as 'The Pink Triangle') at the eastern end of New Town. Although not as mad, bad and dangerous to know as the Glasgow scene, there are enough pubs and clubs to keep the boozing and cruising crowd happy. You can find out what's happening through the listings in *Scotsgay* magazine (**W** www.scotsgay.com) and *The List*. For community contacts see the Gay & Lesbian Travellers section in the Facts for the Visitor chapter.

Blue Moon Cafe *(☎ 556 2788, 1 Barony St)* **Map 3** Open 11am-11.30pm Mon-Fri, 9am-12.30am Sat & Sun. Set in the heart of The Pink Triangle, the Blue Moon is a friendly caff offering good food and good company.

Out of the Blue *(☎ 478 7048, 1 Barony St)* **Map 3** Open noon-7pm Sat-Wed, noon-8pm Thur & Fri. Set in the basement beneath the Blue Moon, Out of the Blue is a gay and lesbian shop selling books, mags, videos, toys and so on.

CC Blooms *(☎ 556 9331, 23 Greenside Place, Leith Walk)* **Map 3** Open 6pm-3am Mon-Sat, 8pm-3am Sun. The raddled old queen of the Edinburgh gay scene, CC's offers two floors of deafening dance and disco. It's a bit overpriced and overcrowed but worth a visit – if you can get past the bouncers and the crowds of drunks looking for a late drink.

Planet Out *(☎ 524 0061, 6 Baxter's Place, Leith Walk)* **Map 3** Open 4pm-1am Mon-Fri, 2pm-1am Sat & Sun. Planet Out pulls in a younger crowd than CC's and has a better party atmosphere at the weekends – it's a bit quieter through the week, when you can chill out on the sofas and chat.

New Town Bar *(☎ 538 7775, 26b Dublin St)* **Map 3** Open noon-1am Mon-Thur, noon-2am Fri & Sat, 12.30pm-1am Sun. Dark and smoky, with a suspiciously sticky carpet, the New Town mainly attracts older males and lots of leather. The cellar bar has a disco from 10pm on Friday and Saturday.

Claremont Bar *(☎ 556 5662, 133-135 East Claremont St)* **Map 1** Open 11am-1am Mon-Sat, 12.30pm-1am Sun. Scotland's only sci-fi theme pub (no, you have to see it), the Claremont is a friendly, gay-owned bar and restaurant. The first and third Saturdays of the month are men-only nights, when leather, rubber, skinheads and bears are the order of the evening. If that's not your bag, Monday nights see the weekly meeting of the Edinburgh Doctor Who Appreciation Society (honest!).

The Stag & Turret *(☎ 661 6443, 1-7 Montrose Terrace)* **Map 3** Open noon-1am daily. This is a pleasant, gay local with karaoke from 8.30pm on Wednesday, Friday and Sunday. It is good for cruising – as the locals say, 'If ye're gaggin' fur it, try the Stag and Turret'.

The Townhouse Sauna & Gym (☎ 556 6116, w www.townhouse-sauna.co.uk, 53 East Claremont St) **Map 3** Admission £6-9. Open noon-11pm Sun-Thur, noon-midnight Fri & Sat. Gay-owned and -operated, The Townhouse is Scotland's biggest gay sauna, spread over four floors of a Georgian town house. Facilities include two sauna cabins, steam room, Jacuzzi, gym, video lounge and bar.

Gay & Lesbian Club Nights
There are several clubs that are gay- or lesbian-only or that attract a large gay contingent. A few of the more permanent fixtures are mentioned here, but as club nights and venues change often, it's best to check *Scotsgay* or *The List* for the latest situation.

Joy @ Ego (☎ 478 7434, 24-hour information ☎ 467 2551, w www.clubjoy.co .uk, 14 Picardy Place) **Map 3** Admission £10. Open 10.30pm-3am Sat. Joy is Edinburgh's longest-running and most upfront gay club night, playing dance music in a vast, wood-panelled venue with an air of faded grandeur. Don't miss it.

Mingin' @ Studio 24 (☎ 558 3768, 24 Calton Rd) **Map 3** Admission £5. Open 10.30pm-3am Sat, fortnightly. In the Scots language, 'minging' means 'dirty'; it also means 'drunk'. That's all you need to know really. Mingin' is a gay-friendly club night pumping out hard house, sexy trance and techno. Sweat till you're wet.

Divine Divas @ The Venue (☎ 556 8997, 15-17 Calton Rd) **Map 3** Admission £6. Open 10pm-3am, 2nd Sat of the month. The top floor of The Venue hosts this monthly, women-only club night, where a mixed-age crowd dances to indie, house, disco and Latin classics. Profits go to the Lothian Gay & Lesbian Switchboard.

Tackno @ Club Mercado (☎ 550 3716, 36-39 Market St) **Map 3** Admission £6. Open 10.30pm-3am, last Sun of the month. Drawing a mixed gay and straight crowd, the ever-popular Tackno thrives on cheesy music and themed fancy dress. Who could resist dressing up for Tackno at the Beach, Tackno in Space, Eurovision Tackno or Tackno Down Under – check *The List* or DJ

Trendy Wendy's Web site at w hello.to/ trendywendy for the next Tackno theme.

ROCK, BLUES & POP
In the last decade many of Edinburgh's live-music venues have closed down or been converted to clubs and bars, and the capital's live-music scene today is not a patch on Glasgow's. There are occasional rock gigs at clubs such as The Venue, Studio 24 and The Bongo Club (see Clubs earlier in the chapter).

Big-name bands and solo artists tend to play at the SECC in Glasgow these days; those that include Edinburgh usually play at the Edinburgh Playhouse (see Theatre later in the chapter). In summer, promoters take advantage of the seating installed for the Military Tattoo to stage a few spectacular concerts on the Castle Esplanade. These shows are atmospheric but potentially cold and wet. Tickets to major gigs are usually sold at *Virgin Megastore (Map 3;* ☎ 220 3234) at 125 Princes St and *Ripping Music (Map 3;* ☎ 226 7010) at 91 South Bridge.

Edinburgh Corn Exchange (☎ 443 0404, w www.ece.uk.com, 10 Newmarket Rd, Chesser) **Map 1** Ticket prices vary. A new venue opened by Blur in 1999, and home to the annual 'T on the Fringe' and Blues festivals, the Corn Exchange is a 3000-seat hall in a converted market building.

The Liquid Room (☎ 225 2564, 9c Victoria St) **Map 8** Tickets £9-15. One of the city's top live-music venues, boasting a superb sound system, the Liquid Room stages all kinds of music from local bands to The Average White Band. Check the programme at w www.liquidroom.com.

The Mercat (☎ 225 3861, 28 West Maitland St) **Map 2** Tickets £2.50. The Mercat is a large, West End pub and sports bar with live bands at 7.30pm on Saturday nights.

NB's (☎ 556 2414, 1 Princes St) **Map 3** Admission free. NB's is the public bar in the Balmoral Hotel and hosts live blues and rock from 9pm Thursday to Saturday.

Timberbush (☎ 476 8080, 28 Bernard St, Leith) **Map 6** Admission free. A cool cafe-bar that serves good food, Timberbush also stages live rock and cover bands from 9pm

ENTERTAINMENT

Friday night, live bands or DJs on Wednesday, Thursday and Saturday, and jazz on Sundays.

Whistle Binkie's (☎ *557 5114,* W *www .whistlebinkies.com 4-6 South Bridge)* **Map 8** Open 7pm-3am daily. This crowded cellar bar just off the Royal Mile has live music every night, including rock, blues and folk. Open mic night, from 10pm on Monday, showcases new talent.

JAZZ
The climax of the jazz calendar is the week-long International Jazz & Blues Festival in late July/early August, but there are plenty of regular gigs throughout the year. Gigs are advertised in *The Gig Guide* and in the free quarterly *Jazz* booklet. Visiting bands often play at the Queen's Hall (see Classical Music later in the chapter).

Harry's Bar (☎ *539 8100, 7b Randolph Place)* **Map 2** Admission free. Harry's is a laid-back basement bar with free live jazz sessions at 3.30pm on Saturday afternoons.

Henry's Jazz Bar (☎ *538 7385, 8a Morrison St)* **Map 3** Edinburgh's hottest jazz joint, Henry's has something going on every night, from traditional and contemporary jazz to soul, funk, hip hop and drum'n'bass.

The Auld Hundred (☎ *225 1809, 100 Rose St)* **Map 3** Tickets £2. Home to the Centre Stage Jazz Club, this old Rose St pub, complete with original cast-iron fittings and leaded windows, hosts a regular Tuesday night jazz session upstairs.

Fairmile Inn (☎ *445 2056, 44 Biggar Rd)* This Art Deco, 1930s-style pub, right on the southern edge of the city, is home to the Edinburgh Jazz 'n' Jive Club. The Friday night gigs put the emphasis on traditional, from Ragtime to New Orleans to swing.

Henderson's vegetarian restaurant (see the Places to Eat chapter) has live music, mainly jazz and classical guitar, at 7.30pm most evenings.

FOLK
The capital is a great place to hear traditional Scottish (and Irish) folk music, with a mix of regular spots and impromptu sessions.

Castle Bar Cafe (☎ *225 7432, 6 John-stone Terrace)* **Map 8** Admission free. The Castle has folk-music sessions at 9pm on Tuesday, Thursday, Friday and Saturday.

Finnegan's Wake (☎ *226 3816, 9b Victoria St)* **Map 8** Admission free. Finnegan's is a cavernous Irish theme pub with a stage where you can catch a live band – mostly Irish and Scottish folk and folk-rock – seven nights a week.

Pleasance Cabaret Bar (☎ *650 2349, 60 The Pleasance)* **Map 3** Admission £6. The Pleasance is home to the Edinburgh Folk Club, which runs a programme of visiting bands and singers at 8pm on Wednesday.

The Royal Oak (☎ *557 2976, 1 Infirmary St)* **Map 8** Admission free, £3 Sun. The popular 'Wee Folk Club' in the downstairs lounge, with a tiny bar and room for only 30 punters, is ticket only, so get there early (9pm start) if you want to be sure of a place. Saturday night is an open-session night – bring your own instruments (or a good singing voice).

Sandy Bell's (☎ *225 2751, 25 Forrest Rd)* **Map 8** Admission free. This unassuming bar has been a stalwart of the traditional music scene since The Corrs were in nappies. There's music almost every evening at 9pm, and also from 2.30pm on Sunday afternoon.

The Shore (☎ *553 5080, 3-4 The Shore, Leith)* **Map 6** This is a fine, traditional waterfront bar, with lively folk sessions on Wednesday night at 9pm.

The Tass (☎ *556 6338, 1 High St)* **Map 8** Admission free. This Royal Mile pub has regular folk sessions on Tuesday, Wednesday and Friday, but musicians are welcome to bring along their instruments any time.

CINEMAS
Film buffs will find plenty to keep them happy in Edinburgh's art-house cinemas, the Filmhouse and the Cameo, while popcorn munchers can choose from a range of multiplexes. Most offer concessions for school kids, students, the unemployed and senior citizens. You can check cinema listings daily in *The Scotsman* and *Evening News* newspapers.

The Cameo (box office ☎ *228 4141,* information ☎ *228 2800, 38 Home St)* **Map 5**

Admission £2.50-5.20. The three-screen, independently-owned Cameo is a good, old-fashioned cinema showing an imaginative mix of mainstream and art-house movies. There's a good programme of midnight movies, late-night double bills and Sunday matinees, and the seats in Screen 1 are big enough to get lost in.

The Dominion (☎ 447 2660, 18 Newbattle Terrace) **Map 4** Admission £3.70-5.90. The much-loved Dom is a delightful, independent, family-run four-screener in a 1938 Art Deco building. The programme is unashamedly mainstream and family-oriented.

The Filmhouse (☎ 228 2688, 88 Lothian Rd) **Map 3** Admission £2.20-5.20. The Filmhouse is the main venue for the annual International Film Festival and screens a full programme of art-house, classic, foreign and second-run films, with lots of themes, retrospectives and 70mm screenings. It has wheelchair access to all screens.

The Odeon (box office ☎ 667 0971, information & credit-card booking ☎ 0870 505 0007, 7 Clerk St) **Map 5** Admission £3.50-4.90. This standard five-screen multiplex shows mainstream, first-run films and special children's matinees.

UGC Fountainpark (Information & credit-card booking ☎ 0870 902 0417, Fountainpark Complex, Dundee St) **Map 4** Admission £3.50-5.50. The UGC is a massive 12-screen mulitplex, complete with cafe-bar, movie-poster shop and scarily overpriced popcorn.

CLASSICAL MUSIC, OPERA & BALLET

Edinburgh is home to the Scottish Chamber Orchestra (SCO), one of Europe's finest and well worth hearing. The Scottish Opera and Scottish Ballet companies and the Royal Scottish National Orchestra (RSNO) are based in Glasgow but regularly perform in Edinburgh. The following are the main venues for classical music.

Edinburgh Festival Theatre (☎ 529 6000, 13-29 Nicolson St) **Map 8** Tickets £6-56. The modern Festival Theatre is the city's main venue for opera, dance and ballet, but also stages musicals, concerts, drama and children's shows.

Greyfriars Kirk (☎ 226 5429, Greyfriars Place) **Map 8** Tickets £5.50-12. The Edinburgh Symphony Orchestra, established in 1963 and composed of amateur musicians, performs concerts here. There are regular recitals and concerts throughout the year.

The Queen's Hall (☎ 668 2019, 89 Clerk St) **Map 5** Tickets £5.50-19. Box office open 10am-5pm Mon-Sat, until end of interval on day of performance. The Queen's Hall is home to the SCO. It also hosts jazz concerts and a whole range of other events.

St Giles Cathedral (☎ 225 9442, High St) **Map 3** Tickets free-£6. The big kirk on the Royal Mile hosts a regular and varied programme of classical music, including popular lunchtime and evening concerts and organ recitals. The cathedral choir sings at the 10am and 11.30am Sunday services.

Usher Hall (☎ 228 1155, Lothian Rd) **Map 3** Tickets £5.50-19. Box office open 10am-5pm Mon-Sat, until 8.15pm on day of performance. The architecturally impressive Usher Hall hosts concerts by the RSNO and performances of popular music.

THEATRE, MUSICALS & COMEDY

Despite the huge international popularity of the Edinburgh Festival and Fringe, theatre audiences during the rest of the year have been falling in recent years, prompting much doom and gloom regarding the future funding of Edinburgh's theatres.

Royal Lyceum Theatre (☎ 248 4848, 30b Grindlay St) **Map 3** Tickets £7-17.50. Box office open 10am-8pm Mon-Sat (6pm on nonperformance days). A grand Victorian theatre located beside the Usher Hall, the Lyceum stages drama, concerts, musicals and ballet.

Traverse Theatre (☎ 228 1404, 10 Cambridge St) **Map 3** Tickets £4-10. Box office open 10am-6pm Mon, 10am-8pm Tues-Sat, 4pm-8pm Sun. The Traverse is the main focus for new Scottish writing and stages an adventurous programme of contemporary drama and dance. The cafe-bar here is a hip place to hang out.

ENTERTAINMENT

Netherbow Theatre (☎ 556 9579, 43-45 High St) **Map 8** Tickets £4-6. This small theatre on the Royal Mile features modern Scottish and international drama, and is home to the Scottish Storytelling Centre.

King's Theatre (☎ 220 4349, 2 Leven St, Bruntsfield) **Map 5** Tickets £7-16.50. The King's is a traditional theatre with a programme of musicals, drama, comedy and its famous annual Christmas pantomime.

Edinburgh Playhouse (☎ 557 2692, bookings ☎ 0870 606 3424, 18-22 Greenside Place) **Map 3** This restored theatre at the top of Leith Walk stages broadway musicals, dance shows, opera and popular-music concerts.

Bedlam Theatre (☎ 225 9893, 11b Bristo Place) **Map 8** Tickets £3-4. Box office open for performances only. Situated at the southern end of George IV Bridge in a converted church, Bedlam is home to the Edinburgh University Theatre Company. As well as staging EUTC productions, it hosts performances by visiting theatre companies. Improverts – improvised comedy spot – is held at 10.30pm every Friday.

The Stand Comedy Club (☎ 558 7272, 5 York Place) **Map 3** Tickets £1-7. The Stand, founded in 1995, is Edinburgh's main comedy venue. It's a cabaret bar with shows every night (free Sunday lunchtime).

A handful of bars, notably *The Gilded Saloon* (☎ 226 2151, 233 Cowgate) **Map 8**, *Finn MacCool's* (☎ 622 7109, 161 Lothian Rd) **Map 3** and *The Outhouse* (☎ 557 6668, 12a Broughton St Lane) **Map 3** have occasional stand-up comedy nights.

SPECTATOR SPORTS
Football
Edinburgh has two rival football (soccer) teams playing in the Scottish Premier League – Heart of Midlothian (aka Hearts, Jam Tarts, Jambos) and Hibernian (aka Hibs, Hibbies). The domestic football season lasts from August to May and most matches are played at 3pm on Saturday or 7.30pm on Tuesday or Wednesday.

Tynecastle Stadium (☎ 200 7200, W www .heartsfc.co.uk, Gorgie Rd) **Map 4** Hearts – winners of the Scottish Cup in 1998 – have their home ground south-west of the centre in Gorgie.

Easter Road Stadium (☎ 661 2159, W www.hibs.co.uk, 12 Albion Place) **Map 3** Hibernian's home ground is north-east of the centre. Hibs – who have not won the Scottish Cup since 1902 – came close in 2001, making it to the final only to lose 3-0 to Glasgow Celtic.

Rugby Union
Each year, from January to March, Scotland's national rugby team takes part in the Six Nations Rugby Union Championship. The most important fixture is the clash against England for the Calcutta Cup. At club level, the season runs from September to May.

Murrayfield Stadium (☎ 346 5000, W www.sru.org.uk, 112 Roseburn St) **Map 1** Murrayfield, about 1½ miles west of the centre, is the venue for international rugby matches.

Golf
For golfing enthusiasts, the Old Course at St Andrews is 55 miles north of Edinburgh across the Firth of Forth (see the Excursions chapter). The Alfred Dunhill Cup, the world's most renowned international team tournament, takes place here in mid October. The British Open Championship is also held here regularly.

Other Sports
Most other spectator sports, including athletics and cycling, are hosted at *Meadowbank Sports Centre* (Map 1; ☎ 661 5351 139 London Rd), Scotland's main sport arena, east of the centre.

Horse-racing enthusiasts should head 6 miles east to *Musselburgh Racecourse* (☎ 665 2859, W www.musselburgh-racecourse.co.uk, Linkfield Rd, Musselburgh). Scotland's oldest racecourse (founded 1816), where meetings are held throughout the year.

ENTERTAINMENT

Shopping

ART & ANTIQUES

The main areas to go hunting for period pieces include Thistle and Broughton Sts in New Town, Grassmarket in Old Town, and the northern end of Causewayside in Southside. *The Courtyard Antiques* (Map 5) (☎ 662 9008, 108a Causewayside) has a good selection of furniture, toys and militaria. *Just Junk* (Map 3) (☎ 557 4385, 87 Broughton St) has lots of desirable furniture from the 19th century to the 1970s, and some fascinating bric-a-brac.

Down in Leith, *Georgian Antiques* (Map 6) (☎ 553 7286, 10 Pattison St, Leith Links) claims to have the largest selection of antiques in Scotland with three floors of Victorian and Edwardian furniture, clocks, brass and porcelain.

Another happy hunting ground in Leith is the *Edinburgh Architectural Salvage Yard* (Map 6) (☎ 554 7077, Unit 6, Couper St), where you can find everything from original Georgian and Victorian cast-iron fireplaces and kitchen ranges to gleaming chrome, Art Deco bathroom fittings.

BOOKS & MAPS

As the centre of the Scottish publishing industry since the 18th century, Edinburgh has always been well supplied with bookshops, both new and second-hand.

James Thin (Map 8) (☎ 556 6743, 53-9 South Bridge), founded in 1848, is the city's principal home-grown bookstore and Edinburgh University's main supplier. There's another James Thin branch at 59 George St. *Bauermeister* (Map 8) (☎ 226 5561, 19 George IV Bridge) is another good general bookshop. In New Town there are big branches of the nationwide *Waterstone's* (Map 3) chain at Nos 13 and 128 Princes St and 83 George St. Both James Thin and Waterstone's have frequent book signings and author events. *Word Power* (Map 5)(☎ 662 9112, 43 West Nicolson St) is a radical, independent bookshop that supports small publishers and local writers. It stocks a wide range of political, gay and feminist literature, as well as non-mainstream fiction and non-fiction.

The Stationery Office Bookshop (Map 3) (☎ 606 5566, 71 Lothian Rd) has a good selection of books on business, Scottish history, travel (including LP guides), computers and probably the widest range of Ordnance Survey maps in town. There are many specialist bookshops in the city, including *The Cook's Bookshop* (Map 8) (☎ 226 4445, 118 West Bow), owned by Clarissa Dickson-Wright of TV's *Two Fat Ladies* fame.

Second-hand & Antiquarian

If you're looking for second-hand and antiquarian books, there's a cluster of bookshops along West Port, just west of Grassmarket, and others on Canongate on the Royal Mile, and in New Town.

West Port Books (Map 3) (☎ 229 4431, 147 West Port) has a good range of material covering Scottish history and has published its own edition of *An Atlas of Old Edinburgh*, a collection of antique maps from 1544 to the 19th century. It also specialises in Indian and Himalayan history and art. *Old Grindle's Bookshop* (Map 6) (☎ 229 7252, 3 Spittal St) just along the street from West Port, is another good place for second-hand Scottish history and literature.

Second Edition (Map 3) (☎ 556 9403, 9 Howard St) is a place for serious collectors buying and selling rare editions, while the maze of shelves at *McNaughtan's Bookshop* (Map 3) (☎ 556 5897, 3a-4a Haddington Place, Leith Walk) houses a broad spectrum of general second-hand and antiquarian books.

Carson Clark Gallery (Map 3) (☎ 556 4710, 181-3 Canongate), near the foot of the Royal Mile, has an interesting range of original and facsimile antique maps, charts and plans of Scotland, Europe and the rest of the world.

CASHMERE & WOOL

Woollen textiles and knitwear are one of Scotland's classic exports. Scottish cashmere – a fine, soft wool from young goats and lambs – provides the most luxurious and expensive knitwear, and has been seen gracing the torsos of pop-star Robbie Williams and England footballer David Beckham.

Designs On Cashmere (Map 8) *(☎ 556 6394, 28 High St)* and *The Cashmere Store* (Map 8) *(☎ 225 5178, 2 St Giles St, Royal Mile)* are good places to start, with a wide range of traditional and modern knitwear, while colourful designs at *Joyce Forsyth Designer Knitwear* (Map 8) *(☎ 220 4112, 42 Candlemaker Row)* will drag your ideas about woollens firmly into the 21st century.

Edinburgh Woollen Mill (Map 3) *(☎ 226 3840, 139 Princes St)* is an old stalwart of the tourist trade with a good selection of traditional jerseys, cardigans, scarves, shawls and rugs.

CRAFTS & SOUVENIRS

During the Festival period there's a good *Crafts Fair* (Map 3) in the churchyard at St John's Church, on the corner of Princes St and Lothian Rd, with a wide range of jewellery, ceramics and leather goods.

The Meadows Pottery (Map 5) *(☎ 662 4064, 11a Summerhall Place)* sells colourful stoneware, all hand-thrown on the premises. *The Adam Pottery* (Map 3) *(☎ 557 3978, 76 Henderson Row)* also produces its own ceramics, mostly decorative, in a wider range of styles.

Flux (Map 6) *(☎ 554 4075, 55 Bernard St, Leith)* is an outlet for contemporary Scottish arts and crafts, including stained glass, metalware, jewellery and ceramics.

The Edinburgh History Shop (Map 8) *(☎ 477 3522, 24 St Mary's St)* has a range of unusual and high-quality gifts, from old maps and history books, to traditional horn spoons, to casts of the stone carvings in Rosslyn Chapel.

Mr Wood's Fossils (Map 8) *(☎ 220 1344, 5 Cowgatehead, Grassmarket)* has a wide range of minerals, gems, fossils and other geological gifts.

DEPARTMENT STORES

Jenners (Map 3) *(☎ 225 2442, 48 Princes St)*, founded in 1838, is the grande dame of Scottish department stores. It stocks a wide range of quality goods, both classic and contemporary. *John Lewis* (Map 3) *(☎ 556 9121, St James Centre)* is the place to go for good-value clothes and household goods.

Aitken & Niven (Map 3) *(☎ 225 1461, 77-9 George St)*, founded in 1905, is another independent Scottish store with a good range of quality tartans and tweeds, and a wide selection of rugby shirts and accessories.

The city centre branch of *Marks & Spencer* (Map 3) *(☎ 225 2301, 54 Princes St)* has an excellent food hall.

FASHION

All the usual high-street chains can be found along Princes St, and in the St James Centre and Princes Mall. More upmarket shops such as Jigsaw, French Connection, Phase 8, Hobbs and Karen Millen are on George St.

Corniche (Map 8) *(☎ 556 3707, 2 Jeffrey St)* and *Cruise* (Map 8) *(☎ 556 2532, 14 St Mary's St)* are good places to shop for designer labels. *Sam Thomas* (Map 2) *(☎ 220 1126, 18 Stafford St)* has a good range of affordable designer gear, from casual to evening wear.

Flip (Map 8) *(☎ 556 4966, 60-2 South Bridge)* is a vast student emporium purveying all things denim, leather and retro at marked-down prices.

Several shops specialise in second-hand fashion. *Armstrong's* (Map 8) *(☎ 220 5557, 83 Grassmarket)* is an Edinburgh institution offering everything from elegant 1940s dresses to funky 1970s flares. *Gladrags* (Map 3) *(☎ 557 1916, 17 Henderson Row)* has a range of clothes, shoes and jewellery from Victorian petticoats to 1950s suits and dresses. *Greensleeves* (Map 4) *(☎ 447 8042, 203 Morningside Rd)* goes for high-quality second-hand clothes, handbags and shoes, including many with designer labels.

FOOD & DRINK

The acknowledged queen of Edinburgh delicatessens is *Valvona & Crolla* (Map 3

(☎ 556 6066, 19 Elm Row) at the top of Leith Walk, established in the 1930s and packed with Mediterranean goodies. Other good delis include **Peckham's (Map 4)** (☎ 229 7054, 155 Bruntsfield Place), **Herbie's (Map 2)**(☎ 332 9888, 66 Raeburn Place) and **Fleur's (Map 6)** (☎ 554 8841, 52 The Shore, Leith).

Crombie's (Map 3) (☎ 557 0111, 97-101 Broughton St) is a top-quality butcher shop where you can buy excellent home-made haggis. **MacSween of Edinburgh** (☎ 440 2555, Dryden Rd, Loanhead), the most famous haggis-makers in the city, closed their Morningside butcher shop a few years ago to concentrate on making haggis. You can buy direct from the factory, from Jenners, or around the UK from Harrods, Selfridges and Fortnum & Mason.

Another place where you can find the best of Scottish produce is the monthly **Edinburgh Farmers' Market (Map 3)**, held on the first Saturday of the month at Castle Terrace car park. Check the latest dates and opening times with the TIC.

If it's a drap of the cratur ye're after, head for **Royal Mile Whiskies (Map 8)** (☎ 225 3383, 379 High St), which stocks a vast selection of single malts, in miniature as well as full-size bottles.

In the USA it's candy, in Australia it's lollies, but in Scotland it's always been sweeties. **Casey's (Map 8)** (☎ 556 6082, 52 St Mary's St) is a good, old-fashioned sweetie shop where you can buy soor plooms, kola cubes, butter nuts and Carluke balls (don't ask) by the quarter (OK, 125g). **Fudge House of Edinburgh (Map 3)** (☎ 556 4172, 197 Canongate) on the Royal Mile has fudge to die for, including chocolate and peppermint, rum and raisin, hazelnut, and tasty Highland cream. Mmmmm.

JEWELLERY
Mappin & Webb (Map 3) (☎ 225 5502, 88 George St) are jewellers to HM the Queen, and offer jewellery, watches and silverware of the highest quality.

For something a little different, take a look at **Montresor (Map 3)** (☎ 220 6877, 35 Stephen St), which has a range of antique

costume jewellery, particularly from the 1920s and 30s.

Ortak (Map 3) (☎ 557 4393, Unit 29, Princes Mall, 3 Princes St) produces beautiful gold and silver jewellery based on Celtic and Art Nouveau designs, as well as pieces inspired by Charles Rennie Mackintosh. **Palenque (Map 8)** (☎ 557 9553, 56 High St) specialises in silver jewellery and hand-crafted accessories.

Scottish Gems (Map 8) (☎ 557 5731, 24 High St) creates gold and silver jewellery to traditional – mostly Celtic – and modern designs.

MUSIC
There are lots of good record shops in Edinburgh. Try **Avalanche Records (Map 3)** (☎ 228 1939, 28 Lady Lawson St) for indie, rock and punk; **Backbeat (Map 5)** (☎ 668 2666, 31 East Crosscauseway) for blues, rock and soul; and **Underground Solush'n (Map 8)** (☎ 226 2242, 9 Cockburn St) for techno, house, jungle and hip hop. **Fopp (Map 8)** (☎ 220 0133, 55 Cockburn St) is a good place for cheap CDs and vinyl, and the staff know what they're talking about.

Ripping Music (Map 8) (☎ 226 7010, 91 South Bridge) has a huge range of CDs, and **Virgin Megastore (Map 3)** (☎ 220 2230, 125 Princes St) is, well, a megastore.

McAlister Matheson Music (Map 3) (☎ 228 3827, 1 Grindlay St) is the place to head for classical music, Scottish folk and Celtic music, and books music.

OUTDOOR
Tiso (Map 3) (☎ 225 9486, 123-5 Rose St) has four floors of outdoor equipment, including camping, hiking, climbing, canoeing, skiing and snowboarding gear. At their macho branch, **Tiso Outdoor Experience (Map 6)** (☎ 554 0804, 41 Commercial St) in Leith, you can try before you buy with their Goretex-test shower, boot-bashing footpath, rock-climbing wall, ice-climbing wall and stove-testing area.

Boardwise (Map 3) (☎ 229 5887, 4 Lady Lawson St) supplies all the gear – and the cool threads – you'll need for any board-based sports, be it snow, skate or surf.

A Kilt Above the Rest

The kilt, as it is worn today, is a relatively modern invention. In the 17th century the traditional garb of the Highlander was the *plaid* (Gaelic for 'blanket'), a long piece of material that was pleated and then wrapped around the body and held with a belt at the waist, with the upper part drawn over the shoulders. (Check out the Highlanders in the film *Rob Roy* – their dress is pretty authentic.) A cut-down version of the plaid – involving the lower, skirt-like part only – was known as the *feileadh beag* (phillibeg, or 'little wrap'), in contrast to the full plaid or *feileadh mor* (phillimore, or 'big wrap').

All manner of Highland dress was made illegal after the Jacobite rebellion of 1745, and in the following decades the Highlanders were drafted into the British army. The Highland regiments proved to be courageous fighters, and in order to foster a sense of identity and national pride, a formalised Highland dress, based around the phillibeg, was reintroduced as a regimental uniform after 1782.

Aided by Sir Walter Scott's tireless promotion of all things Scottish, Highland dress soon became all the rage in high society; even King George IV and the lord mayor of London wore kilts during the royal visit to Scotland in 1822. It is this formal version of Highland dress that gets worn to countless weddings, Burns suppers and clan gatherings today. Dedicated followers of fashion, however, have not ignored the kilt – everyone from Siouxsie Banshee to Madonna has donned the tartan in the name of chic. But there is one Edinburgh designer who has gone a step further and has made the kilt a cult fashion item.

Howie Nicholsby, of *21st Century Kilts* (Map 8) (☎ 557 0256, fax 556 0615, **W** *www.21stcentury kilts.com, 57-9 High St*), has targeted the style-conscious market with his fashion kilts, retaining the traditional design and cut but experimenting with different fabrics and accessories. Choose a plain black barathea kilt – the most popular model – or try on one made from denim, imitation leather, stretchy black PVC, or even camouflage material. Who knows, he might develop a kilt following...

See the boxed text 'Cycling Edinburgh' in the Getting Around chapter for cycle shops.

TARTAN, KILTS & BAGPIPES
There are dozens of shops along the Royal Mile and Princes St where you can buy kilts and tartan goods. One of the best is **Kinloch Anderson** (Map 6) (☎ 555 1390, *Commercial St, Leith*), founded in 1868, and still family-run; they are also the supplier of kilts and Highland dress to the Royal Family.

Geoffrey (Tailor) Inc (Map 8) (☎ 557 0256, *57-9 High St*) can fit you out in traditional Highland dress or run up a kilt in your own clan tartan. Their offshoot, 21st Century Kilts (see the boxed text above), offers modern fashion kilts in a variety of fabrics.

Kilberry Bagpipes (Map 5) (☎ 221 9925, *38 Lochrin Bldgs, Gilmore Place*) are makers and retailers of traditional Highland bagpipes; they also sell piping accessories and learning materials.

TOYS, GAMES & OTHER STUFF
Wonderland (Map 3) (☎ 229 6428, *97-10 Lothian Rd*) is a classic, kids-with-nose pressed-against-the-window toy shop b also caters to the serious train-set an model-making fraternity.

Aha Ha Ha (Map 8) (☎ 220 5252, *9 West Bow*) have enough plastic poo, fak vomit, stink bombs and electronic fartin machines to keep your average Dennis th Menace happy for a month.

Forbidden Planet (Map 8) (☎ 225 861 *40-1 South Bridge*) stocks a wide range sci-fi comics, videos and T-shirts, as well Star Trek, Simpsons and South Park me chandise. It's also the place to shop for yo Rocky Horror Show gear.

Another Planet (Map 4) (☎ 337 0072, *Ashley Terrace*) – no relation to the above sells things that fly, sail or are otherwise o erated by the breeze – from £1.50 plas boomerangs to £1500 Blokarts (mini la yachts – the latest, ultracool, big boys' toys

WHERE TO SHOP

Princes St is Edinburgh's principal shopping street, lined with all the big high-street stores, from Marks & Spencer to Dixons to Virgin Megastore, with many smaller shops along pedestrianised Rose St. There are also two big shopping centres – Princes Mall, at the eastern end of Princes St next to the Balmoral Hotel, and the nearby St James Centre at the top of Leith St.

A new shopping complex with a flagship *Harvey Nichols* store is due to open on the eastern side of St Andrew Square in autumn 2002, and the new *Ocean Terminal* (Map 5) in Leith, anchored by Debenhams and BHS department stores, is the biggest shopping centre in Edinburgh.

Other central shopping streets include South Bridge, Nicolson St and Lothian Rd. For more off-beat shopping – including fashion, music, crafts, gifts and jewellery – head for the cobbled lanes of Cockburn, Victoria and St Mary's Sts, all near the Royal Mile in Old Town, or the urban 'villages' of Stockbridge and Morningside.

Markets

Ingliston Market (Ingliston Showground Car Park, Glasgow Rd; open 10am-4pm Sun), 8 miles west of the city centre and close to the airport, sells household goods, clothes and bric-a-brac; there's also a car boot sale.

Greenside Place Car Boot Sale (Map 3) *(Level 2, Greenside Place Car Park, Leith St; open 10am-2pm Sun)* offers the usual attic-clearance crowd leavened with a few semi-professional traders. There are usually some bargains hidden among the acres of junk. Get there early though or all the good stuff will be gone. Most stall-holders start packing up at 1pm.

Excursions

If you have time, it's worth getting out of Edinburgh to get a taste of the surrounding regions – the beaches and castles of East Lothian, the Border hills, the golfing capital of St Andrews, and of course Glasgow, Scotland's biggest city and Edinburgh's great rival in the west. The following places can all be reached easily using public transport.

To check details of timetables and fares for all public transport services in East and West Lothian, call Traveline (☎ 0800 232323) between 8.30am and 8pm Monday to Friday. For buses to Peebles and Melrose call First Edinburgh (☎ 0131-663 9233), and for buses to Fife call Stagecoach Traveline (☎ 0870 608 2608). For train times and fares, call National Rail Enquiries ☎ 0845 748 4950.

If you want to stay overnight in any of the places mentioned in this chapter, you can book accommodation through the Edinburgh & Scotland Information Centre (Map 3; ☎ 0131-473 3800) at Princes Mall, Edinburgh.

West

GLASGOW
☎ 0141 • pop 611,500

Although lacking the instantly inspiring beauty of Edinburgh, Glasgow is one of Britain's largest, liveliest and most interesting cities, with a legacy of appealing Georgian and Victorian architecture. It is the most Scottish of cities, with a unique blend of friendliness, energy, black humour and urban chaos. The city also boasts excellent art galleries and museums, most of them free – including the famous Burrell Collection – as well as numerous good-value restaurants, countless pubs, bars and clubs and a lively performing arts scene.

Information
The main Tourist Information Centre (TIC; ☎ 204 4400) is opposite Queen St train station at 11 George Square. It opens 9am to 6pm Monday to Saturday (till 7pm in June and September, and till 8pm in July and August) and 10am to 6pm Sunday, Easter to September. It has a Web site at [W] www.see glasgow.com.

There are currency exchange desks at the TIC and at the post office on the corner of Buchanan and St Vincent Sts. You can check your email at easyEverything (☎ 222 2365) at 57–61 St Vincent St; it opens 24 hours.

A Walk Through the Merchant City
An interesting hour-long walk will take you from George Square to Glasgow Cathedral through the Merchant City, a planned 18th century civic development. The Tobacco Lords were the entrepreneurs who opened up Europeatrade with the Americas, importing tobacco, rum and sugar in the 18th century, and their profits went to build these warehouses, offices and gracious homes. The current redevelopment trend has turned the warehouses into apartments for Glaswegian yuppies, and stylish shopping centres such as the Italian Centre have sprung up to serve their retail needs.

George Square is surrounded by imposing Victorian architecture, including the grand **City Chambers**, the seat of local government, built in the 1880s. The extravagant interior has been used in films as a double for the Kremlin and the Vatican. Cross George Square and walk one block south down Queen St to the **Gallery of Modern Art** (1827). This four-storey colonnaded building was once the Royal Exchange where business transactions were negotiated.

The gallery faces Ingram St, which you follow east for two blocks. To the right, down Garth St, is **Trades House**, designed by Robert Adam in 1791 to house the trade guild. A farther two blocks east along Ingram St brings you to **Hutchesons' Hall**, built in 1805 to a design by David Hamilton

An illuminating experience: Edinburgh cityscape at dusk, with the Bank of Scotland and Balmoral Hotel

Rock on! Finnegan's Wake hosts Scot-rock and folk bands.

rassmarket beneath the castle

Irn-Bru with ice and a slice? The quieter side of city pub life.

Now moored in Leith, Royal Yacht *Britannia* spent her heyday riding the waves with a conspicuous cargo

Glasgow's Kelvingrove Art Gallery & Museum, opened in 1902, is a feast for fanciers of Scottish art

GLASGOW

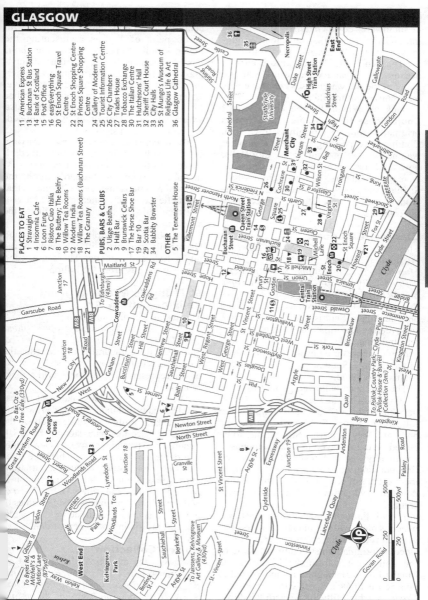

PLACES TO EAT
1 Stravaigin
4 Insomnia Cafe
6 Loon Fung
7 Ristoro Ciao Italia
8 The Buttery; The Belfry
10 Willow Tea Rooms
12 Modern India
18 Willow Tea Rooms (Buchanan Street)
21 The Granary

PUBS, BARS & CLUBS
2 Uisge Beatha
3 Halt Bar
9 Brunswick Cellars
17 The Horse Shoe Bar
19 Bar 10
29 Scotia Bar
34 Babbity Bowster

OTHER
5 The Tenement House

11 American Express
13 Buchanan St Bus Station
14 Bank of Scotland
15 Post Office
16 easyEverything
20 St Enoch Square Travel Centre
22 St Enoch Shopping Centre
23 Princes Square Shopping Centre
24 Gallery of Modern Art
25 Tourist Information Centre
26 City Chambers
27 Trades House
28 Tobacco Exchange
30 The Italian Centre
31 Hutchesons' Hall
32 Sheriff Court House
33 City Halls
35 St Mungo's Museum of Religious Life & Art
36 Glasgow Cathedral

EXCURSIONS

Retrace your steps one block and continue southwards down Glassford St, turn right into Wilson St and first left along Virginia St, lined with the old warehouses of the Tobacco Lords. The **Tobacco Exchange** became the Sugar Exchange in 1820 and many of the old warehouses here have now been converted into flats.

Back on Wilson St, the bulky **Sheriff Court House** fills a whole block. It was originally built as Glasgow's town hall. Continue east past **Ingram Square**, another warehouse development, to the **City Halls**, now used for concerts. The city's markets were once held here. Turn right from Albion St into Blackfriars St. Emerging onto the High St, turn left and follow the street up to the cathedral.

Glasgow Cathedral

This cathedral (*☎ 552 6891, Cathedral St; admission free; open 9.30am-6.30pm Mon-Sat & 2pm-6.30pm Sun Apr-Sept, 9.30am-4.30pm Mon-Sat & 2pm-4.30pm Sun Oct-Mar*) is a shining example of pre-Reformation Gothic architecture, and the only mainland Scottish cathedral to have survived the Reformation. Most of the current building dates from the 15th century, and only the western towers were destroyed in the turmoil. Sunday services are held at 11am and 6.30pm.

This has been hallowed ground for over 1500 years. The site was blessed for Christian burial in 397 by St Ninian. In the following century St Mungo brought the body of a holy man from Stirlingshire to be buried here. He stayed to found a monastic community, and built a simple church. The first building was consecrated in 1136, in the presence of King David I, but it burned down in 1197 and was rebuilt as the lower church.

Entry is through a side door into the **nave**, which is hung with regimental colours. The wooden roof has been restored many times since its original construction but some of the timber dates from the 14th century. Much of the stained glass is modern and to your left is Francis Spear's 1958 work *The Creation*, which fills the western window.

The cathedral is divided by a late 15th-century stone choir screen decorated with seven pairs of figures representing the Seven Deadly Sins. Beyond is the **choir**. Also by Francis Spear, the four stained-glass panels of the eastern window, depicting the apostles, are particularly effective. At the north-eastern corner is the entrance to the 15th-century **upper chapter house** where Glasgow University was founded. It's now used as a sacristy.

The **lower church**, reached by a stairway, is the most interesting part of the cathedral. Its forest of pillars creates a powerful atmosphere around St Mungo's tomb, the focus of a famous medieval pilgrimage that was believed to be as meritorious as a visit to Rome. Edward I paid three visits to the shrine in 1301.

Behind the cathedral is the renovated **Necropolis**, crowded with the tombs of the city's rich and famous. There are good views of the city from the hilltop.

St Mungo's Museum of Religious Life & Art

This award-winning museum (*☎ 553 2557, 2 Castle St; admission free; open 10am-5pm Mon-Thur & Sat, 11am-5pm Fri & Sun*) near the cathedral is named after the patron saint of Glasgow, and displays works of art representative of the world's main religions.

The building may look like a bit of restored antiquity, but in fact it's just a few years old – a £6.5 million reconstruction of the bishop's palace that once stood here. A 10-minute video provides an overall view before you delve into the exhibits. There are three galleries, representing religion as art, religious life and, on the top floor, religion in Scotland. In the main gallery Dali's *Christ of St John of the Cross* hangs beside statues of the Buddha and Hindu deities. Outside you'll find Britain's only Zen garden.

Burrell Collection

Glasgow's top attraction, the Burrell Collection (*☎ 649 7151, 2060 Pollokshaw Rd; admission free; open 10am-5pm Mon-Sat & 11am-5pm Sun Apr-Sept, 10am-5pm*

Mon-Thur & Sat, 11am-5pm Fri & Sun Oct-Mar), was amassed by wealthy industrialist Sir William Burrell before it was donated to the city. It's now housed in a prize-winning museum in Pollok Country Park, 3 miles south of the city centre. This idiosyncratic collection includes everything from Chinese porcelain and medieval furniture to paintings by Renoir and Cézanne. It's not so big as to be overwhelming, and the stamp of the collector lends an intriguing coherence.

From the outside, the building seems somewhat of a hybrid but the truly spectacular interior provides a fitting setting for an exquisite collection of tapestries, oriental porcelain, paintings and European stained glass. Floor-to-ceiling windows admit a flood of natural light, and the trees and landscape outside only enhance the effect created by the exhibits.

Carpeted floors maintain the silence to contemplate the beautifully displayed treasures. Carved-stone Romanesque doorways are incorporated into the structure so one actually walks through them. Some galleries are reconstructions of rooms from Hutton Castle, the Burrell residence. Even the public seating is of superb design.

The light and airy cafe on the lower ground floor includes the same floor-to-ceiling windows, hung with heraldic glass medallions. Numerous buses pass the park gates (including Nos 45, 48A and 57 from the centre), and there's a twice-hourly bus service between the gallery and the gates (a pleasant 10-minute walk). Alternatively, catch a train to Pollokshaws West from Central station – there are three trains per hour; on Glasgow's rail and underground map, Pollokshaws West is the third station on the light blue line to the south from Central station; trains on this line are destined for either East Kilbride or Kilmarnock stations.

Pollok House

Also in Pollok Country Park, and a 10-minute walk from the Burrell Collection, Pollok House *(☎ 616 6410, 2060 Pollokshaws Rd; adult/child £4/free; open 10am-5pm daily Apr-Oct, 11am-4pm daily Nov-Mar)* contains a fine collection of Spanish paintings, including works by El Greco and Goya. The house is Georgian and parts have been redecorated with historically correct colour schemes. There's a tearoom in the old kitchens.

The Tenement House

An extraordinary time-capsule experience, the small apartment in the Tenement House *(☎ 333 0183, 145 Buccleuch St; adult/child £3.50/1; open 2pm-5pm daily Mar-Oct)* provides a vivid insight into middle-class city life in the late 19th/early 20th centuries, complete with box-beds, an original kitchen range and all the fixtures and fittings of the Toward family who lived here for over 50 years.

Kelvingrove Art Gallery & Museum

Opened in 1902, this grand Victorian cathedral of culture *(☎ 357 3929, Kelvingrove; admission free; open 10am-5pm Mon-Sat & 11am-5pm Sun Apr-Sept, 10am-5pm Mon-Thur & Sat & 11am-5pm Fri & Sun Oct-Mar)*, and particularly its excellent collection of Scottish and European art, should not be missed.

The impressive central hall is dominated at one end by organ pipes; recitals are an integral part of the museum programme. An authentic museum smell emanates from the natural history of Scotland section, popular with school tours. Also downstairs there's a rather dowdy presentation of some interesting artefacts, including archaeological finds of prehistoric Scotland, European arms and armour, and silver.

The art gallery upstairs houses the city's art collection of 19th- and 20th-century works. Scottish painters of luminous landscapes and still lifes are comprehensively represented – Arthur Melville, McTaggart, Cadell, Joseph Crawhall; and Eduardo Paolozzi, Bruce McLean, David Hockney and Jasper Johns are among the moderns. Other paintings include Rembrandt's wonderful *Man in Armour*, and works by Monet, Botticelli, Van Gogh and Picasso.

The art gallery and museum are grandly set back from the road in Kelvingrove Park, just west of Kelvin Way. Any bus heading for Dumbarton Rd passes this way, including Nos 6, 6A, 57, 64 and 64A. Kelvin Hall is the nearest underground station.

Organised Tours

From March to October, *Scotguide Glasgow Tour* (☎ 204 0444) runs daily hop-on hop-off tourist buses every 30 minutes along the main sightseeing routes; the full circuit takes about 40 minutes and it costs £7/2.50 for a day ticket. *Guide Friday's* (☎ 556 2244) Discover Glasgow tour is similar and runs from April to October.

Places to Eat

Glasgow has an excellent selection of eateries and many are moderately priced. The city's top restaurants can be found in the West End and in the city centre.

West End This area probably has the greatest range of restaurants, everything from Glasgow's most famous place to eat, the upmarket Ubiquitous Chip, to cheap cafes where they really do serve chips with everything.

The Ubiquitous Chip (☎ 334 5007, 12 Ashton Lane) 2-course dinner with coffee £27.95. The Chip has earned a solid reputation for excellent Scottish cuisine, fresh seafood and game, and for the length of its wine list. Set among potted plants of arboreal proportions, this is an excellent place for a night out. There's a cheaper restaurant, *Upstairs at the Chip*, where a two-course lunch costs less than £10.

Ashoka (☎ 357 5904, 19 Ashton Lane) 2-course pre-theatre menu £7.95. The Ashoka is one of Glasgow's most popular Indian restaurants.

Grosvenor Cafe (☎ 339 1848, 31 Ashton Lane) Evening specials under £4. The cheapest place to eat in Ashton Lane is the Grosvenor, where you can get soup, filled rolls and hot meals all day; it's a popular student hangout.

Mitchells (☎ 339 2220, 35 Ashton Lane) Mains £8-12, 2-course pre-theatre meals £8.

Open for dinner only, this is an informal bistro with some excellent Scottish dishes.

Stravaigin (☎ 334 2665, 28 Gibson St) 2-course dinner £20. Stravaigin's Scottish fusion cuisine is highly recommended. The chilli con carne, Thai green curry and rack of blackfaced lamb are particularly good. There's a cheaper menu upstairs.

Bay Tree Cafe (☎ 334 5898, 403 Great Western Rd) Mains under £5. The vegetarian Bay Tree Cafe is excellent value, with generous salads and a good range of hot drinks. If you're in a hurry, it serves takeaways too.

Insomnia Cafe (☎ 564 1700, 38 Woodlands Rd) Mains £4-6.25. Scotland's first 24-hour cafe, this place has never closed since it first opened in October 1995. There are sandwiches, a wide range of meals, herbal teas and coffees.

Janssens (☎ 334 9682, 1355 Argyle St) Mains £6-11. Near the Kelvingrove Art Gallery & Museum, friendly Dutch-run Janssens serves good lunches and everything from adventurous sandwiches to full meals. There's a specials blackboard and vegetarian choices.

University Cafe (☎ 339 5217, 87 Byres Rd) Meals under £4. A Glasgow institution, the University Cafe is very cheap, offering fish and chips and salad, excellent pizzas and superb home-made ice cream.

City Centre There are a number of good choices in this area, especially along Argyle and Sauchiehall Sts.

The Buttery (☎ 221 8188, 652 Argyle St) 3-course lunch £16.85. Open Mon-Sat. Although it's surrounded by tower-block flats just west of the M8, The Buttery is one of the best restaurants in the city. The decor is Victorian and the menu is Scottish-Mediterranean.

The Belfry (☎ 221 0630, 652 Argyle St) 2/3-course pre-theatre dinner £9.50/11.95. The Belfry is a less expensive bistro downstairs from The Buttery. Reservations are advised.

The Willow Tea Rooms (☎ 332 0521, 217 Sauchiehall St) Lunch £5-6. Designed by Charles Rennie Mackintosh in 1904, and set above a jewellery shop, the Willow is pure Glasgow. Last orders are at 4.15pm, and for lunch and tea the queues can be long. Avoid them by arriving when it opens, and splash out on a superior breakfast of smoked salmon, scrambled eggs and toast. There's another branch at 97 Buchanan St.

Modern India (☎ *331 1980, 51 West Regent St*) 3-course lunch £5.95. An Indian restaurant with a difference, this place combines traditional tandoori dishes with more modern, experimental ones.

Loon Fung (☎ *332 1240, 417 Sauchiehall St*) 3-course lunch £6.30. This is one of the best Chinese places in town, with a good selection of chicken, seafood and vegetarian dishes. On Thursday to Saturday nights it has an all-you-can-eat banquet (£13.95).

Ristoro Ciao Italia (☎ *332 4565, 441 Sauchiehall St*) 3-course lunch £6.50. This is an efficient Italian restaurant where you can eat well for under a tenner.

The Granary (☎ *226 3770, 82 Howard St*) Mains £3.50-4.50. Near the St Enoch Shopping Centre, the Granary is a relaxed and inexpensive place serving mainly vegetarian food but with a few non-veggie choices.

Entertainment

Some of the liveliest nightlife in Scotland is to be found in Glasgow's pubs and bars. Most pubs also do food, although many stop serving around 8pm. For the latest information, get a copy of *The List*. Also look out for the monthly *Go!* magazine, and the free *city live!*, a listing of live music.

West Regent and Bath Sts have a plethora of small, subterranean hang-outs; Merchant City is full of larger, hip joints but there's no shortage of fun places to drink anywhere. The best thing about Glasgow is that it has maintained an unpretentious and welcoming atmosphere while keeping up with the funky beat of fashion. Try the city centre and the West End for the trendiest spots.

City Centre This is where the pre-club and club action is focused.

Bar 10 (☎ *221 8353, 10 Mitchell Lane*) Bar 10 is a stylish and popular cafe-bar off Buchanan St, designed by Ben Kelly who

was responsible for Manchester's famous Dry Bar and Hacienda.

Brunswick Cellars (☎ *572 0016, 239 Sauchiehall St*) The subterranean Brunswick Cellars is a popular bar that also does cheap lunches (main courses between £4 and £5).

Scotia Bar (☎ *552 8681, 112 Stockwell St*) This is Glasgow's oldest pub, boasting a history that goes back to 1792. It serves real ales and bar lunches. There's live folk music on Wednesday evenings and blues on Sunday afternoons.

Babbity Bowster (☎ *552 5055, 16 Blackfriars St*) A popular Merchant City pub with a good range of real ales, BB's also has excellent pub grub from £4 to £6 and live folk music on Saturday and Sunday.

The Horse Shoe Bar (☎ *221 3051, 17 Drury St*) The Horse Shoe may have one of the longest bars in Europe but its more important attraction is what's served over it – real ale and good food that's also good value. A three-course lunch costs just £2.40; evening meals in the upstairs lounge are only a little dearer. The pub's been here for over 100 years and it's largely unchanged.

West End This area offers a cool nightlife alternative for the post-college crowd.

Halt Bar (☎ *564 1527, 160 Woodlands Rd*) This is a popular university pub that hasn't yet been tarted up. There's a great atmosphere and free live music most nights. It serves toasties, rolls and soup until 9pm or 10pm.

Uisge Beatha (☎ *564 1598, 246 Woodlands Rd*) Farther along Woodlands Rd than the Halt Bar, the Uisge Beatha is a friendly place with eclectic decor, including church pews, and a huge range of malt whiskies.

Bar Oz (☎ *334 0884, 499 Great Western Rd*) Bar Oz is an Australian theme pub serving a good range of bottled beers, lagers and wines from Down Under.

Curlers (☎ *338 6511, 256 Byres Rd*) Curlers is very popular with students who come for the bargain food (until 7pm) and stay on for the comedy club on Wednesday night and the DJs Thursday to Sunday.

The Ubiquitous Chip (see Places to Eat earlier) has a good bar upstairs.

EXCURSIONS

Getting There & Away

Scottish Citylink runs frequent buses from Edinburgh's St Andrew Square to Glasgow's Buchanan St bus station (£7/5 peak/off-peak return); there are departures every 15 to 25 minutes, and the journey time is around 1¼ hours.

ScotRail trains shuttle back and forth between Edinburgh Waverley and Haymarket stations and Glasgow Queen St station every 15 minutes (£14.30/7.50 standard/cheap day return); the journey time is only 50 minutes.

You can drive the 56 miles from Edinburgh to Glasgow along the M8 motorway in an hour, but avoid the rush-hour traffic.

Getting Around

The St Enoch Square Travel Centre (☎ 226 4826), in the centre of St Enoch Square, provides information on all transport in the Glasgow region. It opens 8.30am to 5.30pm Monday to Saturday. Here you can get a copy of the free *Guide to Getting Around Glasgow*, which includes a map. The Roundabout Glasgow ticket (£3.50/1.75) covers all public transport in the city for a day; it also gives a £1.50 discount on city bus tours.

Bus Frequent services are provided. You can buy tickets when you board buses but on most you must have exact change. Fares are 70p for short trips in the city.

Train The small, circular underground train line – known to Glasgwegians as the Clockwork Orange – serves 15 stations in the city's central and western parts (both north and south of the river). Single tickets cost 80p, and the Discovery Pass (£2.50) gives a day's unlimited travel on the system.

Glasgow also has an extensive suburban rail network; tickets should be bought before travel if the station is staffed, or from the conductor if it isn't. The network connects with the underground at Buchanan St station.

Taxi You can hail taxis in the street or pick them up at a rank. If you order a taxi from Glasgow Wide Taxis (☎ 332 6666) by phone, you can pay by credit card.

LINLITHGOW
☎ 01506 • pop 9500

This ancient royal burgh, 15 miles west of Edinburgh, is one of Scotland's oldest towns, though much of it 'only' dates from the 15th to 17th centuries. Its centre retains a certain charm, except for the appallingly ugly modern buildings just west of the palace and the Cross (marketplace).

The TIC (☎ 844600), in the Burgh Halls at the Cross, opens 10am to 5pm daily, April to October.

Things to See & Do

The town's main attraction is the magnificent ruin of **Linlithgow Palace** (☎ 842896, *Church Peel; adult/child £2.80/1; open 9.30am-6.30pm daily Apr-Sept, 9.30am-4.30pm Mon-Sat & 2pm-4.30pm Sun Oct-Mar*). Begun by James I in 1425, the palace was under construction for over a century. It was a favourite royal residence – James V was born here in 1512, and his daughter Mary (later Queen of Scots) in 1542. Cromwell billeted his troops here in the 1650s and Bonnie Prince Charlie briefly visited in 1745 – legend has it that a cooking fire left by retreating Jacobite soldiers caused the blaze that gutted the palace in 1746.

Beside the palace is the Gothic **St Michael's Church** (☎ 842188, *Church Peel; admission free; open 10am-4.30pm daily May-Sept & Easter weekend*). Built between the 1420s and 1530s, it is topped by a controversial aluminium spire that was added in 1964, and is said to be haunted by a ghost that foretold King James IV of his impending defeat at Flodden in 1513.

The **Linlithgow Story** (☎ 670677, *Annet House, 143 High St; adult/child £1/60p, admission free Sun; open 10am-4pm Mon & Wed-Sat & 1pm-4pm Sun Easter-Oct*) is a small museum that tells the story of the Stewart monarchy and the town's history.

Just 150m south of the town centre lies the Union Canal and the **Linlithgow Canal Centre** (☎ 671215, **w** *www.lucs.org.uk, Manse Road Canal Basin; admission free;*

open 2pm-5pm Sat & Sun Easter-Sept). A little museum records the history of the canal, and there are three-hour **canal boat trips** west to the Avon Aqueduct (adult/child £6/3; departures at 2pm Saturday & Sunday Easter to June and September to October, and 2pm daily July and August). Shorter, 20-minute cruises leave every half-hour (adult/child £2.50/1.50; departures between 2pm and 4.30pm Saturday & Sunday Easter to June and September to October, and 2pm to 4.30pm daily July and August).

Places to Eat
The Four Marys (☎ 842171, 65-76 High St) Mains £4.95-6.95. Just across the street from the TIC, this attractive traditional pub serves real ales and good pub grub – try the haggis, neeps and tatties for £4.95.

Marynka (☎ 840123, 57 High St) 2-course dinner £16.50. Open daily except Sunday. For something a little more formal, head a few doors down to this pleasant little gourmet restaurant.

Champany Inn (☎ 834532) Mains £5.95-12.95. Two miles north-east of town, on the A804 road towards Queensferry, this is an excellent lunch spot famous for its steaks and lobsters. The 'Chop and Ale House' is a less expensive alternative to the main dining room.

Getting There & Away
Buses (Nos 38, 38A, 38B and 138 from St Andrew Square) and trains between Edinburgh and Falkirk stop at Linlithgow. Buses stop at the Cross, and the train station is 250m east of the centre. The M9 motorway passes north of the town.

North

The region to the north of the Firth of Forth refers to itself as the Kingdom of Fife – it was home to Scottish kings for 500 years. Now just another Scottish county, it maintains an individual Lowland identity quite separate from the rest of the country.

The main attraction for visitors is undoubtedly St Andrews. It's an ancient university town and ecclesiastical centre that's also world-famous as the home of golf.

DUNFERMLINE
☎ 01383 • pop 52,000
Six Scottish kings, including Robert the Bruce, are buried at Dunfermline Abbey. Once the country's capital, Dunfermline is now a large regional centre surrounded by sprawling suburbs, but the abbey's well worth a visit.

Orientation & Information
The post office is on Pilmuir St. The train station is 600m west of the town centre, and the bus station is in the centre, both within easy walking distance of the abbey.

The TIC (☎ 720999), 13 Maygate, is close to High St and the abbey, and opens 9.30am to 5.30pm Monday to Saturday year round; and 11am to 4pm Sunday, April to October.

Things to See & Do
In the 12th century King David I built **Dunfermline Abbey** *(☎ 739026, St Margaret St; adult/child £2/75p; open 9.30am-6.30pm daily Apr-Sept, 9.30am-4.30pm Mon-Wed & Sat & 9.30am-1pm Thur & 2pm-4.30pm Sun Oct-Mar)* here as a Benedictine monastery. It grew into a major pilgrimage centre, eclipsing the island of Iona (off Mull, on the west coast) as the favourite royal burial ground. The original 12th-century Romanesque nave, with its decorated columns, survives. The choir has been converted into the parish church (closed in winter).

Next to the abbey are the ruins of **Dunfermline Palace** *(same details as Abbey)*, rebuilt from the abbey guesthouse in the 16th century for James VI. It was the birthplace of Charles I, the last Scottish king born on Scottish soil.

The award-winning **Abbot House Heritage Centre** *(☎ 733266, Maygate; adult/child £3/free; open 10am-5pm daily)*, near the abbey, dates from the 15th century. It has interesting displays about the history of Scotland, the abbey and Dunfermline.

The most famous former inhabitant of Dunfermline is Andrew Carnegie, who was

EXCURSIONS

Edinburgh's Other Castles

Edinburgh is famous for *the* castle, but few people take time to seek out the dozen or so other castles that lie within and around the city. Some are ruins, some are restored, and some you can actually stay in (see the boxed text 'A Scotsman's Home...' in the Places to Stay chapter). The following are six of the best.

Ship-shaped **Blackness Castle** (☎ 01506-834807, *Blackness, West Lothian; adult/child £2/75p; open 9.30am-6.30pm daily Apr-Sept; 9.30am-4.30pm Mon-Wed & Sat & 9.30am-1pm Thu & 2pm-4.30pm Sun Oct-Mar*) is 15 miles west of Edinburgh. It's a massive artillery fortress jutting into the sea, built in the 15th and 16th centuries. Take bus No 47/47A from St Andrew Square to Bo'ness and get off at Mannerston; the castle is a 1-mile walk north.

Craigmillar Castle (*Map 1;* ☎ 661 4445, *Craigmillar Castle Rd; adult/child £2/75p; open 9.30am-6.30pm daily Apr-Sept; 9.30am-4.30pm Mon-Wed & Sat & 9.30am-1pm Thu & 2pm-4.30pm Sun Oct-Mar*) is 2½ miles south-east of the city centre. Dating from the 15th century, the tower house rises above two sets of machicolated walls that enclose an area of about half a hectare. Mary Queen of Scots took refuge here after the murder of Rizzio; it was here too that plans to murder her husband Darnley were laid. Look for the prison cell complete with built-in sanitation, something some 'modern' British prisons only finally managed in 1996. Take bus No 33 from Princes St to Old Dalkeith Rd and walk 500m up Craigmillar Castle Rd.

Ruined **Crichton Castle** (☎ 01875-320017, *Pathhead, Midlothian; adult/child £2/75p; open 9.30am-6.30pm daily Apr-Sept*) is 10 miles south-east of the city. It enjoys a delightful location overlooking a valley, and has a beautiful, Italianate courtyard with faceted stonework. Take bus No 29 or 30 from Waterloo Place to Pathhead village, then walk 2 miles south on B6367 road.

Medieval **Dirleton Castle** (☎ 01620-850330, *Dirleton, East Lothian; adult/child £2/1; open 9.30am-6.30pm daily Apr-Sept; 9.30am-4.30pm Mon-Sat & 2.30pm-4.30pm Sun Oct-Mar*) is 20 miles east of Edinburgh. It's surrounded by beautiful gardens, has massive round towers, a drawbridge and a horrific pit dungeon. Take bus No 124 from George St or St Andrew Square, or take the train to North Berwick and walk 2 miles west to Dirleton.

Lauriston Castle (*Map 1;* ☎ 336 2060, *Cramond Rd South; adult/child £4.50/3; open 11am-1pm & 2pm-5pm Sat-Thur Apr-Oct; 2pm-4pm Sat & Sun Nov-Mar*) is 3 miles north-west of the city centre. It started life in the 16th century as a tower house, built by Archibald Napier (whose son, John, invented logarithms). The castle was extended and 'modernised' in 19th-century baronial style and now contains a collection of fine art and furniture. It's set in peaceful grounds with great views north across the Firth of Forth to Fife. Take bus No 40 from Hanover St to Cramond Rd South.

Thirlestane Castle (☎ 01578-722430, *Lauder, Berwickshire; family/adult/child £13/5.20/3; open 10.30am-5pm, last admission 4.15pm, Sun-Fri Apr-Oct*) is 25 miles south-east of Edinburgh. Thirlestane is the home of the Maitland family – the dukes of Lauderdale – and is one of the finest country houses in Scotland. Bonnie Prince Charlie stayed here in 1745 after the Battle of Prestonpans. The extensive grounds include an adventure playground for kids. Take bus No 30 from Waterloo Place to Lauder.

born in 1835 in a weaver's cottage, which now houses the **Andrew Carnegie Museum** (☎ 724302, *Moodie St; adult/child £2/free; open 11am-5pm Mon-Sat & 2pm-5pm Sun Apr-Oct*). He emigrated to America in 1848 and by the late 19th century had accumulated enormous wealth, $350 million of which he gave away. Dunfermline benefited by his purchase of Pittencrieff Park, beside the palace.

Getting There & Away
Scottish Citylink (☎ 0870 550 5050) runs buses hourly from Edinburgh to Dunfermline (£5, 45 minutes). There are half-hourly trains (£6, 30 minutes).

ST ANDREWS

☎ 01334 • pop 13,900

St Andrews is a beautiful, unusual seaside town – a concoction of medieval ruins, obsessive golfers, windy coastal scenery, tourist glitz and a cosmopolitan university where Scottish theology students rub shoulders with aristocratic English undergrads and even with royalty – Prince William is studying art history here.

Although St Andrews was once the ecclesiastical capital of Scotland, both its cathedral and castle are now in ruins.

For most visitors, the town is synonymous with golf. It's the headquarters of the game's governing body, the Royal and Ancient Golf Club, and the location of the world's most famous golf links, the Old Course.

History

St Andrews is said to have been founded by St Regulus, who arrived from Greece in the 4th century bringing important relics, including some of the bones of St Andrew – Scotland's patron saint. The town soon grew into a major pilgrimage centre and later became the ecclesiastical capital of the country.

The university was founded in 1410, the first in Scotland. James I received part of his education here, as did James III.

Golf was being played here in the 15th century and the Old Course dates from the 16th. The Royal and Ancient Golf Club was founded in 1754 and the imposing clubhouse was built a hundred years later. The British Open Championship, which was first held in 1860 in Prestwick, near Glasgow, has taken place regularly at St Andrews since 1873.

Orientation

St Andrews preserves its medieval plan of parallel streets with small closes leading off them.

The most important parts of the old town, lying east of the bus station, are easily explored on foot. The main streets for shopping are Market and South Sts, running east to west.

Information

The TIC (☎ 472021) at 70 Market St opens 9.30am to 8pm Monday to Saturday and 11am to 6pm Sunday, July and August; 9.30am to 7pm Monday to Saturday and 11am to 6pm Sunday, June, September and early October; 9.30am to 6pm Monday to Saturday and 11am to 4pm Sunday, April and May; and 9.30am to 5.30pm Monday to Friday and 9.30am to 12.30pm Saturday, the rest of the year.

The post office is at 127 South St and opens 9am-5.30pm Monday to Friday and 9.30am-12.30pm Saturday.

Shops have half-day closing on Thursday but in summer many stay open until the normal daily closing time. Parking requires a voucher, which is on sale at the TIC and in many shops.

St Andrews Cathedral

At the eastern end of North St is the ruined western facade of what was once the largest and one of the most magnificent cathedrals in the country (☎ 472563, North St; adult/child £4/1.25 including ticket to castle, £2/75p for cathedral only; open 9.30am-6.30pm daily Apr-Oct, 9.30am-4.30pm daily Oct-Mar). Although founded in 1160, it wasn't consecrated until 1318 and was a focus of pilgrimage until the Reformation, when it was pillaged in 1559. Many of the town's buildings were constructed using stones from the cathedral.

St Andrew's bones lay under the high altar; until the cathedral was built, they had been enshrined in the nearby Church of St Regulus (St Rule). All that remains is **St Rule's Tower**, well worth the climb for the view across St Andrews and a great place for taking photographs. In the same area are parts of the ruined 13th-century **priory**.

The visitors centre includes the **calefactory**, the only room where the monks could warm themselves by a fire. Masons' marks on the red-sandstone blocks, identifying who shaped each block, can still be clearly seen. There is also a collection of Celtic crosses and gravestones that have been found on the site.

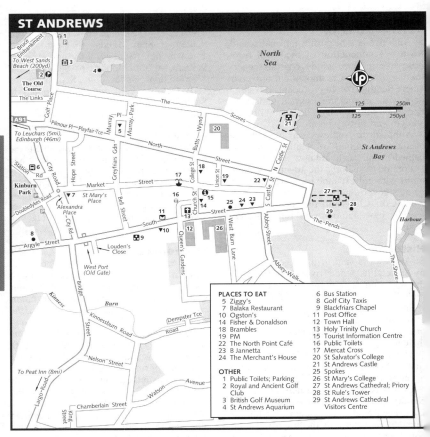

ST ANDREWS

North Sea

St Andrews Bay

Harbour

PLACES TO EAT
5 Ziggy's
7 Balaka Restaurant
10 Ogston's
14 Fisher & Donaldson
18 Brambles
19 PM
22 The North Point Café
23 B Jannetta
24 The Merchant's House

OTHER
1 Public Toilets; Parking
2 Royal and Ancient Golf Club
3 British Golf Museum
4 St Andrews Aquarium

6 Bus Station
8 Golf City Taxis
9 Blackfriars Chapel
11 Post Office
12 Town Hall
13 Holy Trinity Church
15 Tourist Information Centre
16 Mercat Cross
17 St Salvator's College
20 St Andrews Castle
21 St Andrews Castle
25 Spokes
26 St Mary's College
27 St Andrews Cathedral; Priory
28 St Rule's Tower
29 St Andrews Cathedral Visitors Centre

St Andrews Castle

A short distance north of the cathedral, jutting over the sea, is the castle (☎ *477196, North Castle St; adult/child £4/1.25 including ticket to cathedral, £2.80/1 for castle only; open 9.30am-6.30pm daily Apr-Oct, 9.30am-4.30pm daily Oct-Mar*). It was founded around 1200 as the fortified home of the bishop, and the young King James II often stayed here in the 1450s. A visitors centre gives a good audiovisual introduction and has a small collection of Pictish stones.

In 1654, part of the castle was pulled down to provide building materials for the harbour wall, but enough survives to give you an idea of what each part was used for. After the execution of Protestant reformer in 1545, other reformers retaliated by murdering Cardinal Beaton and taking over the castle. The cardinal's body was hung from a window in the Fore Tower before being tossed into the bottle-shaped dungeon. The reformers then spent almost a year besieged in the castle; one of the most interesting things to do here is to explore the **siege tunnels**, said to be the best surviving example of siege engineering in Europe.

The Scores

From the castle, follow the Scores west past St Salvator's College. At the western end is **St Andrews Aquarium** *(☎ 474786, The Scores; adult/child £4.50/3.50; open 10am-6pm daily Sept-Jun, 9am-7pm daily July & Aug)*, which has the usual displays of marine life and an interesting sea-horse exhibition.

Near here is the **British Golf Museum** *(☎ 478880, Bruce Embankment; adult/child £3.75/1.50; open 9.30am-5.30pm daily Apr-Oct, 11am-3pm Thur-Mon Nov-Mar)*. It's a surprisingly interesting and modern museum with good audiovisual displays and touch screens, as well as golfing memorabilia.

Opposite the museum is the clubhouse of the Royal and Ancient Golf Club; beyond stretches the **Old Course** and beside it the West Sands, the beach that starred in the film *Chariots of Fire*.

Places to Eat

The North Point Café (☎ 473997, 24 North St) The North Point is a good place for coffee, cream tea or a light lunch; soup and a roll costs £2.

Brambles (☎ 475380, 5 College St) Open for lunch only. One of the busiest lunchtime spots, this place has excellent soups, salads and vegetarian dishes.

The Merchant's House (☎ 472595, 49 South St) Mains £4.95-7.95. Open 10am-5.30pm. Located in a venerable building, it serves delicious home-made soup (£1.50) and excellent home-baked fare.

Balaka Restaurant (☎ 474825, 3 Alexandra Place) 3-course lunch around £5.95. The Balaka is a Bangladeshi restaurant that prepares excellent curries flavoured with home-grown herbs; Sean Connery has eaten here.

Ziggy's (☎ 473686, 6 Murray Place) Popular with students, Ziggy's offers good burgers starting at £3.95, plus a range of steaks, Mexican, seafood and vegetarian dishes.

Ogston's (☎ 473473, 116 South St) Mains £4.50-5.50. Ogston's is a cafe-bar and bistro, offering an eclectic evening menu in its conservatory restaurant.

B Jannetta (31 South St) Don't leave town without sampling one of the 52 varieties of ice cream here. Most popular flavour? Vanilla. Weirdest? Irn Bru!

If you're on a tight budget, *PM*, on the corner of Market and Union Sts, does inexpensive breakfasts, burgers, and fish and chips. *Fisher & Donaldson* on Church St has more upmarket snacks such as Selkirk bannocks (rich fruit bread), cream cakes and a wonderful range of pastries.

Peat Inn (☎ 840206) 4-course set lunch £19.50, set dinner £28, excluding wine. Open for lunch and dinner Tues-Sat. One of Scotland's top restaurants, the Peat Inn is 6½ miles south-west of St Andrews. Meals are prepared by David Wilson, one of Scotland's leading chefs. The set dinner includes excellent fresh seafood. To get there, go 5 miles along the A915 then turn right on the B940 for 1½ miles.

Getting There & Away

St Andrews is 55 miles north of Edinburgh. Stagecoach Fife (☎ 0870 608 2608) runs a

---

The Witches of North Berwick

In 1590, the Church of St Andrews was the scene of a gathering of witches of both sexes under the leadership of 'the Devel', who was in reality Francis Stuart, earl of Bothwell. He tried by means of witchcraft to cause a storm in the Forth, which he hoped would drown James VI as he returned by sea from Denmark, accompanied by Princess Anne of Denmark, his wife.

The attempt failed and several witches were subsequently tortured, tried and executed. Bothwell was imprisoned but later escaped. The North Berwick events became widely known. James VI took a great interest in the trial and even wrote a book about witchcraft.

Nearly 200 years later, it's believed that Robbie Burns drew on stories about the witches when writing *Tam O'Shanter* and the *Old Kirk of Alloway*.

half-hourly bus service between St Andrew Square in Edinburgh and St Andrews (£5.70, two hours).

There is no train station in St Andrews, but trains run from Edinburgh to Leuchars, 5 miles north-west (£12.90, one hour). The St Andrews Railbus scheme is a combined ticket (£15.80), covering trains and buses.

Getting Around

Try Golf City Taxis (☎ 477788), 23 Argyle St. A taxi between Leuchars train station and the town centre costs around £7.

You can rent bicycles from Spokes (☎ 477835) at 77 South St; mountain bikes and hybrids cost from £9.50 per day.

East

Beyond the former coalfields of Dalkeith and Musselburgh, the fertile farmland of East Lothian stretches eastwards along the coast to the seaside resort of North Berwick and the fishing harbour of Dunbar. In the middle lies the attractive county town of Haddington.

SCOTTISH MINING MUSEUM

About 9 miles south-east of Edinburgh city centre is the impressive Scottish Mining Museum (☎ 0131-663 7519, Lady Victoria Colliery, Newtongrange; adult/child £4/2.20; open 10am-5pm daily). Exhibits explain the story of coal and the history of coal mining in Scotland, including the harsh life of a 19th-century mining family, before you visit the pithead, a noisy re-creation of a working coalface and the massive winding engine. Ex-coal miners act as guides.

First Edinburgh bus Nos 80, 80A, 86 and 89 run from Princes St, Edinburgh, to Newtongrange.

HADDINGTON & AROUND

☎ 01620 • pop 8000

Haddington, straddling the River Tyne 18 miles east of Edinburgh, dates back to the 12th century when it was made a royal burgh by David I. Most of the modern town, however, was built between the 17th and 19th

centuries during the period of prosperity that resulted from the Agricultural Revolution. It's still a prosperous market town and the administrative centre for East Lothian.

The prettiest part of Haddington is the tree lined Court St, with its wide pavement and grand 18th- and 19th-century buildings. Haddington gets congested with traffic, especially on Market and High Sts where, during the day at least, cars jostle for the limited parking spaces.

Things to See & Do

From the eastern end of High St, Church St leads to **St Mary's Collegiate Church** (☎ 823109, Sidegate; admission free; open 11am-4pm Mon-Sat & 9.30am-4.40pm Sun). Built in 1462, it is the largest parish church in Scotland. Buried in the churchyard is Jane Welsh (1801–66), wife of Thomas Carlyle. The **Jane Welsh Carlyle Museum** (☎ 823738, 2 Lodge St; adult/child £1/75p; open 2pm-5pm Wed-Sat Apr-Sept) is the house in which she lived until her marriage.

A mile south of Haddington is **Lennoxlove House** (☎ 823720, Lennoxlove Estate, adult/child £4/2; guided tours 2pm-4.30pm Wed, Thur & Sun Easter-Oct). The oldest part of the house dates from around 1345 with extensions added over the following centuries. It contains some fine furniture and paintings, and memorabilia relating to Mary Queen of Scots. Chief among these are her death mask and a silver casket given to her by Francis II of France, her first husband. The house has been the seat of the duke of Hamilton since 1947.

Places to Eat

The Waterside Bistro & Restaurant (☎ 825764, 115 Waterside) Mains £6.95-13.95. With a lovely location overlooking the river, the Waterside is a great place to have lunch on a summer's day, watching the swans and ducks go by. The bistro does good quality light meals, while the upstairs restaurant is more formal.

The Garden Cafe (☎ 823720, Lennoxlove House) Open 11am-5pm Tues-Sun. This cafe is a delightful spot for morning coffee, a light lunch (noon-2pm) or afternoon tea.

Getting There & Away

First Edinburgh bus No 106 runs between Edinburgh and Haddington every 20 minutes. The nearest train station is at Drem, 3 miles to the north.

NORTH BERWICK & AROUND
☎ 01620 • pop 4860

An easy day trip from Edinburgh, North Berwick is an attractive Victorian seaside resort with long sandy beaches, three golf courses and a small harbour. The TIC (☎ 892197), Quality St, opens 9am to 6pm Monday to Saturday.

Things to See & Do

North Berwick's big new attraction is the **Scottish Seabird Centre** (☎ 890202, **w** www.seabird.org, The Harbour; family/adult/child £12.50/4.50/3.20; open 10am-5pm daily Apr-Sept, 10am-4pm daily Oct-Mar). The centre uses remote-control video cameras on the Bass Rock and other islands to relay live images of nesting gannets and other seabirds, and screens films and multimedia shows. There are also high-powered telescopes on the viewing deck that you can use to scan the coast and islands.

Beside the harbour are the remains of the **Auld Kirk**, the 12th-century Church of St Andrews, the first parish church of North Berwick. Off High St a short steep path climbs up **North Berwick Law** (184m), a conical hill that dominates the town. When the weather's fine there are great views.

Several small islands lie offshore. **Bass Rock**, 3 miles east, was once used as a prison for Covenanters but is now home to thousands of gannets and other seabirds. Puffins nest in burrows on nearby **Craig Rock** and **Fidra Island**.

Fred Marr (☎ 892838) runs trips out daily in summer (at weekends the rest of the year). Trips around Bass Rock and Fidra island cost £5/3 and take about one hour 30 minutes. Fred can also drop you off on Bass Rock for two to three hours then return and pick you up (£12).

Tantallon Castle

Built around 1350, spectacular Tantallon Castle (☎ 01620-892727; adult/child £2.80/1; open 9.30am-6.30pm daily Apr-Sept, 9.30am-4.30pm Sat-Wed & 9.30am-1pm Thur Oct-Mar), 3 miles east of North Berwick, was a fortress residence of the Douglas Earls of Angus (the 'Red Douglases'). On one side it's an almost sheer drop to the sea below, and fulmars nest in the cliffs.

Getting There & Away

First Edinburgh bus No 124 runs between Edinburgh and North Berwick every 20 minutes during the day and hourly in the evenings (£4, one hour). There are frequent trains to Edinburgh (£7, 33 minutes).

DUNBAR
☎ 01368 • pop 5800

Dunbar is a small fishing port and holiday resort on the east coast, 30 miles from Edinburgh. It was the site of two important battles, both resulting in Scottish losses. Edward I invaded in 1296 and General Monck defeated a larger Scots army in 1650, facilitating Cromwell's entry into Edinburgh. John Muir (1838–1914), pioneer conservationist and 'father' of the US national park system, was born here.

The TIC (☎ 863353), 143 High St, opens 9am to 5pm Monday to Friday, October to March; and daily, April to September (extended hours in July and August).

Things to See & Do

In the Middle Ages, Dunbar was an important Scottish fortress town, but little remains of **Dunbar Castle** except for some tottering ruins, inhabited by seabirds, overlooking the harbour. From the castle a 2-mile cliff-top trail follows the coastline west to the sands of Belhaven Bay and **John Muir Country Park** (☎ 863886).

John Muir House (☎ 862595, 128 High St; admission free; open 11am-1pm Mon-Sat & 2pm-5pm daily June-Sept) is Muir's childhood home, and has a small exhibition and audiovisual display on his life. The **Dunbar Town House Museum** (☎ 863734, High St; admission free; open 12.30pm-

4.30pm daily Apr-Oct) gives an introduction to local history and archaeology.

Dunbar Leisure Pool *(☎ 865456, Castle Park; adult/child £3.50/2; open 10am-9pm Tues & Wed, 10am-5pm Thur-Sun),* on the hilltop above the harbour, is a modern pool with flumes and a separate children's pool.

Getting There & Away

Dunbar is well served by buses from Edinburgh including bus Nos 251, 253 and 256. Great North Eastern Railway (always referred to as GNER) trains run from Edinburgh Waverley (£11.50, 40 minutes) every half-hour or so.

South

If you head south from Edinburgh, you'll find the lovely Tweed Valley, and the rolling hills, forests, castles, ruined abbeys and sheltered towns of the Borders, which have a romance and beauty of their own. This is excellent cycling and walking country. The region survived centuries of war and plunder and was romantically portrayed by Sir Walter Scott.

PEEBLES & AROUND
☎ 01721 • pop 7080

Peebles is a prosperous little town set among rolling wooded hills on the banks of the River Tweed. It has a broad, attractive High St, and makes a pleasant base from which to tour the Tweed Valley.

The TIC (☎ 720138), High St, has complex opening hours but generally opens 9am or 10am to between 4pm and 8pm Monday to Saturday, and 10am to 2pm Sunday, April to October; and 9.30am to 12.30pm and 1.30pm to 4.30pm, Monday to Saturday, the rest of the year.

Tweeddale Museum & Gallery

The museum *(☎ 724820, High St; admission free; open 10am-noon & 2pm-5pm Mon-Fri & 10am-1pm & 2pm-4pm Sat & Sun Easter-Oct)* is in the Chambers Institute, which was given to the town by publisher William Chambers in 1859. It houses

an interesting collection of displays including copies of the frieze taken from the Parthenon in Athens by Lord Elgin and also the 19th-century *Alexander Frieze.*

Neidpath Castle

This castle *(☎ 720333; adult/child £3/1; open 11am-5pm Mon-Sat & 1pm-5pm Sun Easter-Sept)* is a 14th-century tower house perched on a bluff above the River Tweed. It's in a lovely spot with good views from the parapets, although there's little to see inside. It's 1 mile west of Peebles on the A72 and can be reached by following a footpath along the river.

Traquair House

About 6 miles south-east of Peebles is Traquair House *(☎ 01896-830323; adult/child £5.20/2.60; open 10.30am-5.30pm daily June-Aug, 12.30pm-5.30pm daily Apr, May, Sept & Oct),* one of Britain's great country houses. There are many that are more aesthetically pleasing but this one has a powerful, atmospheric beauty – exploring it is like travelling back in time. Parts of it are thought to have been built long before the first official record of its existence in 1107. The massive tower house was expanded over the next 500 years but has remained virtually the same since 1642.

Since the 15th century, Traquair House has belonged to various branches of the Stuart family and the family's unwavering Catholicism and loyalty to the Stuart cause is largely why development ceased when it did. The family's estate, wealth and influence was whittled away after the Reformation, and there was neither the opportunity nor, one suspects, the will to make changes.

One of the most fascinating rooms is the concealed **priest's room** where priests secretly lived and said Mass until 1829, when the Catholic Emancipation Act was finally passed. Other time-worn rooms hold fascinating relics, including the cradle used by Mary for her son, James VI of Scotland, and many letters written by the Stuart pretenders to their supporters.

In addition to the house, there's an art gallery, a garden, a maze, a small brewery producing Bear Ale, and an active crafts community. The Scottish Beer & Jazz Festival takes place here in late May (contact Traquair House for details).

Getting There & Away

The bus stop in Peebles is beside the post office on Eastgate. First Edinburgh bus No 62 runs hourly from Waterloo Place and South Bridge in Edinburgh to Peebles and Innerleithen.

For a local taxi, call ☎ 01896-831333.

By car, leave Edinburgh via Morningside and Fairmilehead and follow the A703 to Peebles. The A72 heads east from Peebles to Innerleithen.

MELROSE

☎ 01896 • pop 2276

Melrose is the most charming of the Border towns, lying at the foot of the three heather-covered Eildon Hills. It's spick-and-span, with a classic market square, some attractive parks, rugby pitches (Melrose is the birthplace of the Rugby Sevens) and the ruins of one of the great Border abbeys.

Information

The TIC (☎ 822555), Abbey House, Abbey St, opens 10am to 5pm Monday to Saturday and 10am to 1pm Sunday, April to October (extended hours May to August). The post office is around the corner on Buccleuch St.

Melrose Abbey

Founded by David I in 1136 for Cistercian monks from Rievaulx in Yorkshire, this red-sandstone abbey (☎ 822562; adult/child £3.30/1.20; open 9.30am-6.30pm daily Apr-Sept, 9.30am-4.30pm Mon-Sat & 2pm-4.30pm Sun Oct-Mar) was repeatedly destroyed by the English in the 14th century. It was rebuilt by Robert the Bruce whose heart is buried here. The ruins date from the 14th and 15th centuries and were repaired in the 19th at the behest of Sir Walter Scott. They are famous for their decorative Gothic stonework – see if you can glimpse the pig gargoyle playing the bagpipes on the roof.

Next to the abbey are the walled Priorwood Gardens (☎ 822493; admission £1; open 10am-5.30pm Mon-Sat & 1.30pm-5.30pm Sun Apr-Sept, 10am-4pm Mon-Sat & 1.30pm-4pm Sun Oct-25 Dec), which specialises in cultivating plants used for dried flower arrangements. The gardens are an NTS property.

Trimontium Exhibition

This small, interesting exhibition (☎ 822651, Market Square; adult/child £1.30/80p; open 10.30am-4.30pm daily Apr-Oct) tells the story of the Roman 'three hills' fort and archaeological digs at nearby Newstead. You can also follow a guided Trimontium Walk to the Roman sites around Melrose.

Places to Eat

Melrose Station Restaurant (☎ 822546, Palma Place) Open for lunch noon-2pm Wed-Sun, dinner 6.45pm-10pm Thur-Sat. This acclaimed restaurant, with a French-inspired menu, is popular so book ahead for evening meals. Lunches are cheaper.

There's excellent pub food at the Kings Head (☎ 822143, High St) and Burts Hotel (☎ 822285, Market Square).

Getting There & Away

First Edinburgh's bus No 62 runs hourly to Melrose via Peebles and Galashiels.

Melrose is about 38 miles south of Edinburgh via either the A7 or A68.

AROUND MELROSE
Abbotsford

The country home of Sir Walter Scott, Abbotsford (☎ 01896-752043; adult/child £3.80/1.90; open 10am-5pm Mon-Sat & 2pm-5pm Sun mid-Mar-Oct, 10am-5pm Sun Jun-Sept) is definitely not an architectural masterpiece but it's in a beautiful setting. It contains a fascinating collection of the great man's possessions, including many historical curiosities, and is well worth visiting.

The house is about 2 miles west of Melrose between the River Tweed and the B6360 road. Frequent buses run between Galashiels and Melrose; alight at the Tweedbank traffic island and follow the signs; it's a 15-minute walk.

Dryburgh Abbey

Seven miles south-east of Melrose is Dryburgh Abbey (☎ *01835-822381; adult/child £2.30/1; open 9.30am-6.30pm Mon-Sat, 2pm-6.30pm Sun Apr-Sept, closes 4.30pm Oct-Mar)*. It's the most beautiful and most complete of the Border abbeys, partly because the town of Dryburgh no longer exists (another victim of the wars), and partly because it has a lovely site in a sheltered valley by the River Tweed. The abbey belonged to the Premonstratensians, a religious order founded in France, and was built from about 1150.

The pink-stoned ruins were chosen as the burial place for Sir Walter Scott and later for Earl Haig, the WWI Allied commander. Attractive picnic spots can be found nearby.

MARTIN MOOS

Birdie-watching on the Old Course at St Andrews

JONATHAN SMITH

DAVID TIPLING

...uined St Andrews Cathedral, founded in 1160

Once a prison, Bass Rock is now a bird haven.

NANCY FREY

...ant to escape the hoards? Take a trip to the verdant Pentland Hills, a great spot for hiking and cycling.

MARTIN MOOS

The high arches of beautiful Dryburgh Abbey

NANCY FREY

The lone ranger: rambling in the Pentland Hills

DAVID TIPLING

A gannet as seen from the Scottish Seabird Centre

MARTIN MOOS

Stunning, red-sandstone Melrose Abbey (1136

Glossary

See the boxed text 'Scottish Gaelic' in the Facts about Edinburgh chapter for more information about the language.

Auld Reekie – Edinburgh (Old Smokey)
aye – yes/always

bairn – baby or child
ben – mountain
brae – hill
bridie – pie filled with meat, potatoes and onion
brig – bridge
burgh – town

cairn – pile of stones to mark path or junction; also peak
ceilidh – (pronounced '**kay**-ley') informal entertainment and dance
close – entrance

dram – glass of whisky
dun – fort

firth – estuary

glen – valley

haar – fog off the North Sea
haggis – traditional Scottish dish made from sheep's offal, oatmeal and suet boiled in a sheep's stomach
Hogmanay – New Year's Eve
howff – pub
HS – Historic Scotland

ken – know
kipper – smoked herring
kirk – church

land – tenement
law – round hill
links – grass-covered, coastal sand dunes; golf course on same

neeps – turnips
NTS – National Trust for Scotland

Pict – early Celtic inhabitants (from the Latin pictus, meaning 'painted')
provost – mayor

rood – cross
RSA – Royal Scottish Academy
RSPB – Royal Society for the Protection of Birds

SNH – Scottish Natural Heritage, a government body responsible for safeguarding and improving Scotland's natural heritage
sporran – purse worn on a chain around the waist, with a kilt
STB – Scottish Tourist Board
SYHA – Scottish Youth Hostel Association

tatties – potatoes
tolbooth – courthouse or jail
tron – public weighbridge

vennel – narrow street

way – walking trail
wynd – lane, alley

LONELY PLANET

You already know that Lonely Planet produces more than this one guidebook, but you might not be aware of the other products we have on this region. Here is a selection of titles that you may want to check out as well:

Scotland
ISBN 1 86450 157 X
US$16.99 • UK£10.99

Walking in Scotland
ISBN 1 86450 350 5
US$17.99 • UK£11.99

Edinburgh City Map
ISBN 1 74059 015 5
US$5.99 • UK£3.99

Britain
ISBN 1 86450 147 2
US$27.99 • UK£15.99

Cycling in Britain
ISBN 1 86450 037 9
US$19.99 • UK£12.99

Walking in Britain
ISBN 1 86450 280 0
US$21.99 • UK£13.99

Europe on a Shoestring
ISBN 1 86450 150 2
US$24.99 • UK£14.99

Read This First: Europe
ISBN 1 86450 136 7
US$14.99 • UK£8.99

Western Europe
ISBN 1 86450 163 4
US$27.99 • UK£15.99

British Phrasebook
ISBN 0 86442 484 1
US$5.95 • UK£3.99

Europe Phrasebook
ISBN 1 86450 224 X
US$8.99 • UK£4.99

Available wherever books are sold

Lonely Planet Guides by Region

Lonely Planet is known worldwide for publishing practical, reliable and no-nonsense travel information in our guides and on our Web site. The Lonely Planet list covers just about every accessible part of the world. Currently there are 16 series: Travel guides, Shoestring guides, Condensed guides, Phrasebooks, Read This First, Healthy Travel, Walking guides, Cycling guides, Watching Wildlife guides, Pisces Diving & Snorkeling guides, City Maps, Road Atlases, Out to Eat, World Food, Journeys travel literature and Pictorials.

AFRICA Africa on a shoestring • Botswana • Cairo • Cairo City Map • Cape Town • Cape Town City Map • East Africa • Egypt • Egyptian Arabic phrasebook • Ethiopia, Eritrea & Djibouti • Ethiopian Amharic phrasebook • The Gambia & Senegal • Healthy Travel Africa • Kenya • Malawi • Morocco • Moroccan Arabic phrasebook • Mozambique • Namibia • Read This First: Africa • South Africa, Lesotho & Swaziland • Southern Africa • Southern Africa Road Atlas • Swahili phrasebook • Tanzania, Zanzibar & Pemba • Trekking in East Africa • Tunisia • Watching Wildlife East Africa • Watching Wildlife Southern Africa • West Africa • World Food Morocco • Zambia • Zimbabwe, Botswana & Namibia
Travel Literature: Mali Blues: Traveling to an African Beat • The Rainbird: A Central African Journey • Songs to an African Sunset: A Zimbabwean Story

AUSTRALIA & THE PACIFIC Aboriginal Australia & the Torres Strait Islands •Auckland • Australia • Australian phrasebook • Australia Road Atlas • Cycling Australia • Cycling New Zealand • Fiji • Fijian phrasebook • Healthy Travel Australia, NZ & the Pacific • Islands of Australia's Great Barrier Reef • Melbourne • Melbourne City Map • Micronesia • New Caledonia • New South Wales • New Zealand • Northern Territory • Outback Australia • Out to Eat – Melbourne • Out to Eat – Sydney • Papua New Guinea • Pidgin phrasebook • Queensland • Rarotonga & the Cook Islands • Samoa • Solomon Islands • South Australia • South Pacific • South Pacific phrasebook • Sydney • Sydney City Map • Sydney Condensed • Tahiti & French Polynesia • Tasmania • Tonga • Tramping in New Zealand • Vanuatu • Victoria • Walking in Australia • Watching Wildlife Australia • Western Australia
Travel Literature: Islands in the Clouds: Travels in the Highlands of New Guinea • Kiwi Tracks: A New Zealand Journey • Sean & David's Long Drive

CENTRAL AMERICA & THE CARIBBEAN Bahamas, Turks & Caicos • Baja California • Belize, Guatemala & Yucatán • Bermuda • Central America on a shoestring • Costa Rica • Costa Rica Spanish phrasebook • Cuba • Cycling Cuba • Dominican Republic & Haiti • Eastern Caribbean • Guatemala • Havana • Healthy Travel Central & South America • Jamaica • Mexico • Mexico City • Panama • Puerto Rico • Read This First: Central & South America • Virgin Islands • World Food Caribbean • World Food Mexico • Yucatán
Travel Literature: Green Dreams: Travels in Central America

EUROPE Amsterdam • Amsterdam City Map • Amsterdam Condensed • Andalucía • Athens • Austria • Baltic States phrasebook • Barcelona • Barcelona City Map • Belgium & Luxembourg • Berlin • Berlin City Map • Britain • British phrasebook • Brussels, Bruges & Antwerp • Brussels City Map • Budapest • Budapest City Map • Canary Islands • Catalunya & the Costa Brava • Central Europe • Central Europe phrasebook • Copenhagen • Corfu & the Ionians • Corsica • Crete • Crete Condensed • Croatia • Cycling Britain • Cycling France • Cyprus • Czech & Slovak Republics • Czech phrasebook • Denmark • Dublin • Dublin City Map • Dublin Condensed • Eastern Europe • Eastern Europe phrasebook • Edinburgh • Edinburgh City Map • England • Estonia, Latvia & Lithuania • Europe on a shoestring • Europe phrasebook • Finland • Florence • Florence City Map • France • Frankfurt City Map • Frankfurt Condensed • French phrasebook • Georgia, Armenia & Azerbaijan • Germany • German phrasebook • Greece • Greek Islands • Greek phrasebook • Hungary • Iceland, Greenland & the Faroe Islands • Ireland • Italian phrasebook • Italy • Kraków • Lisbon • The Loire • London • London City Map • London Condensed • Madrid • Madrid City Map • Malta • Mediterranean Europe • Milan, Turin & Genoa • Moscow • Munich • Netherlands • Normandy • Norway • Out to Eat – London • Out to Eat – Paris • Paris • Paris City Map • Paris Condensed • Poland • Polish phrasebook • Portugal • Portuguese phrasebook • Prague • Prague City Map • Provence & the Côte d'Azur • Read This First: Europe • Rhodes & the Dodecanese • Romania & Moldova • Rome • Rome City Map • Rome Condensed • Russia, Ukraine & Belarus • Russian phrasebook • Scandinavian & Baltic Europe • Scandinavian phrasebook • Scotland • Sicily • Slovenia • South-West France • Spain • Spanish phrasebook • Stockholm • St Petersburg • St Petersburg City Map • Sweden • Switzerland • Tuscany • Ukrainian phrasebook • Venice • Vienna • Wales • Walking in Britain • Walking in France • Walking in Ireland • Walking in Italy • Walking in Scotland • Walking in Spain • Walking in Switzerland • Western Europe • World Food France • World Food Greece • World Food Ireland • World Food Italy • World Food Spain **Travel Literature:** After Yugoslavia • Love and War in the Apennines • The Olive Grove: Travels in Greece • On the Shores of the Mediterranean • Round Ireland in Low Gear • A Small Place in Italy

Lonely Planet Mail Order

onely Planet products are distributed worldwide. They are also available by mail order from Lonely Planet, so if you have difficulty finding a title please write to us. North and South American residents should write to 150 Linden St, Oakland, CA 94607, USA; European and African residents should write to 10a Spring Place, London NW5 3BH, UK; and residents of other countries to Locked Bag 1, Footscray, Victoria 3011, Australia.

INDIAN SUBCONTINENT & THE INDIAN OCEAN Bangladesh • Bengali phrasebook • Bhutan • Delhi • Goa • Healthy Travel Asia & India • Hindi & Urdu phrasebook • India • India & Bangladesh City Map • Indian Himalaya • Karakoram Highway • Kathmandu City Map • Kerala • Madagascar • Maldives • Mauritius, Réunion & Seychelles • Mumbai (Bombay) • Nepal • Nepali phrasebook • North India • Pakistan • Rajasthan • Read This First: Asia & India • South India • Sri Lanka • Sri Lanka phrasebook • Tibet • Tibetan phrasebook • Trekking in the Indian Himalaya • Trekking in the Karakoram & Hindukush • Trekking in the Nepal Himalaya • World Food India **Travel Literature:** The Age of Kali: Indian Travels and Encounters • Hello Goodnight: A Life of Goa • In Rajasthan • Maverick in Madagascar • A Season in Heaven: True Tales from the Road to Kathmandu • Shopping for Buddhas • A Short Walk in the Hindu Kush • Slowly Down the Ganges

MIDDLE EAST & CENTRAL ASIA Bahrain, Kuwait & Qatar • Central Asia • Central Asia phrasebook • Dubai • Farsi (Persian) phrasebook • Hebrew phrasebook • Iran • Israel & the Palestinian Territories • Istanbul • Istanbul City Map • Istanbul to Cairo • Istanbul to Kathmandu • Jerusalem • Jerusalem City Map • Jordan • Lebanon • Middle East • Oman & the United Arab Emirates • Syria • Turkey • Turkish phrasebook • World Food Turkey • Yemen **Travel Literature:** Black on Black: Iran Revisited • Breaking Ranks: Turbulent Travels in the Promised Land • The Gates of Damascus • Kingdom of the Film Stars: Journey into Jordan

NORTH AMERICA Alaska • Boston • Boston City Map • Boston Condensed • British Columbia • California & Nevada • California Condensed • Canada • Chicago • Chicago City Map • Chicago Condensed • Florida • Georgia & the Carolinas • Great Lakes • Hawaii • Hiking in Alaska • Hiking in the USA • Honolulu & Oahu City Map • Las Vegas • Los Angeles • Los Angeles City Map • Louisiana & the Deep South • Miami • Miami City Map • Montreal • New England • New Orleans • New Orleans City Map • New York City • New York City City Map • New York City Condensed • New York, New Jersey & Pennsylvania • Oahu • Out to Eat – San Francisco • Pacific Northwest • Rocky Mountains • San Diego & Tijuana • San Francisco • San Francisco City Map • Seattle • Seattle City Map • Southwest • Texas • Toronto • USA • USA phrasebook • Vancouver • Vancouver City Map • Virginia & the Capital Region • Washington, DC • Washington, DC City Map • World Food New Orleans **Travel Literature:** Caught Inside: A Surfer's Year on the California Coast • Drive Thru America

NORTH-EAST ASIA Beijing • Beijing City Map • Cantonese phrasebook • China • Hiking in Japan • Hong Kong & Macau • Hong Kong City Map • Hong Kong Condensed • Japan • Japanese phrasebook • Korea • Korean phrasebook • Kyoto • Mandarin phrasebook • Mongolia • Mongolian phrasebook • Seoul • Shanghai • South-West China • Taiwan • Tokyo • Tokyo Condensed • World Food Hong Kong • World Food Japan **Travel Literature:** In Xanadu: A Quest • Lost Japan

SOUTH AMERICA Argentina, Uruguay & Paraguay • Bolivia • Brazil • Brazilian phrasebook • Buenos Aires • Buenos Aires City Map • Chile & Easter Island • Colombia • Ecuador & the Galapagos Islands • Healthy Travel Central & South America • Latin American Spanish phrasebook • Peru • Quechua phrasebook • Read This First: Central & South America • Rio de Janeiro • Rio de Janeiro City Map • Santiago de Chile • South America on a shoestring • Trekking in the Patagonian Andes • Venezuela **Travel Literature:** Full Circle: A South American Journey

SOUTH-EAST ASIA Bali & Lombok • Bangkok • Bangkok City Map • Burmese phrasebook • Cambodia • Cycling Vietnam, Laos & Cambodia • East Timor phrasebook • Hanoi • Healthy Travel Asia & India • Hill Tribes phrasebook • Ho Chi Minh City (Saigon) • Indonesia • Indonesian phrasebook • Indonesia's Eastern Islands • Java • Lao phrasebook • Laos • Malay phrasebook • Malaysia, Singapore & Brunei • Myanmar (Burma) • Philippines • Pilipino (Tagalog) phrasebook • Read This First: Asia & India • Singapore • Singapore City Map • South-East Asia on a shoestring • South-East Asia phrasebook • Thailand • Thailand's Islands & Beaches • Thailand, Vietnam, Laos & Cambodia Road Atlas • Thai phrasebook • Vietnam • Vietnamese phrasebook • World Food Indonesia • World Food Thailand • World Food Vietnam

ALSO AVAILABLE: Antarctica • The Arctic • The Blue Man: Tales of Travel, Love and Coffee • Brief Encounters: Stories of Love, Sex & Travel • Buddhist Stupas in Asia: The Shape of Perfection • Chasing Rickshaws • The Last Grain Race • Lonely Planet ... On the Edge: Adventurous Escapades from Around the World • Lonely Planet Unpacked • Lonely Planet Unpacked Again • Not the Only Planet: Science Fiction Travel Stories • Ports of Call: A Journey by Sea • Sacred India • Travel Photography: A Guide to Taking Better Pictures • Travel with Children • Tuvalu: Portrait of an Island Nation

LONELY PLANET

ON THE ROAD

Travel Guides explore cities, regions and countries, and supply information on transport, restaurants and accommodation, covering all budgets. They come with reliable, easy-to-use maps, practical advice, cultural and historical facts and a rundown on attractions both on and off the beaten track. There are over 200 titles in this classic series, covering nearly every country in the world.

Lonely Planet Upgrades extend the shelf life of existing travel guides by detailing any changes that may affect travel in a region since a book has been published. Upgrades can be downloaded for free from **www.lonelyplanet.com/upgrades**

For travellers with more time than money, **Shoestring** guides offer dependable, first-hand information with hundreds of detailed maps, plus insider tips for stretching money as far as possible. Covering entire continents in most cases, the six-volume shoestring guides are known around the world as 'backpackers bibles'.

For the discerning short-term visitor, **Condensed** guides highlight the best a destination has to offer in a full-colour, pocket-sized format designed for quick access. They include everything from top sights and walking tours to opinionated reviews of where to eat, stay, shop and have fun.

CitySync lets travellers use their Palm™ or Visor™ hand-held computers to guide them through a city with handy tips on transport, history, cultural life, major sights, and shopping and entertainment options. It can also quickly search and sort hundreds of reviews of hotels, restaurants and attractions, and pinpoint their location on scrollable street maps. CitySync can be downloaded from **www.citysync.com**

MAPS & ATLASES

Lonely Planet's **City Maps** feature downtown and metropolitan maps, as well as transit routes and walking tours. The maps come complete with an index of streets, a listing of sights and a plastic coat for extra durability.

Road Atlases are an essential navigation tool for serious travellers. Cross-referenced with the guidebooks, they also feature distance and climate charts and a complete site index.

LONELY PLANET

ESSENTIALS

Read This First books help new travellers to hit the road with confidence. These invaluable predeparture guides give step-by-step advice on preparing for a trip, budgeting, arranging a visa, planning an itinerary and staying safe while still getting off the beaten track.

Healthy Travel pocket guides offer a regional rundown on disease hot spots and practical advice on predeparture health measures, staying well on the road and what to do in emergencies. The guides come with a user-friendly design and helpful diagrams and tables.

Lonely Planet's **Phrasebooks** cover the essential words and phrases travellers need when they're strangers in a strange land. They come in a pocket-sized format with colour tabs for quick reference, extensive vocabulary lists, easy-to-follow pronunciation keys and two-way dictionaries.

Miffed by blurry photos of the Taj Mahal? Tired of the classic 'top of the head cut off' shot? **Travel Photography: A Guide to Taking Better Pictures** will help you turn ordinary holiday snaps into striking images and give you the know-how to capture every scene, from frenetic festivals to peaceful beach sunrises.

Lonely Planet's **Travel Journal** is a lightweight but sturdy travel diary for jotting down all those on-the-road observations and significant travel moments. It comes with a handy time-zone wheel, a world map and useful travel information.

Lonely Planet's eKno is an all-in-one communication service developed especially for travellers. It offers low-cost international calls and free email and voicemail so that you can keep in touch while on the road. Check it out on **www.ekno.lonelyplanet.com**

FOOD & RESTAURANT GUIDES

Lonely Planet's **Out to Eat** guides recommend the brightest and best places to eat and drink in top international cities. These gourmet companions are arranged by neighbourhood, packed with dependable maps, garnished with scene-setting photos and served with quirky features.

For people who live to eat, drink and travel, **World Food** guides explore the culinary culture of each country. Entertaining and adventurous, each guide is packed with detail on staples and specialities, regional cuisine and local markets, as well as sumptuous recipes, comprehensive culinary dictionaries and lavish photos good enough to eat.

OUTDOOR GUIDES

For those who believe the best way to see the world is on foot, Lonely Planet's **Walking Guides** detail everything from family strolls to difficult treks, with 'when to go and how to do it' advice supplemented by reliable maps and essential travel information.

Cycling Guides map a destination's best bike tours, long and short, in day-by-day detail. They contain all the information a cyclist needs, including advice on bike maintenance, places to eat and stay, innovative maps with detailed cues to the rides, and elevation charts.

The **Watching Wildlife** series is perfect for travellers who want authoritative information but don't want to tote a heavy field guide. Packed with advice on where, when and how to view a region's wildlife, each title features photos of over 300 species and contains engaging comments on the local flora and fauna.

With underwater colour photos throughout, **Pisces Books** explore the world's best diving and snorkelling areas. Each book contains listings of diving services and dive resorts, detailed information on depth, visibility and difficulty of dives, and a roundup of the marine life you're likely to see through your mask.

LONELY PLANET

OFF THE ROAD

Journeys, the travel literature series written by renowned travel authors, capture the spirit of a place or illuminate a culture with a journalist's attention to detail and a novelist's flair for words. These are tales to soak up while you're actually on the road or dip into as an at-home armchair indulgence.

The range of lavishly illustrated **Pictorial** books is just the ticket for both travellers and dreamers. Off-beat tales and vivid photographs bring the adventure of travel to your doorstep long before the journey begins and long after it is over.

Lonely Planet **Videos** encourage the same independent, tough-minded approach as the guidebooks. Currently airing throughout the world, this award-winning series features innovative footage and an original soundtrack.

Yes, we know, work is tough, so do a little bit of deskside dreaming with the spiral-bound Lonely Planet **Diary** or a Lonely Planet **Wall Calendar**, filled with great photos from around the world.

TRAVELLERS NETWORK

Lonely Planet Online. Lonely Planet's award-winning Web site has insider information on hundreds of destinations, from Amsterdam to Zimbabwe, complete with interactive maps and relevant links. The site also offers the latest travel news, recent reports from travellers on the road, guidebook upgrades, a travel links site, an online book-buying option and a lively traveller's bulletin board. It can be viewed at **www.lonelyplanet.com** or AOL keyword: lp.

Planet Talk is a quarterly print newsletter, full of gossip, advice, anecdotes and author articles. It provides an antidote to the being-at-home blues and lets you plan and dream for the next trip. Contact the nearest Lonely Planet office for your free copy.

Comet, the free Lonely Planet newsletter, comes via email once a month. It's loaded with travel news, advice, dispatches from authors, travel competitions and letters from readers. To subscribe, click on the Comet subscription link on the front page of the Web site.

Index

Text

Bold indicates maps.

172

Places to Stay

Places to Eat

Boxed Text

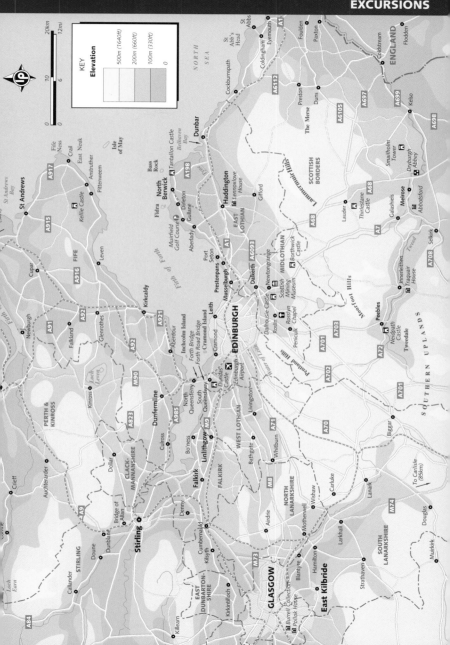

KEY

Elevation

500m (1640ft)

200m (660ft)

100m (330ft)

0

20km

12mi

10

6

0

0

NORTH SEA

St Abbs
St Abb's Head
Eyemouth
A1
Coldingham
Foulden
Coldstream
ENGLAND
Flodden
Paxton
Cockburnspath
A6112
Preston
Duns
The Merse
A697
A6105
A698
Kelso
Dunbar
Tantallon Castle
Belhaven Bay
SCOTTISH BORDERS
Smailholm Tower
Dryburgh Abbey
Bass Rock
North Berwick
A198
Haddington
Lennoxlove House
Gifford
Lammermuir Hills
A68
Thirlestane Castle
Lauder
Galashiels
Melrose
A7
Abbotsford
Fidra
Dirleton
Gullane
EAST LOTHIAN
A1
A68
Muirfield Golf Course
Aberlady
A917
Crail
East Neuk
Anstruther
Pittenweem
Fife Ness
Kellie Castle
St Andrews Bay
St Andrews
A915
FIFE
A916
A91
Cupar
Newburgh
Leven
Glenrothes
Kirkcaldy
A92
A921
Falkland
Kinross
Loch Leven
A90
M90
A985
Aberdour
Incholm Island
Forth Bridge
Forth Road Bridge
Cramond Island
Leith
Cramond
EDINBURGH
Musselburgh
Prestonpans
Port Seton
South Seton
A6093
Dalkeith
Newtongrange
Scottish Mining Museum
MIDLOTHIAN
Borthwick Castle
Dalhousie Castle
Rosslyn Chapel
Roslin
Penicuik
A701
A703
Peebles
Neidpath Castle
Tweeddale
A72
Traquair House
Innerleithen
A708
Selkirk
SOUTHERN UPLANDS
Pentland Hills
A702
A70
A701
Moorfoot Hills
Water of Leith
Edinburgh Castle
Edinburgh Airport
Dunbar
South Queensferry
North Queensferry
WEST LOTHIAN
Livingston
Bathgate
Whitburn
A71
Linlithgow
M9
Bo'ness
A803
Culross
Dunfermline
PERTH & KINROSS
Crieff
Auchterarder
A9
Dollar
CLACKMANNANSHIRE
Bridge of Allan
Dunblane
Doune
Callander
Loch Earn
A84
STIRLING
Stirling
Denny
Falkirk
FALKIRK
Cumbernauld
Kilsyth
Kirkintilloch
EAST DUNBARTONSHIRE
M73
M80
Killearn
GLASGOW
Burrell Collection
Pollok House
East Kilbride
Blantyre
Hamilton
Strathaven
SOUTH LANARKSHIRE
Muirkirk
Larkhall
Douglas
Lanark
M74
Carluke
Wishaw
Motherwell
NORTH LANARKSHIRE
M8
Airdrie
Carnwath
To Carlisle (85km)
Biggar

MAP 1 GREATER EDINBURGH

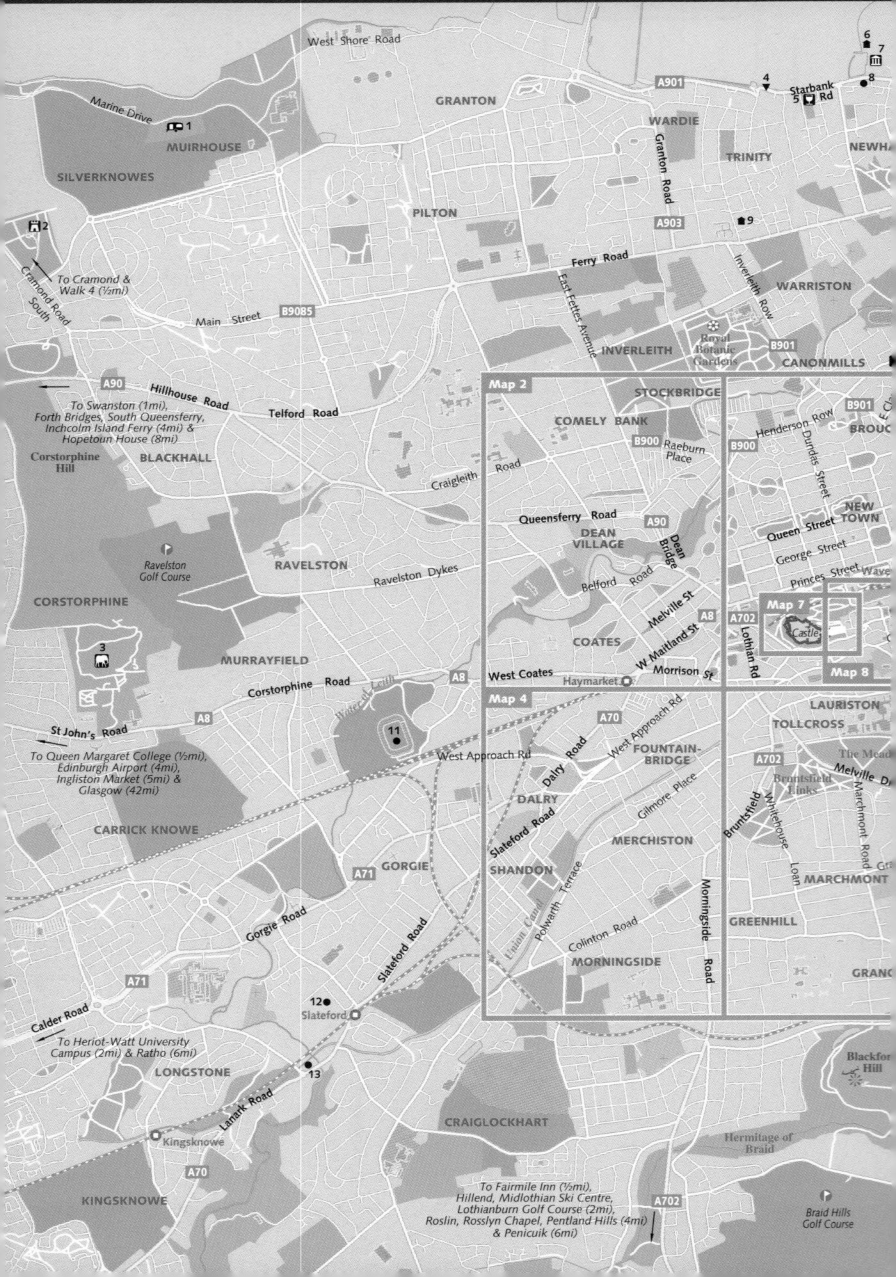

MAP 1 GREATER EDINBURGH

FIRTH OF FORTH

Western Harbour

LEITH DOCKS
Map 6

NORTH LEITH
Lindsay Rd
Commercial St
Ferry Road
ONNINGTON
Great Junction St
Bonnington Road
South Leith
ILRIG
Leith Walk

A901
A199
Constitution Street
Salamander Street

Map 3
A900

GREENSIDE
CALTON
London Road
Regent Rd
A1
rloo
ce
Mile
Canongate
ABBEYHILL
CANONGATE
Holyrood Rd

PORTOBELLO
Portobello Road   A1140
A199

London Road   ● 15

Portobello High Street
A199   ● 23

Queen's Drive
Holyrood Park

St Margaret's Loch
🏛16
Whinny Hill
WILLOWBRAE

Walk 3

A1   Duddingston Road   A6106

To Musselburgh (2mi),
Prestonpans (5mi) &
North Berwick (18mi)

A1

Map 5
Walk 3

ARTHUR'S SEAT (251m)
Dunsapie Loch

18 ☐   17
🏛19

DUDDINGSTON

St LEONARD'S
Holyrood Park Road
Old Church La
Duddingston Loch
● 20

BINGHAM
A6106

A1
A199

WINGTON
A7
Dalkeith Road
Minto Street
Mayfield Gdns
A701
Causewayside
ge Loan
West Savile Terrace

A6095

NIDDRIE

CRAIGMILLAR
Craigmillar Castle Road
21 🏛

LACKFORD

Gilmerton Road
Old Dalkeith Road

22 ●

DANDERHALL
A6106

To Mortonhall Caravan Park (¾mi),
Penicuik (7mi) & Peebles (22mi)
A701
A772
A7
MOREDUN
Melville Golf Centre (2mi)

To Dalkeith (2mi), Newtongrange
Scottish Mining Museum (4mi),
Lauder (20mi) & Melrose (32mi)

Mayfield Rd

0   0.5   1km
0   0.25   0.5mi

MAP 2

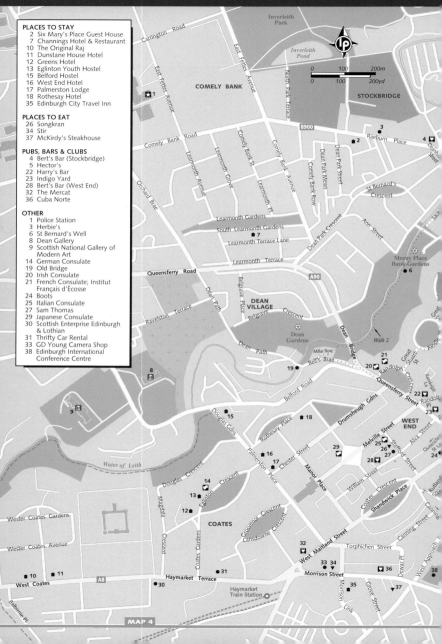

PLACES TO STAY
2 Six Mary's Place Guest House
7 Channings Hotel & Restaurant
10 The Original Raj
11 Dunstane House Hotel
12 Greens Hotel
13 Eglinton Youth Hostel
15 Belford Hostel
16 West End Hotel
17 Palmerston Lodge
18 Rothesay Hotel
35 Edinburgh City Travel Inn

PLACES TO EAT
26 Songkran
34 Stir
37 McKirdy's Steakhouse

PUBS, BARS & CLUBS
4 Bert's Bar (Stockbridge)
5 Hector's
22 Harry's Bar
23 Indigo Yard
28 Bert's Bar (West End)
32 The Mercat
36 Cuba Norte

OTHER
1 Police Station
3 Herbie's
6 St Bernard's Well
8 Dean Gallery
9 Scottish National Gallery of Modern Art
14 German Consulate
19 Old Bridge
20 Irish Consulate
21 French Consulate; Institut Français d'Écosse
24 Boots
25 Italian Consulate
27 Sam Thomas
29 Japanese Consulate
30 Scottish Enterprise Edinburgh & Lothian
31 Thrifty Car Rental
33 GD Young Camera Shop
38 Edinburgh International Conference Centre

MAP 3

PLACES TO STAY
- 4 Wayfarer Guest House
- 5 Dene Guest House
- 11 Marrakech Guest House & Restaurant
- 28 Sibbet House
- 35 Christopher North House Hotel
- 41 Roxburghe Hotel
- 57 Caledonian Hilton Hotel; The Pompadour
- 60 Sheraton Grand Hotel
- 77 The Point Hotel
- 80 The Knight Residence
- 93 rick's Hotel & Restaurant
- 100 Hanover Hotel; Robertsons 37
- 112 George Inter-Continental Hotel
- 120 Old Waverley Hotel
- 123 Balmoral Hotel; Number One; Hadrian's Bistro; NB's
- 127 City Centre Tourist Hostel
- 136 Royal Garden Apartments
- 142 Parliament House Hotel
- 154 Greenside Hotel
- 155 Royal Terrace Hotel
- 156 Ailsa Craig Hotel
- 157 Carlton Greens Hotel
- 178 Macdonald Holyrood Hotel
- 181 Pleasance Youth Hostel

PLACES TO EAT
- 16 Blue Moon Cafè; Out of the Blue
- 17 Cafè Mediterraneo; LGBT Centre
- 23 The Basement
- 24 Stac Polly
- 33 Howie's Stockbridge
- 42 Wok Wok
- 48 No 27
- 53 Starbuck's
- 62 Bar Italia
- 63 Rainbow Arch; Ho Ho Mei Noodle Shack; Henry's Jazz Bar
- 67 Dario's; Lazio
- 70 The Atrium; blue bar cafe
- 76 It's Organic
- 82 Favorit
- 92 La P'tite Folie
- 94 Caffé D.O.C.
- 95 Fishers in the City
- 96 Café Marlayne
- 98 Mussel Inn
- 110 Tampopo; Henderson's
- 111 Nargile
- 116 The Dome; Frazer's; Why Not?
- 116 The Garden Cafe
- 117 Rhodes & Co; The Abbotsford
- 128 Café Royal Oyster Bar; Café Royal Circle Bar; Guildford Arms
- 146 Modern India
- 148 Gurkha Brigade
- 149 Valvona & Crolla Caffé Bar
- 152 No 3 Royal Terrace

PUBS, BARS & CLUBS
- 13 The Cask & Barrel
- 19 Ego
- 20 The Outhouse
- 21 PopRokit
- 22 Mathers
- 25 New Town Bar
- 26 The Cumberland Bar
- 27 Clark's Bar
- 31 The Antiquary
- 34 The Bailie
- 36 Kay's Bar
- 38 The Oxford Bar
- 39 Tonic
- 40 Bar 38
- 46 Ryan's
- 64 Finn MacCool's
- 83 Gaia
- 85 The Kenilworth
- 97 Po Na Na
- 101 The Standing Order
- 107 The Auld Hundred
- 130 Tiles Bar-Bistro
- 137 The Stand Comedy Club
- 140 Pivo Caffé
- 141 The Venue
- 145 CC Blooms
- 147 Planet Out
- 158 The Stag & Turret
- 168 Studio 24
- 180 Pleasance Cabaret Bar

OTHER
- 1 Glenogle Swim Centre
- 2 The Adam Pottery
- 3 Gladrags
- 6 Second Edition
- 7 Canonmills Dry Cleaners & Launderette
- 8 City Cycles
- 9 Townhouse Sauna
- 10 Europcar
- 12 Sundial Launderette; Lost Sock Diner
- 14 Crombie's
- 15 Just Junk
- 18 Edinburgh Printmakers' Workshop & Gallery
- 29 The Scottish Gallery
- 30 Robert Louis Stevenson's House
- 32 Montresor
- 37 Spanish Consulate
- 43 Bute House
- 44 Georgian House
- 45 West Register House
- 47 Post Office
- 49 National Trust for Scotland
- 50 American Express; Edinburgh Woollen Mill
- 51 Waterstone's
- 52 Virgin Megastore
- 54 St Cuthbert's Parish Church
- 55 St John's Church; Crafts Fair
- 56 Watch Tower
- 58 Jessops Photo & Video Centre
- 59 Canadian Consulate
- 61 The Filmhouse
- 65 Web 13
- 66 Wonderland Toys
- 68 The Stationery Office Bookshop
- 69 Usher Hall
- 71 Traverse Theatre
- 72 Castle Terrace Car Park; Edinburgh Farmers' Market
- 73 Royal Lyceum Theatre
- 74 McAlister Matheson Music
- 75 Old Grindle's Bookshop
- 78 Boardwise
- 79 West Port Books
- 81 Avalanche Records
- 84 Ross Bandstand
- 86 Tiso
- 87 Mappin & Webb
- 88 Waterstone's
- 89 Aitken & Niven
- 90 Australian Consulate
- 91 Post Office
- 99 easyEverything
- 102 Thomas Cook
- 103 Floral Clock
- 104 Royal Scottish Academy
- 105 Marks & Spencer
- 106 Lothian Bus Travelshop
- 108 George IV Statue
- 109 Swiss Consulate
- 113 Dutch Consulate
- 114 Church of St Andrew & St George
- 118 Jenners
- 119 Scott Monument
- 121 Princes Mall; Ortak
- 122 Edinburgh and Scotland Information Centre
- 124 Waterstone's
- 125 National Archives of Scotland
- 126 New Register House
- 129 Bank of Scotland
- 131 Melville Monument
- 132 The Royal Bank of Scotland; Dundas House
- 133 Site of St Andrew's Shopping Centre
- 134 New Bus Station; First Edinburgh Bus Shop
- 135 Scottish National Portrait Gallery
- 138 Main Post Office
- 139 St James Centre; John Lewis
- 143 Greenside Place Car Boot Sale
- 144 Edinburgh Playhouse
- 150 McNaughtan's Bookshop
- 151 Lothian Buses Lost Property Office
- 153 Calton Gallery
- 159 Easter Road Stadium
- 160 US Consulate
- 161 National Monument
- 162 Nelson Monument
- 163 City Observatory
- 164 Monument to Dugald Stewart
- 165 St Andrew's House
- 166 Royal High School
- 167 Burns Monument
- 169 Canongate Kirk
- 170 Canongate Tolbooth; The People's Story
- 171 The Fudge House of Edinburgh
- 172 Huntly House; Museum of Edinburgh
- 173 Carson Clark Gallery
- 174 Queen Mary's Bath House
- 175 Holyrood Abbey
- 176 Palace of Holyroodhouse
- 177 Site of New Scottish Parliament Building
- 179 Our Dynamic Earth

MAP 3

Inverleith Terrace

Water of Leith

Howard St 6

Huntly St

Canon Mills

Broughton Rd

West Annandale St

Annandale St

Glenogle Road

Eyre Place

B901

8

Rodney Street

9 East Metgund Tce

Bellevue

Bellevue Pl

Bellevue Grove

Annand

STOCKBRIDGE

Henderson Row

B900

4 5

3

B900

East London St

10

Hamilton Place

Clarence St

2

Fettes Row

Dundas Street

Cumberland Street

27

26

London Street

11

12 13

14

15

16 17

Barony St

Albany St La

Broughton St

Forth

22 20

Brough

Hart St

St Stephen

Walk 2 End
33 32

31

34

Great King Street

Drummond Place

Northumberland St NE La

Northumberland St

Dublin St

Dublin St La N

Broughton Market

Albany Street

York St

York

23

Pla

35

NW Circus Pl

SE Circus Pl

Circus Pl

Royal Circus Pl

India St

Cloucester St

Cloucester Pl

Doune Tce

Gloucester La

Jamaica St

Jamaica St La

Northumberland St NW La

Northumberland St SW La

28

Northumberland St SE La

29

Abercrombie

Northumberland Pl

Northumberland Pl La

25

24

Dublin St S

Dublin Meuse

Albany Street

York Place

Elder St

James St

Little King St

St Cathedral La

138

Moray

Darnaway Place

Wemyss Place

Heriot Row

Jamaica St

36

30

Northumberland Row

Queen St Gardens W

Queen Street Gardens

Queen St Gardens

Queen Street

136

135

137

134

Clyde St

St Andrew

133

132

139

MAP 2

Forres St

N Charlotte Street

Queen Street

NEW TOWN

Frederick Street

Thistle St La NW

Thistle St NW

Thistle St NE

Thistle Street

Hanover Street

Thistle St La NE

Thistle St SW

Thistle St La SE

113

Walk 2 Start

131

St Andrew Square

126

129

128

127

125

Leith

140

St Colme

Glenfinlas St

44 43

Charlotte

42

45

37

Hill St La N

Hill Street

Hill St La S

Young St La N

Young Street

Young St La S

38

39

92

91

95

96

94

97

88

90

89

87

George Street

86

110

109

108

101

100

99

102

98

107

111

112

115

116

105

106

117

114

Rose St N La

Rose Street

Rose St S La

118

120

121 122

119

124

123

St David St

S St David St

Hanover Street

St Andrew St

130

Princes Street

Waverley Bridge

Waverley Train Station

Waterloo Place

Walk 3 Start

40

41

Square

48 49

46

50

47

51 52 53

Hope St

Rose St La

Rose St N La

Rose St S La

85

103

104

Princes Street

East Princes Street Gardens

See Map 8 Central Edinburgh

North Bridge

West Princes Street Gardens

84

The Mound

Market

Cockburn Street

North St

Jet

55

54

58

57

56

Rutland St

A702

See Map 7 Edinburgh Castle

Edinburgh Castle

Castle Bank

Esplanade

North Bank St

Bank St

High Street (Royal Mile)

Lawnmarket

Victoria St

George IV Bridge

Cowgate

OLD TOWN

Chambers Street

Guthrie

Street

59

West Approach Rd

Lothian Road

Castle Terrace

Cornwall

72

Castle Stables Road

Johnston Terrace

King's Stables Rd

King's Stables La

83

Grassmarket

Candlemaker Row

Forrest Rd

Bristo Pl

Lothian St

South

60

Festival Square

Newport St

69

73

70

68

67

66

65

74

77

76 75

78

79

81

80

64

63 62 61

Grindlay St

Spittal St

Lady Lawnwnd

West Port

Edinburgh College of Art

Lauriston St

Keir St

Heriot Pl

82

Teviot Pl

Bristo Square

Marshall

Bread St

East Fountainbridge

Morrison St

MAP 5

MAP 3

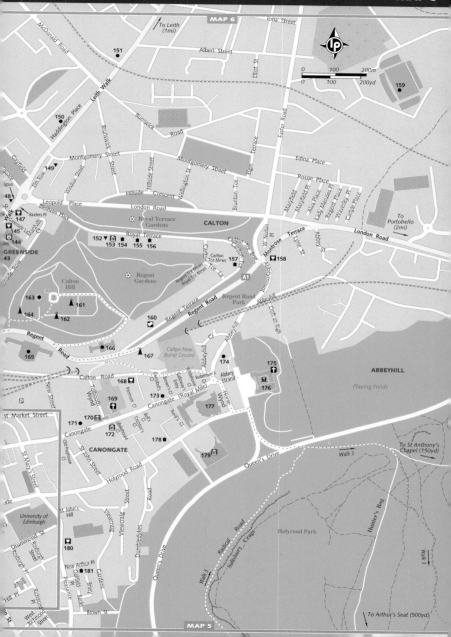

To Leith
(1mi)

MAP 6

Iona Street

Albert Street

151

McDonald Road

Leith Walk

Elliot St.

159

0   100   200m
0   100   200yd

Easter Road

150

Haddington Place

Brunswick

Road

Elgin Terrace

Edina Place

149

Elm Row

Windsor Street

Brunswick Street

Montgomery Street

Montgomery Street

Brunton Tce.

Rossie Place

Maryfield

Mayfield Pl.

Ava Place

Lady Menzies Pl.

Regent Place

Waverley Pl.

Carlyle Place

To
Portobello
(2mi)

Hillside Street

Wellington Street

Hillside Crescent

London Road

London Road

48

147

Leopold
Place

Blenheim Place

Baxters Pl.

Marshalls Ct.

Greenside Row

145

144

GREENSIDE

43

Royal Terrace Gardens

CALTON

W. Norton Pl.

Montrose Terrace

Abbey St.

Lyne St.

152   153 154 155 156

Royal Terrace

Clifton

Carlton Tce. Brae

158

157

Regent Gardens

Carlton Tce. Mews

Carlton Terrace

Regent Tce. Mews

Royal Tce. Mews

A1

Clifton Tce.

163

164

161

Calton
Hill

162

Regent Terrace

Regent Road

Regent Road Park

Abbeyhill

Clock-in-Rush

165

Regent   Road

166

160

167

Calton New
Burial Ground

Cr

Abbeyhill

174

175

176

ABBEYHILL

Playing Fields

Calton Road

168

New Street

Tolbooth Wynd

169

173

Pirrie's Cl.

Campbell's Cl.

Chessel's

Old Tolbooth Wynd

Reid's Cl.

Bakehouse

Bull's Cl.

177

Abbey Strand

Horse Wynd

Canongate (Royal Mile)

170

171

172

178

179

To St Anthony's
Chapel (150yd)

St Market Street

P

CANONGATE

Canongate

Holyrood Road

Queen's Drive

Walk 3

St Mary's Street

Old Playhouse

St John's
Hill

Viewcraig Street

Holyrood Road

Dumbiedykes

Queen's Drive

Walk 3

St John's Street

Radical Road

Salisbury Crags

Holyrood Park

Hunter's Bog

E WPM

University of
Edinburgh

Drummond St.

Roxburgh Street

180

New Arthur Pl.

181

Oldfield

Pleasance

Brown St.

Hill Pl.

West Richmond Street

Richmond St.

ate

To Arthur's Seat (500yd)

MAP 5

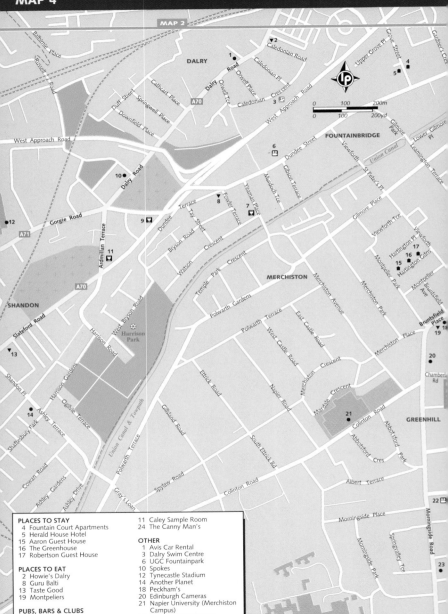

MAP 4

MAP 2

DALRY

FOUNTAINBRIDGE

MERCHISTON

SHANDON

GREENHILL

Harrison Park

Union Canal & Towpath

Great Scot! The ornate Scott Monument

Mighty William Wallace, St Margaret's Chapel

St Cuthbert's Parish Church, built in the 1890s, and St John's Church sit side-by-side on Princes St.

MAP 5

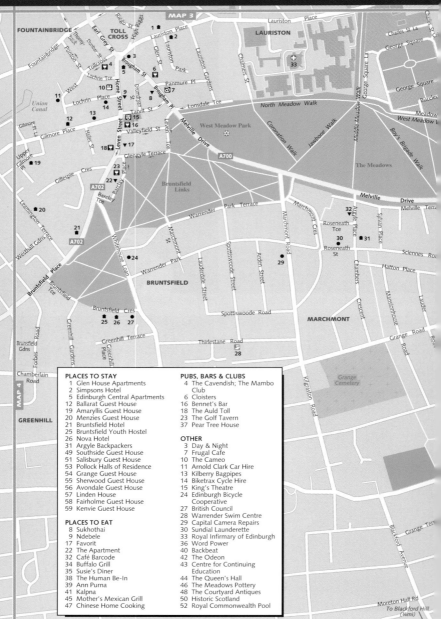

MAP 3

FOUNTAINBRIDGE

TOLL CROSS

LAURISTON

Union Canal

North Meadow Walk

West Meadow Park

The Meadows

Bruntsfield Links

BRUNTSFIELD

MARCHMONT

Roseneath Tce

Roseneath St

Grange Cemetery

GREENHILL

MAP 1

To Blackford Hill (½mi)

PLACES TO STAY
1 Glen House Apartments
2 Simpsons Hotel
5 Edinburgh Central Apartments
12 Ballarat Guest House
19 Amaryllis Guest House
20 Menzies Guest House
21 Bruntsfield Hotel
25 Bruntsfield Youth Hostel
26 Nova Hotel
31 Argyle Backpackers
49 Southside Guest House
51 Salisbury Guest House
53 Pollock Halls of Residence
54 Grange Guest House
55 Sherwood Guest House
56 Avondale Guest House
57 Linden House
58 Fairholme Guest House
59 Kenvie Guest House

PLACES TO EAT
8 Sukhothai
9 Ndebele
17 Favorit
22 The Apartment
32 Café Barcode
34 Buffalo Grill
35 Susie's Diner
38 The Human Be-In
39 Ann Purna
41 Kalpna
44 Mother's Mexican Grill
47 Chinese Home Cooking

PUBS, BARS & CLUBS
4 The Cavendish; The Mambo Club
6 Cloisters
16 Bennet's Bar
18 The Auld Toll
23 The Golf Tavern
37 Pear Tree House

OTHER
3 Day & Night
7 Frugal Cafe
10 The Cameo
11 Arnold Clark Car Hire
13 Kilberry Bagpipes
14 Biketrax Cycle Hire
15 King's Theatre
24 Edinburgh Bicycle Cooperative
27 British Council
28 Warrender Swim Centre
29 Capital Camera Repairs
30 Sundial Launderette
33 Royal Infirmary of Edinburgh
36 Word Power
40 Backbeat
42 The Odeon
43 Centre for Continuing Education
44 The Queen's Hall
46 The Meadows Pottery
48 The Courtyard Antiques
50 Historic Scotland
52 Royal Commonwealth Pool

MAP 5

MAP 3

Holyrood Park

To Arthur's Seat
(400yd)

0   100   200m
0   100   200yd

Walk 3

Carnegie St

Nicolson St

Davie St

Gilmours St

Carnegie St

4
35
38
37

Nicolson St

Haddon's Ct

Hardwell Cl

40
E Crosscauseway
W Cross-causeway

Boxmont St

St Leonard's St

New John's Pl

St Leonard's Craig

St Leonard's Ln

39
41

St Patrick Square

43

42

Clerk St

A7

Rankeillor St

St Leonard's St

St Leonard's Bank

Queen's Drive

Hermit's Croft

Terars Croft

East Parkside

Gifford Park

Montague St

Parkside St

Borough Loch Ln

Buccleuch Tce

ST LEONARD'S

44

Bernard Terrace

45

Dalkeith Road

Parkside Tce

Meadow Park

Summerhall

46

Summerhall Pl

Sciennes Road

South Clerk Street

Lutton Place

Holyrood Park Road

52

NEWINGTON

53

West Preston St

East Preston Street

47

Newington Road

49

Gladstone Terrace

St Catharine's Pl

48

Causewayside

51

Salisbury Road

SCIENNES

50

Salisbury Place

54

A701

Blacket Place

Dalkeith Road

Marshall Crescent

Findhorn Place

Sefton Place

Causewayside

Upper Gray Street

55

Blacket Avenue

Priestfield Road

Kirkhill Road

Kirkhill Gardens

Cumin Place

Duncan Street

Minto Street

56

Mayfield Terrace

East Mayfield

Kilmaurs Road

59

Place

South Gray Street

A7

Grange Loan

West Mayfield

MAYFIELD

McLaren Road

Fountainhall Road

Findhorn Place

57

Mayfield Gardens

Clinton Terrace

Morton Terrace

St Alban's Road

Mayfield Road

58

South Lauder Road

Relugas Road

Craigmillar Park

West Savile Road

West Savile Terrace

MacDowall Road

Ross Gardens

Langton Rd

Suffolk Gardens

Cranby Road

Gilmour Road

To Penicuik (2mi);
& Peebles (22mi)

Lady Road

MAP 6

Western Harbour

Imperial Dock

LEITH DOCKS
● 1

2 ●

3

Ocean Drive

To Newhaven (¾mi) & Granton (2mi)

Lindsay Road

Britannia Way

■ 4
● 5

Ocean Drive

Victoria Dock

Albert Dock

0   100   200
0   100   200

NORTH LEITH

10

Tower Place

■ 11

Commercial Street
7 ●

9 ●

A199

8 ●

Dock St

Dock Pl

Tower Street

12 ☑
☑ 13

Timber Bush

■ 14

16

Bernard Street

Shore Pl

☑ 15

Constitution Street

To Portobello

North Junction Street

Portland Street

Madeira Prince Regent Street

Madeira Street

6 ●

Couper St

Coburg Street

Sandport Place

Water of Leith

Ferry Road

Mill Lane

Sheriff Brae

21 ●

20 ■
22

Baltic Street

Assembly St
Cadiz St

23 ☑

▼ 24

Great Junction Street

Cables Wynd

Henderson Street

Giles St

26 ●

Coley St

27 ●

Maritime Lane

Maritime Street

Mitchell Street

Queen Charlotte Street

Constitution Street

Links Plac

Leith Links

A901

South Fort Street

Anderson Place

Bangor Road

Bonnington Road

Tenant Street

Jane Street

Leith Walk

Duke Street

Academy St

Wellington Place

John's Place

East Hermitage

SOUTH LEITH

Pilrig Park

Pilrig Cdns
Pilrig St

28 ■
29 ■

Rosslyn Crescent

Balfour Street

Cambridge Gardens

Cambridge Avenue

Lorne St

30 ■

31 ●

32 ■

33 ●

Leith Walk

To Central Edinburgh (1mi)

Dalmeny Street

Buchanan Street

Iona Street

PLACES TO STAY
4 Express by Holiday Inn
11 Malmaison Hotel & Brasserie
28 Balquhidder Guest House
29 Balfour House
30 Ardmor House
31 Barrosa Guest House
32 Balmoral Guest House

PLACES TO EAT
5 Britannia Spice
9 Daniel's Bistro
12 Fishers; Signal Tower
19 Martin Wishart
21 The Raj
22 (fitz) Henry
24 Khublai Khan

PUBS, BARS & CLUBS
13 The Shore
14 Timberbush

15 Carriers Quarters
17 The King's Wark
23 Port o'Leith

OTHER
1 Britannia Visitor Centre
2 Royal Yacht Britannia
3 Ocean Terminal
6 Edinburgh Architectural Salvage Yard
7 Tiso Outdoor Experience
8 Kinloch Anderson
10 Scottish Executive
16 Flux
18 Fleur's
20 The Leith Gallery
25 Georgian Antiques
26 Scotch Malt Whisky Socie
27 Trinity House; Kirkgate
33 Bendix Launderette & Dry Cleaners

MAP 3

Forty winks at the Firth of Forth: sit back and take in the breathtaking vistas or simply have a nap.

MARTIN MOOS

St Giles Cathedral, the High Kirk of Edinburgh, is a testimony to the city's chequered religious history.

MAP 7 EDINBURGH CASTLE

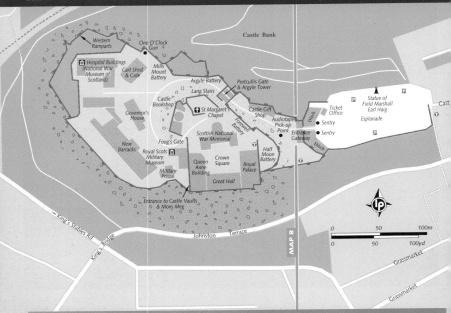

Western Ramparts

One O'Clock Gun

Castle Bank

Hospital Buildings (National War Museum of Scotland)

Cart Shed & Cafe

Mills Mount Battery

Argyle Battery

Portcullis Gate & Argyle Tower

Castle Bookshop

Lang Stairs

St Margaret's Chapel

Castle Gift Shop

Governor's House

Foog's Gate

Scottish National War Memorial

Foreweil Battery

Audiotape Pick-up Point

Entrance Gateway

Ticket Office

Statue of Field Marshall Earl Haig

Esplanade

Cast

Ditch

Sentry

Sentry

Ditch

New Barracks

Royal Scots Military Museum

Military Prison

Queen Anne Building

Crown Square

Great Hall

Royal Palace

Half Moon Battery

Entrance to Castle Vaults & Mons Meg

King's Stables Rd

King's Bridge

Johnston Terrace

MAP 8

Grassmarket

Grassmarket

0   50   100m
0   50   100yd

BETHUNE CARMICHAEL

Indulge in Scottish fare and wash it down with a wee dram of whisky at one of Grassmarket's pubs.